DUE DATE

EC 19 2001

NOV 28 Rec'd

Rhetoric and the Arts
of Design

David S. Kaufer
Brian S. Butler
Carnegie Mellon University

# Rhetoric and the Arts of Design

LAWRENCE ERLBAUM ASSOCIATES, PUBLISHERS

1996    Mahwah, New Jersey

WITHDRAWN
OESTERLE LIBRARY
NAPERVILLE, IL 60540

Copyright © 1996 by Lawrence Erlbaum Associates, Inc.
All rights reserved. No part of this document may be reproduced
in any form by photostat, microform, retrieval system, or any
other means without prior written permission of the publisher.

Lawrence Erlbaum Associates, Inc., Publishers
10 Industrial Avenue
Mahwah, New Jersey 07430

Cover design by Gail Silverman

Library of Congress Cataloging-in-Publication Data

Kaufer, David S.
    Rhetoric and the arts of design / David S. Kaufer, Brian S. Butler.
        p.   cm.
    Includes bibliographic references and index.
    ISBN 0-8058-2145-7.—ISBN 0-8058-2146-5
    1. Rhetoric.   2. Design.   I. Butler, Brian S.   II. Title.
    P301.K375   1996
    808—dc20                                                    95-50513
                                                                   CIP

Books published by Lawrence Erlbaum Associates are printed on
acid-free paper, and their bindings are chosen for strength and
durability.

Printed in the United States of America
10  9  8  7  6  5  4  3  2  1

308
<16r

This book is dedicated to:

Barb, Aaron, and Mollie, whose presence is the gift
D.S.K.

Michelle—My patient, supportive wife
B.S.B.

YALE LIBRARY
JUNIOR COLLEGE
MORRELL

# Contents

# Preface

What is the difference between rhetoric and "mere" rhetoric? What is "public" about the public discourse that has been associated with rhetoric since Aristotle? What kind of skill and knowledge underlies rhetoric and why has that skill come to be valued so lowly in contemporary culture? How should it be valued? Is there such a thing as rhetorical expertise? What underlies such expertise? Can we extract it from the behavior of canonical specimens of rhetorical discourse, such as Lincoln and Douglas? Are there goals of rhetoric beyond power and profit? Are there plans in rhetoric? Tactics? Strategy? In what sense is the rhetor an architect of social reality? In what sense a chess player seeking an edge on an opponent? In what sense a poet, seeking to bring fresh, surprising, and edifying words to classify an audience's here and now? What would it take to build a cyber-rhetorician from component parts? In this book we take a perspective on all of these questions. We offer answers, but more importantly, from our view, we offer a framework—rhetoric as design—for asking them, a framework that we hope others after us continue. We have written this book for readers who are well versed in rhetoric but who are open to seeing the familiar in new ways. We have also written this book for those who have never entertained rhetoric as a cohesive and intellectually challenging area of study and who are open to engaging it as one.

## ACKNOWLEDGMENTS

We owe debts to many people. The first author wants to thank Lawrence Rosenfield, Lloyd Bitzer, Edwin Black, and Mike Leff, who offered early exposures to rhetorical theory at Wisconsin, and to thank his peers who overlapped his time in graduate school: Kathleen Jamieson, Thomas Farrell, Christine Oravec, and John Lyne, with whom he learned what he believes is a distinctly Wisconsinesque approach to rhetoric. The rich Wisconsin environment made Kaufer know early on he wanted to "do" rhetoric. He did not know at the time it would take a career to unpack what that initial commitment already involved. Thanks go to Donald Cushman, who taught Kaufer what rhetoric could be outside Wisconsin, and Phil Tompkins, who gave him his first job and has remained a close colleague. Moving to Carnegie Mellon meant moving to a new field (English) and growing out of touch with the field of communication. Yet the migration has always been more physical than intellectual. Kaufer would also like to acknowledge his colleagues in the Departments of English and Design at Carnegie Mellon, where the head of the Department of Design, Richard Buchanan, is a rhetorical theorist in design theory and where Dan Boyarski, another professor of design, teaches convincingly how much rhetoric in the culture gets communicated with the eye as the primary audience. Richard Young, Erwin Steinberg, and Alan Kennedy are members of the Department of English who have worked hard to build the English/design coalition that has influenced the perspective of the book. Thank you. David Fleming, a PhD student doing his own innovative work in rhetoric and graphic design, read many drafts and gave much cogent advice. Thanks also to the (literally) score of Carnegie Mellon students who have gone on to their own distinctive successes in English. Cheryl Geisler (chair at Rensselaer Polytechnic Institute), Chris Neuwirth (Carnegie Mellon), and Chris Haas and Davida Charney (both of Pennsylvania State University) have remained close colleagues and sounding boards. Rosa Eberly of the University of Texas and Jerry Hauser of the University of Colorado share an interest in "publics" for rhetoric and clarified some of our thinking about publics. Readers familiar with David Zarefsky's fine study of the Lincoln/Douglas debates will see his influence on our discussion. We also hope they will appreciate the complementarity between a consummate historian of rhetorical practice (Zarefsky) and our efforts to explore expert rhetorical design from expert rhetoricians (who are, incidentally, historical figures). Wayne Booth, a member of the advisory board to the Department of English that Kaufer now heads, influenced this book by insisting (when we told him about it) that we not forget the ethical dimension of rhetoric. We haven't. Faculty at the Universities of Colorado and the Annenberg School of Communication at the University of Pennsylvania were kind enough to bear through some of these ideas in early stages. Kaufer would finally like to thank his family, Barb, Aaron, and Mollie, for their unwavering support.

Butler would like to thank Deborah Gibbons, Shyam Sunder, and most importantly his wife Michelle Butler for reading, discussing, and patiently listening to his work.

—*David S. Kaufer*
—*Brian S. Butler*

# Introduction

"It ain't rocket science." The phrase has become a colloquialism for practices considered too slight to require deep thought, training, or reflection. Rocket science, so the phrase makes apparent, requires all these things, and then some. It requires focused and disciplined training over time, typically in a face-to-face apprenticeship to masters. It requires most newcomers quitting or peaking not much beyond the novice stage. It requires those who stay with the training having to endure failure and false starts before enjoying whatever successes they come to enjoy. It requires a wide gradient of skill between low novice and high expert. It requires, not insignificantly, a learning commitment beyond anything offered through a casual print relationship. One can't expect to stroll to the nearest bookstore and pick up a pocket "how to" on being a rocket scientist. The cultural stereotype for rocket science applies, in more muted and modest shades, to the arts in the family of arts we associate with design— engineering, architecture, graphics, musical composition. The principal argument of this book is that rhetoric belongs in this family of arts as well. Why this argument is necessary and its consequences for a reconceptualization of rhetoric furnishes the larger background we seek to fill in.

In the process of framing a theory of rhetoric as design, we pursue two convergent lines of inquiry. The first is to present a theory that responds to the new rhetorician's long-standing interest in invention as original composing (Flower & Hayes, 1981; Young, Becker, & Pike, 1970). In the 1980s, writing programs in English departments were challenged to incorporate invention, the design of original argument, into their conception of written argument. Yet viewing rhetoric as an art of original design posed a challenge that existing theory was only beginning to come to grips with. The first author spent much of the 1980s trying to come to grips with it further. In 1984 he, along with Cheryl Geisler and Chris Neuwirth, working with Preston Covey in philosophy at Carnegie Mellon, began the WARRANT project, a Department of Education funded protocol study of novice and expert writers engaged in the composition of original academic argument.

That project led to various research papers (Geisler, 1990; Kaufer and Dunmire, 1995; Kaufer and Geisler, 1989), a curriculum on composing original written argument (Kaufer, Geisler, & Neuwirth, 1989), a book that overviews and reports on the 10-year empirical effort (Geisler, 1994), and a series of evolving software environments (reviewed in Kaufer, Neuwirth, Chandhok, & Morris, 1992).

The theory expressed in the 1989 curriculum was cognitive in nature, focusing on the mental activities (e.g., reading, summarizing, analyzing) of the single writer working with the texts of previous authors but otherwise in a social vacuum. Social context played no role in the theory of writing expressed; nor did the evolving conventions of academic writing; nor the social history in which these conventions evolved; nor the institutions—publishing houses, universities, and professions—that supported academic writing and that structured competition between authors; nor the issue of the writer's motivation or mobility to find new readers, or the reader's to find new authors; nor the technologies used by the writer or available to the reader. None of these factors played a role in the theory of written argument expressed in Kaufer et al. (1989). To supplement the 1989 theory, Kaufer collaborated with a sociologist to produce a sociological history of academic writing (Kaufer & Carley, 1993a).

The 1989 theory was based in the forensic, past-oriented, model of case-based reasoning, a type of reasoning familiar in law—how similar is the present case to previous cases that are better known and analyzed?—as a starting point for helping students compose original written argument from source readings and their everyday experience. Writers were encouraged to invent new positions that described and resolved a collection of "problem cases" from "similar" cases drawn from their own experience or from their reading. Original composition, according to the 1989 theory, involved the application of similarity judgments from previous cases to the case at hand.

The authors of this book now see the 1989 theory as a limited theory of argument design—one in need of expansion into a deliberative, future-oriented, theory, with the expanded theory more interactive with the public rhetorics of the Aristotelian tradition. We have come to see a theory of written argument as needing to involve not just reasoning from prior cases but also what the ancient rhetoricians understood as "probable" argument encouraging audiences into the uncertain future. We have come to believe that, despite the influence of classical rhetoric, current theories of written argument, including the 1989 theory, cannot accommodate either the ubiquity or the diversity of probable reasoning or the public narratives they inform. What is the probable? As the classical rhetoricians understood, the power of an argument does not rely on case analysis or deductive validity alone. Audiences can be swayed by an argument even when, on further examination, they discover that they have insufficient information to confirm it with certainty or even with statistical probability. The probable in the rhetorical sense does not mean a 99% or even a 50% or greater probability of occurrence. The latter are statistical judgments based on the mathematical theory of probability. The probable is a vaguer and more qualitative judgment, what the ancient rhetoricians understood as creating in the audience a vivid impression of the truth, or impending truth, of the premises and conclusions offered. Using probable argument, a skilled rhetor can make air travel seem more dangerous than ground travel even when, in terms of statistical frequency, ground travel is the more dangerous.

Judgments of the probable thus seem to depend less on the strict mechanics of deductive or inductive inference than they do on the way the mind creates vivid and pressing images of impending realities. In this sense, the probable deals as much with the psychology of belief as with logic proper. McCloskey's (1985, 1990, 1995) work on the rhetoric of economics has beautifully illustrated the probable as an underlying, but typically hidden, basis of economic science. He has exposed the extent to which economic argument relies on "metaphors and ethos, implied readers and ruling stories." And he has cautioned that for any discipline to try to get by on "fact and logic" alone is to fall "a few bricks short of the load" (1995, pp. 7, 11). By foregrounding rhetoric as the design of plans into probable public narratives, we propose a theory of rhetoric that, better than the 1989 installment, expresses the continuities between public rhetoric and academic expression.

The second line of inquiry is to address the recent movements to "rescue" rhetoric for the academy by turning it into an analytical and critical art while diminishing its ties to production. Many modern commentators on rhetoric have suppressed the probable and productive aspects of rhetoric in favor of definitions that seek to make rhetoric over into a body of analytic knowledge, apart from practice. The reason for this suppression of rhetoric's fundamental characteristics has been, ironically, to "promote" rhetoric in the modern academy, to create a more prestigious disciplinary space for it. As Janet Atwill (1993, p. 112) wrote in her critique of modern Aristotelian scholarship, "in order to institute rhetoric as a formal discipline, [some modern writers] transform it. In particular, they must extricate rhetoric from the epistemological model of productive knowledge and refashion it according to the specifications of the foundationalist paradigm."

The problem, we came to see, crystallized into a dilemma:[1] As rhetoric has tried to prove itself in the modern academy, it has had to reshape itself to look more like an organized body of analytical knowledge and less like a form of productive knowledge, the latter considered more craft-like and heuristical than principled and lawfully regular. Yet as rhetoric has "succeeded" in remaking itself to fit the modern standard, it has lost its bearing as an art of production. One route out of the dilemma is to champion rhetoric as an object of analytic study and to ignore its ancient ties to production. This brings rhetoric into the academy but only after transforming it beyond recognition. A second path of escape is to champion rhetoric as a productive art and to accept the fact that the modern academy has left it behind. This preserves rhetoric as it was and has been but keeps rhetoric and modern academe on a noninteractive course. A third form of escape, one less tested or taken, is to reject the terms of the dilemma altogether by insisting that the arts of production are no less organized and regular in their internal structure than the knowledge we now associate with the disciplines. The problem, on this third route, is that there has been far too little serious academic attention paid to the arts of production.

The promise of this third route was an impetus for the first author's collaboration with Butler, a PhD student in management and information systems who is interested in communications and learning. We determined that not only modern theories of written composition but also modern formulations of classical rhetoric could benefit from an account of rhetoric as a type of productive knowledge, a member in full of the family of design arts. This is the account of rhetoric we offer in this book. We suggest that neither the ancients[2] nor moderns fully envisioned rhetoric in the family of arts we associate with modern design: architecture, engineering, graphics. We show what it would be like to envision rhetoric this way and the advantage of doing so for integrating classical theories of rhetoric and modern theories of written argument. Although we were not aware of it when we started this project, our account comports with Lanham's (1983, 1993) characterization of rhetoric as an art that oscillates between serious truth-telling, gaming, and play. A theory of rhetoric as design, we hope to

---

[1]There is a good deal of overlap between the dilemma cited here and that formulated recently by Gaonkar (1990, 1993); see Kaufer (in press).

[2]It is always tricky to speak for the ancient rhetoricians and what they did or did not entertain in their particular visions of rhetoric. Perhaps our point should be that, irrespective of ancient views of rhetoric, no modern commentator on the ancients has brought to the surface the ties between rhetoric and the family of design arts with the systematicity that we aim for in this book.

show, allows us to comprehend these oscillating faces of rhetoric within a single theory. It offers us the promise of finding a single hat to fit a many-headed hydra.

The two lines of investigation—a theory of written argument as original design and a philosophical justification of rhetoric as a productive design art—are interspersed throughout the book. We have merged them because we have come to conclude that theories of written argument, formed for purposes of description or instruction, must be based on sound general theories of rhetoric, and that sound general theories of rhetoric are, at their base, theories of design.

# One

# Rhetoric And Design: The Ancient Art Meets the Modern Science

*Rhetoric is the art of finding the available means of persuasion.*
—Aristotle (1991)

*The proper study of mankind is the science of design.*
—Simon (1969, p. 159)

## THE FALL OF RHETORIC AND THE RISE OF DESIGN

To moderns, *rhetoric* is a word of odium, signifying uses of language that are self-serving and unprincipled. *Design*, as Simon's statement hints, is a word of prestige, meaning the use of method to change "existing situations into preferred ones" (Simon, 1969, p. 121). In the global economy, design method has gained currency as the capacity to produce ideas and products meeting high standards of quality and consumer acceptance (Norman, 1988). As industrial societies have become increasingly professionalized and reliant on technology, rhetoric has become a popular signifier for the ideas and products of a society that cannot compete in a world of high quality design. It has come to depict markets in which verbal smoke and mirrors are peddled as feeble compensation for low-grade ideas and products. Even the ancient art of politics, reconfigured as the modern discipline of political science, seems to have left rhetoric behind. The international press associates the hot ravings of a political demagogue or a third-world strongman with "rhetoric," and the firebrand radio host as the purveyor of "hate rhetoric," but identifies the cool discourse of a major world leader with "professional diplomacy."

Rhetoric, in short, has come increasingly in the popular culture to be cast aside as a cultural anachronism, a practice out of step with the best of current thinking. It has come to stand for verbal posturing masquerading as genuine

1

insight and innovation. It is shunned as the very antithesis of substance. Economies that can compete will win, we are told, like the Japanese and the quiet hero of Capra's Hollywood, in the silence of their actions, not the seduction of their words. Within this narrative, rhetoric is the villainy of the loose tongue, the modern emblem of dishonorable persuasion. The pejorative usage is so pervasive that it scarcely needs comment. Many politicians would rather admit to isolated crimes and misdemeanors than confess to the systematic use of "rhetoric" in their symbolic behavior.

Rhetoric's decline in the west has a history, of course, and that history has been chronicled in many places. As Roberts and Good (1993, p. 85) observed, rhetoric's decline is not a "simple occlusion," but a more subtle suppression, where groups in power have come to rely on a curious rhetoric of antirhetoric, disclaiming all "rhetorical antecedents or affinities." Ruegg (1993) chronicled this rise of an antirhetoric rhetoric in 19th century German social science; Salazer (1993) offered a comparable analysis in his account of the rise of social science in 19th century France. Cahn (1993) noted that rhetoric in the 18th and 19th century shifted its focus from public speaking and persuading to a more staid form of textual interpretation in order to secure a footing in the evolving university structures of Europe.

The most cited and celebrated account, that of Ong (1971), associated the fall of rhetoric with the rise of print technology. The notion was that print promoted a natural selection toward longer, more complex, and more technical ideas, ideas fixed in the mental space of private individuals rather than in the public space of oral/aural memory. The ideas favored by this selection came eventually to support a document-centered law, science, and technology. Such ideas, moreover, fixed in print, captured a precision in detail that could not be supported by an oral art. As the ideas native to print grew in importance to society, the oral/aural art of rhetoric fell into disrepair.

Elsewhere, one of us (Kaufer & Carley, 1993a) has argued that Ong's thesis, left unqualified, seems not quite right, especially insofar as Ong framed his history as a cognitive hypothesis, one suggesting that print attuned our inner consciousness to think of words as spatial patterns more than bursts of sounds. As Kaufer and Carley argued, it is fantasy to assume that an external technology, like the printing press, could change, in the course of a few generations, fundamental structures of mind.

One strand of the print hypothesis seems, however, more sustainable: the association of rhetoric's downfall with the imposition of one standard for disseminating cultural ideas over another. The original standard might be thought of as classical persuasion, fundamental to ancient rhetoric. In classical persuasion, the speaker uses the premises of the audience as a standard against which to measure the quality of the ideas presented. In classical persuasion, cultural ideas are of high quality because of their cultural resonance and wide social acceptance. The quality of an idea is tied directly to its cultural reach.

The cultural standard that came to replace classical persuasion in prestige circles, one accompanying the rise of Enlightenment science and technology, might be called *novelty*.[1] Bender and Wellbury (1990, pp. 1–39) traced the fall of rhetoric in the Enlightenment to five causes, all of which inform the antirhetoric rhetoric of novelty. These causes are the rise of science, the emergence of authorship and subjective expression, and the rise of liberalism, of the nation-state and national languages, and print.

Supported by each of these antecedents, advocates of the novelty standard came to utilize the *absence* of an idea's cultural precedent as the basis for assessing its potential quality. The potential value of an idea, in other words, is based on its being not fully accepted or anticipated in advance, on its setting its own historical precedent in the culture. On a novelty standard, the question of an idea's potential quality is thought of prior to and independent of its eventual cultural acceptance. The speaker trying to be new wants to persuade audiences; however, on the novelty standard, persuasion means little if it is not also seen as innovation, as ideas pushing the boundaries beyond what is currently known or archived.

Spreading new ideas would be hopeless, of course, if the long term for acceptance were too long and if the ideas disseminated were not in a medium durable enough to guarantee even the possibility of a long term. Here is where print fits into the story, because print specifically colludes with the novelty standard, and the novelty standard, with print.

Print, and the electronic modes of communication, claimed three important properties for making "newness" a feasible standard for cultural dissemination. The first property is archivability. Archivability is the capacity to store and retrieve huge quantities of information in the exact form in which it was composed. Ancients and medievals stored information in hand-written documents, but even the most careful of scribes introduced errors and corruptions as one copy was made from another. Print added mechanical reproducibility. This capacity allowed ideas to be fixed across time, space, and cultures. Print's role in bringing about such fixity has been commented on at length by cultural historians such as Ong (1971) and Eisenstein (1979).

---

[1]The theory of Kaufer, Geisler, and Neuwrith (1989) cites "novelty" as the standard for academic argument. Kaufer and Geisler (1989) explored this standard in detail; see the introduction.

The second property is boundedness. Boundedness means that a text contains all the content it will ever contain at the time it is composed. Readers bring their own learning and background experience into their reading of a text. But the texts that circulate among readers are not themselves augmented by this learning and experience. The textual content remains physically fixed across readings. Like archivability, boundedness is a property of documents, but the speed, scale, and lowered costs of printed documents made boundedness a material reality for an expanding market of readers. Kaufer and Carley (1993) argued that boundedness speeds the human potential to access new information. This is not because new ideas are unavailable in face-to-face interaction. It is because, in face-to-face interaction, new ideas compete in an ocean of commonly shared, ritualistic information. Face-to-face interaction evolved to perform many functions for the survival of collectives; the imparting of new information is only one of these functions. Interaction with written information has a much shorter history and a much smaller set of functions to perform for human survival. Because of the boundedness of texts, moreover, the sharing of new information becomes a prominent textual function. Boundedness allows texts to be artificially constructed to minimize the amount of ritual that passes between author and reader and to contain the reader's search for new information.

The third property of print that supported the novelty standard is speed. Kaufer and Carley demonstrated that print (and, in general, media that support one-to-many communication) can greatly decrease the time it takes new ideas to diffuse across a society. Their mathematical argument rests on an intuitive one—if you can reach 10 readers at the same time, you will soon reach many more readers than if you need to address only one at a time.

Through these three material properties, print made it possible to foreground novelty as a new paradigm for the cultural dissemination of ideas. We do not mean to suggest by this that print alone subverted classical persuasion and enshrined novelty as a new standard of communication. Strictly speaking, the older rhetorical standard of persuasion was never overthrown as much as reinterpreted. We suggest rather that print was a powerful factor in what came to be the reinterpretation of an older rhetorical standard in terms of a newer scientific one. Print, and especially the explosion of print capacity during the industrial revolution, made it a feasible expectation from the mid 19th century on that the prestige cultures of persuasion could, and should, also be cultures of innovation.

Not coincidentally, we think, the reinterpretation of classical persuasion in terms of novelty in prestige circles of cultural communication brought with it the decline of rhetoric and the ascension of design. In the post-Enlightenment world, design has come to be known as what innovators must do to persuade. Scientists design theories and experiments in order to uncover the design in nature. Richard Dawkins (1986), in his book *The Blind Watchmaker,* identifed the fundamental problem of biology as explaining nature as a "complex design" of random convergences. Engineers design machines. Architects design buildings. Politicians design policies and programs. Novelists, poets, and playwrights, asked to speak to the innovations in their writing, now talk about the design of character, image, mood, and scene. Until the mid 19th century, rhetoric was the central discipline for teaching speakers how to motivate and direct organizations. Now we have management *science,* where MBAs are trained how to design optimal organizations and procedures. In every case where design has overtaken rhetoric, the agent of study, and sometimes even the object (nature), is recast as an innovator who seeks to work with an audience, but only through a design.

In an era that makes design the privileged site of prestige persuasion, rhetoric is either an important absence or an outright failure of design. Rhetoric has not comfortably survived the Enlightenment because it is seen as bald persuasion, persuasion outside of the innovative context of design, or bad persuasion, relying on a failed or seriously flawed design.

## THE RECENT REEMERGENCE OF RHETORIC

Recent developments, however, have altered this picture of rhetoric and design as arts in opposition. Such developments have tried, self-consciously, to incorporate older notions of rhetoric and argument into the leading edge of novelty cultures. Serious students of the design process, for example, have come to recognize that reflective processes are an important and recurring element in guiding the productive aspects of a design, and that these reflective processes often rely on the strategic uses of language consonant with rhetorical practice. Schon (1983) was the first to make this point in book length. The case for language, even rhetoric, in design was explored with even greater specificity by Fisher, Lemke, and McCall (1991). These researchers posited that the design process is divided between constructing things and using language to discuss, analyze, and finally advise the constructive process as the design evolves. When multiple designers favoring different priorities are involved, the language in design must be explicitly rhetorical, adapted to persuade other agents about the direction in which the design should go. In this more recent understanding of the relationship between rhetoric and design, commentators are willing to acknowledge that persuasive words can profitably direct design. This view gives rhetoric a more honorable face. This face of rhetoric is given more prominent exposure still in two movements that came to the fore in the 1980s: the rhetoric of inquiry (Bazerman, 1988; Lyne, 1985; McCloskey, 1985; Nelson, McGill, & McCloskey, 1987), and writing in the specialized disciplines (see Kaufer & Young, 1993, for a review). Both movements make it common practice to expose rhetorical activity both in the informal practices of science and in the formal channels of published research.

## OUR PROJECT

Our project is consonant with efforts to move an older rhetoric into the center of creative activity that animates the novelty cultures of today. There are also notable differences between our project, the rhetoric of inquiry, and writing in the specialized disciplines. At the risk of oversimplification, the purpose of the latter projects is to show how rhetoric, as a practice, is pervasive in sciences that are thought to be "mature" enough to have surpassed, to have evolved beyond, rhetoric. Within the scope of these projects, rhetoric is "exposed" in places that have attained their eminence by denying their reliance on rhetoric. Work in the rhetoric of inquiry and writing in the specialized disciplines tries to show, in sum, how rhetoric, assumed to be a loosely knit and relatively unstructured bundle of practices, finds its way into disciplines considered too highly structured to need rhetoric.

Significantly, work in both these areas tends to view rhetoric as a common meta-knowledge needed to understand where the logical and methodological foundations of a discipline fall short and where discursive practices of speaking, writing, and persuading begin. As a *lingua franca*, rhetoric is cast as a way to foster intellectual exchange across disciplines that otherwise share little in common. Like a Cicero holding together Rome's warring factions, rhetoric is portrayed as offering the open hand of a civic culture to close-fisted specialists. But even within these positive constructions, rhetoric itself remains without an intellectual center or an indigenous founding knowledge. Rooted in atheoretical practice, it is judged "ill-suited to founding theories." It is rather "an antiepistemological epistemology that breaks down the walls dividing disciplines" (McCloskey, 1995, p. 17).

We certainly don't diagree with McCloskey's characterization of rhetoric if rhetoric is touted to be, or to rival in logical systematicity, an axiomatic science. Rhetoric never has defended itself or could defend itself, against the charge that it does not proceed, lawlike, from universal assumptions to universal conclusions. But rhetoric has paid a higher price for this absence than perhaps even Plato could have imagined. An implication of rhetoric's decline in the modern academy, we later argue, has been to diminish it into a caricature of itself, into a practical art, serving the ends of persuasion, but lacking a substantive basis beyond the value of the ends sought.

Our project begins with the concession that rhetoric is not axiomatic science. But we go on to suggest that such a concession need not force rhetoric to flatten itself from a body of knowledge into a bridge. We argue that rhetoric has remained institutionally unstable as an indigenous knowledge because the academy has failed to place it where it deserves to be placed—in the family of design arts. Our project, in short, is to reconceive rhetoric as an art of design, and to present a theory based on that reconception. Our reconception, and the theory drawn from it, in no way threatens the aims and uses of rhetoric in writing in the disciplines and the rhetoric of inquiry. On the contrary, it promises to bring a more systematic and centered notion of rhetoric to those enterprises. But our reconception and theory also strive to situate rhetoric, as an art of design, in activities that go beyond the walls of the academy. We hope to show how even traditional expressions of rhetorical knowledge, public address in civic forums, meet the requirements of highly structured design knowledge, a knowledge needed to create "new" artifacts from the creative oragnization of known materials. Design knowledge is the knowledge associated with the architect, engineer, and computer specialist. It is standardly described as (a) modular, able to be broken into parts; (b) cohesive, allowing the parts to be related back into a working whole; and (c) problem-focused, allowing persons with the knowledge to apply it to do so for pragmatic ends.[2] Our thesis is that rhetorical knowledge, whether practiced in civic communities or by schooled professionals, is a type of design knowledge.

The requirements for design knowledge are seldom articulated, but in chapter 3, drawing from the work of Goel and Pirolli (1992), we enumerate them and compare them with the knowledge underlying the rhetoric of public address. We use this comparison to propose an architecture for rhetorical design (chapter 4), and the rest of the book is an effort to demonstrate the viability of that architecture.

Why does such a project matter? It matters because in the modern revival of rhetoric, we have often mistaken rehabilitating rhetoric with salvaging it for the ivory tower. The thinking is that rhetoric for the world remains fallen, but its academic reputation can at least be restored by showing how traces

---

[2]This is not intended as an exhaustive definition of design knowledge. For a fuller description, see chapter 3.

of it show up in academic argument. Such thinking slights rhetoric's historical tradition and recurring potential as an agent of effective change in the world of practical and political action. It filters the richness of the rhetorical tradition through the narrow lens of the contemporary academy rather than permitting us to expose the narrow academic reinterpretation of rhetoric through the lens of the tradition.

Geisler (1994) wrote at length on this matter. She showed that important changes took place in the discourse of philosophy as it moved in the 19th century from the sphere of generalist publics to audiences composed only of academic philosophers. The language became more specialized and technical. The textual representation of the author and the author's opponents also changed. From a generalist discourse reflecting a chorus of voices competing for control, the specialist discourse of academe turned the speaker's voice into a solution of a linear puzzle, the best way to get from A to B on a particular issue. The opponent's voice, represented in the text, was forced into the cul-de-sac of citation, transformed either into a supporting citation or a "faulty path" (Kaufer et al., 1989), a negative citation distracting the reader from the true solution. The rich and often inconclusive interplay between a live speaker and a live opponent was lost in the narrow bandwidth of the written medium. The human dimension of civic argument, played out in register shifts, false starts, and intellectual hiccups, was expunged when the advocacy discourse of civic society became professionalized. Geisler concludes that much can be lost when a generalist rhetoric becomes professionalized.

We concur. Yet without a framework of a generalist rhetoric as design, we remain in the dark about all there is to gain or lose when rhetoric is taken to a disciplinary context. Our project offers a baseline for understanding the various additions and accommodations that a civic rhetoric must make when it expresses itself in physics, biology, diplomacy, engineering, and other specialized contexts. We don't mean by this choice to devalue the study of rhetoric in the disciplines. We mean rather to say that all professions and disciplines are also publics, and by following a theory of rhetoric as design within a general public, we can begin to track how public rhetoric is transformed or elided when taken further into a professional or disciplinary context.

The account we offer is essentially a rhetoric of words, a verbal rhetoric. This flies in the face of contemporary experience, where many, if not most, of the rhetorical arguments we receive in the general culture come from static and kinetic images, packages, and products in addition to words. In a recent, innovative volume on design thinking, Richard Buchanan (1995, p. 44) related the broad multimodal context of design thinking to rhetoric:

> Rhetoric is still perceived by many people in its Renaissance orientation toward poetry, belles lettres, and beaux arts, rather than in its twentieth-century orientation toward technology as the new science of art, where theory is integrated with practice for productive purposes and where art is no longer confined to an exclusive domain of fine art but extends to all forms of [visual and three-dimensional] making.

Although we share Buchanan's goal to relate the tradition of rhetoric to modern design, our preference is not to begin straightaway on the project of formulating a multimodal rhetoric, one that combines words with other plastic arts of expression. We are interested first in trying to understand what words alone bring to the mix. As any producer of tabloid news knows, it is more riveting, production value held constant, to show a suicide on television than to report it in words. But in order to appreciate why the image enhances the power of the words, we need a baseline of what the words can do on their own. In 1955, the philospher John L. Austin revolutionized linguistic philosophy when, in his William James lectures at Harvard (published as Austin, 1975), he proposed to his audience that much could be gained by asking, How do we "Do Things" with Words? Now, four decades later, the fundamental question of rhetoric may be, How do we "Design Things" with Words? We consider this question throughout this book. The question may seem strange because we tend to think of words as names for things rather than things, artifacts, products, in their own right. And yet we suggest that what rhetors design, elementally, are abstractions—a public and its trajectory through time and space—that are embodied by and large through the abstractness of language. We demonstrate, for instance, how speakers can use words to design histories, conspiracies, precedents, and even images of themselves as public agents.

A theory of rhetoric amounts to nothing without specific examples to inform and answer to. To make our theoretical work answerable to naturally occuring rhetorical artifacts, we apply the theory throughout to the seven joint debates between Abraham Lincoln and Stephen A. Douglas during the summer and autumn of 1858.[3] We have chosen these debates because they are a celebrated specimen of rhetoric, allied to no other modern discipline, a prime example of what the classical rhetoricians called deliberative rhetoric (arguments about future policy) mixed in with what modern democracies know as campaign rhetoric. Of these debates, Roy Basler observed that, "it

---

[3]Unless otherwise indicated, the debates transcripts we used in our analysis are published in Johannesen (1965).

would be difficult to find in all history a precise instance in which rhetoric played a more important role than it did in Lincoln's speeches of 1858" (cited in Einhorn, 1992, p. 4).

We choose a debate format because rhetorical design always deals, explicitly or implicitly, with an audience's collaborative and an opponent's competitive input. The environment of rhetoric, that is, always involves a context of a speaker or writer's discourse being designed cooperatively, with the real (in the case of speaking) or simulated (in the case of writing) participation of an audience; it further involves the competitive design of discourse with the participation of a real or simulated opponent. The study of a spoken debate format makes it possible to consider rhetorical design in a context where the input of audience and opponent is live and not merely simulated.

The particular Lincoln/Douglas debates are of further interest, moreover, because they allow us to study the importance of media choice in rhetorical design. As Zarefsky (1990, p. 54) noted, the debates " probably represented the first time that campaign speeches had been reported verbatim." This meant that Lincoln and Douglas had the choice of designing their speeches either mainly for the audience in attendance or for the reading audience. Douglas' primary audience seemed to be the immediate, face-to-face audience in each local gathering. Lincoln's, as he himself mentioned in the Galesburg debate, was the print[4] audience, the literate opinion leaders in each town and village who often exerted disproportionate influence by orally relaying, perhaps putting their own spin on, newspaper accounts to nonreaders.

We explain the debates as an artifact designed from the competition between two gifted rhetors. The ultimate worth and test of a productive theory of design is how well it explains the artifact designed.Naturally, an adequate theory of rhetorical design will eventually have to account for many rhetorical artifacts, not just Lincoln/Douglas. But thus far we are lacking theories of rhetorical design that can capture the design of even one realistically complex case. We acknowledge from the start that our account is limited, even for this single example. Through our analysis of Lincoln/Douglas, we are not trying to end the story of rhetoric and design but to open it up for rigorous treatment.

---

[4]Print messages have durability (Kaufer & Carley, 1993) beyond the immediate rhetorical situation. Lincoln's interest in the printed word suggests that he was interested in communicating his long-term plans for the country above and beyond the tactical moves that made him a "winner" or "loser" within the debate.

Ours may be considered a "minimalist" analysis of Lincoln/Douglas insofar as we are trying to map the minimal complexity needed to understand various design decisions in that debate. By a minimalist analysis, we mean an attempt to develop an explanatory framework that accounts for a significant portion of the observed results with minimal conceptual complexity. It is essentially the application of Occam's razor, a basic launching point for the systematic arts, sciences, and theory construction in general. A symptom of rhetoric's long handbook tradition is to view it mainly as a practical "how to" art, an art too inherently commonsensical to merit an analysis of its minimal underlying complexity. By insisting that rhetoric be treated as design, we are also insisting that the appropriate way to approach rhetoric is to seek the minimal and general in an art of overwhelming complexity. This insistence is not to be confused with bringing technical jargon to a handbook tradition, which is more a means for making the simple complex than to make the complex simple. Given our approach, a way to falsify and improve upon our account (and we do think rhetorical accounts should be falsified and improved on) is to show that rhetorical design can be treated with comparable coverage and explanatory power but more simplicity than we have been able to muster. Readers can judge this for themselves based on how well and parsimoniously our account handles the underlying complexity of the Lincoln/Douglas debates. We hope that those interested in these debates and other rhetorical artifacts put our account to the test and suggest better ones. At the conclusion of this book, we tell the reader what to do to prove us wrong. If we can provoke readers to accept our invitation, we will have met our internal standard for success.

Before we enter the world of Lincoln/Douglas, however, we must elaborate the general theory and our specific architecture that links rhetoric to design. This we do over the next few chapters.

# Two

# Overlooking Rhetoric as Design

To begin to understand rhetoric as an art of design, we need to examine why rhetoric is generally overlooked as a design art, why it is not likely to be heard in the same breath as arts like architecture, engineering, and graphic design. In this chapter we explore more received assumptions about the placement of rhetoric, either as a liberal or a practical art. In either of the traditional placements, the fit is not all that good. Rhetoric is typically viewed as more practical than the traditional liberal arts and more liberal than the traditional practical arts. We investigate the consequences of these received assumptions and examine their limitations. We finally develop a definition of the design arts that is compatible with the conception of rhetoric as an art of design.

A good place to begin our analysis is with a definition of rhetoric, which will, in turn, be an invitation to better, more descriptive, elaborations of rhetoric within the family of design arts.

## A DEFINITION OF RHETORIC

Let us define rhetoric as the control of events for an audience. To be more specific, let's say that rhetoric is the strategic organization and communication of a speaker's version of events within a situation in order to affect the here and now of audience decision making.

### Factoring the Definition

There is much in this definition that we ignore for now. Of immediate interest is the notion of "events" and "situation" that figures into it. Let us explore these notions further.

#### Events

Events are clause-size depictions that a rhetor brings to the attention of an audience during a rhetorical situation. A rhetor, either in face-to-face contact with the audience or through a text, punctuates the audiences' here and now with dozens, scores, hundreds of continuous or sporadic events, depending on the duration and interactivity of the communication. Unlike physical phenomena, such as heartbeats or magnetic forces, events, as phenomenological entities, do not exist as independent forces of nature. We cannot count or measure events in the manner of heartbeats and magnetism. Events are constructs of how we view, make sense, and talk about the world around us. As such, events depend on a perspective toward the world that expresses itself in a linguistic consciousness. Consider the following two descriptions of the same physical phenomena:

Event 1
   The pitcher threw the ball. The batter, number 22, swung...and missed. The game, the series, and the season were over. The Cubs had finally won a World Series.

Event 2
   Casey, number 22, brought the bat around expecting to hear the crack of a cleanly hit baseball. But all he heard was a swish, a thud, and the umpire's call of "Strike three." The game, the series, and the season were over. They had lost the World Series to the Cubs! And it was his fault...

These two examples illustrate how it is possible for the same physical phenomenon, in this case a baseball player striking out, to function as the basis for significantly different events (the strikeout that wins the World Series or the missed opportunity that loses it for the opponent). Recording the "same" phenomenon from different perspectives is enough to differentiate Events 1 and 2. Strictly speaking, events span semantic, acoustical, and spatial fields of perception. An event always marks off either a discrete or continuous flow of time. But the dimension of time differs depending on whether the perception of the event resides within a semantic, accoustical, or spatial field. Take, for example, the clause "Casey, number 22, brought the bat around," a subevent of Event 2. Semantically, the movement of time is embedded in the tense/aspect system of English, in the past-tense verb phrase "brought around." Acoustically, as sounds of language, the movement of time is registered as frequencies and pitches that are interpreted by the ear and brain into semantic events. Spatially, as marks of typography, the movement of time is expressed in the spatial-serial organization of the page, allowing for the reader to detect, for example, that the writer of Event 2 has composed visual marks that reference both the batter's swing and hopeful expectation, and that the writer's marks lie, in planar space, "to the left of" and "above" (and so by implication prior in time to) references to the umpire's call and the writer's own registration of disappointment. When we speak of events henceforth, we leave it implicit, up to context, whether we mean the accoustical or spatial features of linguistic events as the source of their temporal meaning. That is, we do not burden the reader with discriminating these sensory contexts on every mention of "event." For the most part, what we have to say about events in rhetorical design is insensitive to the particular field of language processing, writing or speech, as long as the events are eventually processed semantically.

It is not a defining condition for rhetoric that the speaker employ language referencing a world "out there." To be sure, audiences will understand the speaker's language as mattering because of its presumption of making external reference to a world beyond. But the notion of language making contact with an external world is a presumption of everyday reference more than of artistic rhetoric. The presumption of rhetoric is more that the speaker can manage to construct events with enough art and transparency that the speaker's representations, however complex and interested, seem little more than the unveiling of the truth. Elevating the presumption of reference to high art, rhetors seek the optimal intersection between truthful reference and a role definition for the audience to accept and act on that aligns with the speaker's interest.

The rhetor's presentation of events is varied and nuanced, but on a broad spectrum, the presentational format ranges between one pole, canonical event-telling, and a much broader and, for our purposes, undifferentiated class of noncanonical event-telling.

### Canonical Event-Telling.

Canonical event-telling is the basis of what is often called "simple narrative." Narratives are typically thought of as simple when they evince four properties. These properties are abstract and hard to grasp without examples, so we will lay them out briefly and then turn to examples. The simple narrative:

1. Relies on, through finite verb phrases, a sequence of events that are discrete, bounded and completed. The events, having been completed prior to the speaking event, are marked in the past tense.

2. Relies on an omniscient point of view, permitting the speaker to conceal the fact that only a version of the past is being represented whereas the past that is put forward lends the appearance of surviving, or rising above, any version.

3. Relies on verbs early in the sequence to activate semantic expectations that are satisfied by verbs later in the sequence. This is especially true when

the scenic background remains constant. For example, the narrative is more likely to contain semantically related events (e.g., "climbed the slope," "skied down") when the events reside in the same scene (e.g., a ski slope in the Alps) than if they cross scenes (e.g., from a ski slope in the Alps to a café in Paris);

4. Relies on verbs in the sequence being relatively independent, meaning that the onset of one event in the sequence follows the completion of the one before. Within a simple narrative, there is minimal or no overlap in the time of events that constitute the sequence. This yields the overwhelming impression that the events that comprise the simple narrative are easy to isolate and count.

An example clarifies these properties. Encyclopedia entries provide a rich source of canonical event-telling, especially when the entry is anchored to a single scenic background. Consider the following entry for the first battle of Bull Run. (The verb phrase sequences are highlighted in boldface.)

### First Bull Run

On July 21, 1861, roughly equal forces **met** near Manassas, Va., in the first major land battle of the war. McDowell's army (soon to be known as the Army of the Potomac) **attacked** Beauregard's lines along Bull Run Creek. Successful early in the day, the Federals **were** at last **held** on the Confederate left by Gen. Thomas J. Jackson's brigade, rushed to the field by rail from the Shenandoah Valley. Jackson's men **held off** repeated attacks, and as Gen. Barnard E. Bee (1824-61) of South Carolina **sought** to rally his own men, he **cried**: "There is Jackson standing like a stone wall. Let us determine to die here, and we will conquer." Stonewall Jackson **became** an internationally known hero in the wake of that rebel victory, but it **proved** to be costly. Southerners **became** overconfident, and Northerners **buckled down** for a long, hard war.

This passage conforms to the four requirements of canonical event-telling. First, the verb phrases are mostly discrete nondurative verbs, indicating punctuated moments of start and surcease that keep the narrative flow moving at a steady pace, with minimal background exposition. The verbs are what Fleischman (1990) called pointed and completed "achievements" in opposition to more continuous "states" (e.g., Stonewall was brave) or "activities" (e.g., Stonewall's men were fighting bravely). Not until the passage moves from the battle to its aftermath for the South does the author of the entry move from achievements to more static and continuous state verbs (e.g., became overconfident, buckled down). Second, the passage is told from an omniscient point of view, seeming to take no side or even role-play one. The passage is written just to indicate "what happened" in the least contestable terms possible. Third, the earlier verb phrases are semantically related around the scene of a battle. Fourth, while related, the events in the scene do not overlap, as the forces had to meet (i.e., come into proximate contact) *prior* to McDowell's attack; McDowell had to attack *before* he could be held off; Jackson had to be fending off the northern army *before* General Bee could immortalize him in the pose of a stone wall. Earlier events anticipate later ones, but they do not entail them. The past and present could have existed with different futures. They could have been decoupled from the actual future they are assigned. This gives each event within canonical event-telling the look of an independent semantic island in an ocean of non-event-related meaning. As the boldface in this passage indicates visually, the verb phrases are relatively easy to mark off from the rest of the text. From the writer's canonical event-telling, we feel we can literally enumerate what happened at Bull Run that day because the events recounted seem to stand out and apart from the text, like a holographic image.

### Noncanonical Event-Telling

By way of contrast to canonical event-telling, noncanonical event-telling is the telling of events that fail some or all of the requirements of the canonical form. Because noncanonical forms are defined as an unspecific absence of specific criteria, we are not prepared to enumerate the range of noncanonical forms. What we are prepared to do is to glimpse the increasing complexity of bounding "an event" when events are presented noncanonically.

Unlike encyclopedia writers, professional historians openly explore and write from a point of view. Often, their reference point is not the unmediated past but how previous historians, with different points of view, have described the past. They thus self-consciously compose versions of the past that include responses to previous versions. Prior to the 1960s, some historical accounts of the Lincoln/Douglas debates had Lincoln offering to debate Douglas and Douglas accepting the offer. These accounts were often told in canonical form, as a conventional sequence of extending an offer to a second party (Lincoln extending to Douglas the offer to debate) and then noting the second party accepting it (Douglas accepting).

Having researched the origins of the debates in the 1950s and early 1960s, the historian Donald Fehrenbacher (1962) found evidence to contravene this canonical historiography. For one thing, Douglas had not accepted the offer that Lincoln originally proposed. Lincoln had proposed fifty debates, not seven. For another thing, Fehrenbacher found, Douglas never had a fair choice to accept or to reject the offer. The offer was made to trap Douglas in a dilemma, for an uncertain outcome awaited Douglas no matter how he responded. If he accepted Lincoln's offer as is, he would have to share too much of the limelight with Lincoln and expend too much energy giving exposure to his lesser known opponent. Yet if he refused to debate Lincoln, Douglas risked the image of a coward running from a fight. Fehrenbacher found that Douglas' response to the dilemma was to agree to debate but only on his terms, not Lincoln's. And he also found that, despite Douglas' "acceptance," the Republicans still tried to expose Douglas' response as an act of cowardice, as if he had flatly turned Lincoln down. Because of the complexity of the story Fehrenbacher uncovered, he needed to move away from the canonical event-telling of simple narrative. The history he composed (p. 100) is as follows, again with the event phrases put in boldface:

It is inaccurate to say, as so many historians do, **that the Little Giant "accepted" this challenge.** Lincoln's plan, if agreed to, **would have meant at least fifty debates, an exhausting thing even to contemplate. Douglas dared not respond with an outright refusal, but he had no intention of going through the entire campaign yoked to Lincoln.** Explaining that his speaking schedule precluded such a comprehensive arrangement, he **offered instead to "accommodate"** his rival by meeting him seven times. Lincoln, with some unseemly grumbling about the terms, **accepted** this wholesale revision of his original proposal. Republican papers in the state **left no doubt that they considered the challenge declined.** The Press and Tribune **exclaimed:** "The little dodger shirks, and backs out, except at half a dozen places which he himself selects." In Springfield, the State Journal **maintained** that about one hundred debates **ought to have been scheduled,** and that Douglas, by his "inglorious retreat from a public discussion," **had stamped himself as only "seven hundreds of a candidate for the Senate."**

Fehrenbacher's language violates every one of the requirements of canonical event-telling. As for the first requirement, boundedness, each of these event representations depicts the ongoing states of consciousness of a complex content, a content that cannot be bounded by simple, well-delineated, or independent verb phrases. As for the second requirement, the omniscient perspective, Fehrenbacher places scare quotes around the verbs "accepted" and "accommodate" to indicate a more focused and interested point of view, one indicating that the simple narratives of many previous historians won't wash. The events in Fehrenbacher's history do not reference the discrete and bounded acts of offering and accepting; they rather reference the versions of prior historians who have mistakenly offered up the canonical acts of offer/acceptance as descriptions of "what had happened" to start the debates. The events in Fehrenbacher's history reference complex mental representations, in sum, that depart in significant ways from the omniscient point of view.

As for the third requirement, the sequencing of discrete events, Fehrenbacher's account resists a sequential ordering. Earlier events are subsumed in later ones if they do not exactly entail them. The verb phrases constructing Douglas' consciousness are semantically focused around the scene of Lincoln's offer, but they are not independent. They depict Douglas' rejection of a future in which he'd have to share the stump fifty times with Lincoln; they depict Douglas' wrestling with the psychological dilemma into which he felt placed by Lincoln's initiative; they depict Douglas' decision about how to respond to the dilemma; they depict Lincoln's being forced to accept Douglas' acceptance in anything but a gracious state of mind; they depict the Republican partisans hitting back at Douglas' "acceptance" so that the public would see it as a rejection. It is further clear how Fehrenbacher's account defeats the fourth requirement, independence. His description suggests a complex interaction between Douglas' fears, his determination, his strategizing, and his calculation of the relevant risks of entering into debates with Lincoln. No realistic description of an active consciousness at work could, or would, separate these events into independent moments. Within the construction of a consciousness, the past, present, and future are integrated as overlapping horizons of time that unite intention, action, and reflection. This gives each event in a noncanonical presentation the look, not of a semantic island, but of a dispersed mass spread across sentences and paragraphs with no clear boundaries.

Hopper (1995) studied these dispersed forms of events in point of view reporting and called them MAVES (for multiply articulated verbal expressions). The verb phrases associated with MAVES are virtually impossible to mark off from the rest of the text without guesswork or arbitration. From Fehrenbacher's noncanonical event-telling, we feel we know the events that happened when Lincoln approached Douglas to debate, but we do not see the events as discrete occurrences cleanly extractable from the full textual account. Rather than needing the text to "contain" the events, as in canonical event-telling, we feel in noncanonical event-telling that the events depicted form an identity with the textual account.

In summary, we have defined rhetoric as the control of events for an audience. Unless the rhetor buys into some very narrow requirements of simple narrative, the presentation of events will be noncanonical. Noncanonical event-telling allows for a range of psychological attitudes, perspectives, and nuances toward events that is not available in canonical event telling. For this reason, rhetors very often rely on noncanonical forms when they present events to an audience. This increases the sophistication of the events that can be brought to an audience's attention. But it also complicates the analysis of rhetorical products. We revisit events in greater depth in chapter 6 and the presentation of noncanonical events in the Lincoln/Douglas debates in chapter 9.

## Rhetorical Situations

Rhetorical situation is a term of art among students of rhetoric referencing the features of historical occasions that give rise to acts of rhetoric (Bitzer, 1968). The Lincoln/Douglas debates, seen in the grand sweep of history, provide a constellation of such situations. A single situation of rhetoric provides an arena through which rhetoric takes place. An arena is a collection of role and culture-specific factors that qualify a situation as a situation for rhetoric. In western rhetorics, speakers exercise a great deal of individual latitude in determining a particular situation as an arena for rhetoric. Significantly, even in our own culture, not all situations pass muster as rhetorical situations, and it is an interesting point of cultural, and cross-cultural, inquiry to determine the factors, apart from individual discretion, that define rhetorical arenas. Liu's (in press) important work in opening up Chinese rhetoric suggests that the arenas for rhetoric in Chinese culture may be circumscribed in part through the Confucian principles of the person/situations that are "addressable" and "nonaddressable."

Rhetorical situations are rich sensory experiences, relying on experiences far beyond words. Many of the sensory inputs that occur within the arena of a rhetorical situation remain under the control of the rhetor and can shape the events that are associated with the rhetoric. Using visual information, the rhetor can use his or her dress and the backdrop to make a statement about the seriousness or lightness of the rhetorical purpose; using sounds, the rhetor can use the surrounding whirr of factory machines to indicate his or her contribution to a healthy economy; using smells, the rhetor can make use of the disinfectant used to clean the walls and floors of a school house to remind the audience of its own school days.

Much of the rhetor's control of sensory inputs brought to the arena of rhetoric depends on the rhetor's control of the situation. Situation involves the time and place of interaction as well as the technologies, or media, of interaction. Does the rhetor choose to speak at high noon or midnight, deep in a valley, on top of a mountain, in a rose garden? Does the rhetor choose to rely on his or her unaided voice in a small room or a voice amplified by a mike in an auditorium? Does the rhetor choose an audience contained by four walls? Or are electronic media allowed to broadcast the message to more distant audiences? If media are involved, does the rhetor turn to the phone, printed press, telegraph, radio, television, fax? Does the rhetor decide to enter cyberspace, reaching audience members through e-mail or the World Wide Web? Does the rhetor seek to avoid live electronic interaction or encourage it?

Beyond these decision points, the rhetorical situation also involves the inclusion of what might be called "ancillary events." Ancillary events are acts of rhetoric played out in fleeting or short-lived arenas that are designed to stimulate and increase an audience's awareness of more sustained and substantive arenas. A book jacket is a short arena of rhetoric seeking to call an audience's attention to the larger and more sustained arena of the book. A similar analysis applies to a newspaper headline, a movie trailer, a wall poster, a promotional pamphlet, a television ad, a bumper sticker, or a word-of-mouth endorsement. Control of the rhetorical situation involves control of the ancillary events that are meant to call attention to it. Not infrequently, control of the rhetorical situation is labor divided between the rhetor and agents working on his or her behalf. An author controls most of the content of a book, but publishers control most of the ancillary events that allow readers to find it.

In this book, we have nothing to say about the rhetor's control over the arena of rhetoric, including the planning and design of ancillary events. We do not talk about how or why rhetors choose a particular arena of rhetoric in order to best convey the message they want to convey. Rather we restrict ourselves to understanding the rhetor's choice of design options once the arena has been chosen and the ancillary events have performed whatever function they have been designed to perform. This allows us to identify what we take to be robust features of rhetorical design that recur across various rhetorical situations. This further allows us to explore and seek to distill a general architecture of rhetorical design without having to deal with all the possible design options that are situation dependent. We are left to seek out an underlying wholeness to rhetorical reasoning that cannot be called into question merely because rhetoric always falls into a context of one diverse sort or another. Not least important from a methodological point of view, we have the hope of constructing a general theory of rhetorical design from a single sustained historical situation of rhetoric whose complexity provides nothing if not a good starting point for general theory—the Lincoln/Douglas debates.

Our focal interest resides in Lincoln and Douglas as agents of rhetorical decision making. Our goal is to offer a theory of rhetorical design that is expansive enough to understand a wide range of their rhetorical decision making. It is the case that the Lincoln and Douglas decisions are affected, in part, by their assumptions about media. As we indicated in chapter 1, Lincoln targeted primarily the elite reading audience whereas Douglas courted the immediate listening audience. This difference involves our looking at the effect of intended media on rhetorical design. The investigation assumes, nonetheless, a constancy across the rhetorical situation. We assume, that is, that Lincoln and Douglas make their rhetorical decisions within the same arena of rhetoric. The fact that they make their decisions with different media in mind does not mean they are choosing different arenas of rhetoric, just different priorities for the types of messages they plan and put forth in that arena.

## THE ANOMALOUS PLACEMENT OF RHETORIC IN THE ACADEMY

Consider for the moment how our definition of rhetoric, as the control of events for an audience, is related to rhetoric's anomalous placement in the academy and, in particular, the academy's ambivalence toward rhetoric. With its emphasis on the speaker's control of events, our definition affirms a tenet of the traditional humanities, namely, that the human agent lies at the center of inquiry about the surrounding world. Yet our definition also carries with it an element that illustrates rhetoric's difference from the traditional humanities: a focus on the control of specific local phenomena, rather than the understanding of universal causes or conditions.

It has often been difficult to reconcile the dignified universals of the humanities with the interestedness, practicality, and localness of rhetoric. Rhetoric's seeming inattention to universals is one source of the modern suspicion against it as a legitimate member of the liberal arts in the manner of literature and philosophy. Its inattention to "truth for all time" makes it a remote cousin with history, which seeks truth for all time about particular times and places. The liberal arts have historically spoken to matters conducive to leisure and random curiosity more than to tactical doing and the making of artifacts under deadlines. Even when professionalized into "disciplines" in the modern research university, the liberal arts of philosophy, history, and literature have eschewed the "practical," abstracting from routine occupational details and deadlines.

In contrast, beginning with ancient Greece and Rome, the art of rhetoric has been timely and interested, involved in civic, organizational, and commercial life. The study of rhetoric was and remains invested in helping lawyers, legislators, and now a host of other symbol-using professionals perform their everyday jobs. In contrast to a focus on universals, the art of rhetoric is used to seek results in the specific case. To be sure, students of rhetoric should not ignore a general understanding of how local results come to pass. Aristotle affirmed that understanding general truths about the means of persuasion is a direct accomplice and not a casual bystander of effective persuasion. Rhetorical knowledge, nonetheless, refers to a productive knowledge that is mainly local, tactical, and applied.

Being local means that the productive knowledge underlying rhetoric must be evaluated by standards other than the enduring truth associated with the subject matter. Expertise in a subject matter will certainly be necessary to formulate event representations that can persuade other experts. But expertise, in the absence of rhetorical skill, will often fail to convince even insiders. Truth may be a standard for a specific subject matter, but audience interest and acceptance are seldom containable within a subject matter's first principles. They often arise from contingent considerations that are not part of the subject matter proper.

Being tactical means that the productive knowledge underlying rhetoric has a competitive aspect, allowing a speaker to be declared a winner even in the absence of a message that is novel, true, or even principled. Rhetoric always culminates with an audience making a judgment. A rhetorical artifact may undergo many iterations before it is completed, but every iteration culminates in an audience judging the present version to be more or less successful than the last.

Being applied means universals are relevant to rhetoric only when they can explain success in a given context. Traditions of rhetoric have differed in the extent to which successful persuasion and being able to produce reasons for one's success have been allied. The theoretical (*rhetorica docens*) tradition of Aristotle emphasized this linkage more than the practical tradition (*rhetorica utens*) of Cicero. But even the theoretical traditions of rhetoric relied on fundamentally utilitarian reasons for linking production and explanation. It was assumed that being able to explain success in terms of universals would make success more routine.

Given the local, tactical, and applied nature of rhetorical knowledge, it was and has remained impossible to defend rhetoric against the earliest charges made by philosophy that rhetoric has no intrinsic interest in the universals of truth and morality. This is not to deny that rhetors, as all humans, have a stake in truth and morals. It is just to say that this investment for rhetoric is not a defining condition. Rhetoric is too contingent to be too principled. Its contingency makes it necessarily a flexible art. Rhetoric is based on a flexibility in the representation of complex social situations, a flexibility required if the individuals in the situation are ever to accomplish practical goals.[1]

## Rhetoric as a Practical Art?

Defining rhetoric as the strategic organization of one's version of events may seem on its face to do nothing to counter the historical prejudice against it. It seems to keep rhetoric boxed in as a banal art of audience enticements. We intend to show that this is not the case. Admittedly, the handbook tradition of rhetoric, aimed at novice learners, is often couched in a simplistic "how to" style that encourages this view of rhetoric as a practical art. We first consider, and then challenge, the idea of rhetoric as a superficial art of the practical.

### Definition of a Practical Art

When we speak of a practical art, readers should keep in mind that we are speaking of "practical" only in the pejorative vernacular of today's academic culture, a remnant of Enlightenment thought that tends to separate the theoretical and the practical and to associate reason with theory and contemplation more than practice and production. Although Aristotle understood politics as a noble art of the practical, the practical arts since the Enlightenment have fallen from that ancient sense.

Practical arts are now understood as forms of production whose successful execution is predictable on the basis of the person setting the goal to do or make something. Working a photocopy machine is a stereotypical example of practical activity. For most people, having the desire to make a copy is the dominant predictor of success. An art descends into the realm of practicality when the realization of the agent's intentions seems unremarkable. An office assistant needs to inform a group of people about an upcoming deadline. The assistant types a memo with a word processor and uses a photocopier to make hundreds of copies, which are distributed throughout the organization. Operating a photocopier has no daunting learning curve; it seems to be no big deal. Yet it is connected in an intimate way with the original goal, informing everyone about the deadline. Because steps for realizing the goal seem to follow almost trivially from setting it in the first place, the goal and its realization practically collapse on top of one another as actions. Such a

---

[1]It is misleading to characterize the rhetor as compromising truth and honesty for shades of truth and honesty. It is more accurate to say that rhetoriticians, at their moral best, seek the shadings that define the most principled stance one can achieve in the circumstances.

collapse of goal and realization characterizes the arts of the lowly practical. It also characterizes the substantive content of the prejudicial adjective "mere" when one speaks of "mere" rhetoric with a sneer.

Significantly, the imputation of "mere" is not cast on all the arts evenly. The public is not cautioned to beware of "mere" architecture or "mere" software design as shadow arts to the true arts. Yet there is plenty of bad, in the sense of incompetent or dishonest, architecture or software design. And arguably, suffering from bad architecture (increasing devastation in hurricanes and fires) and bad software design (throwing into chaos world financial markets, nuclear power plants, and the air traffic control system) exacts a cultural toll no less steep than incompetent or evil rhetoric. So why has rhetoric become the special object of negative stereotyping?

One possible answer it that the concept of "mere" rhetoric is a result of viewing rhetoric as a practical art offering little challenge beyond the naked intention to power. A speaker wants to be persuasive, stands on a soapbox, and begins to deliver rhetoric. Everything is done with the use of words and images.[2] The speaker's intentions arguably begin as (internal, unverbalized) words and the delivery finishes off in the same medium. No expensive apparatus, external instrumentation, or elaborate setup is required. Only words are required, a medium available to humans with little conscious effort after a few months of life.

The singular danger perceived with rhetoric is not that the speaker will fail to meet his or her goals (rhetorical being a lowly practical art), but that the speaker will lack honorable goals. The cultural anxiety toward rhetoric seems to result from the dual logophobia that words can be both "easy" and "dangerous" at the same time—easy because they can be mastered, unlike the building of atomic bombs, by the lowest elements of society; dangerous because they can have profoundly pernicious effects. Rhetoric thus unleashes to too many a great power to do harm.

An additional dimension of what makes rhetoric "easy" in the mindset of the culture stems from another connotation of the lowly practical. For a practical art, we assume that the agent's intentions are largely unchanged in the course of taking the actions to realize them. The practical arts, in other words, tend to place emphasis on the doer's intended outcome of action with little need for adapting or complicating the original intent. This is not to say that the knowledge required for a practical art is trivial. Often the instructions for operating a photocopier can occupy several volumes. But the

---

[2]As already indicated, we restrict out present discussion to verbal rhetoric, rhetoric as words only. A similar analysis applies if we extend rhetoric to images as well.

hallmark of a practical art is not the volume of what must be learned as much as how that knowledge is organized. In a practical art, it is assumed that, however much there is to learn in some absolute sense, the organization of what there is to learn remains structurally simple. More specifically, it is assumed that the items to be learned are relatively independent. For this reason, the items can be learned in a relatively "flat" linear stream, as a list. There are no complex interdependencies between the items that can make learning fragile and even improbable.

This flat list structure is how handbooks have typically organized the knowledge associated with rhetoric. Rhetorical knowledge is often portrayed as a long list of things to know or do, and because the medium of action is just "words," it is easy to suppress the possibility of there being subtle and complex interdependencies to make the words work as they do. Perelman and Oldbrechts-Tyteca's (1969) treatise on rhetoric is an example of a theory of rhetorical knowledge, insightful in its particular entries, that is nonetheless organized as a phone directory of information about argument. In a practical art, no matter how long the instruction set, the instructions can be understood one at a time, so learning, in essence, remains "easy." It is these very considerations that follow from and reinforce the idea that rhetoric is a practical art. The same idea explains why rhetorical knowledge is too often confused with the list-like books that contain information on the subject. Such confusions would have caused catastrophes for the development of architecture and engineering. But viewed as a practical art, the confusion has seemed less pernicious for rhetoric.

## Some Efforts to Rehabilitate Rhetoric as a Practical Art

Sensing that rhetoric has a more noble, though hidden, face beyond that of practical persuasion, writers in the rhetorical tradition, beginning with Aristotle, have sought to bolster the respectability of this face. They have sought less to change the practical art than to rehabilitate it.

One such strategy is to ennoble the practical art by emphasizing its systematicity and structure through rules. Organizing rhetoric by "rules"[3] does not change the fundamental list structure of the practical art, but it does at least offer navigational paths through the list. Rhetoric is described as a set of "rules" to think about and adhere to as intention refines itself into expression. The rhetor is encouraged to think in prescriptive formulations

---

[3]Rules might be contrasted with the organic tradition of rhetoric, which associates rhetoric with inspiration more than with practical message giving.

through such heterogeneous categories as situation, purpose, audience, invention, logic, organization, character, the emotions, style, and grammar. The rhetor is made to understand, not unreasonably, that the hard work of rhetoric is surveying the components of the message and then assembling them according to prescriptions of good form.

A second strategy is less to ennoble the practical art through rules than to fit rhetoric into a narrower, more tractable, and more honored set of outcomes and practices, such as rational persuasion or dialectic. Although the "ruling" of rhetoric was associated most with the Romans, Aristotle's tack was to make rhetoric the the counterpart or correlative (*antistrophos*) of dialectic (1991, Book I1, p. 28).

True, rhetorical design culminates in (not always rational) persuasion, in changing or at least reinforcing the beliefs and behavior of the target audience. However, persuasion signifies only the final state of this process. It is difficult to reconstruct a complex process simply by knowing the final state toward which it is launched.

In response to this difficulty, rhetoric is often associated with a rational process, notably the process of dialectic. To be sure, a positive consequence of coupling rhetoric and dialectic has been to anoint rhetoric with philosophical prestige by defining it as overt reason-giving behavior. A speaker, under this analog, practices rhetoric by giving reasons for or against a position on an issue, and the quality of the rhetoric is judged to be conditioned on the quality of the reasons given.

Although the close association between rhetoric and dialectical argument may have served, in the minds of some, to rehabilitate rhetoric or at least to expose a rational face, there remain three noteworthy gaps between standard dialectical reason-giving and rhetorical behavior.

First, as understood by Aristotle, dialectical behavior involves the exchange of views by speakers (1991, Book I.12, p. 34n.) interested in exploring an intersubjective truth, in the manner of a Sherlock Holmes or a textbook scientist involved in "disinterested" inquiry. The dialectician needs to be willing to change positions abruptly and often as the preponderance of evidence changes. The dialectician needs to understand the situation with the interlocutor (or opponent) as cooperative rather than competitive, as both are trying to enlighten the other rather than beat him or her into submission. These assumptions conflict with the conditions under which Aristotle describes the exercise of rhetoric. In the rhetorical contexts Aristotle describes (i.e., public speaking in the legislatures and courtrooms), speakers operate as advocates with fixed competing interests that can perhaps be compromised but never fully dismissed or negotiated away by "evidence." In sum, a prerequisite of rhetorical behavior is a context of potentially competing interests, a context that does not characterize dialectical interaction in its purest form.

Second, as understood by Aristotle, the dialectician usually operates in a social context of peers who are not only knowledgeable about the subject matter but also on constant watch for the potential defect of reasoning that would fool an unsophisticated audience. The aim of dialectical exchange is to rout poor reasoning about a subject and to identify promising paths. For those goals, the dialectical partner needs to bring to the mix both knowledge and skepticism. For rhetoric, on the other hand, Aristotle makes no such stipulations about the qualifications of the audience and in fact acknowledges that the audience for rhetorical occasions often lacks the training or alertness to follow a detailed argument.[4] The aim of rhetoric, according to Aristotle, is to bring an audience to judgment in a context of competing interests. Often this goal is easiest to fulfill when the audience for the occasion shimmers with neither knowledge nor skepticism. In such contexts, it is easy, and strategic, for the speaker to behave rhetorically in ways that violate the standards of dialectical exchange.

Third, and perhaps most importantly, anyone who studies naturally occurring instances of rhetorical behavior knows how much "messier" that behavior is than a parlor game played out under stipulated rules of dialectical repartee. Rhetoric is strewn with arguments of various types. But it is also rife with much that strikes one as gratuitous from the point of view of rational argumentation. Rhetoric relies not incidentally on humor, on ridicule, on the emotions and pleading, on characterizations, on wit, word play, and tone, on storytelling, on disclosure, and on excursions into autobiographical worlds. From the standpoint of strict dialectical argument, these aspects of rhetorical behavior are at best diversionary and at worst irrational.

In sum, writers in the rhetorical tradition who have recognized a systematic and rational side of rhetoric have sought to ennoble the practical art either by presenting rhetorical knowledge as ruled or by fitting rhetoric into a more uniform, less complex outcome, process, or method of interactive reasoning or argument. This first effort implies that rhetoric is a practical art of learning many different things loosely strewn together. The second effort implies that rhetoric is a practical art of learning some relatively uniform thing, involving neither diverse nor challenging components. In both cases, rhetoric is reduced to something less interesting and challenging than it in

---

[4]The Platonic tradition of rhetoric made no stipulation that even the speaker was knowledgable.

fact is. It is rationalized as a practical art despite the fact that any rationalization within the practical arts, we submit, is bound to leave rhetoric behind.

Before proceeding further, let us take stock of where we have been and where we are going. One might ask, why associate rhetoric with the design arts at all? What, in the long term, is at stake in this way of looking at rhetoric? What is to be gained if the association can be made compelling?

## Rhetoric as a Design Art

In higher education, one finds special labs and studios for teaching architecture, engineering, and the graphic arts. There are no comparable studios for teaching rhetoric. Rhetoric is not associated with a studio or a lab art. Unlike most design arts, rhetoric is perceived as "common" and "everyday." We do not expect everyone to have consummate rhetorical skill. Yet we expect that everyone in their everyday lives should have a minimal competence in rhetoric if only to meet the responsibilities of collective life.

Historically, this expectation has led to another: that the demands for competence in rhetoric within a free society mean that rhetoric should be a part of every student's education. To those acquainted with rhetoric as a body of knowledge associated with Demosthenes, Cicero, Edmund Burke, and Danial Webster, rhetoric since the Greeks has had an important calling. Along with logic and grammar, rhetoric formed the trivium of education in medieval Europe; until the middle of the nineteenth century, it remained an unchallenged cornerstone of a liberal arts curriculum in American universities; and, to this day, students of the rhetorical tradition recognize rhetoric as an art fundamental to a free society, especially in times and places where democracy and open forums of expression are prized. Rhetoric has thus not been denied a place in the liberal arts. Its place has just not been accorded the same status as those arts considered timeless and universal. In lieu of universality, rhetoric relies on practicality and utility. In lieu of timelessness, rhetoric is enacted in carefully timed performance. To the highmindedness of the classic stance of humanism, rhetoric seems all too worldly and compromised, too concerned with giving its students an edge rather than a good soul.

## Definition of a Design Art

Design arts highlight a distinction between an agent's naked intention, the goals outside of and motivating the design, and the goals of the designer that reside in the design. The goals of the design (e.g., fame, wealth, glory, power) and the goals *in* the design (e.g., balance, symmetry, restraint) coevolve. The defining conditions of a design art are that (1) the goals of the design are perceptually distinct from the goals in it; (2) the artifact produced by the design depends on the coevolution and convergence of these systems of goals; and as an unavoidable consequence, (3) the actor requires considerable effort and skill to bring about this coevolution and convergence.

A moment's reflection suggests that rhetoric matches these defining conditions of design. Viewed as a design art, the goals in rhetoric are distinguishable from the goals of a particular use of rhetoric. Missing this distinction is largely behind the logophobic accusation against rhetoric as "dangerous," for to collapse the distinction is to hold rhetoric hostage to the goals of the persons who practice it. Imagine, for example, that a speaker uses rhetoric skillfully to lie. The charge of "rhetoric" can be dropped for a more specific ethical lapse, a lapse dependent on the goals of the design, but not on the goals in it.

Aristotle made the same point when he offered that rhetoric is an amoral art that can be used for good or ill. Yet many rhetorical theorists are also moralists who disagree with Aristotle on this point. They refuse to condemn only the external goals of rhetoric while leaving the internal goals beyond good and evil. They base their refusal on the fact that skilled rhetoric can greatly enhance the evil of a person who is bent to do evil. For example, moralists often blame Hitler's evil in no small measure on his powers of rhetoric. They can't find reason to exonerate the skills in his rhetoric when those skills seemed so consequential to bringing about the goals of it.

On this issue, our inclination is to side with Aristotle and against the moralists. It seems folly to condemn Hitler for his "rhetoric" when other moral labels that evaluate his naked intentions, such as "mass murderer," remain available. Granted, the fact that Hitler's rhetoric was so "good" is needed to explain how the depths of his evil were achievable. But this acknowledgment only induces one to want to put a stop to Hitler, not to rhetoric. In most cases, when a speaker acts through intentions that are evil, the charge of "rhetoric" can be thrown out as irrelevant. In the study of rhetoric, like other design arts, the evaluation of a speaker's naked intentions and deeds can be separated from the evaluation of the design in the rhetoric. The example of evil but brilliant rhetoricians suggests only that the art of rhetoric can be misused, has the potential for being directed toward malfeasance. Were this potential sufficient to condemn every art and discipline, then all would be condemned.

An ethical consideration more intrinsic to rhetoric is whether the audience is empowered to see the design behind the events constructed. The question is not whether audiences will always see the design or even sometimes see it. For, as art, rhetoric is always produced not to be seen. The question is, rather, will the audience be empowered to see the design if the audience makes the concerted effort to look for it? And from this question we can rightfully ask, what is the responsibility of the designer to motivate the audience to make the effort to look? Further, we can ask, what is the responsibility of the designer to train the audience in what to look for?

These questions resist blanket answers because they depend on the perceived importance of the circumstances for rhetoric. In designing a commercial for bottled water, neither the audience's responsibility to look nor the designer's to teach what to look for seem pressing. But in designing a message for nuclear power, the stakes, and so the ethical responsibilities, appear to increase on both sides. What is clear is that the demand for ethical scrutiny must come from both sides or the assumption of responsibility is only incompletely examined. If the designer of rhetoric does not demand it, he or she will see nothing that audiences must learn before they are fit to be audiences. If the audience does not demand it, they will have, at best, only the patience to learn what the designer wants them to know.

The goals of rhetoric are as vast as human motive and intent. Yet the design goals within rhetoric, we argue, are surprisingly finite. They are based on the notions of predictiveness, responsiveness, and humanness, to be discussed at greater length in chapter 5.

The ethical issues involving rhetoric are only scratched, not resolved, on the strength of these considerations. There is a hidden complexity in the issue of the moral independence of the design from the designer, the rhetor from the rhetoric. We do not open up this issue until the next chapter.

Because the goals in a design art change as the design proceeds, designers need to rely on a variety of representations to understand and communicate their various intermediate results as they proceed. In a prototypical design art such as architecture, for example, sketches, blueprints, models, mock-ups, thumbnails, and storyboards are created at intermediate stages preceding the creation of the final artifact. In *The Sciences of the Artificial*, Simon (1969) stated that to design and manage the information needed to create truly complex artifacts, designers must organize the work-in-progress into relatively independent, hierarchical collections of elements. It is through organizing information into modules and levels, he claimed, that we can design very complicated physical and symbolic artifacts such as jet airplanes and large computer programs.

Although the coevolution of the designer's goals and the artifact and the utilization of hierarchies of elements to assist in this coevolution are both prime characteristics of the design process, they also are what makes so-called good design hard to study. This is because so-called "good" design is often judged to be design that hides the very characteristics of its making. A central perception of good design is that the designer has managed to hide the collections of different elements involved in the design, to make the artifact seem as if it were produced in a single seamless burst of creativity. Plenty of not-so-great musicians, one can imagine, share the basic intentions of the great ones. Plenty of nonmusical instrument makers share with musicians the knowledge of the instrument's capacity to make sound. Only the exemplary musicians, presumably, can interleave their goals with their knowledge of the physical aspects of the instrument. Although a trained judge may be able to detect and recover intricate details of the coevolution, and laypersons can at least appreciate that integration has taken place, the perception of different elements at work and the designer's ability to interleave them seamlessly within a single artifact are what allow us to appreciate good design.

In many design arts, such as architecture, the interaction of the various elements associated with the creation of artifacts can be depicted as in Fig. 2.1.

For the architect, the design process draws on his or her knowledge of three-dimensional space and how forms map onto esthetic, functional, and livable space. In addition to using this domain knowledge, during the design

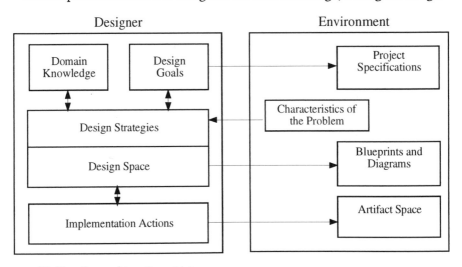

FIG. 2.1.   Elements of the architectural design process.

process the architect must develop a battery of specific design goals, strategies, and plans that can be applied to satisfy the needs of a particular client. Because the architecture design process typically involves multiple people, an architect must encode many of these goals and plans in a symbolic form for clients and other designers. A project description or specification captures a snapshot of the goals, whereas blueprints and engineering diagrams attempt to capture the lower level plans. Each documents captures different aspects of the design process that must be integrated to complete the final physical structure.

The goals, strategies, and plans within a design are likely to change throughout the design process. In reviewing the blueprint or the specifications, the client is reviewing much less than the final artifact. These symbolic representations are meant to capture as much of the client's "choice set" as possible, making it feasible for the client to track how his or her own goals and intentions are being embodied in the design so far. Externalizing the goals and plans assures that the client can participate in the design process. It further assures that the architect does not stray too far from the agreed-on goals or go too far into the costly, material phase of the design process without approval from the client.

As the process continues, the designer enters, or oversees, the implementation phase. To implement his or her plans, the architect must understand a set of complex operators that map the features of the design onto the characteristics of the material artifact. Taken as a set of coordinated actions, these transformations convert the plan into the material design. Although the architect needs to know about the existence of these operators for implementation, he or she may end up overseeing, rather than carrying out, the actual implementation. There are different reasons why this may be so. First, the actual implementation may require too much labor for one person to accomplish in a reasonable time. Second, the material components involved in the implementation can vary widely, requiring many areas of expertise outside of design expertise. For a building, material components include foundational structures, wood, wire, and water pipes. The architect needs as a result to turn to structural engineers, carpenters, electricians, and plumbers to implement many of the plans for a building from a blueprint. However, it remains the responsibility of the architect to ensure that the various material elements are seamlessly integrated in the final structure.

In summary, a design art is a production process that involves the interdependent development of goals and a material artifact, relying on knowledge about the nature of the artifact to be produced. Because of its complexity, this knowledge is organized as a hierarchical collection of different elements. The challenge of a design art is to develop an artifact that is, ideally, a seamless integration of the knowledge and goals of the designer. Because much of the design process is externalized through symbolic representations, it is relatively easy to see that prototypical design arts, such as architecture and engineering, have these characteristics. Yet, for various reasons that we consider later, it is much more elusive to perceive, and so appreciate, these features in rhetoric.

### Consideration of Rhetoric as a Design Art

In architecture and other forms of design in which implementation involves physical materials, there is a dichotomy between the symbolic representations and the "real" artifact. As shown in Fig. 2.2, the symbolic includes the goals and proposals down to the blueprints and plans. The real includes the physical materials shaped by these plans.

This dichotomy has relevance as a stereotype in the sense that design arts that culminate in a material (nonsymbolic) artifact are often considered to be more "real" than design arts that result in a purely symbolic artifact. Examples of design arts that end in material artifacts are architectural, mechanical, product, and hardware design. Examples of design arts that end in a symbolic artifact are software, instructional, and graphic design. In the hierarchy of design arts, the first set of examples are considered, prejudicially, to be "real" design arts, and the second set, more "quasi-real."

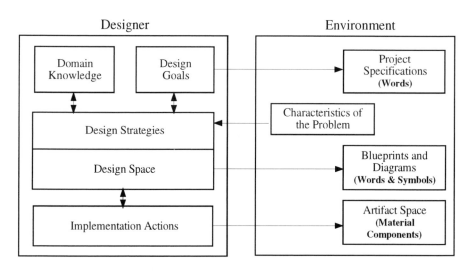

FIG. 2.2   Different symbol systems of the elements in the architectural design process.

Because of the stark and visible difference between physical materials and pure symbolic materials, the boundaries between the components in a real design art, mediating symbolic and material worlds, are themselves more stark and visible than those involved in quasi-real design. The seams in quasi-real design, nonetheless, typically retain a certain degree of visibility. For even in quasi-real design, the designer's goals and intentions have a symbolic embodiment that is different from the symbols in which the plans are expressed and the plans, a symbolic embodiment that is different from the symbols comprising the final artifact. For example, in software design, the highest level goals and strategies are embodied in words, the planning space in a more restricted logical English, and the final artifact is embodied in a set of statements coded in the syntax of a programming language.

However, rhetoric remains suspect as a design art because it seems not to fit within either the stereotype of the real or quasi-real design arts. Like quasi-real design, rhetorical "design" results in an artifact that is symbolic rather than material. But unlike the more acknowledged quasi-real arts, the seams involved in rhetorical design all consist of one uniform symbolic type—words—leaving the very boundaries that could conceivably discriminate levels of the symbolic, much less the symbolic from the real, blurred.

This feature of rhetoric encourages the belief that the internal logics coordinating words with more structured knowledge types, evident in the quasi-real design arts, are utterly absent in rhetoric. And this belief, in turn, has bequeathed to rhetoric the appearance of pseudo-design rather than real or even quasi-design. Rhetorical design, on this common belief, accommodates few parts requiring intricate integration and few intermediate channels from which or to which information must flow when moving back and forth from conception to utterance. Rhetoric is rather seen as clever and deceptive wordplay all the way down, a house of verbal cards lacking solid foundation.

However, like good design, well-done rhetoric is characterized by a balance of many factors: the point of view of the speaker, the opponent, and the audience, various rhetorical goals, strategies, and plans that a speaker may have for a given rhetorical situation, and the numerous ways that these plans can be transformed into the spoken or written word (Fig. 2.3).

In fact, the various factors that are juggled in rhetorical design all depend on the audience in the end, for it is the audience whose response determines the success of the rhetor. If rhetoric is considered to be a design art, "mere" rhetoric is no longer the result of simplicity or danger but rather is a consequence of poor design. "Mere" rhetoric occurs when it is recognized that a speaker has not successfully integrated the various elements of rhetorical design, deciding instead to attempt an expedient, and so less than

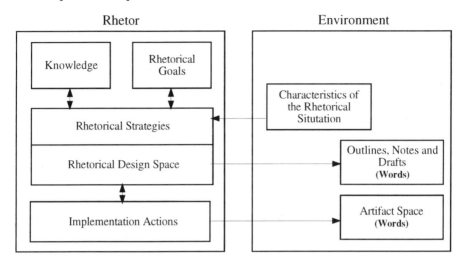

FIG. 2.3.   Uniform symbol systems in the elements of the rhetorical design environment.

fully deserved, resolution with the audience. In other words, the rhetor fails when audience members realize that they are being accommodated at the expense of other considerations, including, but not limited to, the speaker's credibility and the truthfulness of the remarks. When rhetoric seems overly compromised, it is because it is poorly designed and the audience is forced to come to the conclusion that the speaker must be pandering to them, or the clients of the rhetoric (e.g., the tobacco industry) themselves insist on messages that pander to targeted audiences and hire rhetoricians (e.g.. advertising agencies) who are willing to collude with them. The first compromise is a failure of design; the second is a failure of will behind the design.

As Plato and Aristotle seemed to understand, bad rhetoric, in either guise, is a visible misfiring within the engine of a less visible art. Associating rhetoric with an art of design is a call to systematize this ancient insight into explicit theory, for a mark of all skillful design is that its regularities are deep structures that cannot typically be caught at the surface. Like any design process, the results of skillful completion of the rhetorical process is characterized by purposeful, and seamless, integration of the elements of rhetorical design.

To summarize, for an adequate conceptualization of rhetoric, we contend that it is necessary to leave behind the practical arts and associate rhetoric with the arts of design. We must seek to recover, if not to consider for the first time, rhetoric as an art within the family of design arts, an art depending on the interplay of diverse elements that mediate intention and artifact. Rather than rehabilitate rhetoric through wishful normative theories that beg the principle questions about rhetoric before we get a chance to study it—for example, by identifying rhetoric with free speech and democracy—we advocate developing a solid base of description for an art of rhetoric as design.

# Three

# The Environments of Rhetoric and Design

In the previous chapter, we focused on understanding why rhetoric often gets overlooked as an art of design. There we concluded that the classification (or misclassification) of rhetoric as a practical art had a significant bearing on the matter. In this chapter we enumerate the characteristics of design arts in general and consider rhetoric in term of each characteristic. We define the concept of *module* in rhetorical design and overview the major modules in the design space of rhetoric. We conclude by examining how the notion of topics from classical rhetoric provided a practical means for writers on rhetoric to address the modular structure of rhetorical knowledge without having to explicitly theorize about it.

## THE ENVIRONMENT OF DESIGN

We begin by examining some family resemblances between rhetoric and design. Our claim is that rhetoric and design are structurally similar. We take for our starting point the work of the cognitive scientists Goel and Pirolli (1992). These authors posited that the activity of design involves formulating future states of affairs in one's head and then designing products that are externalized representations of these futures. In the case of the architect, there is the future state of a building under design and its gradual realization in material form. In the case of rhetoric, we have argued, the speaker must plan ahead to control the events in the here and now of an audience. Granted, most of the words used by the rhetor are chosen at the point of utterance and not prestored as complete sentences. But the same holds true for the architect, who does not carry in his or her head a true-to-scale physical model but a logical abstraction of what, through refinement, will become a completed material artifact. On this very point, Goel and Pirolli argued that "design is too complex to be specified by necessary and sufficient conditions." Rather, they claimed, one must consider general characteristics that are more or less central to, but not strictly required for, a generic design art. They went on to elaborate eleven of these characteristics and contrasted design environments with nondesign problems in logic and math. In the following paragraphs, we examine their ideas of what design environments have in common. We then compare these features with the environment of rhetoric to determine the features that rhetoric shares with the other design arts.

The first prototypical feature of a design environment is what Goel and Pirolli call the underspecified distribution of information. Unlike the information in an algorithmic environment (e.g. an algebra problem), the information in a design environment underspecifies a solution. There is incomplete information about how to start, where to end, and how to move from start to finish. In other words, the nature of a design problem does not strictly determine what the designer can (or should) do. Thus, the choices made by the designer impact the resulting artifact in a way that exposes the designer's own style and personality, beyond the artifact's strict success or failure as a "correct" solution. By contrast, for a well-defined problem in logic or arithmetic, the nature of the correct solution is defined strictly by the structure of the problem and not by the profile of the problem solver.

A second related characteristic of design is that design problems come with two very different sets of constraints. The first set, similar to nondesign problems, are the logical constraints that constitute the problem description. These constraints cannot be changed without fundamentally altering the problem. For example, it is generally not acceptable to randomly ignore one of the variables in a system of equations with three unknowns on the premise that to do so makes the problem easier to solve. A problem solver who seeks to modify the constraints in this case "cheats" by changing the problem before solving it. The second set of constraints, unique to design problems, are the constraints that underlie the choice set of the designer. Because of the underdetermination of the design problem, these constraints are often based on historical, social, and cultural information that is incorporated into the design space. A designer may do some things because a client is very insistent or delegates decision-making power to a proxy who is. A designer must be open to refining the constraints of the design on this contingent information. Consequently, there is no sense of the designer "cheating" when he or she modifies these constraints. These modifications are understood as the designer's needing to refine the problem prior to solving it, a necessary step whenever the initial information is too vague to begin serious work.

A third common feature underlying prototypical design environments is the size and complexity of the problem. Logic and math problems with well-known and converging solutions are typically small and well-constrained, requiring minutes for experts to complete but seldom longer.

Design problems, on the other hand, are large and complex, requiring hours, days, months, sometimes years to complete, often involving many people across many workspaces.

A fourth characteristic is the contingent modularity of design environments. In the previous chapter, we described a collection of elements that comprise a design art, including domain knowledge, goals, strategies, plans, and actions. Because of the size and complexity of design problems, it is necessary to decompose the design space into modules. A modular decomposition is a breakdown of a complex, hard-to-manage activity into a set of smaller, easier to manage activities called modules. *Module* is the generic name given to any of these smaller activities. Computer programmers, for example, designing a large program to solve a large problem, find it useful to break the problem down into smaller modules, design programming solutions for each module, and then assemble the small solutions into a large one. The underspecification of design constraints often means there is wide latitude in how the work of a large problem can be divided into modules. However, the need for the designer to develop the design constraints as he or she goes means that the basis for insisting on any particular breakdown is weak. Working with a master, an apprentice may learn that many design decisions are structured, not random, and so some modular breakdowns are more useful than others. But no breakdown is absolutely necessary for a successful design, especially when the definition of a "successful outcome" is itself a parameter that can be negotiated by the style and experience of the designer and the goals of the design.

A fifth feature typical to design environments is the interconnections of modules within a design. Many "clean" nondesign problems in logic and math arise because the problem can be broken down into a few independent modules. The independence of the modules means that the problem can be approached using a simple divide-and-conquer strategy. The problem, in other words, can be solved in parts and the solution determined by simply combining the partial solutions. In nondesign problem solving, that is to say, each module can be worked on separately and, when all the modules are completed, there is a strong guarantee that the modules can be "assembled" into a whole that works.

However, because of the complex relationships between modules in true design problems, it is much harder to approach such problems through a pure divide-and-conquer strategy. Decomposition remains desirable, un-avoidable in fact. But pure or complete decomposition resulting in modules that are fully independent and noninteractive, is impossible. One part of the design affects other parts in complex and often unforeseen ways. Consequently, designers often find themselves faltering when they discover they have failed to track these interactions, or, when working in teams, they realize they have forgotten to keep other members updated about changes they have made that affect other parts of the design. The interconnection of modules in design means that a design solution is more than the sum of the parts.

A sixth aspect common among design environments is that there are no right or wrong answers, only better or worse ones. Design is not a commitment to relativism; all outcomes are not the same. But neither can the outcomes be partitioned into binary absolutes, like right or wrong. What makes an outcome better or worse has to do with the fit of the design to the client's purposes.

A seventh commonality concerns the open versus closed process of design versus nondesign problem-solving. A process is closed when it can be enacted in full from information that is given at the start. Theorem proving is an example of a closed process. A process is open when it can only be completed by seeking more information from the outside environment. Because it is created on behalf of people (clients) and for the use of people (audiences, consumers, users), a design process is inherently open. The goals, desires, needs, and expectations of clients and consumers must be taken into account in order for the design to succeed. These are never fully communicated at the start of the process and must keep being communicated throughout.

An eighth feature is the lack of "real" feedback as a way of building the user's goals and expectations into the final design. According to Goel and Pirolli, designers receive no real user feedback until the design has been released to the client. Goel and Pirolli acknowledged that users may be selectively tested before release time, but this testing is only formative, helping to improve the current design in piecemeal fashion. It is far from a summary overview of the entire design. That level of feedback must await actual use of the artifact.

A ninth family resemblance is the costliness of a design's failing. According to Goel and Pirolli, the cost of a failed design can be very high. As the expectations put on a design increase, seeking some form of feedback (however distant from the actual client base) prior to the completion of the design becomes increasingly important and cost-effective.

A tenth common feature is the independence of the designer from the artifact. At some point, the design is launched and assumes a life of its own, which runs a course parallel with the life of the designer. Independence means that designs can be judged apart from the designers and the rationales that produce them.

An eleventh and final point of commonality is the distinction between specification and delivery. According to Goel and Pirolli, it must be possible to specify a design as an abstract plan prior to its embodiment in a concrete artifact. Moreover, this planning must precede the delivery of the designed artifact.

These eleven characteristics, summarized in the following list, were proposed by Goel and Pirolli as general features shared by most design environments.

1. The underspecification of the design solution.
2. The presence of both logical and design constraints .
3. Problems that are both large and complex.
4. The contingent modularity of the design space.
5. The interconnections of modules.
6. No right or wrong solutions, just better and worse.
7. Design is an open process.
8. The lack of "real" audience feedback during design.
9. The costliness of failure.
10. The independence of the designer from the artifact.
11. The separation of artifact specification and delivery.

## THE ENVIRONMENT OF RHETORIC

Previously, we proposed that rhetoric has the general characteristics of a design art and presented Fig. 2.3 as a conceptualization of the elements of "rhetorical design." Having reviewed Goel and Pirolli's detailed characterization of design environments, we now consider whether the features they cited are also present in rhetorical environments.

We start with the clear matches. Feature 1, underspecification of the problem, and feature 2, the presence of both logical and design constraints, are clearly present in most rhetorical environments. Like design environments, the environment of rhetoric typically offers less information than is needed to address the rhetorical situation. The speaker has more choices than are determined by the external situation, meaning that rarely is the rhetor logically constrained to one specific output, but rather must negotiate the rhetorical environment through contingent decision making. As described in feature 7, while making these decisions, both a rhetor and a designer must balance the needs of a client[1] along with other audiences and their interests.

---

[1] In ancient democracies, the birthplace of formal rhetoric, the speaker, representing him- or herself, was also the client. In a variety of contexts, the rhetor will have clients other than him- or herself.

In addition, as described by feature 9, serious costs can be incurred when a situated act of rhetoric fails. Issues of justice and injustice, life and death, often hang in the balance.

We now turn to the more problematical matches. Consider feature 3: the size and complexity of design problems. Normally one does not gauge rhetorical production at the same level of difficulty as the material production of complex structures such as bridges or buildings. However, this perception is largely based on the fact that the assembly of physical structures typically requires a large team effort, whereas the presentation of rhetoric is most often thought to be accomplished by individuals. Although they may seem easy to assemble, examples of well-done rhetoric involve an internal complexity that is significant enough to suggest an environment of design.

The case for contingent modularity (feature 4) is, or has been, less evident for rhetoric. There is no question that rhetoric involves contingent decision-making. The question is whether rhetoric requires modularity. As we observed in the last chapter, rhetoric has been traditionally conceived as a collection of knowledge that can be presented in an unordered list of "things to do" in various circumstances. Writers in the tradition have commonly thought that the ability to use this list to produce an organized, skilled performance depended on the student having the appropriate knack (in some cases, the knack for following rules of navigation through it). Teachers were thought to have completed their responsibility when they had covered the collection of knowledge and now waited only for students to do something impressive with it. On a design theory of rhetoric, in contrast, a central feature of rhetorical knowledge is knowing how to break down the rhetorical task into interrelated modules.

In the second part of this book, we elaborate a particular modular breakdown of rhetorical design knowledge. As with all design, the modular breakdown we describe for rhetoric tolerates a great deal of contingency, allowing alternative ways of producing rhetoric. Our modularization is intended to demonstrate a reasonable structure for the complex body of knowledge that makes up a rhetorical design. We also use this structure to consider how the various elements of the rhetorical design process (goals, domain knowledge, strategies, etc.) impact the various modules in a rhetorical design.

Another problem match between rhetoric and Goel and Pirolli's categories for design involves the interconnections between modules (feature 5). If classical rhetoric was not highly informative about the structure of rhetorical knowledge, neither was it informative about the interdependencies among different items in the "to do" lists. Instead of positing structures that enabled rhetors to monitor how change in one part of rhetorical knowledge affected changes in others, classical rhetoricians divided rhetoric into separate functions or offices—invention, organization, memory, style, and delivery—that were navigational but otherwise noninteractive steps toward preparing a speech. Each function could be studied as a separate subject, even though practical performance required their thorough integration. If rhetorical design constitutes one practice and not many, the rhetor must coordinate the progress of the design in separate modules. In our model of rhetorical design, this coordination is an important part of rhetorical strategy.

The task of monitoring better or worse performance (feature 6) is also a challenge in relating rhetoric to design. As we observed earlier, an important part of strategy is identifying how the various modules contribute to the overall performance of the design, in terms of meeting the designer's goals. However, specifying rhetorical goals is no simple task. Putative candidates like "persuasion," "truth," "dialectical fairness," or even "cleverness" do not easily work. As we see in chapter 5, the goals of rhetorical design also serve as standards by which to dynamically judge the success (or failure) of a design. It is these goals that inform the rhetor's design and allow him or her to evaluate and potentially improve it.

There are what at first seem to be some failed matches between rhetoric and Goel and Pirolli's features of design. For example, the match between rhetoric and design seems to fail outright in terms of Goel and Pirolli's 8th and 10th features, the lack of real feedback and the independence of the designer and the artifact. Although written, or mass-media, rhetoric can be characterized as lacking real-time feedback, this ostensibly is not the case for live, spoken rhetoric where the audience is available to respond. On closer inspection, however, we might better understand the audience's immediate reaction as equivalent to the formative feedback of a client anticipating what a user of the design will think about it. The genuine feedback, the feedback that matters, only comes about when the design is made available to the user and the user is given a chance to evaluate it. In like fashion, the feedback that most matters to the rhetor is not the feedback in the situation but the feedback that comes about after the situation has passed and the rhetor can monitor whether the audience's beliefs and behaviors match the intended outcome.

As far as independence is concerned (feature 10), the rhetor is never entirely independent from the rhetoric. This is because the evaluation of a rhetorical design is tied to the audience's perception of the designer. The Hitler argument notwithstanding, there is an unmistakable sense in which the worth of a rhetorical message depends on the audience's perception of the messenger. Cherry (1988) pinpointed just the matter at issue when he distinguished between a speaker's ethos (the character resident in the speaker) and his or her persona (the character implied in the speech). A speaker must have an effective persona in order to have an effective speech. But if the persona does not reflect, and purposely masks, the enduring character of the speaker, then the effectiveness of the speaker is not a consideration of technical neutrality alone; it becomes a statement about the speaker's capacity to dissemble about matters of character. Because rhetoric affords complex interactions between the design and the designer, as Cherry demonstrated, the one cannot be neatly judged apart from the other.

In light of these considerations, we do not believe that rhetoric differs from generic design on the matter of design/designer interaction. We rather suggest that Goel and Pirolli were mistaken about the putative independence of the design and the designer in general design. Suchman (1987) noted that designs are never fully autonomous from the designer. According to her, designers continue to stand in for their designs, even after release, and continue to explain their design rationale as they try to get others to understand, accept, and use their designs. Furthermore, the design rationale is so integral to the intended use of the design, and the design rationale is so often embedded in the perspective of the designer, that it is unlikely that the evaluative context of the design can be completely severed from the evaluation of the designer. To judge the designed object is to judge the perspective and priorities of the designer. What seemed a failed match between rhetoric and design reveals itself as a limitation in Goel and Pirolli's analysis. The interdependence of rhetoric and the rhetor moves rhetoric closer to, not farther from, other design arts.

Finally, consider the 11th feature, the expectation that a design be specifiable prior to, and independent from, the delivery of the designed artifact. It is on the basis of this feature that Goel and Pirolli excluded the arts of communication, including writing, from the design arts. In communication, after all, the specification and delivery of the message seem to occur simultaneously. According to Goel and Pirolli, designers tend to rely on strategies of incremental refinement and minimal commitment, and these strategies require a significant time lag between planning and implementing a design. Thus rhetoric, because of the simultaneity of planning and delivery, does not require this gap, and so lacks a feature of design.

However, if we acknowledge what Goel and Pirolli did not, namely that the designer is never fully independent from the design, we also reduce the apparent difficulty of insisting that design actions be planned and nonspontaneous. Because designers may include an image of themselves as part of their design, they can make themselves the objects of their own plans. In some cases, further, the image they may want to cast is one of a person who has used serendipity in some aspects of the design. Dramatic improvisation works just on this principle. In design, there is thus no general way to assure a plan of the design that can be completed in toto without the actual implementation put in front of the user. What is true for design is true for rhetoric. In rhetoric, speakers often find they need to design themselves to seem adaptive to an audience or an opponent. They can do this, in part, by appearing to be spontaneous in their speech or by actually being so. Further, if they have very limited planning time, they may have no choice in the matter other than to act spontaneously even if they would have preferred more time to plan. Thus, characterizing rhetoric as "spontaneous" must be done cautiously because timing can be hard to access (and so assess) from an external point of view; even the "look" of spontaneity does not preclude many exacting decisions about the message as it comes out. Nor does the reality of spontaneity necessarily disqualify an art either from the family of design arts or from rhetoric.

There remains one compelling issue concerning the requirement that a design be specifiable apart from its delivery. Despite all we want to claim about rhetoric as a design activity, it would be small victory if all we could say about rhetorical design is that it exists only in the same form as the delivered speech. Were this so, then our design theory of Lincoln/Douglas would be difficult to distinguish from the textual debate itself. In this case, Goel and Pirolli's skepticism about including the communication arts as members of the arts of design would be more right than wrong. Thus an important consideration in the remainder of this book is to specify modules of rhetorical design that account for but are nonetheless distinguishable from the textual product of the rhetoric. A central contention of this book is that rhetorical design exists as an entity much larger and more encompassing than the textual implementation of rhetorical discourse.

The example of architecture is again an instructive analogy. The design of any complex design artifact requires many modularized views to grasp the requirements that must be satisfied to understand what it means for the artifact to be well-functioning. To grasp what it means for a building to be well-functioning, for example, we must understand the internal workings of the structural plan, the architectural design, the plumbing plan, the electrical plans, and so on. Significantly, each of these modules is distinct but none-theless inderdependent, if only because the ultimate success of the design depends on the simultaneous realization of all of the views in the same artifact. The view we get from any one module fails to comprehend the whole, yet our only glimpses of the whole come from the standpoint of any one module, and perhaps from the vertigo we feel when our mind shifts from one module to another, understanding that no module offers a complete, or stable, view of a dynamic, internally complex whole.

Similarly, a modularization of a rhetorical design is necessary in order to deal with the complex nature of the rhetorical artifact. Each of the modules in the rhetorical design space, introduced in the next section and elaborated on throughout the course of this book, provides a different view of the developing design. Conceptually, these modules can be seen as symbolically different, focused on different aspects of the design. At the same time the modules are interrelated through the design, because like a building design, the success of a rhetorical design is dependent on the simultaneuous realization of all the various views.

## KEY MODULES IN RHETORICAL DESIGN

The fit of rhetoric to Goel and Pirolli's criteria of design leaves us with the notion that specifying an entity called "rhetorical design" is not an idle hope or merely the result of a clever metaphorical construction. Rhetorical design is, in potential, a literal concept with an operational specification. We can move closer to this potential by considering how the concept can itself be (contingently) decomposed into a set of more operational understandings. Every design art worth the name can be modularly decomposed. What does a modular decomposition of rhetorical design look like?

A central argument of this book is that the main modules in the design space of rhetoric are what we call Plans, Tactics, and Events (Fig. 3.1).

These modules account for many of the rich textures and variability that we find across rhetorical artifacts. Rhetorical artifacts vary according to the extent to which the attention of a rhetor shifts across these modules during the process of rhetorical design. At any one time during rhetorical design, one of these modules is the focus of attention. And at any one time, a rhetor can shift the focus from one module to another. With some indirect help from the machinations of the Strategy module, the tactical and event aspects of the design are coordinated with the plan aspects. Later we show, through the Lincoln/Douglas debates, how some of this coordination is accomplished.

Rhetorical artifacts are, to a greater or lesser extent, plan-driven, tactics-driven, or event-driven. Which module is the focus depends on the speaker's goals and knowledge. In chapter 5, we discuss the speaker's goals in more detail; in chapter 6, the speaker's knowledge and memory as both are

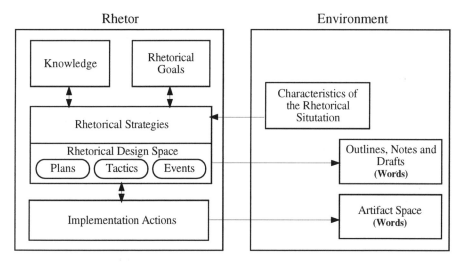

FIG. 3.1    Partitioning the rhetorical design space into plans, tactics, and events.

reflected in the structure of the rhetorical design. Our present interest is to overview plans, tactics, and events as modules involved in rhetorical design.

## Plans

We generally think of rhetoric as a contest between speakers with different interests. But that is to think of rhetoric only as a tactical art, an art more restricted than the conception of rhetoric we take in this book. Before rhetors can contest worlds and interests, they must first create them. This is the business of the Plans module of rhetorical design. In rhetorical design, the Plans module oversees a speaker's construction of the historical world and the means by which it should evolve into the future. Plans are used to build the world that the speaker has inherited, to project future worlds on the normative basis of these alternatives, and to discredit the contingent alternatives offered by other rhetors. Plans are a speaker's blueprints of the temporal world, the way the world "works" for good or ill, with the blueprints often recursively referencing the ill-conceived blueprints of others. The specific construction of the world built from Plans forms a model of a "public", the definition of which we pursue later in this book.

## Tactics

Were there no live opponents in the world, rhetorical design would be primarily plan-driven. Speakers would offer their blueprints to audiences and audiences would accept them, without an active opponent trying to interfere. In the Plans module, there are no live opponents—just wrong-headed thinkers who try to violate the natural blueprint of history and political life. Under the view of Plans, rhetoric would be more the design of Homeric poetry than political debate. There would be heroes and villains, but all pushed by a historical blueprint beyond their control.

The world, however, is full of live opponents, who seek to disrupt a speaker's stories from outside the speaker's design. This means that, as designers, rhetoricians must anticipate having their narratives disrupted by real persons. They must face up to the fact that others will assign to their historical blueprints the same tentative and contingent status that they assign to the blueprints of others. They need to envision their own underlying view of the world as itself part of a gameboard, where positional strength must be fought for and protected, like chess pieces. They must anticipate where they are most vulnerable and they must assess the vulnerabilities of opponents in kind. They must plan preemptively, in ways that are not part of their basic story about the world but that nonetheless minimize disruption from skeptics and opponents. These considerations are the role of the Tactics module in rhetorical design.

Classical rhetoric in the Aristotelian tradition often focused on rhetoric as a contest with an opponent, rhetoric as oppositional tactics in the legislature and the courtroom. When live opponents are in the environment and are not merely frozen stereotypes within a static plan, rhetoricians must also focus on the Tactics module. They must design with a live, counterplanning opponent in mind. Chapter 8 explains the Tactics module in detail.

## Events

The Events module focuses the speaker's attention on the moment-by-moment interaction with the audience at whom the message is aimed. Neither plans nor tactics captures the moment-by-moment interaction with an audience. Working transparently, calling no attention to itself as such, the Events module functions to lexicalize plans and tactics into linguistic objects, prior to their actual public expression before an audience as part of a sequenced presentation. Working more overtly, the Events module makes transformations to plans and tactics beyond lexicalization; it also helps a speaker adapt plans and tactics to the perceived requirements of specific audiences. Finally, working in the open, the Events module oversees a speaker's use of diversions, the capacity of the speaker to "wink" at the audience with lexicalizations that calls attention to the speaker as a human being distanced from the role of public speaker. The internal lexicalization of such diversions becomes the first stage of what eventually may appear to audiences as wit, humor, and irony. Whether such lexicalization does strike that appearance depends on the timing of the words in sequenced presentation as much as their linguistic content. But the Events module assigns the content required to initiate the beginnings of witty, humorous, or ironic expression.[2]

To summarize, Plans, Tactics, and Events are the key modules in the design space of rhetorical design. They represent important, although distinct, parts of such a design. Plans focus the speaker's attention on the construction of the inherited world and the social truths that govern it mechanistically. Tactics focus attention on contesting such worlds with live opponents. Events bring to the here-and-now of an audience the lexicalized worlds, opponents, and the contest that is at stake.

## CLASSICAL TOPICS: A PRACTICAL ALTERNATIVE TO MODULARITY

As we stated earlier, one of the key similarities often missed between rhetoric and design is the need for modularity in the design. The modularity of design environments is a first principle, yet it seems to be an exotic assumption for environments of rhetoric. Why? The answer may be that the rhetorical tradition found ways of teaching rhetoric that encouraged students to apply their knowledge of rhetorical design without having to come to a modularized understanding of the design space.

This type of instruction was evident in the topics. The elusive notion of the rhetorical topics, or, in Greek, *topos* (singular) or *topoi* (plural), is central to classical rhetoric, beginning with Aristotle. In his authoritative translation of Aristotle's *Rhetoric*, George Kennedy (1991, p. 320) defined *topos* as a "mental "place" where an argument can be found or the argument itself...a form or strategy of argument usable in demonstrating propositions on any subject to be distinguished from an idion, which is a proposition specific to some body of knowledge."

This definition is dense and multifaceted. Topics refer at once to a mental place and to the objects located there (a form or strategy of argument). They refer to a process (demonstrating) and to the results of applying the process (the propositions demonstrated). Propositions are always about some specific knowledge, yet the rhetorical topics are described as resisting an "aboutness"

---

[2]Later on, we make a further refinement by distinguishing the Events and Presentation modules. At this point, we collapse the work of these two modules.

relationship to such knowledge. When topics are about a particular body of knowledge, they are *idia* or special topics, knowledge unrelated to rhetoric. A central distinction in Aristotle is between special topics, which reside within the specialized disciplines, and rhetorical or common topics.

Here, we try to make sense of classical topics as a notion whose complexity is explained by understanding rhetoric as a design art. The process of rhetorical design requires pushing information to refinement by submitting prelexicalized knowledge to various views, from the view of this knowledge as fitting into plans, to the view of this knowledge on a gameboard with an opponent, to the view of this knowledge as lexicalized into "sayables."

Systems of topics also incorporate these views. Their incorporation of them, however, is implicit rather than explicit. Unlike modules, as we define them here, topics are associative patterns that are extremely permeable across modules. One and the same topical pattern, say, opposition, can trigger the mind to associate across different views without forcing the mind to recognize that boundaries have been crossed. The generic pattern opposition, for example, can help the speaker cleave to a specific and fruitful way of thinking about the historical world (as mechanistic forces and counterforces), a specific and fruitful way to think about the opponent in the contingencies of the situation (my opponent just said X and Y, which I must counter with Z), or a specific and fruitful way to lexicalize a piece of knowledge ("Let me not concede that...but rather..."). When the classical rhetoricians discovered the rhetorical topics, they discovered robust associative patterns that hold their shape well across hetereogeneous views of knowledge, across modules of rhetorical design. They discovered that one and the same pattern can mnemonically induce an argumentative plan from a memory of events, can induce an anticipated tactical advantage over an opponent, and can further help in the development of specific patterns of language with which to hold the moment with an audience. They came to understand that with special associative patterns, verbal gestalts, a speaker could perform a variety of diverse functions: tell the truth, turn the tables, and anchor the audience's drifting attention to the weight of the moment.

The referent of the topics was similarly diffuse. To speak of the topics was, at one and the same time, to speak of memories of events warehoused in long-term memory; to speak of the actualization of these events as plans in real-time interaction; to speak of the manipulation of these plans for the purpose of monitoring one's leverage in the situation; and to speak of the complex field of linguistic choice, determining the events that would ultimately find their way into the presentational stream of events.

The topics are inherently diffuse because they are verbal gestalts with no single module or environment of application. The topics can be understood precisely if understood as enabling a diffuse reference within a rhetorical design. Table 3.1 provides a look at 14 of Aristotle's 28 rhetorical topics as patterns holding their shape across argument plans, relational tactics, and linguistic events. The examples come from the Lincoln/Douglas debates. The table shows how a topic as used by Aristotle and other classical rhetoricians, seems to simultaniously establish internal coherence for an argument (as a plan), leverage for a speaker (as a tactic), and a linguistic stream of variable and opposing information (as events). To speak of the topics that inform rhetorical design is to speak of the refinement of information at all these sites.

An example can guide how to read the table. Take the first category of opposites. At the level of plans, speakers construct the historical world. They construct that world by aligning objects into complex object classes (chapter 7). The topic of opposition is evident at the plan level because, among other things, Lincoln and Douglas are opposed in the object classes they cite as instigating the primary issues, the reasons for rhetoric. Lincoln associates the problem with the object class "slavery" and Douglas with the object class "abolition." For Lincoln, all would be well were there no slavery, and for Douglas, were there no abolitionists. "Slavery" and "abolition" are opposing fillers for the same slots in the plans of Lincoln and Douglas.

At the level of tactics, speakers compete for leverage. They make their plans major weapons in the competition, but they also rely on nondiscursive objects—non sequiturs, nonresponsiveness, face threats—to compete. One way of competing is to play defense, to try to disrupt the opponent's plans. Both Lincoln and Douglas construct plans that tie the problem-bearing and the problem-resolving object classes with winning and losing positions, respectively. Both speakers want to claim that their plans produce winning positions and avoid losing ones. For both, a winning position is tied to the object class "making things calm" and a losing position "stirring things up." These represent oppositions at the tactical level.

The actual words slavery, abolition, agitation, and calm embody this tactical opposition as a series of linguistic or event oppositions. Lincoln makes Douglas' position on "slavery" a basis for "agitation" and his own antislave position a basis of "calm." Douglas makes Lincoln's position on "abolition" a basis for "agitation" and his own "don't care" position about slavery a basis of "calm."

We could say that topics occur independently at the level of plans, tactics, and events. But to say that is to miss the elegance of the topic, for the topic

TABLE 3.1
A Topic as a Pattern Activating Plans, Tactics, and Events

| Topical Pattern | Plan | Tactic | Event |
|---|---|---|---|
| 1. Opposites | Show that argument of self leads to unexpected and strengthening event classes; show that argument of opponent leads to unexpected and weakening object classes. | Reverse leverage by showing that the ground of the opponent's winning position seeds a losing one, and vice versa. | Lincoln: "Slavery is the source of agitation; its elimination, the source of calm." Douglas: "Abolition is the source of agitation; freedom to choose slavery in the territories, the source of calm." |
| 2. Correlatives | Show, through correlative slots, that argument of opponent is missing crucial information or contradictory. | Reverse leverage by showing correlatives that expose the opponent's argument as having less force. | Lincoln: "Douglas endorses freedom to choose slavery in the territories. Every choice implies the slot of chooser. But who gets to choose and when? Any answer smokes out Douglas as having no clear position." |
| 3. More or less | | Reverse leverage by showing that self's own weak arguments are still stronger than opponent's; and strong, stronger; or arguments weaker than self's have been accepted; arguments stronger than the opponent's have been rejected. | Douglas: "Illinois rejects anti-Nebraska Republicans, much less abolitionists, like Lincoln." Lincoln: "Douglas accuses his opponents of lying. Have I ever done anything remotely like that?" Lincoln: "Douglas and I both argue for a conspiracy. But mine is more probable than his." |
| 4. Reversing the charge | | Reverse leverage by showing that the opponent's attack is self-indicting. | Lincoln: "Douglas argued that only Lincoln could thank a conspiracy to nationalize slavery was afoot. But Douglas made the same charge only a few months back." |

TABLE 3.1 (*Continued*)

| Topical Pattern | Plan | Tactic | Event |
|---|---|---|---|
| 5. Variation in meaning | | Reverse leverage by showing that the weight of the opponent's meanings can be counterweights. | Douglas speaks of the "enormity" of Lincoln's abolitionist principles. But "enormity" also modifies a reputation. The relative unknown Lincoln asks, "How can my ideas be so enormous when I am such a little man?" Douglas dismisses him with the left-handed compliment, "Lincoln is conscientious,," only to have Lincoln return the compliment many more times. |
| 6. Precedent | Show that the argument of self descends from a chain of events carrying positive principles. | Reverse leverage by showing that history smiles on the self's argument more than that of the opponent. | Both Douglas and Lincoln trace their argument in the "sacred principles of the founding fathers." |
| 7. Consequences | Show that the argument of self generates reasonable event outcomes and the reverse for the opponent. | Reverse the leverage by tying the opponent's argument to negative outcomes (often, like opposites). | Douglas: "Lincoln's house-divided policy will lead to civil war." Lincoln: "Douglas' ideas will nationalize slavery." |
| 8. Dilemma | Show that the opponent's argument, in order to involve reasonable assumptions and outcomes, must also involve unreasonable ones. | Reverse the leverage by showing that the opponent can only answer pertinent questions acceptably by leaving behind other unacceptable answers. | Douglas: "Either Lincoln is an abolitionist or he doesn't very well understand the Republican platform he was nominated to represent." |
| 9. Private/Public | Show that the opponent's public argument is dependent on private events that weaken its structure. (Basis of conspiracy.) | Reverse the leverage by showing that the opponent's public mission bundles various compromising private ones. | Douglas: "Lincoln's private motive is to abolitionize the country.' Lincoln: "Douglas' private motive is to nationalize slavery." |

TABLE 3.1 (Continued)

| Topical Pattern | Plan | Tactic | Event |
|---|---|---|---|
| 10. From different results to different antecedents. | Show that if a line of argument has the same outcome as the present, it is well grounded in the past; otherwise, not. | Reverse the leverage by showing that if the present is not as the opponent says, then neither is the past. | Douglas: "If Lincoln's house-divided were historically true, we would now be a slave-holding country north and south. |
| 11. Shifting behaior after event | | Reverse the leverage by showing that opponent broke precedent when it should not have been, or remained within precedent when it should have been broken. | Douglas: "Republicans seized their opportunity only after the north gained economic superiority." Lincoln: "Democrats acknowledged blacks in the Declaration until the Nebraska Bill passed." |
| 12. Results as purposes | Show that if an argument culminates in an event, it was/was not intended. | Reverse the leverage by showing that opponent's results were intended; if the opponent objects, show that unintended results can be just as harmful as intent. | Lincoln: "Douglas may have been a dupe in a conspiracy to nationalize slavery, but he let himself be used nonetheless." |
| 13. Presumption of action/nonaction | | Reverse the leverage by showing that the opponent's action should have been a nonaction; the opponent's nonaction, an action. | Lincoln: "Douglas said nothing when I made the charge and I took a default on him. Instead of being insulted, a good debater would have refuted me." |
| 14. Meaning of a name | | | Douglas calls Lincoln "spot" to recall his controversial record in the Mexican War. Lincoln calls Douglas "judge" in a context where Douglas' ascension to the bench is under fire. |

is a pattern that spans all these levels. Once our minds are attuned to the pattern at one level, they are attuned to recognizing it at others. Topics offer the mind a redundancy across the modules of rhetoric that, for the practitioner, makes understanding the disparate views of the rhetorical modules less crucial.

The remaining topical patterns in Table 3.1 can be worked through using a similar analysis. We leave it to the reader to do that.

If this analysis has merit, we can begin to appreciate the difficulty of characterizing rhetorical knowledge in a single way. The temptation is to localize such knowledge within a single module—as long-term event memory, as plans, as tactics, or as linguistic knowledge. For a practical art of rhetoric, the genius of the topics is to allow speakers, through simple verbal gestalts, to move fluidly and tacitly across the modules of rhetorical design without requiring a technical understanding of the individual modules through which they are moving. This allows perfection of the craft with a minimal technical understanding of the art. For an art of rhetoric as design, however, it is not enough to rely on mnemonic gestalts to assure that the different modules will be visited for the purposes of able performance. To understand the fit of rhetoric to the criteria of modern design, we must investigate each of the modules on its own terms, as part of a systemic understanding.

One may object that what we are calling a modular approach to rhetoric is not fundamentally different from a topical approach. The objector may argue that a modular approach is just a topical approach with, perhaps, more topics specified, or more topics specified at a more overarching level, in the manner of plans, tactics, and events. On this view, plans, tactics, and events are just another proposed topical system of rhetoric. The problem with this objection is that it fails to comprehend the chief difference between a topical and a modular approach to design. In a topical approach, associations can be judged to be effective whether there is a structure to them or not. As long as their application meets some performance criterion (e.g., wins the debate; makes the sale), the performance is effective regardless of its structural antecedents. It is in this sense that topical approaches to rhetoric are inherently "practical" and frame rhetoric as a practical art. In a topical organization of rhetoric, rhetoric that does not work is not interesting. The focus is not the morphology of rhetorical design as an art of design, but the consequences of applying the design to specific situations.

In a modular approach to rhetoric, consequences are not the dominant concern. The end of rhetoric is to evolve our understanding of the morphology of rhetorical design. This relies on an interest in particular instances of rhetoric (like Lincoln/Douglas) as a practical archive from which to work. An adequate morphology must be realistically descriptive of actual instances. The data from actual instances should, in turn, cause us to revise our existing morphologies. The value of a sophisticated morphology of rhetorical design is comparable to the role it plays in any art of design. It allows us to classify practical instances in systematic ways. It allows a common framework within which to describe different approaches or "schools" of rhetorical design. It provides a ready vocabulary for describing what a particular approach highlights and what it tends to ignore. It becomes a working theory from which to identify where our collective knowledge of rhetoric is dense and where it is sparse. It provides a vehicle for exposing contradictions and gaps in our collective understandings and points out directions for resolving the inconsistencies and filling in the gaps.

Significantly, Aristotle began his *Rhetoric* with statements sympathetic to a modular theory of rhetoric and for some of the reasons we have just suggested. He called for understanding rhetoric as a general body of knowledge for which the reasons for success or failure (with words) can be understood and explained. But the dominant shape of his treatise on rhetoric is that of a practical handbook, listings of heuristics and hints offered to increase the chances of successful speaking.[3]

A good example of the difference between topical and modular design can be found in thinking through Aristotle's three modes of proof: pathos, logos, and ethos. Pathos is persuasion that relies on the emotions of the audience. Logos is persuasion that relies on the content of the speech. Ethos is persuasion that relies on the credibility and character of the speaker. On a topical approach, these modes of proof are common members of a single category, an unordered list of members in a set. A modular approach, however, reveals that each mode of proof arises from starkly different and distributed source points in an architecture of rhetorical design. As we see in chapters to come, a speaker creates pathos primarily through the Events module, by lexicalizing displaced situations that stir the audience's emotions (chapter 9). The emotive force of the rhetoric is dependent on the force of the words utttered and this is why events figure prominently in pathos. Logos and ethos, by way of contrast, are primarily controlled within the interaction of the rhetor's dominant goals (chapter 5) and the Plans (chapter 7) and Events (chapter 9) modules. Logos depends on the speaker's goal to be predictive (chapter 5) and the plans the speaker uses to lay out the social

---

[3]This seeming inconsistency is no negative judgment against Aristotle, for he never composed the *Rhetoric* as a single work. His treatsie evolved over many years as lecture notes and was compiled by his students after his death.

world as an unfolding mechanism. Ethos, in the service of credibility, depends on the goal to be predictive (chapter 5) coupled with plans to reveal one's entitlements to formulate and to make good on those goals. Ethos, in the service of character, depends on the goal to be human, plans to reveal the principles that reflect character, and expression at the level of events that creates a symbolic identification with the audience (chapter 9). In all cases, tactics (chapter 8) are required in rhetorical proof to make sure that these proofs carry against the resistance put up by an opponent.

A virtue of a modularized theory of rhetorical design is that it can help us appreciate the very different sources of rhetorical elements that have received undifferentiated treatment in traditional theory. A modular organization transforms rhetoric into a full-bodied discipline of study, with the possibility of evolving rigor and consensus. As we indicated earlier, rhetoric has never had a comfortable fit in the modern research university. The absence of a serious modular understanding of rhetorical design, we submit, has had profound implications on why this is so. In the modern academy, the precision of knowledge is associated with referential discreteness. Yet rhetorical knowledge, typically seen as referentially diffuse, is stigmatized as imprecise. At the same time, the modules that are rhetorical get boxed and reduced into more discrete knowledge bundles. Plans become the province of psychology; tactics, the province of political science and management; language events, the province of linguistics. Each discipline has become very successful in its own right. Rhetorical knowledge, the knowledge applied in rhetorical design, is the link between them. If we are to make rhetoric a more focused target for research, we first accept rhetorical knowledge as the relationships that cross different elements and design modules. Otherwise, we are in danger of doing what so many post-Enlightenment thinkers who decline to investigate rhetoric do: mistake, on a priori grounds, the diffuseness of rhetoric for imprecision; mistake its apparent lack of density as an art for a lack of structure. What we have to say in this book falls short of offering an exhaustive road map, a finished architecture as it were, of rhetoric as an art of design. But we believe that it is a useful start.

# Four

# An Architecture of Rhetorical Design

Our discussion up to now has shown how rhetorical design fits within the family of prototypical design arts like architecture. In this and the remaining chapters, we continue to isolate and further hone those features of design that distinguish rhetorical design from other generic types. Compared with the broad analysis we have taken in previous chapters, our analysis in forthcoming chapters is more microscopic, examining in greater depth the features that make rhetorical design what it is. In the spirit of this shifting focus, we introduce in this chapter an architecture of rhetorical design. We combine what we have said in previous chapters and fix them as components in a unified architecture so that we will know where to train our microscope in the chapters to come.

## COMPONENTS

We now overview the various components of the architecture. Our model of rhetorical design, as we saw in previous chapters, consists of two main parts, the rhetor and the external environment. The external environment captures the significant elements of the rhetorical situation, such as the audience and the opponent. It also includes the various artifacts that the speaker uses for external memory and communication, such as notes, outlines, sketches, and the speech or text produced throughout the design process. The components of the design process itself reside within the rhetor's internal environment. These components include the rhetor's knowledge, goals, rhetorical strategies, and the rhetorical design space. The rhetor's knowledge, along with much of the incoming information about the rhetorical situation, comprises the structural content, or simply "structure," of the rhetorical design. Working under the direction of specific goals, the rhetor can work on assembling structures from three different perspectives: Plans, Tactics, and Events. Each one of these views of the design structure plays an important decision-making role in determining the outcome of the rhetorical design process.

Components that make decisions are also referred to as modules. Goals and structure provide information to decision-making modules rather than make decisions themselves. The components that are also modules are the Strategic, Plans, Tactics, Events, and Presentation modules. Throughout this book, we use the convention of capitalizing the name of a component or a module when we mean to refer to the component or module as a whole entity. We move to the lower case when we mean to refer to specific products that emanate from the decisions of this module. Thus goals are the products of Goals (the component); plans, the product of Plans (the module); tactics, the products of Tactics (the module); events, the product of Events (the module), and so on.

In the following chapters we consider the Goals (chapter 5) that establish and represent goal priorities for the current design. In chapter 6, we consider the structures out of which rhetorical designs are fashioned. The remaining chapters detail the rhetorical design space itself, in which structures are shaped into a rhetorical artifact. The design space is internally partitioned into the Plans (chapter 7), Tactics (chapter 8), and Events (chapter 9) modules, each providing alterations to the evolving structure through distinct "views." The application of Plans, Tactics, and Events to the design structure within the design space is itself partially coordinated though the application of the Strategic module. The Strategic module coordinates the behavior of the modules within the design space based on the current goal priorities. We offer some discussion in the concluding chapter about how this coordination works (chapter 10). The Presentation module (chapter 10) makes decisions about how best to implement, as expression, the results of a specific rhetorical design when that portion of the design is considered "rhetorically complete" and "ready for expression." In the sections to follow, we overview the various components of the architecture in slightly more detail. A more microscopic analysis of each component is forthcoming in the remaining chapters.

## Goals

Goals is a component that stores information about the speaker's goal priority in light of information about the speaker's purposes and the external environment, including the rhetorical situation and the larger culture in which the situation is embedded. In the next chapter, we make a detailed case that the primary goals in rhetorical design are predictiveness and adaptiveness.

With respect to predictiveness, the rhetor needs to present a message that insists on some constants over time and space: needs to strike the audience as "standing firm" in positions that preceded and will outlast the immediate rhetorical situation. In this way, the rhetor fulfills the goals of predictiveness. Rhetors rely on the Plans module in the design space to demonstrate predictiveness in the design. With respect to adaptiveness, the rhetor needs to present a message that reflects the states of change that naturally accompany the rhetor's learning new information about the world. Adaptiveness is decomposable into the subgoals of responsiveness (to the opponent) and humanness (with the audience). Lacking responsiveness to outside interrogation, a speaker's rhetoric and, by implication, the speaker him- or herself can seem inert and inflexible. Lacking humanness, a speaker's words can fail to connect to the everyday reality of the audience. The rhetor relies on the Tactics module to demonstrate the responsiveness of his or her position to outside scrutiny and the Events module to achieve humanness goals. Figure 4.1 overviews the relationship of goals in rhetorical design.

Using converging input from the speaker and outside environment, the Goals component "decides" whether the speaker's current priority should be predictiveness or adaptiveness. Although this decision-making responsibility would entitle Goals to be a module rather than a mere component, we leave it to future theory to specify how the current goal priority is established from the incoming stream of information about the speaker and the environment. We treat Goals in this book only as a component rather than a module, one

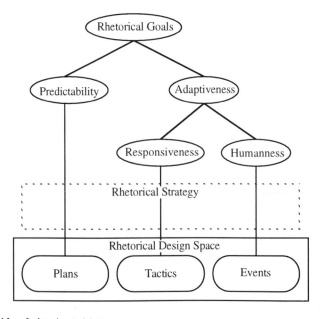

FIG. 4.1.   Goals in rhetorical design.

that represents predictiveness and adaptiveness as goals and is able to establish which goal should take priority in directing, for some allocated amount of time according to the rhetor's internal clock, the current design.

## Structure

In rhetorical design, the outcome of design consists of expressions and their strategic presentation before audiences. What is the input to this process? Where does rhetorical design begin? Or, more precisely, what is the raw material that gets shaped by the design and where does it originate? One obvious answer is the speaker's knowledge, either as it exists in long-term memory or as it is learned through books and interaction with others. But "knowledge" is not the most accurate description of this raw material because the speaker must have a way of representing this knowledge so that it can be manipulated as part of a design, so that existing patterns can be decomposed and reassembled into new patterns as needed. The better term for this raw material, then, is *knowledge representation.* A knowledge representation is defined as a structure for thinking about knowledge as a designed entity, one that, like a language, has a syntax for decomposition into parts and recomposition into new structures. Because the idea of structure figures centrally in the idea of a knowledge representation; because the notion of structure applies equally well to the mental terrain (knowledge) and the terrain of physical symbols (content), and because the rhetor's design space is an open system, constantly being altered by information sources outside the rhetor's immediate knowledge, we prefer "structure" or "the structure of the design" to "knowledge"as names for the contents of the rhetorical design space that are viewed by Plans, Tactics, and Events.

Were this book to describe a computer program that could design like a rhetorician, a robot Lincoln or robot Douglas as it were, we would need a very long description of how knowledge is structured, much longer than the space we have given it here (chapter 6). These details would be crucial in explaining how this knowledge is formed and manipulated within the design space and then sequenced into expression adaptive to the audience and the situation. Because our aims in this book are to discuss the components of a cyber rhetorician without implementing one, we supply enough of the detail of structure (chapter 6) to fit into an architecture of rhetorical design without claiming that the architecture is a complete specification of a full-fledged artificial rhetor.

## The Rhetorical Design Space

The rhetorical design space is essentially the rhetor's internal workbench. The design space is a conceptual place to create and organize structure forming the building blocks of a rhetorical design. Were rhetorical artifacts as simple, as linear, and as list-like as they are sometimes portrayed in practical handbooks, rhetoric could be accomplished by the rhetor's doing "memory dumps" of these structures in the design space and then parceling out packets of these retrieved memories into sentences of English. As a design art, however, rhetorical artifacts involve enormous internal complexity, too much to be explained by anything other than a design space that is expressly organized to deal with complexity. A rhetorical artifact, in other words, is too complex to manage within a single conceptual view. Multiple views are needed. Much of the fragility and delicacy of rhetorical design involves balancing these views opportunistically to meet the demands of the external situation.

Thus, we posit a design space of rhetoric partitioned into Plans, Tactics, and Events modules. To manage the complexity inherent in rhetorical discourse, the rhetor shifts back and forth across these modules. Each module provides its own "view" of the structures that comprise the evolving artifact; each view makes tacitly apparent to the speaker certain decision requirements for the structures under examination that the other views can't or don't capture. Each view functions much like a draftsman's stencil, which is superimposed over a structure, used to give the structure a particular shape and definition, and then removed. If one looks carefully and systematically at the final artifact, it is possible to reconstruct the result of applying a particular view. It is reasonable to suppose that each view can be used to manipulate structures in ways that permanently alter them. Still, the views themselves are separate from the finished design, allowing the speaker to offer the design as an "organic whole" with no one noticing the intricate seams in its development. This is how the emergent artifact, spoken or written, can look seamless. The product is unveiled incrementally or as a whole only after the stencils are taken off.

Every rhetorical product that emerges in final form benefits from the careful shaping of the abstractions afforded by Plans, Tactics, and Events. The inductive problem we face in formulating a theory of rhetorical design is that, once we have a rhetorical product in final form, the stencils have long been removed and so their shape, and the shape they contribute to the evolving structure, remains an unknown. Think-aloud protocols of rhetors working over tens of hours (Geisler, 1994; Kaufer & Geisler, 1989) are extremely useful in learning about aspects of their design activity. However we wanted to base our understanding on an example of public rhetoric and not of individual writers. Gathering process data across native situations with realistically complex rhetorical design is more elusive. In addition, we wanted to work with data close to finished form (namely, text) so that we would be in a position to capture as many of the design requirements as possible.

Our way of searching for these unknowns, then, has been in the study of Lincoln/Douglas. We have approached the debates not as historians of rhetoric but as theorists of rhetorical design. We have approached them not to appreciate them as wondrously rich artifacts of rhetoric but to assume that, and then inquire into how such a wondrously rich artifact of rhetoric is designed. More specifically, we have sought to induce from the debates the various abstractions that give them their shape and definition as prize rhetorical artifacts. Searching for these abstractions is how we arrived at the modular partitioning of the design space into Plans, Tactics, and Events.

Although there is much overlap in the structures that are viewed from the vantage of Plans, Tactics, and Events, each view provides its own internal vocabulary and set of priorities for what constitutes assembling the structures into a "good" design. The idea of multiple views overseeing an evolving structure to judge a process as "good" is fairly common in the culture, although we tend to understand it more as Freudian conflict than effective design. Imagine an adult who wants to be a "good" driver. In many respects, attaining this designation requires driving, at times, as if a state patrolman were in the passenger seat; at times, as if a senior citizen were riding along; and at times, as if a seasoned racer of vintage cars were the companion. Each passenger would share much tacit knowledge about a "good" ride but they would have different ways of describing what they would be experiencing and they would offer conflicting descriptions in specific cases. The "conflict" the driver would feel in satisfying each of these passengers would be a healthy one insofar as one's standing as a good driver relied on the mutual satisfaction of all concerned. Having abstractions in the design space that hold the evolving structure accountable to multiple requirements, to these multiple "voices," increases the speaker's chances of making the rhetoric effective.

Plans, Tactics, and Events represent multiple views overseeing the assembly of structures in the rhetorical design space. Rhetorical discourse freely accommodates and, typically, is held accountable to the range of these assumptions. Some important and contrastive characteristics of the Plans, Tactics, and Events modules will be previewed in Table 4.1 and discussed at greater length in forthcoming chapters. Here we simply overview some of the salient differences among the different views of the rhetorical design space provided by the Plans, Tactics, and Events modules, respectively.

## The Plans Module

The purpose of the Plans module is to construct a model of a public and to help the speaker organize structures within the rhetorical design. The definition of public and cognates (e.g., public model) are matters we pursue through to chapter 7. A useful preliminary definition of public is a particular way of thinking, and speaking, about the world from the perspective of a collective. This particular mode of thinking/speaking envisions normative principles that bind individuals in their everyday lives as forces that move collectives through history in better or worse directions. The Plans module is focused on developing and supporting a particular abstracted representation called a public space. This abstract representation is used to characterize a world of principled forces that move ideological history in right (precedent) or wrong (counterprecedent) directions. There are no unaffiliated individuals within the public space, nor individuals personally involved in contest, conflict, opposition, controversy, emotions, or humor. The conflicts that exist are between abstract principles and the human collectives that try to instantiate them. Impersonal blueprints of principles and counterprinciples guide competing groups in how the historical world is to be viewed (and normed). Individuals in historically entitled category affiliations (e.g., "Founding Fathers," "Republicans," "Democrats") moving through time and space in institutionally defined events are the focus of this module. The Plans module knows about telling relatively simple stories about truth and falsehood in the social world.

Within the Plans module, chronological or calendar time moves only by carrying principles or counterprinciples forward from one event to the next. Calendar time, in effect, is compressed into precedent time. All events have public meaning and are aligned either with the right or wrong forces of history. In the public space, there are no routine or generic events, like closing doors and opening windows; nor are there voiceless events, events with no lessons to teach. All events are test cases, pregnant with incipient principles, that either have been aligned with historical forces or are awaiting such alignment in the present decision making context. Under the lens of Plans, rhetoric is understood to be an occasion for creating and manipulating a model of a public and the abstraction of a public space that lies at its kernel. The definition of public is pursued in chapter 5 and again in chapter 7, where we introduce the notion of a model of a public and the plans that serve to focus attention on the model in patterned ways. In chapter 7, we illustrate plans at length by tracking them through specific examples within Lincoln/Douglas.

## The Tactics Module

Rhetors derive various plans by taking different angles of focus on a public model. Live[1] opponents, listeners and readers, often dispute and seek to interrupt these public models, either in the process of their being delivered (face-to-face interaction) or after their composition and publication in texts (interaction in print). The Tactics module helps a rhetor respond to a live opponent's actions, or (with print) to anticipate the responses of a simulated live opponent reading from a distance. Under both face-to-face and print assumptions, the speaker uses tactics to repair a part of his or her design structure that the live audience questions (or anticipates the reader to question), or to attack alternative structures brought to, or expected to be brought to, the rhetorical situation by opponents.

The Tactics module presupposes a viewpoint different from Plans. Although Plans only knows about truth and falsehood in the social world, Tactics knows only about a world of gaming between a speaker and live opponents in a specific rhetorical situation. Plans knows nothing about the particulars of rhetorical situations. Plans stays somewhat aloof from the actual details of any specific situation of rhetoric. Tactics and Events are the modules that actually "forage" rhetorical situations, modules that directly manipulate situational inputs that can change the design structure.

The Tactics module, in particular, views structures in the design space that are influenced, and modifiable, by the live opponent in the situation. It modifies the design structure in direct response to opponent input. The inert and abstracted historical blueprints under the viewpoint of Plans becomes, under the shifting viewpoint of Tactics, an interactive game of move and countermove with a live opponent. Individuals in the tactical world are implicated in a live contest through face-to-face, print, or electronic inter-

---

[1]Tactics always deal with opponents who are living and at least interactive in potential (face-to-face or in print) with the speaker. Persons who are cited unapprovingly are "faulty paths" (Kaufer, Geisler, Neuworth, 1989). They are a part of the roadside of the speaker's plan, pointed out only to avoid. For the contemporary writer, Aristotle (or any dead writer) can never be a tactical opponent. Although a speaker can also cite the work of a tactical opponent negatively (and so assign ideas of the opponent to a faulty path), tactical opponents, so defined, are not conceptually part of the speaker's constructed plan. Live opponents have a capacity to act independent of the speaker, and they have the capacity to perceive, through an autonomous consciousness, that for their own actions to go through, the plans of the speaker must be blocked.

action. The Tactics module opens the way for actions that are beyond the notice of the Plans module—the ability to play offense or defense. Playing offense, the tactical speaker tries to push into the rhetorical situation elements of the design structure that reflect his or her point of view, including structures that reflect intact plans. Playing defense, the speaker seeks to take leverage away from the opponent's structure, including his or her obstructionist counterplans.

The Tactical view is also sensitive to an important requirement that social anthropologists call "face" (Brown & Levinson, 1987; Goffman, 1959). Speakers who agree to duel, on the offense or defense, typically maintain the face of the opponent. Both tactical offense and defense build from the premise that the opponent is a qualified public agent. A speaker threatens face by sheathing the sword and complaining about the poor quality of the opposition. Threatening face, thus, is often coincident with the suspension of an offensive or defensive orientation. A speaker threatens the opponent's face by questioning the opponent's basic knowledge of the subject, his or her preparation, credentials, good will, or motives. In doing so, the speaker offers a direct challenge to the opponent's fitness to share the same platform. In the Plans module, by way of contrast, "face" is a meaningless notion because there is no concept of an active opponent who can support or threaten it. Individual characteristics that fill in a notion of "face" in the social world are abstracted out, within Plans, as entitlements that enable an individual to engage in public discourse.

In later chapters, we see that one of the key differences between Lincoln and Douglas is their preference for tactical actions. Lincoln, who prefers to play defense, is a master at blocking his opponent's plans. Douglas is an able offensive debater but weak on defense. He is good at reasserting his own position but bad at blocking anything of value Lincoln has to say. He responds to many opportunities for defense merely by threatening Lincoln's face. Thus, against many of Lincoln's more devastating attacks, rather than defend himself, Douglas questions the credentials of the attacker.

## The Events Module

The Plans module constructs publics as abstracted realities; the Tactics module contests these abstractions in specific rhetorical situations with live opponents. In neither Plans nor Tactics are lexicalizations, words, part of the visible design. To be sure, Plans and Tactics are abstracted views that need to be lexicalized in order to be brought to expression. But in the normal case, there is nothing unique or even distinctive about the words used to implement Plans and Tactics. Many lexical variations on the same theme would get the job done and no one variation is more or less effective than another. In the normal case, in other words, the words used to express the design have no standing in the design; they are just there to implement the design. The audience is intended to see through the words to the larger structures of argument (tactics, plans, strategies, goals), rather than looking at the words as an independent layer of design. (See Lanham, 1983, for the distinction between looking "through" and "at" language; Brown and Levinson, 1987).

The Events module works in the special cases where the words chosen for rhetorical expression are thought to be part of the rhetorical design. Like the Tactics module and unlike Plans, the Events module views the design structure from elements that are affected by the rhetorical situation. Unlike Tactics, the Events module homes in on the audience in the situation, not the opponent. It seeks to identify parts of the design structure whose lexicalization would contribute to the local audience effect. When captured as unique lexicalizations, such structure forms the basis of language that is thought to be part of the rhetorical design. It forms the basis of language we call rhetorical performatives, like adaptations, nondeclaratives, indirection, emotives, and reflexives like wit, humor, and irony.

## Comparing Plans, Tactics, and Events

The various views of Plans, Tactics, and Events direct the speaker's notice differently, and these differences speak to different requirements of rhetorical design. What are taken as inert, impersonal forces of social truth within Plans become dueling social narratives in the Tactical view, as each speaker tries to claim a privileged vantage from which to recount how the forces of temporality and experience impact the present decision context, and each seeks leverage over the other in proclaiming this vantage. The Events view in the rhetorical design space presupposes a more personal environment than Plans and a more cooperative environment than Tactics. Like Tactics, Events assumes a world of live interaction. Unlike Tactics, the basic impulse of Event interaction is cooperative, not competitive, the impulse that sharing language is sharing culture, and that much useful persuasion can be captured from cultural sharing alone. In contrast, for Plans and Tactics, language is transparent and a nonentity in their take on design. For Plans, sharing language is an unremarkable precondition for telling what is true and false about the social world. For Tactics, it is an unremarkable precondition for doing battle in the situation with an opponent.

Each module focuses the rhetor's attention on different aspects of the structures within the design space. Each predisposes the rhetor to notice certain features of the design and to fail to notice others. Under the viewpoint of Plans, the significant structures are the truths and falsehoods of the social world, entitled individuals and the groups that entitle them to tell their stories about truth and falsehood. Stories about falsehood are described in the actions of counteragents who, though entitled by their groups, nonetheless represent groups that seek to endorse social falsehoods. From the viewpoint of Tactics, the significant structures noticed are interactive moves in rhetorical situations used for offense, defense, and face threats. Under the viewpoint of Events, the significant structures noticed are those that can be opportunistically and artistically lexicalized in order to reflect complex timing dependencies between the structure of the design and audience involvement with that structure (see Table 4.1).

Plans, Tactics, and Events carry different responsibilities for the final rhetorical artifact produced. Plans contributes to blocks of discourse that indicate any single speaker's repeatable, predictable, and on-the-record lines of argument concerning truths and falsehoods about the social world. Tactics contribute to the places in the final artifact where we learn what the speaker in fact does during the delivery (in speech) or composing environment (in writing) to enhance the persuasiveness of his or her plans against the resistance of an opponent. Events contribute to the artifact, the words and phrases that we understand and appreciate as unique lexicalizations, wordings that reflect unique timing dependencies between the design structure and the audience input on that structure.

Finally, each module, taken by itself, poses a potential liability for rhetorical design because of its narrow focus on what rhetoric is about. Viewed only from Plans, rhetoric is a stilted script about how to abstract true and false trajectories of the social world. Viewed only from Tactics, rhetoric is a way of bloodying an opponent with nothing more at stake. Viewed only from Events, rhetoric is a way of engaging the audience in the here and now without offering to take it anywhere. The myopia of Plans can cause a speaker to talk right past an opponent's questions without answering them. The myopia of Tactics can cause a speaker to contradict a long-held position in order to win a few minutes' leverage with the opponent. The myopia of Events can cause a speaker to lose sight of an intellectual direction and an opponent trying to head it off. Table 4.1 summarizes some of the major contrasts across Plans, Tactics, and Events in the rhetorical design space.

Our architecture of rhetorical design is not yet complete. There remain two further modules that we need for our architecture and that we will return to in the final chapter: the Presentation and the Strategic modules.

TABLE 4.1
Overview of the Different "Views" of the Rhetoric Design from Plans, Tactics, and Events

| Module | Plans | Tactics | Events |
|---|---|---|---|
| Relevant goals | Predictiveness—Tell stories about truth and falsehood in the social world. | Responsiveness—Win the immediate conflict with the opponent. | Humanness. Win the moment with the audience by identifying with its everyday reality. |
| Viewpoint | Discourse that projects a world apart from consciousness. The social world is constructed in precedent time. History is a branching line splintering the here and now of the audience into precedent and counterprecedent directions. Generic plans are points of focus for moving the social world in better or worse directions. | Discourse as a weapon of offensive and defense leverage that can maintain or threaten the opponent's face. | Opportunistic, uniquely lexicalized discourse used as a social bond. Creates moments in which language sharing can also be appreciated as culture sharing. |
| Liabilities | Makes rhetoric into a scripted monologue. No knowledge of live opponents and audiences. Focused on a story to tell for a long time and clueless about the next thing to say in the situation. Good for telling what to do in the course of history; but feeble at telling what to do in the course of the debate. | Makes rhetoric into boxing match. Can't distinguish beating the opponent with the larger issues needed to take the audience into the future. Good for breaking down the opponent but, without careful coordination with Plans, nothing but ridicule and name-calling can result. | Makes rhetoric into a form of entertainment and sometimes self-reflection through linguistic and cultural identification. Although offering useful reflexive moments for self-understanding, no content for which it alone is responsible is important enough to explore or disagree with as a basis for future action. |
| Significant structures | Groups, entitled individuals. | Speaker, opponent, offensive actions, defensive actions. | Words, phrases, cultural/linguistic memory, reflexive memory. |
| Design actions | Constructing what is true and false about the social world. | Offensive actions, defensive actions, face-threatening actions. | Rhetorical performatives. |
| Artifact focus | Blocks of discourse revealing forces of truth and falsehood in the social world. | Blocks of discourse monitoring what speakers do to improve their leverage with an opponent. | Weighted discourse moments reflecting unique timing opportunities to relate content and audience convergences. |

## The Presentation Module

This module handles the lexicalization and organization of linguistic structures that are considered outside the design of rhetoric. It "decides" to bring aspects of the rhetorical design—the combined output of Plans, Tactics, and Events—to expression when it represents these aspects of the design as "rhetorically complete" and "ready for expression." This judgment can be driven by the content or context of the expression. But it can also be driven by the tempo and rhythm of the speaker's expression. It is instructive to contrast the Presentation and the Events modules. The Events module makes words part of the rhetorical design. It anchors the content of the design to the momentary weight of a unique lexicalization. As we said earlier, this is not the normal case for rhetoric, or for language use in general. The default is that language implements a design that is formed outside itself, a design that many linguistic paraphrases could implement equally well. Not all linguistic aspects of a rhetorical design, in other words, are assigned to the design itself. They are only integral to the grammar implementing it.

This means that we need a way for rhetorical designs to be implemented through linguistic events that are not understood or treated as unique lexicalizations. The Presentation module provides this mechanism. The Presentation module "looks" into the design space for structure to lexicalize. Unlike the Events module, where lexicalization changes the design, the Presentation module implements the design structure in "structure-preserving" ways, in ways where many variations on (nonunique[2]) linguistic events would express the same design and where the job of the Presentation module is to choose any variation that gets the job done.

The Presentation module also must perform an organizing, as well as a lexicalizing, function. It must organize multiple-clause structures into patterns of nonunique events that are understandable to an audience. It seems that much of this organization can be taken directly from the organization of structure in the design structure. But other forms of organization may be more specific to presentation, such as the dramatic narrative, transforming one's internal rhetorical plans and tactics into a setting, conflict, and resolution.

---

[2]To be distinguished from the unique events created by the Events module. Notice that our definition of rhetoric (chapter 2) as the strategic organization and communication of events, does not specify the uniqueness or nonuniqueness of the events organized and communicated. Rhetoric results from language that is judged to be part of the design, and language that is not so judged.

## The Strategic Module

The Strategic module takes goal priorities from the Goals component and seeks to coordinate the behavior of the internal design modules—Plans, Tactics, and Events—in line with the current priorities. In chapter 10, we discuss specific ways the Strategic module can affect the behavior of the internal design modules, effectively steering the design toward the current goals. For now, it is important only to recognize that any shift in a speaker's priority toward predictiveness needs to elicit patterns that change, on average, the speaker's focal attention in the design space from Tactics and Events to Plans. This is because the Plans module is more likely, on average, to have an effect on the design structure that is consistent with increasing the speaker's predictiveness. It is also important to understand that such strategic shifts in goals are hardly foolproof for shifting behavior. Plans, ultimately, can't get anything accomplished in rhetorical design without some cooperation of Tactics and Events. Tactics and Events, however, privilege goal priorities other than predictiveness and can neutralize or counter the original shift in goal priority toward predictiveness. The Strategic module, like the head of a large, diffuse, and nonhierarchical organization, can only communicate high-level priorities for the company established by an outside board of directors (Goals). The degree to which these priorities are assimilated or mangled depends on many machinations of the internal bureaucracy, which are only indirectly affected by the Strategic module.

Every module in our architecture tracks a different, incommensurable, view of the speaker's position. Plans tracks the speaker's position in a social world directed by forces of truth and falsehood. Tactics tracks the speaker's position in a tactical game with the opponent. Events tracks the speaker's relational position with the audience. Although the different notions of speaker's "position" across modules are not commensurable, they nonetheless retain the capacity of being artfully coordinated. It can't be a random accident when a speaker's planned position aligns with a tactical position in an argument or with a (relational) position, or stance, with the audience. Were there not this capacity to coordinate actions across incommensurable elements, to create the appearance of a seamless artifact, successful rhetoric would be primarily a result of luck. In chapter 10, we discuss coordination across modules.

## THE ARCHITECTURE AT A GLANCE

So far we have considered the components of the architecture. We now take a final look at the architecture from the top down (Fig. 4.2). An analogy

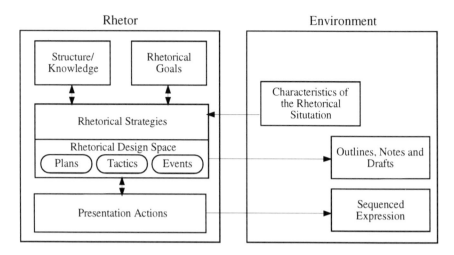

FIG. 4.2.   The architecture of rhetorical design.

from chess[3] can help us fix the way we think about how these components are coordinated in rhetorical design. The goals of rhetorical design are analogous to the goals of chess. Although the goals of chess are convergent on a single state of the board (capture of the opponent's king), the goals of rhetoric are mixed across three goals that must be held in balance for the rhetoric to succeed: predictiveness, responsiveness, and humanness. Strategies in rhetoric are analogous to the long-term strategies in chess to satisfy goals and shifting goal priorities as situations on the board change. Plans in rhetoric are analogous to the abstract board positions that a chessmaster knows how to associate with the furthering or blocking of strategy. In rhetorical design, what we call the structure of the design space is analogous to the game board. The rhetor plans by taking abstract views on the design structure called a model of a public. Generic and specific plans of rhetoric result from different ways of focusing on this model. The chess master can recognize and respond to concrete patterns on the playing board (structure) that match the interior of an abstracted plan, either the chess master's own plan or a plan driven by the opponent. The ability to recognize and respond to specific moves of the opponent is tactics in chess. A similar ability to recognize and respond to specific moves of the opponent is tactics in rhetoric. An event in chess is the physical manifestation of a move in terms of the

---

[3]Chess is a design art that, like rhetoric, incorporates competitive gaming. Unlike most design arts, it "makes" no physical artifact apart from the process of moves made. For some, this is enough to exclude it as an art of design.

repositioning of a piece on another square on the board. The presentational layer in chess is the working through of multiple events into a sequence. Rhetoric's presentational layer allows a speaker to compose many events in a macro sequence.

From our description, it might seem that goals, strategies plans, tactics, events, and presentation work in assembly-line fashion. Each shouts orders to the one immediately lower in the structure and the subordinate obediently follows the order. This is conceivable in theory but highly doubtful as a description of practice. Our architecture does not impose a hierarchy across components. Goals and strategies are more abstract than tactics and events. Still, we do not mean to suggest that the more abstract components are higher in the design process than the more concrete ones. We avoid the idea of a centralized "intelligence" in rhetorical design guaranteeing that it all works out in the end. It often does not, in any case. If doing rhetoric well was usual and expected, it is not likely that we would see so many abysmal instances of it in the real world. Failure, incremental success, and more failure is the rule more than the exception in the design arts. Rather than assume a practical rhetoric that builds success into the definition by setting the appropriate goal, we assume that rhetoric involves intricate coordination of components throughout the design process.

In contrast to a practical art, where the goal means almost everything toward successful performance, we need to think of goals in rhetoric as meaning very little. There is no deterministic way of guaranteeing that a strategic shift will result in behavior in the direction of the shift. Each component has an indispensable job to do, a range of responsibilities, with respect to satisfying the goals of rhetorical design, and each tries to do that job within its own limited set of assumptions. Each produces information that can change the design structure and each looks for notification of a change when the design structure has been altered by another component. One module's being notified about a change in the design structure brought about from another module can never be taken for granted as a fait accompli. In addition, the modules look at the design structure in different ways and from different sets of interests and assumptions. So their ability to communicate with one another is like multiple cars negotiating a busy intersection, with each driver having slightly different conventions for who should yield the right of way. Coordinating the modules in rhetorical design, as in every genre of design, is a difficult issue, which we return to in the final chapter.

Before closing, let us take stock and consider from a larger perspective why we associate rhetoric with design and why we propose an architecture that cuts the joints of the design space at constructing (Plans), competing with (Tactics), and creating the horizon of linguistic acts (Events) that flow within a rhetorical situation.

In classical rhetoric, rhetors were understood to need to impose their own lens on the flow of the external situation, a lens called a stasis. A stasis was a "pressure point" in an issue at which rhetors could train their focus and plan the generation of discourse.

Our take on rhetoric is somewhat different. We believe that the main external reference point "out there" for speakers is the here and now of the audience. The speaker's job is to have the audience associate the near future with the historical world that best suits the speaker's purposes. But this is a world that must be carefully designed to adjust the audience to the speaker's purpose and vice versa. To design it, the speaker must rely on a battery of tools taken from the tool kit of rhetorical design. Some of these tools supply the goals about what to do. Others supply the symbolic bricks and mortar out of which historical worlds are built. Still others are the offensive and defensive maneuvers through which the alternative designs of opponents are discredited. And others still are the linguistic events that stick social categories onto conceptual design so that it can be public and recorded.

Our differences with classical theory speak to the different relationships we see between rhetoric and power. Classical theory did not emphasize as much the malleability of the social world and the rhetor's role in shaping and reshaping it. Rhetors do not simply submit utterances to a social world around them. Such acts of submission, literally and figuratively, describe the culturally impotent, not the rhetor. Rhetors rather design the social world around them and bring it to the here and now, a new orientation to rhetoric pioneered by Kenneth Burke and recently brought to the attention of social scientists by the British social psychologist Michael Billig (1987, 1990, 1992). This, perhaps, is the most important reason why it is more illuminating to think of rhetoric as a design art. The rhetor is an architect of the social world. Aristotle spoke of different kinds of rhetoric as focusing on the past (judicial), present (encomium), and future (policy), respectively. But in constructing the social world, the rhetor must design the here and now to accommodate every horizon of time so as to influence the audience's decision making. The rhetor must be timeless enough to retrofit the audience to its historical past and destined future, timely enough to foil any live opponent with similar but competing goals, and well enough timed to give the audience pleasure in the now.

# Five

# Goals

The design arts, we have claimed, highlight a distinction between an agent's naked intention, that is, the goals outside of the design, and the goals of the designer that reside in the design. More succinctly put, the design arts bring to the fore the contrast between the goals *of* the design versus the goals *in* the design. The former are material or substantive goals; the latter are formal goals. In chapter 3, we suggested that substantive and formal goals are not fully independent, either in rhetoric or in the other arts of design. The designer's material and ethical responsibilities to the client and the culture permeate and so can be reflected in the formal character of the artifact.

This truth notwithstanding, the design arts allow for the abstraction of formal goals in the art from the contingent range of material goals that a designer brings to it. What are these formal goals in rhetorical design? In the previous chapter, we identified them as predictiveness and adaptiveness. We indicated how adaptiveness consists of the subgoals of responsiveness and humanness. We further indicated how these formal goals are related to one another and how they influence different modules within the rhetorical design space. In the chapters to come, we show how these formal goals of rhetorical design are expressed in Lincoln/Douglas. However, we cannot talk about the specific content and subjective alignments within a rhetorical design until we understand the interaction of goals, structure (chapter 6), and plans (chapter 7). And we cannot talk about the specific rhetorical situations of the debates themselves until we consider the interplay of plans and tactics (chapter 8). Consequently, in this chapter, our focus is on rhetorical goals as an independent component, still abstracted from a singly focused content or context. The context of Lincoln/Douglas is mentioned, but only as it illustrates some of the concepts and distinctions we draw out about rhetorical goals. Our primary purpose in this chapter is to make the case for the relationship we have posited between the formal goals of rhetorical design and their differing influence on modules within the design space.

Our discussion begins with pointing out limitations in the received view about the "goals" of rhetoric. Since the ancients, the goal of rhetoric has been associated with persuasion, moving an audience to a favorable judgment. However accurate, this traditional answer remains less than fully informative. Persuasion, after all, is a hidden motive term, thought to work best when it works undercover, a side effect of a verbal argument rather than a head-on goal. Few things are more off-putting, more likely to hinder persuasion, than the perception that persuasion is what the speaker is most about. Persuasion is better understood both as the overall goal of rhetoric and as a hoped-for side effect when the speaker's rhetoric is working. But if that is the case, one then needs to ask, what is the image we entertain of rhetoric when we imagine it to be working? Our answer to this question is that when the rhetoric is working, the speaker seems to be both predictable and adaptive. Let us factor out each of these appearances in turn.

## PREDICTIVENESS

Predictiveness, as a rhetorical goal, is based on the idea that speakers claim an "identity" that endures both before and after the rhetorical situation. In systemic terms, a system is predictable if a knowledgeable observer is never surprised as a result of viewing its performance over time. The system may spit out a wide variety of behaviors, but all of the behaviors conform to the observer's underlying "model" of how the system is supposed to work. In the case of rhetoric, a speaker achieves predictiveness in a similar way—when all of the speaker's verbal utterances conform to an audience's underlying model of what the speaker is about, what the speaker stands for.

A speaker's predictiveness does not mean that the audience can correctly guess in advance exactly what the speaker will say. Predictiveness accommodates a great deal of variability, which may preclude "predicting a speaker" in the way a meteorologist seeks to predict the weather. Predictiveness does mean, however, that, despite the variability of the speaker's utterances, no utterance of the speaker will be without an "explanation" within the audience's model of the speaker. The predictable speaker, in effect, is a "system" that the audience understands. The audience has "figured out" the speaker in the way an experienced gambler can figure out the odds of a fair roulette wheel. Every action can be understood and categorized after the fact even if no specific action can be forecast in advance.

In the purest case of predictiveness, a speaker is predictable when his or her utterances reflect a model of knowledge that is completely intersubjective, unambiguous, and determined for the audience. A teacher explaining multiplication is expected to be a perfectly predictable system to a group of capable students ready and eager to learn how to multiply. In comparison to arithmetic, rhetoric relies on an impure notion of predictiveness. A speaker's predictiveness in rhetorical design typically implies a subject matter that is, in contrast to arithmetic, neither well structured, unambiguous, nor complete. Predictiveness in rhetoric need not imply even internal consistency. In typical situations of rhetoric, a speaker can be predictable even when the knowledge animating his or her utterances is inconsistent, as long as the inconsistency committed is accommodated in the audience's model of the speaker. The only true consistency implied in rhetorical predictiveness is that between the internal model underlying the speaker's utterances and the audience's model of the speaker. It is the consistency of recognizing where the speaker is "coming from" no matter how many different, even incompatible, source points this might represent. The speaker with a multiple personality syndrome can be predictive to a person who knows the various personalities and the consistent world each personality inhabits.

As for training and exposure time, constraints imposed by the communication medium, the format of interaction, and the speaker's conscious decisions all limit the audience's information about the speaker and the model of information the speaker brings to the rhetorical situation. As we see later in this chapter, these constraints play an important role in determining the actions in the design space that a speaker uses to achieve predictiveness.

## ADAPTIVENESS

The teacher of multiplication has a subject matter to teach that does not change as a result of interacting with students. The teacher may adjust his or her utterances to make the structure of multiplication more revealing or better motivated for students. But the purpose of these adjustments is to help the students acquire a knowledge whose structure is itself nonadaptive, nonnegotiable. The teacher of multiplication thus is a predictable speaker who must show enough flexibility at the level of utterance to make the predictiveness of what is being taught accessible. The teacher is a flexibly predictable communicator. But that is not the same as being an adaptive one. Flexible predictiveness allows for changes in lexicalizations without causing changes in the underlying knowledge model. Adaptiveness requires changes, perhaps minimal changes but changes nonetheless, in the underlying knowledge model as changes are made in the lexicalization of a message. The distinction between flexible predictiveness and adaptiveness rests on a philosophical assumption about the relationship between knowledge and language.[1] But more important for our immediate purposes, it rests on a pragmatic assumption. The speaker after flexible predictability understands that if adaptations need to be made, they must be short-lived so that the audience can move back to the "right" representations. The teacher of multiplication may state problems in terms of apples and cookies but knows that, sooner or later, the representations of students need to return to abstract numbers. The speaker after adaptation works under no such constraint. The adaptive speaker, other things being equal, can assume that changes in lexicalization need not be short-term conveniences but rather closer approximations to a durable truth. Adaptiveness, unlike flexible predictability, makes empowering assumptions about the audience's right to participate in knowledge design. Adaptiveness is premised on the idea that audiences and opponents are codesigners of the underlying knowledge model exchanged. For an adaptive speaker, the knowledge model underlying the utterances will change. To be more specific, the speaker will augment, qualify, or retract information in the underlying knowledge model according to whom the knowledge is addressed to and the circumstances of address.

At first blush, predictiveness and adaptiveness might seem mutually exclusive, possibly conflicting, goals in a design of rhetoric. However, if one considers the natural limits on a speaker's predictiveness, the limits on the speaker's knowledge, and the circumstances under which audiences can come to know it, it becomes apparent that adaptiveness can be an important complement to predictiveness. Because it is unlikely that a speaker is able, or motivated, to present a complete model of his or her knowledge, the capacity of the speaker to deal with challenges and alternatives from "hostile" opponents becomes an important consideration for the audience. Furthermore, because of the inherent limitations of predictiveness, audiences often give as much attention to a speaker's capacity to respond under critical questioning as they give to an original presentation.

A second misleading impression is that predictiveness is associated with planned rhetorical actions whereas adaptiveness is associated only with

---

[1]The distinction specifically rests on the assumption that knowledge and its lexicalization are independent. This assumption, as any assumption about the relationship between knowledge and language, is obviously controversial and it is beyond our scope to offer a philosophical defense of it. In chapter 2, we argued that events are inherently linguistic and, as we will see, the function of the Events module (chapter 9) is to lexicalize knowledge structures in the rhetorical design space. This implies that the knowledge structures (chapter 6) manipulated by Plans (chapter 7) and Tactics (chapter 8) are not yet or at least not fully lexicalized.

spontaneous, unplanned, ones. This is sometimes true, but not always. Politicians with well-known positions can achieve predictiveness even when speaking off the cuff. And writers can achieve adaptiveness even when their messages are canned. Consider, for example, a couple who need to write a thank-you letter to 200 different wedding guests. The couple surmises that it would take too much time to compose a fully individualized letter to each person. However, they also fear it would be tacky to send out a single mass mailing. The couple decides to "personalize" the letter across a few variables: whether the guest was local or came from out of town, what kind of gift was given, and so on. Using these variables, the couple creates a form letter that is customized on these items. Through such customization, the couple tries to mask a one-shot adaptiveness under the cloak of a fully individualized adaptiveness.

A variation of the last example is the speaker who has committed to memory hundreds of scripts, any of which can be adapted to the immediate context. A case in point is the comedian who knows how to simulate "creative energy and spontaneity" by tying the telling of a joke to events having to do with the latest politics, with breaking news events, or with the local color of the city in which the joke is being told. The trick is to make the telling of the joke seem so inspired by the late-breaking context of utterance that it seems unthinkable that the composition of the joke could have been independent of its telling.

Like predictiveness, as we will see more fully when we discuss the conditions of public discourse, adaptiveness can be affected by the characteristics of the communication medium, the format of communication, and other characteristics of the interaction. For example, the comedian's modifiable scripts may demonstrate spontaneity (and so adaptiveness) on first hearing. However, after repeated exposures to the scripts, audiences may tire of the routine. The comedian's freshness, a judgment based in adaptiveness, can harden into a rigid predictiveness, fatal for comedy. To accommodate the same audience over time, a speaker who wants to remain highly adaptive must in fact change the knowledge model underlying the message and not just its wording. This is not to say that the speaker who only changes wordings with each new audience, as opposed to more encompassing structures of knowledge, is failing at being adaptive. Like predictiveness, adaptiveness is a goal that is satisfied or missed in degree terms. Speakers are more or less predictive insofar as their knowledge models are resistant to rhetorical situations; they are more or less adaptive to the extent that any given rhetorical situation causes a change in their knowledge models. A speaker who changes lexicalizations across rhetorical situations, who, like Douglas, targets the enemy in Northern Illinois as "Republicans" and the enemy in Southern Illinois as "Northerners," has not done much adaptation in terms of his underlying knowledge model, but still has made some interesting changes in lexicalized knowledge, the knowledge the local audiences come to hear in the event stream of rhetorical discourse.

Adaptiveness can be further broken down into subgoals, depending on the target of adaptation. We can distinguish a speaker's adaptiveness with respect to an opponent (what we call *responsiveness*) and with respect to the audience to be persuaded (what we call *humanness*). We next consider each of these subgoals in more detail.

## Responsiveness

In rhetorical situations there are typically opponents, implicit or explicit, who offer challenges and alternatives to the speaker's statements. Speakers tacitly understand opponents as a resource as much as a hindrance because of the limits on their own predictiveness. They understand that because their positions are typically not above criticism in terms of coherence, completeness, or consistency, they must help their audiences make the comparative judgment that their positions are at least better than the available alternatives. To stimulate this kind of comparison thinking, however, is to be responsive to the opponent and to his or her knowledge model. Conversely, should a speaker overlook getting an audience to engage such comparative thinking, the speaker's design will seem "unresponsive" to alternative views and the opponents who advocate them. Interestingly, many of the tactics listed by Aristotle under the common topics are formulated to encourage speakers to be responsive to their opponents. They are formulated to help rhetors satisfy the adaptive subgoal of responsiveness.

In our own age of dirty politics, we confuse comparative argument with negative and dirty tactics. We say we prefer political speakers who take the "high road" by focusing on their own positive accomplishments and leaving negative talk about the opponent out of their speeches. This modern ideal is confused because it neglects the role of responsiveness as a rhetorical goal. It mistakes being able to respond to a fair challenge, the reason for being responsive, for unfairly misrepresenting an opponent, the action of many speakers nowadays who happen to include the opponent in their rhetoric.

## Humanness

As we noted earlier, audiences rarely have the information or the inclination to develop complete models of each speaker's views. Lacking such models, audiences are often faced with very impoverished grounds for "objectively" evaluating speakers' positions. It is therefore not surprising that audiences fall back on judgments of a speaker based on personal and human characteristics, and also not surprising that writers on rhetoric have incorporated such judgments into heuristics for speakers seeking to do well on the human or personal dimension of rhetoric. Two of these heuristics are that, other things equal, (a) audiences will accept your model of the world to the extent they can identify with you as a person (Burke, 1969),[2] and (b) audiences will accept your model of the world if they think you, as a person, are more like them than they are like the opponent (Kaufer & Carley, 1993). Lacking either one or both of these heuristics, speakers can seem insensitive to the personal dimension of argument. The rhetorical goal of humanness serves as the basis for actions such as wit, humor, and the sharing of autobiographical information with an audience.

## BALANCING GOALS

Each of the three rhetorical goals described earlier, predictiveness, responsiveness, and humanness, contributes in different ways to rhetorical design. These goals act as translators, converting the rhetor's substantive goals and pertinent information about the context into terms that are relevant for rhetorical design. In their capacity as translators, goals in the design function as the gateway through which the high-level material goals of rhetoric are converted into low-level design actions.

Formulating what he called "stances" for rhetoric, Wayne Booth (1970) noticed that a rhetor must have balance, because it is easy to focus exclusively on part of the rhetorical situation to the detriment of the other parts. Our analysis of goals in rhetorical design offers a different but complementary perspective on Booth's insight. The goals in a rhetorical design are mutually necessary but singularly limiting with respect to the overall purposes of rhetorical design. Predictiveness without responsiveness leads to dogmatic behavior and, ironically, unpredictability, insofar as important unstated conditions and implications are bound to remain implicit and undocumented; predictiveness without humanness leads to robotic and bureaucra-

---

[2]Burke's notion of identification with the audience is often offered as the whole of persuasion. But this view is incomplete. A statement of identification, such as "I was a worker too," said to an audience of worker, still leaves out the speaker's public platform (predictiveness) and the implications of that platform under various conditions (expressed in the speaker's goal to be responsive).

tized behavior, leads to people so well rehearsed going into the rhetorical situation that they don't dare set the script aside and engage the audience as a fellow human. Without predictiveness, adaptiveness can turn into a destabilizing inconsistency, leaving the speaker's behavior in the situation unanchored to any cross-situational direction-giving. Without predictiveness, more specifically, being responsive leads to a deceptive kind of attentiveness that can be more discomfiting than assuring to audiences: The speaker makes many tactical adaptations to beat the opponent in debate, but the audience senses that the speaker has no purpose beyond being declared the winner. Without predictiveness, being human provides only a form of immediate entertainment that takes no responsibility for the future: The audience is grateful for the attention but loses sight of whether anything more enduring is at stake than their applause.

Goals define what a rhetor needs to balance. The Strategic module must work to maintain the balance of goals in specific situations of rhetoric.

## Rhetorical Balance and Aristotelian Theory

How does our analysis of rhetorical goals and the need to balance them compare with Aristotle's? In chapter 3, contrasting topical versus modular organization, we suggested that a modular organization of rhetoric can capture better than a topical organization the distributed sources of pathos, logos, and ethos. Now, having investigated the goals indigenous to rhetorical design, we can say more. Aristotle did not focus on logos, ethos, and pathos as goals in a rhetorical design. He focused on them instead as different sources of proof. But there is a way to connect them to our discussion of goals.

The scholarship on Aristotle, influenced by the 18th century divorce of reason and the passions, has tended to valorize logos as a "rational" source of persuasion to be favored over the "irrational" sources thought to animate ethos and pathos. Logos, in this 18th century view, denotes proofs that rely on the reason-bearing aspects of argument; ethos is understood as a form of irrational proof derived from the image of the speaker overwhelming the substance of the speech. The audience taken in by the ethical proof mistakes image for substance. Pathos is interpreted as a type of proof that can work its magic only when in contact with the emotional—that is, irrational—states of the audience. The audience taken in by the pathetic proof mistakes emotion for substance. In these 18th century interpretations of Aristotle, ethos and pathos are crutches used by the dishonorable speaker to compensate for having too little of worth to say.

The 18th century interpretation of Aristotle's types of proof eventually succumbed under the weight of two simple observations. The first is that both personal image and the emotions have a rational basis and need not occupy seats of irrationality. As Aristotle himself recognized, there are routine situations when we are inclined, rationally, to believe people just because of our image of who they are: routine situations when anger, pride, shame, and other emotions are not only rationally expected but absolutely required for rational behavior. We would be irrational to believe an astrologer over an economist on the future of the economy. We would be irrational not to be angry with a person who is to blame for harming us gratuitously or with base motives. Personal image and the emotions both claim a "logic" that makes compelling claims on our rationality. The speaker who understands the rational conditions underlying personal image and emotional states and who uses these conditions for persuasion can hardly be accused of irrationality.

The second observation that defeated 18th century interpretations of Aristotle's types of proof is that so-called rational discourse, the stuff of logos, comprises a range of more complex and heterogeneous entities than is generally acknowledged. We already hinted at this observation when we noted that rhetorical argument is filled with many devices beyond those required for the progression of conclusions from premises. Arguments whose "logic" strikes readers as "close" and "taut" also typically include humor, pleadings, colorful and leading characterizations, witticisms, word play, confessions, and so on. These aspects of rhetorical behavior are never captured in logic textbooks that describe the closed forms of syllogistic or propositional logic.

To sum up, 18th-century interpretations of Aristotle's types of proof seem to have failed because they underestimated the rationality of ethos and pathos and overestimated the uniformity of what normally falls under the category of logos.

More recent interpretations of Aristotle's categories divide logos, ethos, and pathos according to the different sources of the proof involved. Ethos is said to reside in the speaker; pathos, in the hearer; logos, in the speech itself. These interpretations have a certain verbal appeal, especially when a speaker wishes to insist that the loci of certain audience effects are the innocent result of an effective content.

This way of understanding Aristotle's categories is not without merit, but on closer examination, it comes undone as well. To be part of a verbal art, all three categories of rhetorical proof must, at some level, be mediated from speaker to hearer through the speech. One cannot imagine any rhetorical proof that does not implicate all three components at all times. One might hedge that the distinction in question is one only of emphasis—that ethical proof relies on the speaker to a degree greater than logical or pathetic proof, that pathetic proof relies on the hearer to a greater degree than ethical and logical, and so on. But to resort to an argument from emphasis is still to beg the principal question by assuming the very distinction that is being argued for. That is to say, it is dubious to proclaim some types of rhetorical proof as more or less "inside" or "outside" the speech when no rhetorical proof can pass from speaker to hearer without simultaneously occupying, in rich ways, both sides along the spatial metaphors of "in" and "outside" the speech.

Given how easy it is to fail to make good sense of Aristotle's seemingly simple categories of logos, ethos, and pathos, what kind of interpretation can begin to make good sense of them? Our theory of goals in the design of rhetoric—predictiveness, responsiveness, humanness—supplies at least a constructive way of understanding how the Aristotelian categories might coherently break down. Our interpretation envisions logos, ethos, and pathos as relating to the different goals that need to be balanced simultaneously for the ends of rhetorical design to be met. Viewed as rhetorical goals that are interwoven, logos, ethos, and pathos occupy simultaneous placements in the speaker, hearer, and speech. What distinguishes logos from ethos and pathos is that logos focuses on on-the-record information, driven by the rhetorical goal of predictiveness. Ethos and pathos, which are accountable for mixtures of on-and off-the-record information, are associated with scaled combinations of predictiveness, responsiveness, and humanness.

As we see in the next section, rhetorical actions are on the record when they are intended to result in information that can be summarized or quoted intact outside the immediate context of utterance. In his introduction to Book III of Aristotle, Kennedy (1991, p. 216) noted that the Greek term *lexis* (Latin, *elocutio*) is the "way of saying something" as opposed to the Greek *logos*, which is "what is said." This distinction seems without a difference when we consider the message in the presentness of its being uttered or delivered. For in the present moment, what is said and how it is said are accomplished through the same channel of actions. It is only when we divide the content and manner of saying by time, only when the content of the message (logos) is understood as that which can be gisted or abstracted into future reporting contexts, as on-the-record information, that Aristotle's distinction between *lexis* and *logos* makes operational sense.

According to our account, then, it is informative to associate the speaker's logos with that part of public discourse that goes on the record. This association captures how logos may seem disproportionately essential to public discourse in relation to ethos and pathos, but also explains, in ways less vague than much of the scholarship, how logos involves some, but hardly all, of the various information that resides "in" the rhetoric itself.

Strategies used to satisfy adaptiveness are, by and large, mixtures of on- and off-the-record goals. As we have suggested, adaptiveness goals are needed, over time, to complement predictiveness goals, so we would expect, as seems the case, that ethos and pathos would be supportive of a speaker's position but in ways not as visibly on the record as actions driven purely by predictiveness, the stuff of logos. Ethos under this description results from (a) responsiveness goals that seek to win the competition with the opponent on role qualification and (b) humanness goals that seek to win character points with the audience. Pathos follows from any of the goals—predictiveness, responsiveness, humanness—resulting in events that move, for strategic purposes, the audience to pleasure (joy, gratification, gratitude) or pain (distress, pity, anger).

We do not claim to be offering an original exegesis of Aristotle. That is, we do not claim that our explanation of rhetorical goals explains what Aristotle meant by his three categories of rhetorical proof. We do claim that our account of rhetorical goals offers a surprising coherence to traditional categories that, as types of proof, have eluded commentators searching for coherence.

## GOALS IN THE ARCHITECTURE OF RHETORICAL DESIGN

In the last chapter we outlined an architecture of rhetorical design and explained where the Goals component fits. We offered that the function of Goals is to monitor the speaker's internal and external environment, to represent predictiveness, responsiveness, and humanness as goals, and to "decide" which goal should take priority at any point in time in directing the design further. We also indicated we would leave it to future theory to determine how this decision making works. In the rest of this chapter, we outline a wide range of contextual considerations that must go into informing this theory. Although we do not yet have a decision making theory detailing how goal priorities emerge from the speaker's context, we do know that those contextual factors include information about the speaker and the speaker's position (e.g., public relevance, social position), information about the speaker's message (verbatim reports, directness), and information about the medium used to carry the message (its formalness and seriousness, its reach, immediacy, and durability). Within our architecture, the Goals component—functioning as a decision maker—seems to sample all of these factors, internal and external to the speaker's environment, to determine whether the speaker will make a priority out of being public, predictive, and on the record in his or her discourse or whether the speaker will try to pursue adaptiveness goals that are more off the record. The rest of this chapter details these contextual inputs as a way of establishing goal priorities for the design of rhetoric.

## CONTEXTS OF PREDICTIVENESS

Predictiveness is distinctive of the goals driving the Plans module. Adaptiveness is distinctive of the goals driving Tactics and Events, modules that work on structures from the input of the specific situation. In an important sense, however, what defines adaptiveness goals is the absence of predictiveness. Consequently, understanding the goal of predictiveness and its contexts can take us far in understanding all three goals of rhetorical design as well as the modules that affect the design space.

To begin to appreciate the contextual constraints on the predictiveness goal in particular, we need to consider how predictiveness interacts with factors of the communication medium, the format of interaction, and the speaker's decision making. To bring these constraints to the surface, we organize our discussion around the distinction between on- and off-the-record expression. This distinction turns out to be central in explaining the goal of predictiveness from a discourse-based perspective.

### Going on the Record and Predictiveness

The notion of "on the record" is a central concept for understanding predictiveness as a goal of rhetorical design, but it is largely unexamined. The first thing to note about speaking on the record is that it is an artificial form of behavior. People do not normally speak on the record. It is an artifact of public life.

To understand why, let us back up and consider everyday expression. Normally, we expect that what people say in one context will bear some resemblance to what they say in others. Were there no commonalities holding together the style and content of a person's speaking patterns, it would be impossible to arrive at a uniform image of the speaker across different contexts. Yet we arrive at these representative images all the time—at least we make the effort to distil consistent images of a speaker across diverse contexts. This effort is common and natural in everyday interaction.

Yet although it is natural to expect speakers to establish some relationship between what they have and do say, and what they will say and do, it is unusual to expect people to be willing to hang themselves if their future actions are not fully determined by their past words. This willingness to submit one's own words as standards for judging one's future behaviors is what going on the record is all about. A speaker going on the record intends that the information put on the record be carried, intact, into future contexts as a standard of evaluation.

## Going on the Record Versus Promising

Going on the record, like promising, is the use of utterances to make a commitment to the future. It is unlike promising in other respects. Imagine Mary *going on the record* with Bill that she will adopt birdwatching as a hobby. Now imagine Mary *promising* Bill that she will adopt birdwatching as a hobby. In both cases, Mary makes an attempt to hold her future behavior accountable to her words. In both cases, Mary assumes a posture where she wants to appear predictable to Bill. She wants Bill, through her words, to be able to predict a hobby she will be taking up in the future.

There is a striking difference, however, between Mary's going on the record with Bill about the future and promising him about her future actions. The difference involves assumptions of audience and the speaker's obligations to the audience. A promiser obligates future behavior to the specific audience addressed. When Mary promises Bill to take up birdwatching, she puts herself under a moral yoke to Bill. Should her actions fail to make her words true, should she not take up birdwatching, she owes Bill an apology for a broken commitment. Suppose Tom overhears her promise to Bill and Mary still breaks the promise. Can Tom claim to be misled? Does Tom have a bone to pick with Mary over her broken promise? No, because the promise was made to Bill and not Tom. Promises are individuated; audience specific. They target specific persons.

A speaker going on the record claims a predictiveness of speech and behavior into the future, irrespective of audience. A speaker who does not live up to the record, moreover, does not necessarily break a moral commitment. Imagine a politician who goes on the record not to raise taxes if elected. Suppose when in office the politician raises taxes. We often speak of a politician breaking a promise at this point (and often accurately so), but this is not necessarily the case. Going on the record often comes with an implicit "all things being equal" clause. The politician who goes on the record not to raise taxes is often implying that, all things being equal, he or she will not raise taxes. "Factors as they now stand would impel me not to raise taxes—but factors could change." If factors do change, the politician owes the electorate an explanation, but not necessarily an apology. The politician who violates on-the-record behavior understands that being predictable is a useful asset but a potentially limited one in a rapidly changing world. Politicians must also be elected for their judgment, for the right to change their mind and to alter their course as circumstances change. Naturally the electorate can decide whether the politician's change of mind was justifiable; they can factor this decision in their overall rating of the politician's job performance. They can decide not to return the politician to office. But these considerations are independent of the moral violations of broken promises.

That said, it is possible for a speaker both to go on the record and to make promises to the electorate. As voters have become more suspicious of politicians generally, they have often demanded that politicians make promises in addition to going on the record. They demand, in other words, that politicians do more than assert their predictiveness as an attractive trait for holding office; they demand that politicians promise, as a personal and moral gesture, to behave according to the same underlying knowledge model once in office. This forces modern day politicians to run on a platform that they personally guarantee not to change. Although they are public figures, they stake their personhood on not changing. They entitle voters to throw them out of office, as promise breakers, should they make decisions that contradict their campaign statements. George Bush was arguably elected in 1988 because he promised ("read my lips") not to raise taxes. He was arguably thrown out of office when he broke that promise in 1990. In chapter 9, when we consider emotions and rhetoric, we suggest that the collapse of on-the-record utterance results from the cynicism and disappointment of an electorate that expects being lied to by its leaders and that therefore insists that its leaders put up their personhood as collateral for the right to hold a public trust.

Assumptions of audience cynicism and disappointment notwithstanding, going on the record and subsequently failing to live up to the record does not in and of itself constitute a moral violation. Unlike promising, the subsequent comportment or failure to comport with the record is not an audience-specific success or violation. Mary cannot go on the record with Bill without also being willing to go on the record with Tom. Mary can, of course, disclose off the record to Bill in a way she refuses to do with Tom. But once she goes on the record with Bill, she has, for all intents and purposes, gone on the record with Tom, or anyone else for that matter. Going on the record means submitting information to the public domain, and it does not matter whether the information was intentionally put into the public domain by the speaker or leaked by spies or eavesdroppers.

Although violating an on the record statement need not indicate a broken promise, it does indicate the giving of recourse to the persons affected.

Information that is on the record was at one time negotiated or otherwise hashed over in some public forum of give and take. When such information is no longer predictive of what has come to pass, or no longer offers listeners a set of reliable expectations within which to proceed, tacit, often historical, agreements are suspended and those affected have the right to a public forum to renegotiate them. We have more to say later about the relationship between going on the record and public discourse.

## Verbatim on the Record

An interesting aspect of going on the record is that it can narrow the space of potential meaning so that only the verbatim utterance, frozen from further implication, elaboration, inference, is understood as the accepted meaning. The verbatim lexicalization, in other words, is sometimes the only unique lexicalization (a structure designed from Events) allowed to stand in for what the speaker means when the speaker goes on the record. As we see later, this condition for on the record is relaxed when a speaker's utterances interact with certain styles and media that are themselves considered on the record.

A good example of the verbatim on the record and its importance in the resolution of predictive meanings is the discussion in the Lincoln/Douglas debates regarding the Chase Amendment. Chase, a Senator opposed to slavery, had wanted to amend the Kansas Bill. The original bill had allowed that the citizens of Kansas had the right to vote "to include" slavery as they saw fit. Chase wanted to amend the bill to say they had the right "to include or exclude" slavery as they saw fit. Douglas saw no need for the change of wording and voted it down. He took inclusion as the unmarked term of a generic pair, meaning that the right to vote to include slavery implies the right to vote to exclude it. Include is the unmarked pair of exclude just as thickness is the unmarked pair of thinness. Measuring the thickness of a tree therefore also implies its thinness is being measured, yet the implication is never brought to the surface as such as verbatim utterance, nor normally need it be. On-the-record discourse, however, is consistent with the lawyer's requirement that saying something verbatim is the only way to mean it—that everything meant must be spoken verbatim to the exact meaning intended. Lincoln used this verbatim requirement of on the record to argue that Chase wanted only to put the Kansan's right "to exclude" slavery on the record and so on equal footing with the right to include it. The reason for the verbatim requirement of on the record is to allow recourse when the language is not followed to the strict letter.

### Factors in Perceiving On-the-Record Behavior

Various factors are at issue in perceiving whether a speaker's utterances are submitted on the record or not. Four factors in particular seem central to this perception.

#### Public Relevance.

The first and perhaps most important factor is the perception that the speaker's discourse addresses or seeks to address a public forum. The speaker addresses topics or issues that are matters of ongoing deliberation by a collective body in which the speaker participates. We have more to say about the concept of public later.

#### Social Position.

Second, the perception is shaped by the social position of the speaker. The more public the speaker's position, the more the speaker's statements, regardless of content, will be taken on the record. One of the hazards for celebrities and politicians in the age of mass media is that any of their statements are likely to be quoted if overheard. For this reason, they can seldom speak off the record if they think there is any chance of their statements being misappropriated.

#### Stylistic Directness.

The third factor affecting the perception of on-the-record behavior is stylistic directness. At its most explicit, a speaker telegraphs on-the-record information through a verbal formula such as, "For the record...." Generally speaking, the reliable way to put information on the record is to telegraph it as being important, central, and in the foreground of the communication. Information that holds positions of prominence in a message is more likely to be taken on the record than information in positions of less prominence. Consider the following promotional copy written by *Major League Baseball* for 12-year-old baseball fans:

> "No Hits, A Lot of Runs." When a pitcher fires a no-hitter, his team always wins, right? Wrong! On July 1, 1990, the Yankee's Andy Hawkins threw a no-hitter, but New York still lost 4–0 to Chicago. The White Sox scored all of their runs with two outs in the bottom of the eighth inning. A Yankee error and two walks loaded the bases. It looked like Andy would pitch himself out of the jam when the Sox's next hitter lofted a short fly. But the Yankees dropped the ball, and two runs scored. The very next batter hit another fly

ball, and the Yankees committed another error! Two more runs scored, giving Chicago four runs on no hits. The Yankees didn't score in the top of the ninth, making Andy the losing pitcher. (unattributed, 1993)

Some direct statements are made, such as "The White Sox scored all of their runs with two outs," and "The Sox's next hitter batted a short fly." Yet other actions taken by the writer are not at the surface of the prose itself, but only implied in the story. For example, as part of the rhetorical design, the writer seems to be acting on the following strategies: "Set up the expectation that no-hitters means wins—and then defeat it." "Hook readers with the voice of an eyewitness to a no-hitter; then shift gears and take a more didactic tone as you explain how the game was lost." "Capture the Yankee fans' hopeful perspective that their 'hero' Hawkins ("Andy") would get out of the eighth without being scored on." "Indicate through the speed and trajectory ('loft') of the ball the strong expectation that the outfielder should have caught the ball." These last actions are below the surface of the story and much less likely to be seen as information the writer is putting on the record.

Directness seems to be an important cue in how readers learn to track a writer's on-the-record commitments. Texts in logic and argument, interested in helping students trace the chain of inference in an argument, have traditionally encouraged students to focus on the explicit connective words (e.g., because, therefore, if…then) that can help uncover what the speaker gives to the record. The same texts have tended to dismiss a speaker's off-the-record behaviors as "irrelevant" to argumentation. This may explain how otherwise good readers of public discourse, trained on these texts, tend to dismiss the speaker's off-the-record behaviors—the humor, pleadings, characterizations, witticisms, and word play—as if such off-the-record maneuvers were nothing more than "noise" or "window dressing" obscuring the speaker's "real" (on-the-record) commitments.

### The Medium.

The fourth factor is the medium of communication, as some media are seen as being more inherently formal than others and so more likely to be understood as media of record. Aspects of formality that can affect the boundaries of on the record are seriousness, reach, immediacy, and durability.

### Seriousness

Actions increase in their likelihood of being taken on the record with the *seriousness* of the medium. Even in the early era of steam print, Lincoln understood that newspapers were a more "serious" medium of record than word of mouth. During the debates, Douglas regularly taunted Lincoln for being "afraid" to debate him, especially in the southern counties. Douglas mentioned that he had beaten Lincoln so decisively in the first debate at Ottawa that Lincoln "had to be carried off." Prior to the Jonesboro debate in southern Illinois, Douglas was quoted in the press as saying that the very idea of going to Jonesboro made Lincoln "tremble in the knees." At the Jonesboro debate, Lincoln acquitted himself very well. With a sense of pride in his performance, Lincoln recalled Douglas' earlier taunts and offered that the judge must be "crazy" to risk the truth against 4000 or 5000 eyewitnesses at Ottawa that he "had to be carried off." At that point, to defend himself, Douglas interrupted: "Didn't they carry you off?" Lincoln noted Douglas' subtle change in syntax and its implications for the serious-minded print audience: "That shows you the character of Douglas." "Only before he said Lincoln 'had to be carried off.' Now he says 'They carried you off.'""He puts [the earlier syntax] in print for the people across the nation to read as a serious document."

### Reach

Generally speaking, the greater a medium's potential *reach* across time and space, and the wider the social spectrum reached by the medium, the more likely the medium is to function as a medium of record. In this sense, going on the record is more likely to occur in formal speech than informal talk, more likely to occur in formal print publications than in formal speech not covered by print, and more likely to occur on network television than on an obscure tabloid or a public access channel.

### Immediacy

Information that is on the record is meant to have *immediate import*. It is hard to go on the record in a genre or medium that highlights the past, such as reciting a diary entry written years before. As Sturrock (1993, p. 133) noted in his study of the autobiography, autobiography dulls the writer's natural capacity for immediacy. The writer or speaker recounting past moments of grief, even in dramatic display, is not grief-stricken. In the first debate at Ottawa, Douglas ignored Lincoln when Lincoln read verbatim a speech he had written three years before about his views on slavery. Although serious and formal, print lacks the immediacy that makes a reader feel that the writer is speaking now. Print disembodies the writer from the rhetorical situation, creating a schedule where the writer's Plans, Tactics, Events, and even Presentation had to be finished long before a reader could ever think to start an engagement with them, through a text.

Conversely, immediacy can explain how information can be taken on the record even when it is conveyed in an informal and private register. Because of the immediate value and potential audience of the information, the tabloids put on the record the private exchanges of celebrities as overheard by waiters or hotel clerks. The immediacy of power is also a reason why the press like to put the power holder on the record, even when every other cue of the power holder's words suggests off the record. One way we know that immediacy matters to the perception of on-the-record behavior is the violation we feel when people try to go on the record in sneaky ways, ways that are intended to escape the notice of immediate audiences. A legislator who inserts something in the *Congressional Record* but never publicizes it, tries to go on the record in a sneaky and so unflattering way.

### Durability

Yet another consideration affecting the perception of on-the-record predictiveness is the *durability* of the medium. Information that, within cues of stylistic directness, would be considered throwaway and incidental can be used as central on the record information. The long-winded political speeches of the last century have turned into the short media sound bites and photo opportunities of today. This is largely a result of politicians having to compose everything they say and do on camera as if it were strictly on the record and reportable. The practice of oral history was conceived and coined in the 1930s and 1940s based largely through the efforts of Alan Nevins (Dunaway & Baum, 1984). Nevins' basic insight was that historiography should not be held hostage to information that has been encoded in durable (even if rare and so low circulating) documents. His thinking was that to produce histories only from the evidence of durable documents and not from the living, but fragile (in terms of durability) recollection of eyewitness survivors is to confine views of the past too much within an "on the record" frame. Joe Smith and Mitchell Fink (1988), echoing Nevin's point, wrote an oral history of popular music, based on never before published, and so preciously nondurable, stories recalled by key figures in the industry, which they titled *Off the Record*.

The Lincoln/Douglas debates were the first major political event covered verbatim by newspapers, a durable medium. Lincoln understood the implications of durability on expanding the range of on the record information. In his opening during the Freeport debate, he made a point of claiming that Douglas "has me on record" only after he had detailed not only his public positions but his complex attitudes toward them. The information Lincoln left on the record was far too long and dense for the listening audience to remember. It was on the record only for a highly involved reader of the printed text.

### Evolving On the Record Standards in New Media.

We have considered how various media can affect on the record information through the factors of seriousness, reach, immediacy, and durability. Yet how any medium uses these factors to define on the record information is a complex interplay of history and social convention. Interesting conflicts between on the record and off the record arise when there is no settled understanding about how a relatively new medium functions as a medium of record.

The use of electronic mail (e-mail) is a case in point. Some users go on the record with e-mail; others never use it as an on-the-record medium. This lack of uniformity about the status of e-mail leads to many conflicts. A dramatic but not far-fetched case is when A sends a message to B. A believes the message is private and should not go beyond B, but does not so indicate that. B thinks the message is semiprivate, useful for C, and so B forwards the message to C. C thinks the message would be relevant to a discussion group and so forwards the message to a distribution list. A member of that discussion group misinterprets the message and places it on the World Wide Web. A is horrified to discover that the original private message has now seeped into the public domain. Were e-mail an uncontroversial medium of record, were A to have understood e-mail as at base a public medium, A would likely have designed the message very differently before sending it to anyone.

However, at times, experienced reporters in an established medium seeking scoops will try to lure newcomers in the medium into headline-making admissions by making the on/off-the-record distinction seem less firm than it is. Connie Chung, interviewing for national broadcast the mother of Newt Gingrich about her son's description of Hillary Clinton ("rhymes with witch" as Barbara Bush once said of Geraldine Ferraro), instructed the elder Gingrich to "whisper" what Newt had said. A whisper is marked as much for its off-the-record status as for its low volume. Like a murmur, mutter, or mumble, a whisper is off the record; unlike these verbs of saying, which are low in volume although indistinct and garbled in content, a whisper is low volume but nonetheless clear and distinct in the channel of communication. Yet a whisper also contrasts with low-volume and clear-channeled communications that are patently public and on the record, such as Teddy Roosevelt's strong and silent leader who was admired for "speaking softly" (with the big stick in hand). Whispers are out-of-channel asides that stop with the confidant. Through her instructions to Mrs. Gingrich to "whisper" her answer, Chung implied to Mrs. Gingrich that she could be assured of off-the-record anonymity in front of millions of gawking viewers. When attacked for issuing such a misleading implication, Chung's comment was that no one, including her interview subject, could be so gullible to take her words at face value.

Different media can be understood as media of record, but they often represent "the record" in different ways. For example, because of the durability of print, print seems to be able to carry a form of public expression that is more complex and less repetitive than formal speech not supported by print. In the continued course of this book, we see that assumptions of the media of record seemed to play a significant role for Lincoln and Douglas in their joint debates. Douglas thought the medium of record for the debates was the oral address themselves; Lincoln thought it was the printed transcripts. For this reason, among others perhaps, Douglas' message tended to be more simple, repetitive, and adaptive to the local audience, and Lincoln's, more complex, more diverse, and less locally adaptive.

### Summary of Factors.

These four factors—public relevance, social position, stylistic directness, and the medium—establish defaults for what is likely to be perceived as on the record behavior. Still, it is important to note that information can be read as on the record even in the absence of all of these factors. That is to say, a hearer can hold a speaker accountable, as going on the record, for information that the speaker believes to be private, casual, and only weakly implied. This failure to coordinate expectations is a common occurrence in couples with marital difficulties, but it can also occur in more public contexts, such as tabloid journalism. The point here is that interpreting information as on the record may be as much a hearer's prerogative as a speaker's initiative.

### Going on the Record and Public Expression

Going on the record, we have suggested, is related to and, in many ways, defining of public expression. Rhetorical design involves as a central assumption the goal of a speaker seeking to impact an audience through public discourse. The word *public* in terms like public discourse and public expression is a notoriously difficult concept—one to be revisited further in this book—but in the present context it can be understood as meaning two things.

First, it means that the expression in question is not localized to the here and now of utterance but potentially reverberates for many times and places beyond the original context. Public expression is never fully localized, indexical expression, although it certainly can contain references to the utterance context. Although the immediate audience can remain important in public expression, its importance can be dwarfed by audiences and contexts beyond the immediate one. The immediate audience and context may provide nothing other than a place-holding occasion to go on the record to a much more diffuse audience and context. A President using a college commencement to address foreign policy issues is a case in point. Public expression can, in principle, exclude no persons as the agents about whom the discourse refers and assigns responsibility into the future. Public expression and expression purposely designed to exclude certain audiences are thus incompatible notions.

Second, this does not mean that, to be public, an expression might not, as a matter of fact and happenstance, exclude some audiences. What is true about a public message that happens to exclude is that the exclusionary restrictions are contributed from the audience side rather than the speaker's side of the equation. If I as a speaker expressly intend my message never to reach some audiences, my message cannot be public. On the other hand, if my intentions are compatible with the message reaching everyone in principle, yet I happen to know it will not do so because of limiting factors in audience characteristics (attention, interest, education, income, time), then the message is not threatened as a public message merely because some audiences miss it and even, in principle, will always miss it. Einstein's theories are part of the public domain but nevertheless remain highly exclusionary because of the requirements they place on audiences. This notion of public, allying itself with the broad reference of on the record expression, comports with Dewey's (1946) idea that the public references an indefinite audience into the indefinite future.

We have come far enough to see that *on-the-record behavior* and *public expression* are terms that can be used to bootstrap increasingly precise characterizations of each other. From the standpoint of the individual speaker, on-the-record actions lend to the speaker an aura of predictiveness, the idea that what the speaker has said and does say in the here and now provides some reasonable indication of what the speaker will say and do in situations to come.

## Going on the Record and Predictiveness

To contribute to public discourse, one must strive for a language that can commit the speaker to a particular future as well as a language that the speaker can use to share that commitment with arbitrary others. To say, this, however, is to say that on-the-record expression is predictive expression, expression designed to satisfy the speaker's goal of predictiveness. Without on-the-record actions, a speaker could not project himself or herself on a line from past to future. Nor could the projection be diffuse, an unrestricted summons to an unrestricted audience, for, as we have mentioned, to go on the record is to put one's words under the yoke of the future to arbitrary individuals, not just to those directly addressed in the utterance context. It is to assume an ongoing responsibility to persons not yet known, perhaps not even born.

Public expression, in turn, is designed to socialize the speaker's lines of individual commitment to the aggregate level, marshaling a public position from a personal commitment. A public position is a line of personal commitment socialized so as to invite arbitrary others to share in the responsibility of making the line evolve as advertised. It is difficult to imagine a rhetoric in which on-the-record expression and public expression are absent, and hence predictiveness is not a goal in the design. Without predictiveness and its various ramifications, a speaker's discourse would fail to be public discourse. The speaker's words would lack the force to bridge a communal past and future, to reinvigorate or change historical processes. The speaker's words would remain in the timeless present of routine.

To summarize, to be predictable, a speaker acts to put information on the record. By doing so, the speaker indicates that the information put on the record can survive intact into future contexts and be used as a standard against which to judge the speaker's future words and deeds.

## STAYING OFF THE RECORD: THE LIMITS OF PREDICTIVENESS

Nonetheless, predictiveness, in isolation, is a limited goal in a rhetorical design. First, there are intrinsic constraints on the predictiveness of an argumentative position. Second, taken to extremes, a speaker's efforts to be predictable can undermine equally important efforts to adapt to the immediate context of interaction. We take up each of these issues in turn.

To appreciate the limits of predictiveness, we need to appreciate that when speakers make predictiveness the goal, they make an abstract position the agent of persuasion. However, there are independent reasons to believe that there are ceilings on how predictable an argumentative position can be, and so how much of a burden of proof it can carry.

A position that is predictable in the ideal case claims to be both complete and consistent. We define both of these terms as they apply to a rhetorical position. A position is *complete* when it determines a way of proceeding for all the cases that people are interested in deciding on. A complete position on, say, abortion determines how to resolve every contested case without the need to make up the rules as one goes along.

A position is *consistent* when, across all formulations, no speaker runs into a contradiction. No speaker, for example, discovers that some formulation of the position forces him or her to conclude both "p" and "not p" at the same time.

Were the goal to be predictable itself sufficient to carry the burden of rhetorical design, we would expect to find rhetors being able to carry the day through the completeness and consistency of their positions alone. Yet no rhetorical argument is flawless, beyond criticism, in this respect. Every rhetor must do his or her best with a position that is in some respects incomplete (causing indecision) and latently or overtly contradictory (causing no consistent decision to result when the whole point of holding a position was to converge on a consistent outcome decision). Even if a rhetor could achieve perfection, furthermore, could formulate a position as intrinsically tight as a mathematical proof, the rhetoric would remain incomplete. Predictiveness allows a speaker to organize his or her memory of events (chapter 6) in a way that plots a consistent trajectory from past to future. Yet a rhetor needs to be more than a force projecting history along a predestined path. A rhetor also needs to enter the here and now of the rhetorical situation.

After all, living on the record is not a very interactive, responsive, or even human way to live. On-the-record information lacks a sense of the here and now because, by definition, a speaker pursuing on-the-record goals is consigned to prior knowledge models binding past to future. The speaker remaining on the record forsakes the world of personal contingency, spontaneity, and engagement for a world of abstract forces propelling individuals and events like puppets through a theater. In the effort to achieve predictiveness, the appearance of thinking and acting according to a prior script, the speaker forfeits the appearance of adaptiveness, the appearance of being able to enter the current here and now of the audience and opponent with energized curiosity about the uncertain.

The foregoing discussion has tried to establish some of the patterned factors that must be considered when a speaker translates rhetorical goals into specific actions. Rhetorical goals are not static factors drawn discretely from a rhetor's decision to take action. They are instead continuous factors that must be dynamically coordinated in a changing context as a rhetor contemplates and takes action. Successful rhetorical design depends on how a speaker trades on this dynamic in building the fabric of his or her message, a fabric woven with off-the-record (private and local) as well as on-the-record (public and global) stitches.

Our focus in this chapter has been on detailing the goals in a rhetorical design rather than on explaining how the Goals component actually represents this information or makes decisions (functioning as a module in its own right) about the current goal priority based on incoming information about the speaker and the changing environment. We leave it to future theory to specify the representation of goals and the decision making that goes into choosing a current priority on the basis of sampling the speaker and the environment at a certain point in a situation of rhetoric. The architecture we go on to develop in this book relies on the Goals component in two ways. First, we show (chapters 7, 8, and 9) how the modules within the design space (Plans, Tactics, and Events) have descriptions that make each better suited for satisfying some goals and worse suited for satisfying others. Second, we show how the Strategic module, cognizant of these descriptions, can affect the behavior of these internal design modules so as to steer the rhetorical design in the direction of the current goal priority (chapter 10).

Six

# Structure

We have examined how goals in rhetorical design affect specific actions within the design space. Besides goals, an architecture of rhetorical design must involve a theory, at least a vocabulary, for describing the basic building blocks that make up the design. A single word for these building blocks, aggregated to reveal the design for what it is, is what we call the *structure* in the design. Our naming conventions for this structure are variable, depending on the source from which we perceive the structure to derive. When we pinpoint the mind as the source of the design, we identify the structure with the designer's knowledge. When we follow the inclusion of the designer's knowledge into the design itself, we are more likely to identify the structure as the design content. Other names for the design structure home in on the precise source of a structure that has arisen from specific linguistic temporalities and moods. When, for example, the design arises from situations in the designer's past or near present, we identity the design structure with the designer's memory. When it arises from situations that are irreal, that is, from situations that are fictive, hypothetical, or projected, we identify it with the designer's imagination.

Scholars across many disciplines have addressed the nature of the building blocks constituting design structure insofar as they have pursued theories of knowledge, memory, linguistics, and the imagination. It is beyond our scope to add to these discussions in the terms in which they are usually couched. The purpose of this chapter is more narrow and pointed: to make explicit the features of a theory of structure in rhetorical design that are sufficient to trace the role of structure in the rhetorical design process, and, specifically, in the design space. Because the ultimate purpose of a rhetorical design is, to a large extent, the creation of a complex linguistic artifact, we start with a notion of structure as linguistic objects and relations and then work our way to an understanding of how that structure can inform a rhetorical design.

## LINGUISTIC STRUCTURE: OBJECTS AND RELATIONS

Linguistic structure consists of objects and relations. An object is anything that can be referenced as an entity in the language. An object can be simple (ball) or complex, one including properties (the red ball) and events (hitting the red ball). Complex objects can be decomposed into smaller object units. "Mary, the 4-year-old, ate her peas" is an event composed of two nominal objects (Mary, peas). Objects can be abstract as well as concrete. Generics (the 4-year-old) are abstract objects, in this case used as a definite description to reference, by association, a specific property ("is 4 years old") of Mary. The word *her* is also an abstract object, indicating "in the possession of a female" who may or may not have been specified.

Simple objects form complex objects through relations. The relations binding simpler objects can be logical, temporal, spatial, conceptual, and so on. Eating is, among other things, a spatial relationship between objects, the one ingested into the physical space of the other's digestive system. Syntax as well as lexical entities imposes relations, as the arrangement of the objects within the event just cited assures that Mary is a 4-year-old eating peas rather than just a female eating 4-year-old peas. It also assures that the peas have already been allocated to Mary's plate (are her possession) and that she has not swiped them off the plate of another child during a lunch at preschool.

Despite many controversies in linguistic syntax and semantics about how to identify and assign objects and relations within a sentence, the fact remains that, in most everyday sentences, speakers and hearers seem to have little trouble coordinating on the objects and relations within the words uttered. Imagine two adults looking at Mary, one uttering the event under consideration, the other nodding in agreement. Arguably, these adults have shared the primary objects and their relations, both in terms of perception and agreement. However, under closer examination, we find that even in everyday discourse, converging on the "same" objects and relations can pose a considerable challenge for understanding, much less agreement-seeking. Consider the following discourse:

Joel was still lounging on the couch. His mother was unhappy about that.

The word *that* in the second sentence is a clausal pronoun taking an entire event for its antecedent. The question is, what is the antecedent? What is the mother unhappy about? Different words in the first sentence offer themselves as contrastive targets for the event affecting the mother. Perhaps the word "Joel" is the target, meaning that the mother is not unhappy about

anyone's lounging on the couch, but only about the particular fact that it is
Joel doing it. Perhaps "lounging" is the target, meaning that the mother
could have tolerated Joel's sitting erect but not his being in some state of
repose and recline. Perhaps the progressive aspect "was...ing" is the target,
meaning that the instant of the mother's reported consciousness is not the
source of her distress but the fact that she has sampled the couch on many
earlier occasions and so (just) now recognizes that Joel's sitting has had an
unacceptably long duration. Perhaps, finally, the "couch" is the target,
suggesting that the mother's concern is not what Joel is doing but what he
is doing it on. The existence of ambiguous targets within a discourse suggests
that the language can reference objects without specifying them in any
simple correspondence between form and meaning. This lack of correspondence and the many inventive paths for trying to restore it at a more abstract
level precipitate many of the debates in linguistic syntax and semantics.

The phenomenon of trying to pin down the "same" event scales upward
in both uncertainty and significance when we move to the problem of
pinning down the "same" issue in the public discourse associated with
rhetorical design. To perceive even the need for rhetoric, speakers must
perceive an actual or potential conflict with reference to some issue. An *issue*
is an ambiguous set of paths through which different speakers can reference
the same, or at least a largely overlapping, set of objects and relations within
a series of events. In addition, the objects in these events are public, meaning
that they are widely referenced across language communities that are
themselves separated in time, space, and culture. The Lincoln/Douglas
debates, for example, can be understood as two rhetors addressing complex
cultural beliefs about public objects and the events in which they participate,
such as the Missouri Compromise, the 1850 Compromise, the Kansas Act,
the Dred Scott decision, and more. Were there no sense of Lincoln and
Douglas addressing the same set of public objects, there would be no sense
of the interactivity or competitiveness that is necessary for rhetorical design.
Consequently, when we want to sample the interactivity and competitive
nature of the Lincoln/Douglas debate, we need first to inquire into the
commonality of their reference: What, if any, are the common referents to
which both refer when they speak of the Missouri Compromise of 1820, the
1850 Compromise, the Kansas Act, or the Dred Scott decision?

On the other hand, were there no sense of some important divergence in
these referents, there would be no debate. An important representation of
ideological history, arguably, is a depiction of public objects and their
interconnections across time. Speakers who share the same ideological
history not only make common references to a past of public objects but

manage to select the same objects or at least manage to make them function in sympathetic and coextensive ways when the referents are different. One fiscal conservative, for example, may use "the Founding Fathers" as the base referent for fiscal conservatism; another may use "Adam Smith." The two referents are different but their function may be equivalent within a certain ideological history. Similarly for the Lincoln/Douglas debates, a Democrat sympathetic to Douglas or a Republican sympathetic to Lincoln could be expected to elaborate events like Kansas and Dred Scott in the ways Douglas and Lincoln would elaborate them. Like the sentence about Joel and his mother, there will be variation and ambiguity in the referents that connect Douglas to a Douglas sympathizer and Lincoln to a Lincoln sympathizer (see Kaufer & Carley, 1993b for an analysis of rhetoric across ideological frames). Nonetheless, the variation and ambiguity should flow in a common direction.

In contrast, speakers who differ in ideological history can be expected to make common references but for the most part with uncommon referents. Lincoln and Douglas, for example, discuss many public objects in common but in incompatible ways. Their differences are not a matter of understanding, but of interest and ideology. Unlike the case of Joel and his mother, where a knowledgeable narrator can resolve the reader's problem by elaborating the description, the differences separating Lincoln from Douglas and the sympathizer of one from the other are beyond matters of comprehension. They rather indicate underlying design structures of rhetoric that move in contrary directions.

To understand the meaning and place of structure in rhetorical design, therefore, we need to conceive of a representation that allows us to depict the interpretation of public objects as belonging to a directional flow that is either common or contrary. The representation in question must also accommodate the normal variability across speakers who interpret the referent of these objects in a common direction. In the next section, we describe what this sought-after representation might look like.

## REPRESENTING STRUCTURE IN RHETORIC

The structure in a rhetorical design centers on the notion of an object class. So far we have defined objects and relations but not object classes. An object class is a label out of which an unlimited number of specific objects can be activated. For example, "The Assassination of Lincoln" is a label for an object class, which in this instance is also subcategorizable as an event class. From this object (event) class, the following events can be triggered.

John Wilkes Booth shot Lincoln.
Lincoln was shot by Booth.
The shooting took place at Ford's theatre.
Mary Todd Lincoln was by the President's side when he was shot.

Object classes are a useful vehicle to help us explain how speakers can retain a unitary notion of "object" in their head and still generate so many discretely different objects from this unity. Object classes are not linguistically dependent objects; they rather trigger the association of language-dependent objects in a particular direction. By thinking of the rhetorical designer's knowledge as organized into object classes, we can tie the structure of the designer's knowledge to the structure of a rhetorical design by way of three important assumptions.

First, we assume that the events, entities, and other objects that appear in public discourse and that are unleashed to the minds of audiences are created on the basis of object classes recalled from a speaker's immediate consciousness, memory, or imagination. Second, we assume that object classes, like objects themselves, may be combined into relations of object classes, resulting in complex object classes. Third, and most telling, we assume that complex object classes array themselves into "lines" of object classes.

Before we go further into the details of lines of object classes, it is useful to make a connection between these "lines" and what the ancient rhetoricians understood as lines of argument. Lines of argument in classical rhetoric were also called *topoi*, but they are different from the topics we described in chapter 3. The topics there were associative cues, single words used to stimulate the mind along fruitful paths. Associative topics might have no internal structure of their own; they could be external prompts used to help the mind begin to structure its own internal pattern of thought. Yet topics could also include more structured patterns for thinking, patterns of thought more intimately connected to the region of experience within which a speaker could find an existing argument or develop an existing argument further (Leff, 1993). This latter notion of the topics takes a view of mental structuring that deeply intertwines structure, content, and experience. The structures of thinking are imbued with content, which in turn derives from the specific experiences and contextual episodes associated with thinking about or through content.

As topical structures become content and context laden, they become more interesting and useful for inference. At the same time, they become an internal description more of what speakers know once they have acquired rhetorical expertise than of what students can be taught through external prompts. Hearing a topic as an external prompt, the student rhetor will need to search memory to find something to say. The search and retrieval will typically be slow and halting. The student will need to take as much as possible from the structure of the external prompt to compensate for the lack of structuring that has yet to go on in the mind. Contrastively, the search and retrieval of the experienced rhetor will be fast and automatic. The issues will already be well known, the lines of argument well rehearsed and both will be deeply tied to content, context, and lexical knowledge. The expert rhetor may find some use in external prompts, but mainly to remember to express well-developed and connected lines of argument that have only been momentarily misplaced or lost sight of.

Designers of rhetoric are experts. Students are nonexperts who are seldom alerted to the possibility that when they are learning skills of strategic communication, they are in fact learning a skill that has promise beyond seeing them through the undergraduate curriculum, the term paper, or the job letter. They are seldom alerted to the possibility that the skills they are learning can evolve into an art of design. Given the students'—and often the teacher's—approach to topics, there is little wonder why. The understanding of topics as external mnemonics fits well within a student tradition of practical pedagogy. Yet if we are to understand rhetorical artists like Lincoln and Douglas, we must understand, at least hypothesize about, their internal systems of topical knowledge, the structures that comprise their rhetorical designs. We start on such hypothesis generation when we seek to represent how complex object classes array themselves into "lines" of object classes. Such representations are meant to get at how the topical expertise of a Lincoln or Douglas might be represented.

A line of object classes (or LOC) is a series of object classes. Every LOC has an identifying header class and a related series of linked object classes. The link has no meaning other than "is associated with." Directionality within an LOC is indicated by prefixing each class with an optional plus (+) or minus (-) to indicate whether the class and, by implication, the specific objects derivable from it are generally supported and endorsed by the speaker or unsupported and unendorsed.

For example, consider the object class "Founding Fathers" in the Lincoln/Douglas debates as the header class in a LOC. This object class and its lines of associated classes comprise a variety of objects that involve the American Founding Fathers. Figure 6.1 indicates how this class, along with an associated set of seven LOCs, can be represented. The header class label is indicated by the double underline. The header label itself is prefixed by a + sign, indicating that every LOC in which this class is involved is a positive reference for both speakers. That is to say, both Lincoln and Douglas make

<u>+Founding Fathers</u>

LOC 1.  + Founding Fathers: Slavery (D, L)

LOC 2.  + Founding Fathers: Slavery: + Popular sovereignty: + National
unity (D)

LOC 3.  + Founding Fathers: + Antislavery: + House divided (L)

LOC 4.  + Founding Fathers: Black rights (D, L)

LOC 5.  + Founding Fathers: + Black rights: + Rights to rise guaranteed
in Declaration of Independence (L)

LOC 6.  + Founding Fathers: Black rights: - Rights to rise guaranteed in
Declaration of Independence: + Treat with Christian charity (D)

LOC 7.  + Founding Fathers: Black rights: - Black citizenship (D, L)

FIG. 6.1.    Illustration of the object class "Founding Fathers" and the various lines of object classes it heads in the Lincoln/Douglas debates.

common reference to "Founding Fathers" in order to create positive historical precedents for their own positions. Lincoln and Douglas shared, in this sense, a common orientation toward the public object class "Founding Fathers."

Yet because Lincoln and Douglas inserts the Founding Fathers within contrary ideological histories, there are notable differences in their references as well. These differences are represented by the different object class structures associated with the speakers. As we indicated earlier, LOCs consist of object classes that are associatively linked.[1] In Fig. 6.1, links are indicated by colons, and each LOC is preceded by a (D) if it belongs to Douglas' orientation only, an (L) if it belongs only to Lincoln's, and a (D, L) if it is shared across the orientations of both speakers.

According to Fig. 6.1, both Douglas and Lincoln share at least a neutral association between the Founding Fathers and slavery (LOC 1), the Founding Fathers and Black rights (LOC 4), and the Founding Fathers, Black rights, and the citizenship rights of Blacks (LOC 7). Of these three shared LOCs, only the last (LOC 7) contains a signed (+ or -) event class (-Black citizenship), indicating an agreement between Douglas and Lincoln on the Founding Fathers' belief that Blacks do not, and should not, enjoy the full social and political rights of whites. Although Douglas tries to muddy

---

[1]Notice that an object class and the LOCs it heads are mutually defining in that object classes consist of a label and a series of LOCs, and LOCs themselves consist of links between object classes. The result is a complex semantic network, much like a thesaurus of associated object classes. Holding together associatively rich classes, the associative trails in an LOC can branch out very quickly.

Lincoln's orientation on this matter, both speakers agree that, to the Founding Fathers, the rights of Blacks are less than the full rights of citizens.

But Lincoln and Douglas disagree about other events concerning the Founding Fathers' views on the rights of Blacks. Lincoln maintains that, according to the Founders, Blacks have the formal rights to rise, the rights of life, liberty, and pursuit of happiness as promised by the Declaration of Independence (LOC 5). Douglas denies that the Founders ever accorded even these formal rights to Blacks. He instead maintains that the Founders only granted Blacks the right to be treated with Christian charity (LOC 6).

Figure 6.1 also highlights how, through the lens of the Founding Fathers, Douglas and Lincoln diverged on slavery. Douglas believes it an officially unsigned or neutral object class, of no intrinsic interest or importance in moral or subjective preference categories. He associates the institution with his doctrine of popular sovereignty, a doctrine that leaves it to the people in each local territory to decide whether to accept or reject slavery. Lincoln, on the other hand, maintains that the Republican Party he led was formed to oppose slavery as a moral evil, and he associates slavery with his house-divided doctrine, which proclaims that the nation cannot exist half slave and half free.

At this juncture, we should step out of the debates long enough to consider how this representation of structure in rhetoric addresses some thorny problems pertaining to rhetoric and reference. First, it clarifies how two opponents can converge on a subject area or topic, even in the face of disagreement. Opposing speakers reference the same topic when they reference the same classes within the context of similar LOCs. Figure 6.1 makes clear, for example, how Lincoln and Douglas can reference the same events, despite their disagreement about where in larger structures of knowledge the events participate. We might understand their point of view on an event as the relationship between the event and the larger structures of knowledge in which it is involved. Speakers can agree on certain referents, or at least certain of their aspects, without agreeing on the line of reasoning that threads them together. Agreement on an event requires sharing points of view on it, which requires threading it through converging lines of reasoning. Lincoln and Douglas shared a variety of object classes but more in an environment of disagreement than agreement. They could focus on the same events but differ in their understanding of how the events fit into the larger scheme of things.

Second, it clarifies the possibility of variability not only across speakers who differ in their orientation to classes and LOCs but also across speakers who share an orientation. Object classes and LOCs are abstractions that define potentials for the construction of linguistic events and entities, but, significantly, they are not the lexicalized events themselves. Two speakers who share an object class and even a point of view on it can nonetheless generate from it an infinitude of different lexicalized events whose truth is nonetheless compatible. Two speakers who thus agree on an event can still express themselves on the event in very different ways.

Third, the availability of a positive or negatively signed (+, -) class addresses a subtle issue about the relationship between the structure of a rhetorical design and the subjective attitudes and affect of the designer. The issue concerns whether a speaker's subjective orientation and affect exist within or apart from their representation of an issue. The representation we propose takes a stand on this controversy, hinting that the subjective attitude and affect of a speaker lie within the speaker's representation of the issue content. It suggests, more specifically, that a speaker's orientation emerges from the way the speaker discovers how he or she annotates object classes retrieved from memory. Our proposed representation thus indicates how subjective attitudes and emotions need not be add-on peripherals to the way we represent the structure of a rhetorical design; but how they can be part and parcel of that representation. As the psychologist Ernst Poppel (1988, p. 147) wrote in his study of time and conscious experience, "Our perception, thinking, and acting is always emotionally shaded." This way of thinking discourages the simplistic view that speakers have intact attitudes and emotion prior to their design activities and then simply search for a design that fits some preexisting mental entity. Rather, speakers retrieve classes from memory all the while they are designing rhetoric. In the process of this retrieval, they discover their responses to what they retrieve, and they discover their attitudes and affect in these responses. Learning one's attitudes and affect as a speaker is, in sum, concurrent with rhetorical design and not a separable activity.

Finally, the representation of object classes and LOCs makes available a measure associated with a rhetor's performance, that of topical diversity. A speaker's topical diversity is the total number of different significant object classes invoked during a rhetorical performance. Topical diversity reflects the variability in the speaker's classes and structures as a performance unfolds. A speaker with requirements to change an argument for persuasive advantage, in response to the unfolding actions/events of an opponent or audience, is benefitted by being topically diverse. Change, though, is not an unequivocal advantage for a rhetorical design. Sometimes the speaker benefits through dogged repetition. And sometimes change only gets the speaker off into diversions and red herrings. Topical diversity only indicates the speaker's use of complex content, tactically motivated or not.

## HOW STRUCTURE INFORMS THE RHETORICAL DESIGN SPACE

The goals and structure in a design act on the rhetorical design space to produce rhetorical artifacts. In the last chapter, we saw at a high level of abstraction how goals interact with the Plans, Tactics, and Events modules. It is now time to consider at a high level the role of structure in the design space of rhetoric. The structure provides the stuff in the rhetorical design space on which the Plans, Tactics, and Events modules work to produce a finished design. The Plans module, as we see later, views structure as the raw material for constructing a public model and for taking specific perspectives on it.

In Fig. 6.1, we saw how LOCs can be associated with individual speakers, like Lincoln, Douglas, or both. Within the rhetorical design space, these structures can be rhetorically primed by also associating a LOC with the likelihood of the speaker using it in the context of an offensive or defensive action. When, for example, a LOC is associated with Lincoln or Douglas' offense, instead of just tagging it with an (L) or (D), we can tag it with an (L, OFF) or a (D, OFF). In an offensive action, a speaker seeks to construct and support a world within his or her own orientation. A LOC with a greater likelihood for defense is represented as (L, DEF) or (D, DEF). In a defensive action, a speaker seeks to block a world, or worlds, within the opponent's orientation. When a speaker wishes to characterize the offense of an opponent we shall use the notation Speaker (Opponent OFF). For example, when Lincoln characterizes Douglas' offense with a LOC, it will be indexed L (D, OFF). When Douglas makes a similar characterization of Lincoln, the LOC will be annotated D (L, OFF).

In light of these notations for offense, defense, and the characterization of the opponent's offense, we can track with reasonable concreteness how the result of the design process can inform the rhetorical design process itself.

In what follows, we overview the tie from structure to rhetoric in the Lincoln/Douglas debates. Every structure in a rhetorical design must be described by the particular object classes relevant to the situation. As it happens, we find it useful to describe the design structures of Lincoln and Douglas in terms of two kinds of object classes: entity classes and event classes.

### Entity Classes in the Structure/Rhetoric of the Lincoln/Douglas Debates

In the public discourse of rhetoric, *entity classes* refer to groups, individuals, and organizations with a presence in the public world. Entity classes play an important role in the debates inasmuch as they reference individuals with the entitlements necessary to change the public world. Important entity classes in the debates include the Founding Fathers, Whigs, Democrats, Republicans, and, finally, Lincoln and Douglas themselves as the nominees of the Republicans and Democrats for the Illinois Senate. By surveying some prominent entity classes within the debates, we can start to illustrate in concrete detail the tie between structure and rhetoric.

## Founding Fathers

The generation in which the debates took place, in 1850s America, held the generation of the American revolution in reverence and awe. A political candidate of mid 19th century America could not succeed without aligning his or her political beliefs with the commitments of Washington, Adams, Madison, Franklin, and Jefferson. Both Lincoln and Douglas wanted to align the intent of the Founding Fathers with their offensive strategies, inferences toward the world they wanted to push through. Lincoln's and Douglas' offense, more often than not, addresses their constructive understanding of ideological history and its normative pull on the future. Douglas' offense was based on aligning the revolutionary Fathers with his doctrine of popular sovereignty and the imperative of national growth. Lincoln's primary offensive maneuver was to align the Fathers with a distaste in the institution of slavery, the belief that the institution was moribund, and the belief that the ultimate health of the country required its gradually moving toward extinction. This antislavery sentiment, as far as Lincoln was concerned, connected the generation of the American revolution to his recently expressed house-divided doctrine. Lincoln's offense also hung on the belief that the Fathers had included Blacks in the Declaration of Independence, guaranteeing at least their formal right to rise in the society.

Lincoln and Douglas also had cause to rely on the Founding Fathers as the basis for defensive actions, actions needed to block inferences rather than push them through. For Douglas, an inference to be blocked was that he was too insensitive to Blacks, even among those moderates on race who thought them inferior and undeserving of citizenship. To block this inference, Douglas couples his racist remarks with a religious call for the humane and charitable treatment of Blacks. For Lincoln, an inference to be blocked was that he was an abolitionist who supported the negro's right to citizenship. To block this inference, Lincoln recurrently denies that Blacks have any legitimate claim to the social and political rights of citizens. A refrain for Lincoln throughout the debates is that just because he would not have a negro for a slave does not mean he would have one for a wife. Figure 6.2

<u>+ *Founding Fathers*</u>

+ Founding Fathers: Slavery: + Popular sovereignty: + National unity(D, OFF)

+ Founding Fathers: + Antislavery: + House divided (L, OFF)

+ Founding Fathers: + Black rights: + Rights to rise guaranteed in Declaration of Independence (L, OFF)

+ Founding Fathers: Black rights: - Rights to rise guaranteed in Declaration of Independence: + Treat with Christian charity (D, OFF)

+ Founding Fathers: + Black rights: D(L, OFF)

+ Founding Fathers: + Black rights: - Black citizenship (L, DEF)

FIG. 6.2.    Illustration of the entity class structure around the "Founding Fathers."

illustrates an object structure focus on the Founding Fathers with the rhetorical potentials of Lincoln's and Douglas' offense and defense indicated.

## Whigs

A major political party until its demise in the early 1850s, the Whigs had stood for federalism, unionism, and banking and financial interests against the populism of Jackson's Democratic Party. One of the Whigs' leading lights had been Henry Clay, the congressman who authored various compromises to protect the union from regional factionalism. The Whigs play only a cameo role in the Lincoln/Douglas debates, and no one speaks ill of them. By the time of the debates in 1858, the Whigs have dissolved and there is little perceived gain in speaking ill of the dead. Douglas cites the Whigs favorably, especially their disinclination to make slavery a matter of national debate. He contrasts the Whigs with Lincoln's new party, the Republicans, who are organized mainly around their opposition to slavery. Lincoln counters that Douglas was never as kindly toward the Whigs while they were a flourishing party, and he accuses Douglas of making the same abolitionist accusations against the Whigs that Douglas now makes of the Republicans. In addition, both Lincoln and Douglas want the most famous of Whigs, Henry Clay, to be perceived as supporting each of their views when they argue for or against the Founding Fathers' intended inclusion of Blacks in the Declaration of Independence. Douglas claims that Blacks were not intended for inclusion; Lincoln maintains they were. Both go to lengths to show that Clay agreed with their particular side. The Whigs were an important point of reference in the debates if for no other reason than that former Whigs remained a major voting block in central Illinois. No one could win central Illinois without winning the old Whigs, and no one could win the election without winning central Illinois.

<u>+ *Whigs:*</u>

+ Whigs: + Princ: + Pop Sov: + National Unity: + Henry Clay (D, OFF)
+ Whigs: + Princ: + Anti-Slavery: + Henry Clay (L, OFF)

FIG 6.3.    Illustration of entity class structure around the "Whigs."

Figure 6.3 depicts how both Lincoln and Douglas use the class "Whig" in the debates. Both used this group and the events instigated by it on the offense. Both align the Whigs with upholding their basic principles, either popular sovereignty (Douglas) or antislavery (Lincoln). Both are concerned that a personal endorsement of their views come from of the mouth of Henry Clay.

## Democrats

The Democrats were the party of Jefferson, localism, nonintervention from the federal government, and Jacksonian democracy. They were also the party of Douglas. Two years before the debates, the Democrats had denied their own Franklin Pierce a second term because of his inability to hold together northern and southern factions. Douglas had enjoyed a base of support in the 1856 presidential election, but the Democrats ended up nominating James Buchanan, whose appeal was based in part on his being out of the country (as ambassador to England) and so out of the fray at a time of strident political debate at home over slavery.

The 1856 Democratic platform endorsed popular sovereignty, the doctrine most closely associated with Douglas. On its face, the doctrine favored the Democrat's sacred cow of nonintervention or local rule. But popular sovereignty was also cast with more narrow and regionalized interpretations. The southern states supported the doctrine on the assumption that it meant a territory could not exclude slavery until the time it chose to enter the union as free or slave. For northern, antislave, and abolitionist interests, the southern interpretation all but insured that slave-holding interests would have time to settle a territory before a referendum could be taken on the desirability of allowing slavery. It would be much harder to vote down slavery once proslave interests had the time to entrench themselves, leaving hollow the promise of true popular sovereignty. Consequently, antislave and abolitionist groups in the North, including Lincoln Republicans, insisted that a condition of a territory's fair vote for or against slavery at the time of admission was that it had excluded slavery for the duration of its territorial charter.

Running in 1856, Buchanan kept the definition of popular sovereignty ambiguous in order to build a coalition of northern and southern voters. He hinted that the implementation details that would disambiguate the doctrine would be decided by a pending decision of the Supreme Court, involving the right of territories to exclude slaves. By the time of the debates, the Dred Scott verdict had been announced and Lincoln understood the court as not only favoring the southern version of popular sovereignty but as having set the stage for a subsequent ruling—a Dred Scott II—that would make it illegal to exclude slavery from states as well as territories. Slavery, Lincoln reasoned, would be nationalized, not contained. Indeed, the most direct result of the Dred Scott verdict was to legally void the Missouri Compromise of 1820 that had contained slavery geographically.

Douglas now faced a difficult choice when it came, in the debates, to upholding the principles of the Democratic party. To hold together the northern and southern voters of Illinois, he wanted to push the principle of popular sovereignty in the regionally ambiguous way Buchanan had pushed it in the Democratic platform of 1856. This for the most part dominates Douglas' offensive maneuverings as a representative of the Democrats, pitting his own popular sovereignty against the Republican's abolition. But the Dred Scott verdict seemed to have disambiguated the Democratic platform to the favor of southern interests. Because the southern Democrats had openly and favorably anticipated the Dred Scott decision, Douglas needed a way to show his support for that verdict without alienating Northern Democrats.

He finds two ways in the debates to walk this tightrope. First, he comes up with the principle of unfriendly local legislation, which means that a territory has the right to rescind a federal ruling if there is no local support for it. Douglas allows that Dred Scott forbids a territory from excluding slavery, and the territory is obligated to abide by the high court decision. At the same time, he argues, the territory has the right to rescind the decision if it is without local support. He likens this rescinding action to the local liquor laws. A federal ruling may grant the abstract right of bringing liquor into a county. But if the local custom does not support that action, the abstract right can be rescinded. Never mind for the moment that Douglas' analogy is imperfect in that it illustrates locally forbidding an action that is federally granted in the abstract rather than (as in the case of unfriendly local legislation) locally granting an action (the exclusion of slaves) that is federally forbidden. For Douglas, unfriendly local legislation is his effort to support Dred Scott without losing the northern vote. For Lincoln, Douglas' support of Dred Scott makes contradictory gibberish of popular sovereignty.

Second, Douglas shows that insofar as the Democratic platform may have moved south, he has resisted the move and is willing to fight southern-lean-

*Democrats:*

+ Democrats: + Principles: + Popular sovereignty: + National unity (D, OFF)
+ Democrats: Slavery in territories: + Popular sovereignty: + Dred Scott: + Unfriendly local legislation (D, OFF)
- Democrats: - Slavery in Territories: (CONTRADICTION) + Popular sovereignty: + Dred Scott: + Unfriendly local legislation) L (D (OFF))
- Democrats: - Lecompton: - Conspiring with Lincoln to defeat Douglas (D, OFF)
- Democrats: + Lecompton: + Conspiring to nationalize slavery (L, OFF)
- Democrats: - Lecompton: - Popular sovereignty (L, DEF)
  Democrats: + Abolitionists (L, DEF)

FIG 6.4.    Illustration of the entity class structures around the "Democrats."

ing factions of the party. Douglas' break with Buchanan and the Southern Democrats came in the event known as Lecompton (considered later). As a gesture to block claims he has moved south with the other Democrats, Douglas spends a good deal of time in the latter debates attacking the Democrats, their stand on Lecompton, and their conspiratorial efforts to hand the election over to Lincoln and the Republicans.

For his part, Lincoln is able to use the Lecompton event to make a stronger offensive maneuver against the Democrats than Douglas can afford to make. Lincoln uses Lecompton to suggest that the Democrats do not really believe in popular sovereignty as a platform. They are instead conspiring to extend slavery to all the states. He uses Douglas' split with Buchanan at Lecompton as a way of crediting his own characterization of the Democrats' platform as working to spread slavery. Finally, Douglas charges that Lincoln must favor abolition because some Republican supporters of Lincoln favor it. Lincoln counters that, using the same reasoning, Douglas must be an abolitionist because he has some Democratic supporters who favor it too. The object class structures for "Democrats" showing this offensive and defensive potential are expressed in Fig. 6.4.

## Republicans

The Republican party was formed in 1856 to fight the Kansas Act, to promote economic growth, to oppose slavery in the territories on moral grounds, and, to weakly push the racist contention that the territories should be left only for free Whites to settle. The party's economic platform gained a following in the North, and its ambiguous stand on slavery appealed to

*Republicans:*

+ Republicans: + Principles: + Antislavery (L, OFF)
- Republicans: + Principles: + House Divided: + Black citizenship: +
  Abolition D(L, OFF)

FIG. 6.5.   Illustration of the entity class structures around the "Republicans."

both abolitionist and racist audiences. The party drew in many antislavery ex-Whigs, including Lincoln in Illinois. The Republican party was a focal point of Douglas' attack during the first three debates, as Douglas portrayed Lincoln as leading a party advocating Black citizenship and abolition, ideas distasteful even to the moderates in central Illinois. Not until the later debates did Lincoln begin to use the Republicans as the basis for an offensive strategy of his own, tracing their basic principles back to the Founding Fathers and their belief in the immorality of slavery (Fig. 6.5).

## Lincoln/Douglas

Although his views on slavery evolved, by 1854 Lincoln had become a staunch opponent of slavery, which he viewed as an evil. Although he was no activist on behalf of slavery, Douglas' top priority was national expansion, and he contended that slavery should remain a local issue resolvable at the state level.

To function as public agents, individuals need the backing of groups or organizations. Lincoln and Douglas were no exceptions. Lincoln had his party organization and Douglas, his. But individuals do not inherit, automatically, all the role characteristics of the groups they lead. Lincoln spends much time in the early debates disavowing the platforms of many local Republican conventions in northern Illinois that passed strongly abolitionist platforms. And Douglas spends much time in the later debates arguing against the Democrats who are trying to defeat him for seeming too northern in his stance on Lecompton. A group identity would count for little if the individual representing it could not use that identity as a way of augmenting his or her own power as an agent of offense, of furthering various normative projects about the way the world should be. Yet public individuals must find ways to defend themselves against their own organization, lest their self identity be swallowed in the liabilities of a group identity they do not fully control. These bids for individual identity in rhetorical design become apparent when we consider how object classes are arranged within the mundane and sensory world of individuals (chapter 7).

### Event Classes in the Structure/Rhetoric of the Lincoln/Douglas Debates

Event classes in an issue context are the primary objects through which the historical progress of an issue is tracked and described through time and space. Principles (another type of object class) typically appear in rhetorical design as properties of event classes judged to have public significance or meaning. Thus public events (e.g., the destruction of the Berlin Wall) do not just happen, they have "meaning." This meaning is captured by associating event classes with public principles (e.g., Berlin Wall = Communism) within the rhetorical design. Of course, the meaning of an event class, the principle it conveys by happening or whether it conveys a principle at all, is an important site of contestation across speakers, as it is with Lincoln and Douglas.

We now consider various event classes that define landmarks for the Lincoln/Douglas debates, such as popular sovereignty, the Mexican War, the 1850 compromise, the 1854 Kansas Act, the 1857 Dred Scott verdict, and the 1858 Lecompton Convention. In each case, as before, we try to say enough to trace the link between the structure and the rhetoric of both Lincoln and Douglas' designs.

#### Popular Sovereignty

Popular sovereignty came to the fore in American politics in the debate over the Wilmot Proviso in 1846, legislation to ban slavery in any territory to be acquired through the Mexican War. The Proviso was passed by the House but defeated by the Senate. Debate over the proviso made it clear that the expansion or restriction of slavery in new territories was an issue that caught the national attention and divided the national interest. Popular sovereignty became both a catchy slogan and an ambiguous policy about how to deal with the issue. Its main popularizer, Lewis Cass, argued that the territories must resolve their own affairs locally, including the issue of whether to allow slaves or not. He contended that the matter of slavery in the territories should remain out of the halls of Congress and contained within the territorial legislatures where they could not paralyze the central government. By late 1848, Douglas was on the popular sovereignty bandwagon. He, like Cass, saw the principle as a way to localize the divisive slavery issue and to free the federal government to get on with the issues he considered most important for the union: railroad, river and harbor improvements, and other policies of land expansion, settlement, and development.

Popular sovereignty is the principle associated with Douglas' primary offense (Fig. 6.6). He wants popular sovereignty—in the ambiguous usage

### *Popular Sovereignty:*

+ Popular Sovereignty: + Free elections (D, OFF)
- Popular sovereignty: -Presumption to extend slavery L (D, OFF)
+ Popular sovereignty: + Free Elections: + prohibit slavery during territorial
   charter (L, DEF)

FIG. 6.6.    Illustration of the event class structures around "Popular Sovereignty."

of Buchanan's 1856 Democratic party—to hold the day. He argues that he is for it; Lincoln, against. And on that basis he believes he is the better, more principled, candidate. Lincoln counters by using popular sovereignty for his own offense, characterizing Douglas' use of the principle as a cover to extend slavery nationally. He insists that Douglas is secretly locked into the southern interpretation of popular sovereignty, which biases a territory toward slavery and so undermines the public and conventional meaning of popular sovereignty. Lincoln can hardly afford to reject the public and conventional meaning, however. He cannot afford to look as if he is against local rule or free elections in the territories, which is the appearance on which Douglas' offense depends. So at places in the debates, Lincoln uses popular sovereignty in a defensive posture, to block Douglas' representation of his (Lincoln's) rejecting the principle in its conventional and uncontroversial interpretation.

## 1846 Mexican War

This war plays a minor role in the debates and is used by Douglas as an offensive manoeuver to block the credibility Lincoln needs to advance his own public program. As a congressman during the war, Lincoln authored what came to be known as the "spot" resolutions, questioning the legality of the war based on where it started. Lincoln was widely reviled and Douglas reports him as having to leave congress for his "unpatriotic" stand. To block Douglas' representation of his conduct during the war, Lincoln maintains that he always supported funds for the troops once the war had commenced (Fig. 6.7).

### *+ 1846 Mexican War:*

+ 1846 Mexican War: - L contested spot of war's beginning (D, OFF)
+ 1846 Mexican War: - L contested spot of war's beginning: + L voted funds
   for war (L, DEF)

FIG. 6.7.    Illustration of the event class structures around the "Mexican War."

## 1850 Compromise

This act involved the territories of Utah and New Mexico that were acquired from Mexico in 1848. The act provided that the states formed from the territories would be admitted as free or slave states as the residents chose. Although it involved many other details, which Lincoln points out during the debates, the act was understood popularly as a case lesson in the power of popular sovereignty to resolve gracefully and without rancor the issue of slavery in the territories. The 1850 compromise was understood as a successful event in American politics and its success was attributed to its embodying the principle of popular sovereignty. As Douglas mentions in the debates and Lincoln acknowledges, both the Whig and Democrat parties ratified this act in their 1852 platforms.

Although the 1850 compromise is an important event for Douglas to push on the offense, Lincoln's eventual defense against it is that the event was more complex than the unitary principle Douglas supposes it to have illustrated. Lincoln argues that the compromise was not a simple principled act, but a compromise, a haggling over many issues decided by parties of competing interests, all of whom gave up some things in order to get other things (Fig. 6.8).

## 1854 Kansas/Nebraska Act

This is a watershed event that sealed Douglas' reputation as a champion of popular sovereignty and that mobilized the anti-Nebraska opposition, including Lincoln. The act provided that the residents of Kansas be given the choice to decide whether to enter the union as slave or free. The act displaced the "sacred" Missouri Compromise (1820) because the territory was situated north of latitude 36 degrees 30 minutes, the boundary designated by that compromise north of which slavery was forbidden. As chairman of the Senate committee on the territories, Douglas had first tried to have the act passed without explicitly repealing the Missouri Compromise. When he was pressed, however, to state the fate of Missouri once the Kansas Act was to go into effect, he insisted that the Missouri compromise had already been repealed by the 1850 compromise and so the repeal of Missouri was, at the time of Kansas, already a fait accompli. Douglas' insistence was widely

<u>1850 Compromise</u>

+ 1850 Compromise: Principles: Popular sovereignty (D, OFF)
  1850 Compromise: Compromise (L, DEF)

FIG. 6.8.    An illustration of the event class structures around the "1850 compromise."

perceived by Northerners as a dangerous revisionism, as the discussion preceding and following the 1850 compromise had never offered that compromise as a direct repeal of Missouri.

Northerners saw the Kansas Act as destroying the only mechanism to contain slavery. Southerners saw it as an attempt to put their economic way of life on a level field with the northern economy. According to Zarefsky (1990), Douglas himself saw it as an expedient linguistic compromise to a problem that would take care of itself through nonlinguistic, nonrhetorical processes. He believed that the extension of slavery was a matter of climate and terrain more than language and law.

Douglas' attention to words as stopgaps rather than solutions is apparent in the Chase Amendment. Senator Chase of Ohio, an advocate of freedom over slavery, wanted the Kansas Act to provide a special clause guaranteeing the right of the people to exclude slavery if they wished. Douglas and the Democrats voted it down, claiming that this condition was already covered in the main clause giving the people the right to vote as they pleased.

After its passage, much controversy lingered about how to implement Kansas. The Toombs Bill of 1856 stipulated procedures for a state constitutional convention with enough federal supervision to assure fairness. Douglas' committee reviewed the bill and deleted a clause that required submitting the constitutional vote to a popular referendum. Douglas' revisions of the Toombs Bill seemed on their face to contradict his doctrine of popular sovereignty. Douglas' apparent hypocrisy became the basis for much of the Charleston debate. To block this inference, Douglas claims that such a popular referendum was an implied result of his revisions, one not requiring explicit language to guarantee.

In the debates, Lincoln and Douglas always use the Kansas Act for offensive purposes (Fig. 6.9). Douglas uses it positively, to push popular sovereignty. Lincoln uses it negatively, to characterize the act as the first in a series of Douglas-induced events—the Chase Amendment and the revision of Toombs—that, together with the Dred Scott verdict, put Douglas in the center of a conspiracy to extend slavery.

*1854 Kansas Act*

+ 1854 Kansas Bill: Principles: + Popular sovereignty (D, OFF)
- 1854 Kansas Bill: - Chase Amendment: -Douglas' revision of Toombs Bill:
      + Dred Scott
      -Conspiracy to limit popular sovereignty to voters of Kansas:
      - Conspiracy to nationalize slavery L (D, OFF)

FIG. 6.9.    Illustration of the event class structures around the "Kansas Act."

<u>*1857 Dred Scott*</u>

+ 1857 Dred Scott: - Denies black citizenship D (L, OFF)
- 1857 Dred Scott: + Denies black citizenship: - Forbids excluding slaves
  in territories: -Unfriendly local legislation L (D, OFF)

FIG. 6.10.    Illustration of the event class structures around "Dred Scott."

## 1857 Dred Scott Decision

Dred Scott was a Missouri slave who accompanied his owner on trips to
Illinois and Minnesota, a free state and territory, respectively. Scott sued for
his freedom based on his passage through free lands. Delivering its verdict
on March 6, 1857, the Supreme Court ruled that, as a negro, Scott was not
a citizen and had no standing in a U.S. court. His residence in Illinois did
not make him free because long-standing agreements between states to
return fugitive slave property were already in effect. Nor did his residence
in the territory of Minnesota make him free because the law excluding slavery
from that territory—the Missouri Compromise —was unconstitutional,
infringing on the right to property affirmed in the Constitution. The Dred
Scott verdict in effect struck down the constitutionality of Lincoln's chief
platform, the exclusion of slavery in the territories prior to admission. Lincoln
and many of his Republican followers had little choice but to rebel against
the decision.

Dred Scott for both debaters had more meaning on the offense than the
defense (Fig. 6.10). Throughout the debates, Douglas equates Lincoln's
objection to Dred Scott with his objection to denying citizenship to Blacks.
Douglas uses Dred Scott, in essence, to make Lincoln's stands seem objec-
tionably abolitionist. Lincoln, on the other hand, uses Douglas' support for
Dred Scott as a means to catch Douglas with a contradictory offense. Popular
sovereignty, after all, affirms that the citizens of a territory have the right to
include or exclude slavery as they see fit. Yet Dred Scott deprives them of
this very choice by repudiating the constitutional right of the residents of a
territory to exclude it. Douglas, according to Lincoln, cannot have it both
ways.

## 1858 Lecompton Constitution

The Lecompton Constitution was a state charter for Kansas written up at
Lecompton, Kansas, by the proslave minority in 1857. The constitution
reaffirmed the Dred Scott finding that slaves were property protected under
the property rights of the federal Constitution. By the time of Lecompton,
it was clear that the residents of Kansas were moving toward an antislave

majority. The aim of the Lecompton conferees was to preempt the antislave majority and to bring Kansas in as a slave state before it had the population of 93,200 normally required for admission. At the time the Lecompton convention was still in session, statewide elections were being held for a new territorial legislature and the antislave forces dominated the election. Knowing that their time in power was limited, members of the Lecompton convention acted quickly to stage a referendum specifically on the slavery clause, whether to submit a state constitution with or without slavery. Before this referendum was voted on, however, the newly elected territorial legislature convened and scheduled its own referendum on the entire charter (including the slave clause) drawn up at Lecompton.

The voters of Kansas were now faced with two separate referenda, the first in late December 1857 and the second in early January 1858. The Free Soilers boycotted the limited referendum of late December and the vote, not surprisingly, was overwhelmingly in favor of bringing Kansas into the union with a slavery charter. The proslave minority boycotted the full referendum of early January and the vote, not surprisingly, was an overwhelming defeat of the entire Lecompton constitution.

In the spring of 1858, Congress was forced to debate which of the two Kansas referenda was legally binding. Buchanan judged that the results of the limited referendum, favoring slavery, were binding. Douglas, however, broke with Buchanan, rejecting the limited referendum on the grounds that, without the requisite population, it was impossible for the will of the people to be expressed. Before the March 23 Senate vote on Lecompton, Douglas attacked the validity of the limited proslave referendum on the Senate floor. Douglas was in turn attacked by the proslave, southern-leaning *Washington Union*, the official press of the Buchanan administration. Douglas charged the editor of the *Union*, and implicitly Buchanan himself, with favoring slavery above the voice of the people.

Validation of the limited proslave referendum was passed by the Senate but defeated in the House. To save the referendum, Senator English of Indiana proposed a bill that would have Kansans vote on it again, but with a sweetened land grant deal if the referendum passed. Douglas opposed the English bill as a "bribe." Buchanan and most of his backers supported the English bill. The English bill passed both bodies of Congress. However, by the time of the debates, the bill was moot. It had required a new vote on August 2, the month of the first debate, and was rejected by an eight to one margin. During the Galesburg debates in early October 1858, Douglas mentions that no one in the Buchanan administration, not even English, now spoke well of the English bill. Yet Buchanan's men, Douglas observes,

_- 1858 Lecompton_

- 1858 Lecompton: - Violates popular sovereignty:
    - Washington union editor's effort to nationalize slavery (D, DEF)
- 1858 Lecompton: - Democrat's conspiracy to nationalize slavery (L, OFF)

FIG. 6.11.   Illustration of the event class structures around "Lecompton Constitution."

are considered heroes because they once supported it. Douglas quips that his only mistake was _never_ to have spoken well of it. Douglas uses Lecompton on the defense during the debate to block the inference that he is in cahoots with southern Democrats to nationalize slavery. Lincoln in turn uses Lecompton in an equivalent way, but from an offensive perspective, not against Douglas, but against the Democrats in general whose support of it indicates their covert intent to nationalize slavery. Indeed, Lincoln and Douglas are almost in perfect agreement about "Lecompton" as an object class. The agreement is so transparent that Lincoln uses Douglas as a supporting witness for his rhetorical use of Lecompton. At one point in the debates, Douglas accuses Lincoln of having no authority beyond his own say-so (his _ipse dixit_) in charging the Democrats with a conspiracy to nationalize slavery. Lincoln replies that, with Lecompton, he has it on Douglas' inside authority that such a conspiracy was underway.

## GAPS BETWEEN STRUCTURE AND RHETORICAL DESIGN

The foregoing discussion, tying the object class design structures of Lincoln and Douglas to their rhetoric, illustrates in the concrete terms of Lincoln and Douglas how structure can inform rhetorical design. From the structural representation alone, we can see the potential of the combatants and, of course, preview a good deal of their actual rhetorical interaction. The structural representation, however, only lays out a blueprint of potentiality, not a running version of the rhetoric as it actually emerges. And although we have traced a line between structure and rhetoric, there is much, in addition to structure, that is needed to explain the rhetoric. We have in this last section, for example, supplied a background of the debates and Lincoln's and Douglas' role in them that uses, but that also goes beyond, the strict content of the object classes and LOCs they invoke. Beyond the structural elements given earlier, our discussion has drawn freely from the view of the debate as seen from the Plans, Tactics, and Events modules. Much of the remaining focus of this book is to differentiate the views these modules prescribe.

# Seven

# Plans

Rhetorical discourse is planned, public behavior, properties secured through the functioning of the Plans module. We have already suggested that Plans in rhetoric are a module in the design space, a particular abstraction on object structures that allows them to be viewed in a particular way, as constructed publics. But we have yet to be very specific or detailed about the status of publics and how they matter to plans. In this chapter, we describe in more detail the characteristics of publics, their relationship to the Plans module, and the generic plans that can be derived from this module. Because Plans are a subtle and often hidden aspect of the seamless discourse of rhetoric we experience, it is best to start from the outmost layer of rhetorical design, as presentation, and work our way into Plans.

Rhetorical design involves the strategic organization and communication of a speaker's version of events. This assumes, of course, that speakers have versions of events to discuss and for audiences to act upon. These versions, furthermore, need to be developed enough to span whole positions or arguments. In light of the complexity of the structural content making up such positions, it is unlikely that speakers bring this content to expression in the form of ready-made mental "pictures," pictures containing all the relevant individuals and events that are organized into a position, and at the level of resolution needed to elaborate and defend it. An important aspect of rhetorical design, more likely, is that speakers must assemble the various parts that go into any systematic version of events. At the outermost level of rhetorical design, this assembly is done by the Presentation module once that module chooses a part, or parts, of the design structure within the rhetorical design space that it assesses as ready for sequencing into locally coherent external expression (chapters 4 and 10). In issue-oriented situations of rhetoric, as they arise in student compositions, politics, academe, and civic discourse in general, the local coherence of the parts presented is determined prior to presentation, by the abstraction of a public brought to the design structure under the lens of Plans. This abstraction is most responsible for making structures in the design classifiable as public discourse when the Presentation module brings them to expression.

In chapter 5, on goals in the design of rhetoric, we devoted a good deal of space to drawing a relationship between public discourse, going on the record, and the goal of predictiveness. We indicated that to be predictive, a speaker aims for public discourse that puts information on the record. By doing so, the speaker indicates that the information put on the record can survive intact into future contexts and be used as a standard against which to judge the consistency of the speaker's future performance. Furthermore, in chapter 4, we cited the Plans module as most responsible for implementing predictiveness goals. There exists, it seems, an intricate, but so far unspecified, relationship between the Plans module, publics, predictiveness, and on the record.

## PUBLICS

These relationships build on a house of cards if we cannot give a substantive definition to *public*. After all, to explain why some information under the lens of Plans satisfies predictiveness goals, we appealed to the notion of putting information on the record. Yet to explain how information gets noticed for the record, we needed to appeal to the notion of public information. Without a noncircular definition of *public*, we are saying no more than a tautology: public discourse = public discourse. And this hardly explains why we are able to distinguish public narratives from, say, children's narratives that do not seem, on their face, to be public discourse. The problem of circularity rears its head because we have allowed the notion of *public* to slide by as an unexamined adjective modifying nouns like *discourse*. We have invoked *public* as if it described a particular type or genre of discourse without offering any criteria for what, precisely, is contained in this description. Without a more firm description of public, we will not achieve an understanding of what plans do. So we first go after the idea of public and work our way to plans.

### The Concept of Public

The concept of *public* in our modern world has become a nominal reality. In terms of what the public "knows," public knowledge has been reduced to polling data, what individuals, in the aggregate, happen to think on a particular issue at a particular time. Thus in statements like "60% of the public believes that..." the knowledge of the public is translated into a statistical percentage of individuals polled or estimated through the use of population parameters. In terms of what the public "hears" or otherwise acquires by way of communication, public communication has been reduced to the notion of mass or one-to-many communication. Information disseminated through the mass media is thought, de facto, to be public information. In the era of Newt Gingrich and the downsizing of government, public has also taken on an economic meaning, (i.e., taxpayer supported). Thus the Public Broadcasting System, National Public Radio, and the National Endowment for the Arts are public because they receive government funding.

In each case, the notion of public has been operationalized into a concrete description that obviates having to confront the notion as a precise abstraction. The modern tendency has been to assume that public is a vague, fuzzy, and metaphysical abstraction and so needs to be salvaged through a more concrete operationalization. This reduces public to an abstraction in name only, a nominal abstraction. Yet students of rhetoric from Dewey (1946) to Bitzer (1978) to Farrell (1993) have been guided by the conviction that rhetoric from ancient times rests on the foundation of *public* as a precise abstraction, not unlike the abstract but precise realities of geometry and physics.

Viewed as a practical handbook art, rhetoric can be taught and used without having to come to grips with the ontological status of *public* as an abstraction. But viewed as an art of design, looking into the mind and the external environment of the person who must compose rhetoric, it becomes imperative to track the status of this abstraction insofar as it lies on the critical path of the Plans module.

## Publics as Abstract Reals

Despite the modern tendency to nominalize the abstraction of public, rhetorical design relies on public being a realist abstraction. Publics are real (albeit abstract) entities whose meaning is changed, rather than clarified, when attempts are made to operationalize them. Because they are abstract, we do not and cannot experience publics with our senses. Much of our linguistic system, although abstract, never intersects with the abstraction of public. For example, many of our generic linguistic descriptions (e.g., the cat is on the mat) do not intersect with the abstraction of public. Even linguistic reports invoking abstracted domains associated with publics can fail to qualify as public discourse. Third-person journalistic descriptions of public agents (e.g., Congress will vote on the crime bill today) only describe, from the outside, groups whose members engage in discourse about publics. In the idealized case of press "objectivity," the talk of the journalists is not about publics but only about the routine activities of those who talk and act on them. The reportage is mass communication about individuals who talk about publics; it is not itself talk about publics.

Yet, increasingly, the press is accused of putting its own spin and bias in political stories. To the extent we perceive the charge as accurate, to the extent we believe the talk of the reporter is itself an illicit contribution to public discourse, to that extent we believe that the reporter functions as a designer of rhetoric and not merely an observer of such designs. The journalist is understood not merely to report on rhetoric but to be making it. We lament that the press has become part of the story. But what is the power, or abuse of power, that we lament? More broadly speaking, what is involved in being a participant in public discourse from the first-person point of view, in actively talking about and taking the authority to shape publics? Were public discourse merely a matter of measuring the opinion of individual voters, then the only power holders would be the statisticians who designed the instruments of measurement. The politician would simply repeat back the results of polls. There would be no creative potential, or potential of abuse, to lament.

Now, of course, some politicians may just listen to and repeat what the polls say. But that is not our point. Our point is that the power to talk about publics is a much more creative power than that. To understand the creative freedom involved, consider a legislator involved in a vote to raise taxes on cigarettes for health care reform. The legislator is a public agent. Public agents are not persons in the mundane sense. They are persons, yes, but their first-person public agency depends, in many cases, on their being authorized to represent others. They have a larger than life quality because in deliberating about how to compose talk about publics, they must respond from an interest larger than the perimeters of their own personal networks and bloodlines. They must respond from the broader interests of the persons and organizations they represent, many of whom they barely know, if at all.

Now suppose the legislator represents 100,000 constituent voters, who are divided evenly on the issue of raising cigarette taxes. Of the constituent voters, exactly half believe that taxes should be raised and half say no. Were the legislator simply trying to capture a real-time reflection of the mood of the voters, like a computer taking running averages of stock prices every minute, the representative might say something like, "I am truly conflicted. I do not know what to do." Let us call this scenario A. Scenario A describes the tensions of a human being but is inappropriate talk for a public agent. The abstraction of public, as the focus of a design, must give the agent a decisive, not a splintered, target to aim at. The public agent is expected and so must be able to talk and act decisively, even in the face of material uncertainty and dissensus in the individuals who are thought to instantiate it.

Public agents must listen to summaries of individual opinion and then decide for themselves what the public wants to do and should do. This seemingly paradoxical truth about representative power often raises fears about publics and their realist character. It encourages us to want to nominalize publics just to avoid leaders who can't distinguish the public interest and outlook from their own. But the fact remains that efforts to nominalize publics, however well intentioned, are doomed because of the unavoidable fact that leaders cannot divorce their own cognitions from their decisions. No matter how much leaders sample opinions on the outside, their decisions always involve convincing themselves about what is the right thing to do. No matter how much outside opinion they solicit, receive, and even claim to have absorbed, leaders will always respond to a public that is an abstraction of their own design.

This conclusion raises a further problem. Earlier, we said that a public agent must be larger than life. Now we seem to be saying that, in addition, the agent must be as small as life. Indeed, we are saying both and we need to understand public agency in a way that allows both.

Imagine that voters on the cigarette tax are still divided, but not evenly. Say now that 75% of the voters want the tax and the remaining 25% do not. The legislator can say with perfect honesty, "I am for the tax because the majority of my constituents want it." Call this scenario B. The talk of this scenario makes it clear that the legislator is responsive to what the voters think. But the legislator's responsiveness to the voters does not absolve him or her from the issue of what he or she thinks. Does the legislator just listen to the voters out of expedience? Or does he or she have principles of her own?

Now change the scenario a bit. This time the voters are overwhelmingly against the cigarette tax, 2 to 1. But the legislator nonetheless votes for the tax. Is it comprehensible how he or she can remain a "good" representative? Suppose the legislator holds a press conference and says, "I am sorry. My parents died from smoking-related health problems and, in good conscience, I cannot support cigarette smoking in this country." Call this scenario C.

From the perspective of the material world, all three scenarios contain a legislator and voters. In scenario A, the legislator tries to produce discourse by describing the material world in its confusing detail. Averaged across all the voters, the legislator's constituents show an ambivalent, conflicted attitude toward the tax. The legislator tries to recirculate this description of material reality as his or her contribution to public discourse, and fails. Public discourse emerges only with the decision to abstract a symbolic perspective out of the relentless ebb and flow of material reality. A public is a particular abstraction. These abstractions, to be credible, must have grounding in material events. But cast as abstract symbols, they are far simpler, more structured and more stable than dynamic reality can ever be.

In scenario B, the legislator has agreed to enter the symbolic realm of public discourse. Although the presence of a majority can be seen in a simple statistical description of reality, as in scenario A, majority rule also is historical warrant for collective decision making in democracies. Thus, although it may at first seem that the legislator in scenario B is attuned to the material reality no less than the legislator in scenario A, there is a significant difference between the two. In scenario A, the speaker, describing only the material reality of indecision, has no abstract representation of the public that can be used as basis for decision making. In scenario B, the speaker relies on the principle of majority rule as a way of shaping a public view of the cigarette tax issue, and the speaker uses this symbolic abstraction to justify a decision.

In scenario C, the speaker seems to resolve the issue at the expense of the aggregated mental set of the voters. From the perspective of the abstraction applied in scenario B, this legislator is a dreadful failure when it comes to responding to majority opinion. Yet the legitimacy of the legislator's response indicates that there are plans for shaping publics that can avoid majority opinion. Such plans involve the strength of personal conviction against the opinion of the masses, the principles that bring a leader down to human dimensions.

These scenarios suggest that the notion of a public shaping decisions is a realist abstraction that cannot be reduced to materialist particulars. At the same time, speakers contributing to a public discourse must contribute more than just a description of the material reality surrounding an issue. The speaker must design a public to shape a decision for action. The public is an abstraction superimposed on a fluctuating and often indeterminate material reality. Needless to say, speakers in representative democracies may act at their peril when their constructions of the public stray too far from material details. But as scenario A clearly shows, they risk no less peril when they heed only the material detail and refuse to abstract from it a symbolic conception of the public.

In sum, the discourse of rhetoric is public in more than a nominal sense. The public discourse of rhetoric is not simply, or even necessarily, discourse that addresses a mass audience. Indeed, discourse can be rhetorical (and public) when it is used in one-to-one communication. The public in "public discourse" is a referential rather than a modifying element. The public discourse of rhetoric is discourse *about* publics as realist abstractions for structuring decision-making. Rhetorical discourse is no less discourse about publics than zebra discourse is discourse *about* zebras. The only difference between public discourse and zebra discourse is that zebras are a set with concrete members and publics are a set containing only symbolic abstractions of material realities.

## MODELING A PUBLIC

The Plans module in rhetorical design is a construction kit for creating a public model for use in a rhetorical design. We should be careful to understand that different genres of rhetoric make different demands on how explicit, elaborate, or systematic this model must be. The demands for a public model being explicit, elaborate, and systematic increase in those rhetorical situations when publics are contested. Only when speakers have very different conceptions of how to proceed into the future must they work to unearth for the benefit of audience decision-making the "public" that authorizes the future each endorses. This is one reason, perhaps, why, despite the number of genres that have come to proliferate under the name *rhetoric,* the paradigm for rhetoric remains deliberative discourse as defined by Aristotle. It is not that other genres of rhetoric do not require the construction of public models. It is that they do not require such models to enter the design space with the care and precision that deliberative argument requires. Focusing on Lincoln and Douglas, our understanding of rhetorical design is heavily weighted toward deliberative rhetoric. Future work will need to explore rhetorical design in genres where public models can be less explicit.

Let us assume that when speakers have applied a plan, or set of plans, in rhetorical design, they have designed from within the Plans module some portion of a model of the public. Generic plans of discourse provide different ways for speakers to attend to this model. Different plans lead to different public models. The legislators in scenarios B and C arrive at different public models because they are focused on different plans.[1] Generic plans impact a design by causing a speaker to attend to particular aspects of a public model and ignore others. Specific plans refer to the actual object structures that

---

[1] The legislator in scenario A had failed to construct a model of the public and so failed at public discourse.

result from the application of generic plans to the construction of particular part of a public model.

## The Functions of the Plans Module

The Plans module performs two functions. First, it supports the creation of a consistent model of the public for the speaker to act on. Second, it applies generic plans and, ultimately, creates specific plans of rhetoric by focusing the speaker's attention on patterned subsets of the developing model. The following two sections describe these functions.

## Composing a Model of a Public

In this section, we discuss how a speaker, through the Plans module, composes a model of a public. The composition process can be usefully examined both from a holistic (top-down) and components (bottom-up) point of view. In the sections to follow, we consider both perspectives.

### A Public Model Composed Holistically

From the vantage of Plans, a vantage indifferent to opponents and rhetorical situations, the reason for rhetoric is to lay out a public model as an abstraction of the social world expressing truth and falsehood. Like a blueprint that holds a house together, Plans monitors whether the structures of a rhetorical plan hold together as a unity. Everything needed to give a rhetorical plan holistic unity, however, is not equally visible. The abstraction of a public model in rhetorical design makes some features of the rhetorical design more visible than others, much like a real estate agent's brochure for a house may showcase the patio and den and give less specific detail about the basement. Within a public model, the Plans module showcases what we call the public space and gives some, but less prominent, visibility to what we call secondary spaces. The public space within a public model consists of the structural abstractions that are considered relevant to the definition and resolution of significant issues within a society. Ultimately, the functioning of a final rhetorical design depends as much on the secondary spaces as the public space. At the same time, the public space is often identified as the "content" of the public model in the way a house is identified with its living space rather than its less visible features. The secondary spaces represent these less visible features, the basement, perhaps, of a rhetorical blueprint. They are necessary for the presentation of a coherent public model, but they are seldom associated on the surface with public discourse. Like a functional but nondescript basement that no one would confuse with the selling point of a house, no one would confuse the secondary spaces of a public model with the contents of the public space.

## A Public Model Composed by Components

From a components perspective, a public model consists of various component structures with different characteristics. Taken together, these components furnish a detailed description of the temporal world from the abstracted vantage of the public space, but with abstractions that are often descriptively serviced from information taken from all realms of lived experience: the sensual and situated as well as the abstract and universal. The Plans module builds a public model from components through the use of two abstractive tools: spaces and plans.

Spaces, which we define later, are regions of experience into which object structures can be classified. The secondary spaces, used to undergird public space abstractions, consist of mundane, entitlement, sensory, and local spaces. Different spaces make varying assumptions about lived experience and, especially, the level of concreteness or abstraction at which one can attend to it.

Plans are ways of focusing on, or creating, links or alignments between object structures either within the same spaces or across different spaces. To compose a public model from components, the Plans module creates and links public and nonpublic spaces in the fashion of Fig. 7.1.

Relying on spaces to classify experience and on plans to focus connections within and across experiences, the Plans module constructs and seeks to maintain a public model consistently over time. To further understand these components and their alignments, we need to look into the nature of the specific spaces that, with plans, emerge as a working public model.

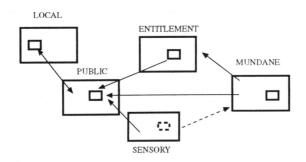

FIG. 7.1.   A public model from components: Aligned spaces within the plans module

## Spaces

Spaces are one of the tools that Plans uses to enable the construction of a public model. A "space" (Facuconnier, 1985) is an abstract collection of items with common properties. Spaces have been posited to explain why certain inferences follow or fail to follow as expected from the standard rules of logic or grammar. For example, the verb "dreams" opens a new space from that of the physical world in sentences like "John dreamed that she was a girl." Although this sentence may first seem illogical and ungrammatical in terms of pronoun agreement, it is fine if we assume that John constructs himself as a female in his dream. Rather than change the rules of logical inference or grammar to handle these cases, it is easier to posit a physical and dream world occupying different spaces. Fauconnier (1985) showed that our reliance on the construction of mental spaces is fundamental and pervasive with respect to our ability, as language users, to correctly infer and disambiguate the meanings of sentences. Although Fauconnier's basic insight has been extended to many areas of language understanding, it has yet to be applied to the organization of rhetorical information. The concept of spaces applies explicitly to the structure viewed by Plans. The Plans module views the design structure with stencils for each of these spaces. The stencil for discriminating spaces is removed when we view the design structure from Tactics or Events. The explicit thus becomes implicit. Nonetheless, we can feel the presence of these boundaries in other modules when they are crossed suddenly and abruptly, as in humor or infelicities. Consider the following dialogues:

> Speaker: You have destroyed my entire game room.
> Friend: I'll pay you for the damage./**I must have been busy to have done that.

> Political Speaker: You have destroyed the country.
> Opponent: I must have been busy to have done that (laughter)./**I'll pay you for the damage.

In the first dialogue, two friends are conversing and the one has accused the other of destroying personal property. The friend, accepting the responsibility, agrees to compensate the first speaker. An inappropriate response (preceded by a double asterisk) would be a flippant remark, indicating the friend's failure to own up to the personal responsibility. Such a remark would strain, if not end, the friendship. The second dialogue has the superficial appearance of the first but is set in a political debate where the speakers are opponents. In a political context, the flippant remark is not necessarily inappropriate; it can even be effective humor. What is inappropriate would be to respond like the friend, as if official acts of leadership implicated the same level of personal culpability as acts of behavior between friends can implicate.

Why we respond differently to the realms of the political and the mundane is not entirely clear on first inspection. After all, destroying a country would seem, if anything, far more serious than destroying a gameroom. And, indeed, in some cases, like Nurenberg, like Robert MacNamara's confessionals about Vietnam, we do hold political leaders, and political leaders hold themselves, morally culpable for their official actions. Nonetheless, this is atypical. The more normal case is to insulate public leaders and their official actions from the way in which we judge the routine acts of individuals. Were this insulation not in place, were there not some invisible boundary between a "public space" for debate and an "individual space" for moral judgment, the opponent's flippant remark would carry no potential for humor whatever. We would see it as lame, off-putting, and irresponsible in the manner of the friend's flippancy. The fact that we do see the humorous potential in the flippancy indicates our recognition that public incompetence need not spill over into personal categories of moral culpability.

Fauconnier argued for the ubiquity of mental spaces in linguistic understanding. Analogously, we argue for the ubiquity of spaces in rhetorical design and comprehension. As we can see from the foregoing dialogues, the knowledge of these spaces and their use in rhetoric is mainly tacit, unavailable to our conscious understanding. To construct an understanding of the Plans module, we need to bring this tacit knowledge to the surface.

The Plans module is called upon to create a unified and consistent public model within the rhetorical design. The Plans module uses an overlay of the five[2] spaces to classify and manage the numerous object classes present in the design. Any object class can be potentially mapped into any space and the same structural content can be mapped into multiple spaces. This allows speakers to use the same content but with very different functions with respect to a public model.

By postulating these spaces, we make no claims about psychological realities, about cognitive or neural divisions in the minds of speakers. We are rather postulating these spaces as a minimal constraint on the complexity of one aspect of rhetoric. That is to say, to categorize rhetorical discourse and its reliance on models of a public, we need, at a minimum, the diversity of assumptions and concepts made available through these five spaces.

---

[2]For Facuconnier, spaces are variable entities. We have found it useful to keep the number of spaces fixed for the composition of public models.

Let us start with the most important space and, often, the most visible to the public context of rhetoric.

*The Public Space.*    The public space is the space housing object classes that function as public abstractions. Although the public and secondary spaces all furnish abstractions of relevance and consequence to a design of rhetoric, only the abstractions from the public space furnish the most direct information for a collective's decision-making. Thus, public space abstractions are considered to be universally accessible and communicable. All information in this space has official status, is considered documented, recorded, "on the record" as it were. An important linguistic marker signaling the elaboration of a public object class is the use of a pledge. What one pledges—as opposed to a personal promise—is offered to an anonymous public as part of a public abstraction. Although what one pledges need not reference one's personal conviction (e.g., the pledge can be forced or based on expedient compromise), there is in Whig liberal ideology the notion that objects put in public spaces reflect simple and unconflicted private devotions. Hypocrisy, conspiracy, blackmail, scandal, and other violations of the public/private divide in liberalism arise whenever it is revealed that alleged "secret," "private," or "compromising" information (i.e., information lacking a publicly communicable or universally acceptable rationale) has been influential behind the scenes in the emergence of public events.

The documented and communicable entity and event classes we overviewed in chapter 6 were by and large used by Lincoln and Douglas as public space abstractions. As we mentioned there, it is part of their rhetorical expertise to know to focus on event classes that function as public space abstractions. The public space is an important focus for the rhetors constructing a historical world to contest, as Lincoln and Douglas used such abstractions to construct their historic worlds. Individuals can be specified as the agents within the world of a public space, but only as holders of official institutional roles or as members of groups empowered by constituencies to initiate, respond to, and define historical events.

The only notion of time that is relevant to the world of a public space is the "before" and "after" of precedent time. Event classes in the world of a public space have a "historical anchorage" attribute to indicate their historic import. Historical anchorage determines the temporal ordering of public event classes as either antecedent, precedent, counterprecedent, or descendant. Antecedent events precede the formulation of a precedent event. Originating precedents and counterprecedents give public voice to the often culturally    hidden    and    tension-ridden    antecedents    that    precipitated them—as child labor exploitation in the early century gave rise to precedent-setting child labor laws, and as the sanctioned use of discipline in child rearing preceded the criminalization of child abusers Precedents and counterprecedents instantiate principles, allowing events to carry positive and negative lessons across time and space. Descendants reinforce these positive and negative lessons across the distance of time and space by "carrying" (like buckets in a fire brigade?) the principle of the original precedents or counterprecedents. Public event classes are further used for representing conspiracy (when a counterprecedent is purposely disguised under the dignified mask of a precedent) and for charging conspiracy against a person. In arguments of venue, speakers appeal to the presence of public event classes to show that the agents in the current rhetorical situation have standing to make a decision; similarly, they appeal to the absence of such classes when they want to argue that they lack such standing.

Public abstractions, in short, are built from events that have lessons to teach. The distribution of public abstractions bearing the same principle—teaching the same positive or negative lesson across time and space—is what allows a collective to envision its past and future within the metaphor of a path along which it commonly travels. Public event classes do not, unlike an ordinary event (e.g., opening a door), merely happen. To bear intact meanings across time and space, public space events must be simpler in resolution than ordinary situated events like "opening a cedar door in the backyard hutch on Tuesday, September 28, 1994." Every public abstraction "stands for" or "means" as well as happens, and its meaning depends on its simplicity. The simplicity of a public abstraction yields the means for inferring a public model from a rhetorical design.

What a public event class means, and the degree of clarity with which it means it, is a highly contested matter among people participating in public discourse. Viewed from the perspective of plans, speakers appeal to structure within other spaces (mundane, sensory, entitlement, local; see later discussion) in order to assure coherence and provide support for their public space abstractions.

Why, within a public model, are public abstractions dependent on information in other spaces? Why isn't the information in the public space autonomous? Unless public abstractions are already firmly embedded in the culture of the audience, public abstractions are simply too abstract and too simple to support a rhetorical design credibility. The public abstractions we already take for granted—mom, apple pie, country—live in their current form because they are the product of much cultural elaboration and semantic filtering. They are tied with the dense events of the culture and yet, with the filtering necessary to make them semantically portable, able to "mean" or "signify" seemingly apart and on their own, like a single word in a conventional dictionary. Most interesting situations of rhetoric require the use of public abstractions that have been neither so thoroughly culturally enriched nor semantically filtered. The alignment of public abstractions with the spectrum of other spaces of cultural experience allows for a speaker to do much of this enriching and filtering of public space abstractions as part of the ongoing design.

We have said enough to indicate, at least in a preliminary way, why public spaces depend on, and so need to be aligned with, nonpublic ones in constructing a model of the public. Let us now look more specifically into the nature of each of the nonpublic spaces.

*The Mundane Space.*   The mundane space includes all the structural information about the world used to provide "facts" or "detail" in the service of abstractions in the public space. When lexicalized, structures in the mundane space may appear as background, backing, and detail for public space abstractions.[3] They illustrate how public space abstractions are nonetheless composed of everyday actions and agents. As such, object classes in the mundane space provide the breadth and nuance of contingent detail that fill in the familiar grounding of public abstractions in the everyday world.

*The Entitlement Space.*   The entitlement space contains information used to legitimize actors (either individuals or larger groups) for agency in the public space. Entitlements are the means through which actors in the mundane space become role agents in a public space. The entitlement space, in other words, provides a mediating link to explain how individuals engaged in routine and situated activities can nonetheless be mapped into the public space as agents of public space abstractions.

Consider that all individuals can instigate ordinary events (e.g., opening windows, closing doors), but ordinary individuals only rarely instigate events within the public space, event classes that carry historical anchorage attributes. To participate in this kind of historical agency, individuals almost always require institutional roles. They need to hold public office or belong to some relevant role category, like voter. Participation in these roles requires qualifications, which are determined by object classes in the entitlement and,

---

[3]This appearance of being backgrounded does not necessarily survive across the Tactics and Events views, where mundane events (e.g., a speaker's having smoked marijuana in college), within these latter views, can be central to the discourse.

ultimately, in the mundane and sensory spaces. The power of an individual to partake in event classes in the public space is, in many cases, a representative power. Most institutional roles inherit their power from constituents, organizations, and groups. The speaker acquires representative power as a function of three factors:

1.  Similarity of conviction—the extent to which his or her fundamental principles and beliefs match those of constituents (an alignment of sensory spaces across the leader and members).
2.  Leadership qualifications—the extent to which the speaker has the accepted qualifications of a leader (an alignment of sensory-mundane and entitlement spaces across the leader and members).
3.  Group solidarity—the cohesiveness of the group itself (an alignment of public models across members of the group).

Throughout the debates, Lincoln and Douglas explore the other's vulnerabilities on all three factors.

The whys and wherefores of how event classes filter into public entitlements is culture—and often class—specific. For example, "going to school" is, in middle-class American culture, an event with little meaning in the entitlement space as a public qualification. On the other hand, "winning a Rhodes scholarship" is thought a substantial qualification for public entitlement among the middle and upper class. We must distinguish failing to qualify for an entitlement (e.g., failing the Rhodes) from disqualifying oneself from one (exposing a Rhodes Scholar's criminal past). In the first case, no alignment between the mundane and the public is established because of the lack of qualification in the entitlement space. In the second case, a possible entitlement was overridden because the individual failed to refrain from an action that had the power to rescind a public entitlement.

Significantly, classical rhetoric stressed arguments from the speaker's ethos, where ethos related to the goodwill, character, and qualifications of the speaker. As students of rhetoric have understood, the mundane actions, qualifications, and entitlements of the rhetor can become an active and effective part of the rhetorical design. The rhetor can present him- or herself as an entitled agent in the public space. When this entitlement becomes an explicit part of the rhetorical design and there is nothing to override it, we recognize the structure as an argument from ethos.

*The Sensory Space.*  The sensory space consists of object classes that are privately "known" to individuals or groups. These differ from the more interpersonally shared "facts" that are placed within the mundane space. The sensory space provides the assumption of prelinguistic experiences that are used for linguistic categorization in the mundane space. Insofar as objects in the sensory space can be referenced (through language), they can only be characterized rather than discretely enumerated as discrete objects. Although all object classes are linguistic (chapter 6), not all mental experiences are (language-dependent) events. The mental experiences that make up the sensory space provide the speaker with a prelinguistic basis for questioning or revising linguistic formulations in the mundane space.

The sensory space captures knowledge thought to be firsthand, independent of the authority of other minds or prior descriptions. This space contains the base of experience out of which speakers test the adequacy of their own words. More basic than language, it is the locus of a person's convictions. The sensory space bridges the gap from sensory experience to enduring beliefs and principles.

In verbal rhetoric, the sensory space is always implicit but hard to distill from the (linguistic) objects in the mundane space, which provide the basis for second-hand knowledge, the knowledge we hear from others and recirculate face to face or through technology. A speaker's depiction of (linguistic) events and objects often indicates only the tip of a large and invisible iceberg of first-hand sensory experiences that provide backing for the words. But it is only the words that reveal themselves, and usually in a far more generic and formulaic way than what the speaker actually sees in his or her mind's eye. The very best literary writers can evoke a rich sensory space through the mundane space of visual language, but such writers are rare in the universe of language users. From a literary point of view, some of the best depictions of the sensory space come in autobiography, where beyond the generic categories of the public words, the speaker must convey what Sturrock (1993) called "a unique human passage" and "self-presentation" (p. 3), a "whole" or "face" (p. 4), in details too singular for a generic transmission (pp. 12–14), with the full authority and conviction of firsthand knowledge (p. 15), against the stereotypes of official accounts (p. 49) or formal dogma (p. 93), external structures (p. 63), or the cultural zeitgeist (p. 193). To write moving autobiography, according to Sturrock, the writer must do what language virtually forbids—speak from a unique singularity that gives voice to the voicelessness of the individuals' own sensory space.

Outside of literary contexts, the sensory space remains eclipsed in the generic and conventionalized expression of the mundane space. Imagine the eyewitness to the crime who, when asked to describe the culprit, smiles at the detailed picture in her inner eye, saying, "He had two eyes, a nose, and a mouth," thinking to have said much more. The advantage of verbal rhetoric supplemented with images and sounds is to externalize the sensory space as a visible companion to the words, to empower the audience to decide for themselves how well the discrete dimension of language comports with the continuous stream of sensory information. Absent nonlinguistic stimuli, the primary evidence of an independent sensory space is that when looking at some natural phenomenon, like constellations in a summer sky, we can revise one another's descriptions of what we are viewing. Such revision would not be possible were there not some independent sensory dimension that we can both consult as a tacit assumption of rhetorical design. This dimension, once again, is the sensory space.

In addition to its invisibility, there is another reason why the sensory space is only indirectly accessible in verbal rhetoric. That is its sense of cumulative experience. Despite the capacity of language to portray history through the use of tense and aspect, the bias of direct and expositional language is to show a world unfolding without showing the learning or human growth that takes place with the accumulation of experience. A Norman Rockwell painting can show the years of wisdom and humbling in the wrinkled smile of an small town doctor as a small child looks with fear and reverence into his eyes. Yet direct language is not as good when it comes to conveying years of accumulated experience. Short of saying "I have had 25 years of experience serving the people of Illinois," how does one get across, in direct words, 25 years of cumulative experience? Skilled writers of fiction or the literary profile can, of course, use the language to describe the accumulation of a subject's experiences, asking the reader to emulate the role of over time viewer or eyewitness. But this is to use language scenically rather than for the purposes of direct exposition. The present perfect ("have had") is the best English (and Lincoln and Douglas) can do in directly conveying the cumulative effects of experience. Short of this linguistic directness, the speaker must rely on sharing with the listener a background of naturally induced or planted visual cues: gray hair, wrinkles, and other cumulative battle scars.

The aspect of cumulative experience conveyed in the sensory space offers the impression, even in verbal rhetoric, that it is the sensory space where speakers are willing to live as authentic human beings with their convictions intact. The sensory space is seen as the wellspring of a speaker's deepest motives and missions. Although it is understood that the speaker is willing to make compromises for the sake of civilization in the public space, that the public person on the record is only a shadow of the person, the sensory space reveals itself as the space where the individual behind the speaker lives in a fairly uncompromising way.

The idea of a unified and authentic person "deep down" is of course a romantic myth. What is important for our purposes is how speakers bring the sensory space to visibility in order to use the myth for rhetorical purposes. There are linguistic markers whose purpose is to show the direct alignment between the sensory and the public spaces. These markers, found in locutions like "frankly," "personally," "I must confess that," "in all candor," and "I'll be honest with you," form a class of confessionals. The purpose of these confessionals is to let the audience know that the speaker has agreed to reveal what he or she normally keeps classified as private. The audience is flattered to know it has been given access. The speaker is able to indicate complete trust in the audience, even if no trust is in fact extended and even if the confessional has a very different effect than exposing the speaker's private vulnerabilities. Often the use of a confessional telegraphs the speaker's interest in passing off false flattery as deep conviction or intimacy. In the age of the tabloid press, George Will, the Tory pundit, regularly laments, and lampoons, the creeping encroachment of the sensory space into our public discourse. He once quipped that "it is axiomatic that when a political person begins a sentence 'Frankly,' a resounding insincerity is on the way" (*Newsweek*, 1994, p. 62). In the introduction to one of his early books (*The Pursuit of Virtue and Other Torry Nations*, 1982), Will offers that commentary worth the name "public" should rise above the sensory, which he considers the root of a scandal-mongering journalism:

> I have made it the aim of my life to die without ever having written a column about which presidential advisors are ascending and descending. I write about the "inside" of public life in another sense. My subject is not what is secret, but what is latent, the kernel of principle and other significance that exists, recognized or not, inside events, actions, policies, and manners.

Even when it is aligned with public abstraction, moreover, the overt presentation of sensory information constitutes a discourse that takes risks. If not properly executed, such presentation can bring to the speaker an unseemly and unwelcome exposure. Faced with exposure, a speaker can try to recover by denying that something public and official had ever been intended. This is what happened to Joseph Biden in the summer of 1994. During the Senate confirmation hearings of Supreme Court nominee Stephen Breyer, Senator Biden, chairman of the Senate Judiciary Committee, pulled rank to get more time for questioning of the nominee. Explaining why he would give himself more time by deducting time from another senator junior to him, Biden said that "that's the privilege of being here [in the Senate] for 22 years." After sensing that his confession had come off as naked power, Biden tried to recover with his next sentence, "But seriously speaking...," framing the aside as if he had never meant more than a joke. Biden's aside was a confessional, indicating years of accumulated experience of public service. He meant it as a serious point about standing and seniority but in a confessional form that (he hoped) would have enough humor to lighten the impact. The execution of the confessional was fumbled, exposing the senator's accumulation of arrogance more than vulnerability. Biden's quick recovery, his effort to reclassify the confessional into a piece of pointless humor, was a way of distancing himself from its smug implications. By unaligning the humor from public abstraction, he was asking us to believe that the Senate had not made him such a bully after all. Or perhaps it had made him a bully, but he was now big enough to admit it publicly, making him endearing in his openness about an otherwise unendearing sense of himself.

The sensory space, aligned with the public space through confessionals, played a significant role in Lincoln/Douglas. For Lincoln, the confessional worked in the debates to allow him to distance himself from public stands he found distasteful even if unavoidable, such as committing himself to the possibility of there being more slave states. Many Republicans in his time had adopted local platforms that denied this possibility. Wanting to avoid the charge of abolitionism, Lincoln took a public stand that allowed for the conceivability of extending slavery beyond its current limits. Yet wanting to hold the Republican alliance, Lincoln used confessionals to indicate that he would be "exceedingly sorry" to see such a thing happen. Lincoln's confessionals drive a wedge between his public pledges and personal convictions, in an effort to keep incompatible audiences mollified.

For Douglas, the confessional becomes a way of eliminating any conceivable wedge between his public pledges and his convictions. He wants in every debate to publicize that popular sovereignty is both his proudest public commitment and his deepest personal passion—a commitment and passion, he is quick to reveal, he shares with the Founding Fathers. His is contrived to appear as a unified position, one having penetrated his heart as well as his head. Despite not being the author of the popular sovereignty doctrine, once Douglas took it up, he took it up as if the wisdom of his accumulated political life had prepared him to preach that doctrine and that doctrine alone. The strength of this use of the confessional is that it makes the speaker seem unified in terms of principle and public policy. The weakness is that the speaker's stance unravels quickly if it is found that the policy is blatantly defective and so could not likely, or wisely, have reflected, as the confessional speaker suggests, years of accumulated thought and personal testing. As the debates progress, Lincoln comes to unravel Douglas in just this way.

*The Local Space*  The local space is used, curiously, to signify public abstractions in a public model that are not part of the speaker's central story to tell about social truth and falsehood. They are abstractions deferred from the public space, temporarily or permanently. From the vantage of Plans, the local space is an uninteresting class of things that never has to be talked about as part of public discourse. From the Plans view, structure that is local consists only of pseudo-public abstractions. Members of the National Rifle Association believe that the object class "gun" is such a pseudo-public abstraction. Ask some to lecture about the truth and falseness of the "gun" in the culture and they will say it's not fit for public abstraction. It's local. It's something that's not scheduled for mention in the public space.

Why should Plans create a public model with a local space of things not to mention? On first blush, the name seems paradoxical. We think of "local" as what belongs to the here and now and not outside or distanced from it. The "local" is normally antonymic with the "external" and the "foreign," yet the Plans module seems to treat the local as foreign. From the view of Plans, the local is not external or foreign in the sense of outside a public model. The local is only outside the public space. It consists of object structures that compete, but fail, as public abstractions. Furthermore, and more importantly, it consists of object structures that fail as public abstractions because of the object structures that do successfully occupy the public space. Responsibility to the local is never dismissed; it is only dispensed with as a result of the public abstractions that are directly addressed. To have definition as a public model, the public space must have sharp and finite contours and a consistent interior. The story about social truth and falsehood cannot become too cluttered or it will fall under the weight of its own complexity and lack of definition. The local space is a way of keeping the public space simple and distinct. You won't hear the NRA members talking about the "gun" as a public space abstraction. But you will hear them talk about the more complex object structure, "the right to bear arms," the freedoms guaranteed by the second amendment to the constitution. The freedoms at issue in the NRA public space abstractions necessarily localize the "gun" as the object class from which not to tell the story, at least not the true story. The issue for the NRA is freedom, not guns.

Although we defer systematic discussion of tactics to the next chapter, the Tactics module views the structure that Plans assigns to local in a different and somewhat more versatile context that is worth noting here. Unlike Plans, Tactics is concerned about the rhetorical situation of which it is a part. Structures that Plans assigns to a local space never to be mentioned become, within Tactics, a set of object classes whose status may just be thought outside the standing of the immediate rhetorical situation and its agents to act on. There are bound to be many worthy public abstractions that exceed the time constraints of the situation to deal with. These abstractions must be deferred if others are to be addressed.

From the Tactics perspective, local structures that Plans views as "unmentionable" may within tactics act as deferrables. This can lead to some interesting coordination problems between Plans and Tactics on common structure that Plans had mapped into the local. Many politicians who oppose abortion know they have a fight on their hands if they also oppose the zoning of abortion clinics in every municipality. The anti-abortion view from Plans is one of high principle, the right and wrong of the social world. The anti-abortion view from Tactics becomes mired in local skirmishes that can easily dull the attentiveness of Tactics to the preservation of the public space abstractions with which Plans knows, and tells, the issue. Imagine that the anti-abortion speaker, operating from tactics and lexical opportunism (from Events), in the heat of battle with a pro-choice foe, concedes, reluctantly, that each municipality must decide on its own zoning restrictions for abortion clinics. The speaker is debating on television, an on-the-record medium, and the speaker is quoted in ways that filter out the fact that the opportunistic utterance was made with reluctance, in a concession, and with a concern of being cut in mid-sentence by a fade-out. The speaker is quoted as saying, "Each must decide," on the abortion issue. Trying to implement Plans' view of a structure that is local, the tactical view mismanaged the local structure and allowed the media to catch Plans in the appearance of a public contradiction.

When Tactics coordinates more fruitfully with Plans, speakers are able to make over the local structures of Plans into tactical deferrables that can diminish, not heighten, the appearance of contradiction, compromise, or going back on one's word that is likely to befall any speakers when their uncontested world of Plans makes contact with a tactical world of opponents. From the view of Tactics, local structures that can be deferred allow a speaker an avenue for eliminating, as irrelevant to the present discussion, aspects of the opponent's plans that might otherwise be perceived as well-motivated and legitimate. Deferring the local structures of Plans to a low priority in the rhetorical situation, tactical speakers can customize the "mentionables" in the rhetorical situation to accommodate the story that they know best to tell.

Speakers can defer object classes from a public to a local space in either a constrained or unconstrained way. Constrained deferrals are the structural and, in some cases, tactical equivalent to what, within Events, are the unique lexicalizations associated with the "verbatim on the record" (chapter 5). In a constrained deferral, the speaker constrains, or tries to constrain, the terms under which the issue will be defined and discussed at a later time and place (by the so-called "local authorities"). This allows the speaker to retain some definitional control of the local space in certain ways. Pro-choice speakers on abortion who leave the zoning of abortion clinics a "local" affair use a constrained deferral if they nonetheless stipulate that local districts must arrive at some zoning resolutions that are favorable to the pro-choice agenda. In an unconstrained deferral, by contrast, speakers place no prior stipulations on how the local agents may decide and act when they finally take up the issue deferred in its designated time and place. Examining the problem at a later time and place, the local agents may convene and decide to outlaw zoning for abortion clinics altogether, thus contradicting the original public model of the pro-choicers who had originally agreed to make zoning a "local" issue.

Even when they do agree on the boundaries between the public and local space, Lincoln and Douglas still disagree, at times, about whether a deferral to local should be unconstrained or constrained. The importance of the debates to American history is that Lincoln and Douglas disagree profoundly on whether slavery, an object class, is to be placed in the public space or deferred to a local space. For Douglas, slavery is a local issue to be decided one state at a time. Slavery is of only marginal interest in Douglas' model of the public, bringing only a yawning "don't care" attitude from him as a public issue. For Lincoln, slavery is the cancer threatening to break apart his model of the public. The country, in his view, can no longer afford to hide the evil of slavery under the rock of localism. Slavery is the quintessential public issue, whose containment and elimination needs to be the nation's top priority.

Having reviewed the various spaces, the reader should come to appreciate the very different realms of experience they carve out. The reader should also appreciate that all the various spaces carving out these realms are necessary tools, coupled with a plan focus, for crafting a public model. Each of these different realms of experience also brings out different assumptions about temporality, to which we now briefly turn.

### Representing Time Across Spaces

Time is represented differently across the various spaces of a public model. The local space inherits its notion of time from the public space; the entitlement space inherits its notion of time from the mundane space. We thus have to consider the representation of time within the public, mundane, and sensory spaces. We should not confuse this with the lexicalization of these representations, which happens in the Events module. It is worth noting that no space in a public model represents time as it represented in scientific practice, as a state-to-state transition description of a physical system (physical time) or as an objective means of dating elements within the physical universe (cosmic time). The mundane space represents time as calendar time, marked by calendar development, the succession of generations, and retaining archived documents and artifacts to keep a trace of the past. The sensory space represents time as lived or phenomenological time, a keeping of time that is internal to states of human consciousness, often violating linear sequence by accommodating flashbacks and abrupt jumps to alternative pasts and imagined futures. Ricoeur (1985/1988) showed that calendar time and lived time are highly interactive, that there can be an important literary aspect to the most pedestrian history writing and a central calendar aspect to the most imaginative of historical fiction. Because of their interactivity, we refer to time in either the sensory or mundane space as sensory/mundane time. The public space relies on precedent time, an abstraction of sensory/mundane time made possible through the ongoing efforts of cultural producers to direct cultural attention and resources to certain events as "founding." Although all histories rely on documents and artifacts from the past, not all documents and artifacts are housed in the Smithsonian or the National Museum of Art. Although all histories rely on marking the succession of generations, not all individuals of a generation have their dates of birth commemorated or turned into holidays. Precedent time is constructed through cultural practices, the allocation of cultural resources, above and beyond verbal narration. Many ongoing practices in the culture are needed to institutionalize sensory/mundane time as precedent time. The very practices involved in this institutionalization make a public space visible to the culture.

## Public Models Versus the Public/Private Distinction

Much better documented in the literature on law and ethics than our notion of public models is the public/private distinction. Why do we avoid this time-honored distinction in favor of a component space view of a public? Some in-depth analyses of the public/private distinction in a 1982 symposium at the University of Pennsylvania devoted to the subject (Kennedy, Klare, Mnookin) concluded that the distinction, although impossible to avoid, is nonetheless difficult to understand in anything but ad hoc terms. Our own breakdown of component spaces illustrates some of the problems with the binary dichotomy between public and private. First, "private" can include very different realms of experience. It can include what we assign to the sensory space: the truly private—an individual's unique sense experiences and lived memories, and the aspects of one's inner life that cannot be transferred to another human being. Yet "private" can also include what we assign to the mundane space, everyday acts of ritual, including language practices, actions, and activities that are widely shared (hence nonprivate) but that have no visible import to a political or commercial sphere of activity (hence nonpublic). Consequently, the category of private becomes seriously overloaded if we try to stuff both sensory and mundane information into it.

Similar considerations led Bensman and Lilienfield (1979), in their classic study of role theory, to add a third "social" category to the public/private distinction. Analyzing data of Lincoln and Douglas, we found that even the category of the "social" became overloaded if we tried to include within it (a) generic acts of social ritual, (b) public entitlements that permit individuals to move from the social to the public sphere of influence, and (c) local authority, the deferral of future decision-making rights by reason of changes in venue. We thus saw the need to split Bensman and Lilienfield's social space into mundane, entitlement, and local spaces, respectively.

To summarize the discussion thus far, we have explored the various spaces out of which a public model is composed. We now turn to the activation of generic and specific plans of rhetoric by directing the speaker's attention to patterned subsets of an emergent public model. Taken together, spaces and plans are the tools the Plans module uses to incrementally build the public model underlying the speaker's discourse. It is the emergence of this public model, incrementally (in speaking) or composed intact prior to delivery (in writing), that gives local coherence to the parts of the speaker's emergent rhetorical design.

## Plans as Focal Subsets of a Public Model

Plans do not emerge whole cloth or from a blank slate. They are ways of focusing on a public model that is in some emergent state of development. Plans and spaces work interactively, incrementally, and—for skilled rhetors—cooperatively to craft an emergent public model. Without spaces, plans would have nothing to focus on when seeking glimmers of an emergent public model; without plans, spaces would be static classifications of experience with no directional focus for the construction and elaboration of abstractions in the public space. Because plans are so highly interactive with spaces, because the Plans module itself is so highly interactive with the goals of rhetorical design and the design structure, it is fair to say that speakers begin on the implicit development of plans when they begin building a rhetorical design from the design structure under the direction of goals. One of the earliest actions skilled speakers know to pursue when they know to satisfy the goal to be predictive is seeing the design structure in terms of an incipient public model. Because rhetorical plans are foci on this emergent model, the public model a speaker seeks to emerge with constrains, and also guides, the universe of plans that the speaker can pursue, making the speaker's competence to build complex plans from the shallow input of "goals" and "content" a more explainable, less mysterious capacity than it otherwise might seem to be.

To be more specific, seven generic plans can be defined as focal patterns on an emergent public model. The generic plans are (a) organizational authority, (b) public confessional, (c) precedent or counterprecedent, (d) conspiracy, (e) historical (f) principle, and (g) venue. These plans are generic insofar as their basic shape falls out merely from the topology of a public model and does not depend on the specific content of the design structure. Generic plans become specific when they are slotted with content from the actual object structure of the design. Each generic plan is generative of hundreds of specific plans, depending on the particular structure used to fill them in.

In the sections to follow, we examine each generic plan and then offer as illustration specific examples of each generic type from Lincoln and Douglas. Throughout our discussion, the reader should note that there is substantial overlap in the patterns representing different generic plans. This fact has a variety of practical implications when the Tactics, Events, and Presentation modules try to draw out structures shared by the Plans module in the course of a rhetorical situation. First, speakers can be following one plan whereas opponents and audiences can take them as following a different but intersecting one. Second, speakers can quickly shift from one plan to a different intersecting plan without needing to telegraph to audiences what they have done and without causing audiences a sense of disruption. Third, speakers can themselves hedge their bets on what plan they are pursuing, taking tactical action with and lexicalizing structures that are consistent with multiple plans and then waiting for the response of opponents and audiences to determine what plan they want to stay with. Fourth, the interactivity of plans is the rule more than inertness. We seldom find speakers staying with specific plans of a single generic type and working through the single generic type to completion. This is hardly surprising given that the Plans module, able to discriminate generic plan structures and the specific instantiations of such structures, is blind to the rhetorical situations in which plans are used, and given the fact that the modules left to forage the rhetorical situation, Tactics, Events, and Presentation, cannot discriminate plans of different types. The modules that forage the rhetorical situation only know what to do to seek an advantage with the opponent (Tactics) or lexicalize structure for the audience (Events, Presentation). The foraging modules know nothing about staying within a discrete plan or maintaining the coherence of a plan. The coordination bottlenecks between Plans on the one hand and Tactics, Events, and Presentation on the other assure that the invocation of plans in the course of rhetorical interaction will be more opportunistic than rigidly scheduled.

Discussed in isolation from real specimens of rhetoric, generic plans of rhetoric are sterile and unbroken monologues about truth and falsehood in the social world. Deployed in real-time interaction, these stories get broken up, mixed up, mangled, collapsed, consolidated, compressed, garbled, distorted, elaborated, and interrupted in the heat of interaction. From the view of Plans, plan structures are glossy and intact, like new cars in a showcase window. From the view of Tactics, Events, and Presentation, the same structures are more like car parts in a junk heap. In real-time tactical interaction, there is nothing discrete or intact about the structures shared with Plans. If there is coordination between Plans and the rhetorical situation, it is only because the Strategic module is hard at work shifting back and forth across Plans, Tactics, and Events views of the design structure, all the while making the effort to coordinate and reconcile information across views. Such coordination and reconciliation of information across disparate modules is at the heart of rhetorical decision making.

Despite their interactivity, we do our best in this chapter to give the reader a view of each generic plan type, as intact and as isolated from other plan types as possible. We are not completely successful in this effort insofar as we cannot really understand a rhetorical plan without comprehending its interactivity with other plans, with tactics, and with the lexicalizations furnished by the Events and Presentation modules. Our best approximation to isolating generic plan types is to discuss each plan type as it is utilized during the debates by both speakers, in chronological order, from Ottawa to Alton. We thus do not consider each plan in its sterile intact state. We rather consider the trajectory of structures associated with the plan as Lincoln and Douglas' Tactics, Events, and Presentation modules call on them to forage the situations of the debates. Our discussion thus does not try to suppress the interactivity of each plan type, but at least it shows this interactivity in the context of a single plan's full trajectory through the debates.

## Organizational Authority

In the modern state, the power of the individual is a representative power, a power conferred by a constituent organization. The words the speaker brings to the here and now carry the authority and backing of a network of individuals and their history as a group. The speaker, through entitlement, has earned the right to meld his or her personal voice with that of the group. In an organizational authority plan, the speaker's sensory experiences and mundane actions align him or her with the entitlement and the public spaces, authorizing the speaker as a public representative. An organizational authority focus is what allows the Plans module to tell its impersonal story about the social world with the weight of many voices behind it.

In Fig. 7.2 and the subsequent figures we consider in this chapter, rectangles refer to event classes associated with the speaker; circles refer to event classes dissociated from the speaker; event classes with solid perimeters indicate events that are shared or that the speaker can directly avow in the public space; event classes with broken perimeters indicate events that are fundamentally private or that the speaker cannot or will not directly avow in the public space; solid lines refer to links that the speaker directly states or strongly implies; and broken lines refer to links that remain private and inaccessible and that audiences only weakly infer if they bother to infer them at all.

There are some interesting things to note about the subset of a public model that constitutes an organizational authority plan. First, there is no direct link between the sensory and the public space. An organizational authority plan cements the voice of the speaker to the voice of the group he or she represents. The assumption of this plan is that the individual and the group are cognitively indistinguishable. Second, and related to the first point, the link between the sensory and the mundane space is private and inaccessible (i.e., a broken line), meaning that audiences are meant to draw weak inferences only with respect to the alignment between how the speaker presents him- or herself as an entitled member of a public group and what the speaker "really thinks" (the sensory space) in the privacy of his or her own mind. To make organizational authority a credible plan, speakers must

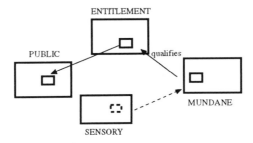

FIG. 7.2.  The organizational authority plan.

suppress cues of compromising, much less concealing, public commitments that would set them apart from other members of the organization.

We now consider the trajectory of organizational authority as a plan carried into the situations of Lincoln and Douglas through their Tactics, Events, and Presentation modules. Although the plan for organizational authority within a public model is a positive one, indicating why an individual, including the speaker, is entitled to represent a group, Tactics can use structures from organizational authority for negative purposes, to implicate the beliefs of an opponent who heads a group with unpopular views. Within organizational authority, Plans tells an innocent story about the need for entitlement in order to have public agency. Tactics seizes on parts of this same structure to use entitlement as a public weakness when the group being led has public standing but low popularity.

This is how Douglas tactically uses organizational authority structures against Lincoln, to indict him for leading a group, Republicans, who espouse abolition. At the time of the debates, the majority of central Illinois voters, the swing vote for the senatorial election, were anti-abolition. Douglas hoped to tie Lincoln to an organization, the Republicans, with negative authority for this key swing vote because of their abolitionism. Lincoln spent much of his reply time at Ottawa denying his physical involvement in the Springfield convention. He also spent some time reading from a speech he had delivered in 1854 in which he indirectly disavowed abolitionist principles. In the speech he recites, Lincoln claims that he does not want to interfere with slavery where it exists and that blacks are not fit to enjoy full social and political equality with whites. By reading from this 1854 speech, Lincoln sought to counter Douglas' tactical use of organizational authority against him. Significantly, Douglas never acknowledges Lincoln's countering move and, arguably, didn't have to. After all, by choosing to read from a speech he had composed four years before, Lincoln opted for a register of very low immediacy (Sturrock, 1993, p. 134), a poor choice for putting information on the record (chapter 5). Never crediting Lincoln with renouncing abolitionist principles, Douglas acknowledged only Lincoln's Ottawa denial of being physically present in the Springfield convention ("I call him an abolitionist and all he can say is that he was never at Springfield"). Like a parent who must confront a child with the basic realities, Douglas warns that he must bring Lincoln "to his milk" about the reality of his organizational alignments. He enumerates a list of facts as premises tying Lincoln to the platform of the Springfield Republicans: "In the first place Mr. Lincoln was selected by the very men who made the Republican organization that day." "He was the leader of the party." Lincoln entertained the sentiments of the Springfield convention and these "have been published on Lincoln again and again and never before has he denied it."

Organizational authority is an entitlement of representation that is not suspended with a leader's physical involvement or lack of involvement in a single convention. Through its alignment between the entitlement and public spaces, organizational authority allows a leader's on-the-record position to be inferred even without explicit vocalization. A speaker's commitments are less a matter of eyewitness, sensory behavior than a matter of an abstract, and public, categorical identity. The leader's on the record is, in effect, the platform of the group. Douglas's tactics are smart enough to bring this aspect of an organizational authority structure to the early debates. In his rejoinder at Ottawa, Douglas says that what concerns him is not the level of Lincoln's participation (or nonparticipation) at the Springfield convention but that Lincoln is the ex officio leader of the Illinois Republicans, so dwelling on his participation at the Springfield convention is "a quibble to avoid the main issue."

As a result of Ottawa, Douglas had tactically used structures from organizational authority to trap Lincoln in a dilemma of category membership: Either Lincoln was a good Republican (and so an unpopular abolitionist) or his views on slavery were more acceptably moderate (and so unrepresentative of Republicans, whose platform he was entrusted to represent). Lincoln's first response to the dilemma is to choose, ostensibly, against his membership as a Republican by refraining to pledge to most of the Republican platform at Springfield. This is a good example of Lincoln's Tactical module working at cross-purposes with his Plans. Douglas' dilemma was skillfully crafted to make Lincoln say something that would force an inconsistency in his Plans. The Plans module, knowing nothing about the rhetorical situation, would have no awareness of the tactical threat against it. Indeed, if the Plans module were able to understand Douglas' questions, it would have no idea how to respond, for it knows only how to tell what is predictably true and what is false about the social world. It is left to Lincoln's Tactics to deal with the dilemma, and the Tactics module understood there is pressure to answer a question even if the answer causes further problems down the road. Lincoln's answer, because it shares the same structure as plans, throws a wrench into the Plans module. When Lincoln's Plan module next sampled the design structure, it finds a structure like "I do not pledge to the Republican platform at Springfield" in the midst of its public model, seeming to disenable Lincoln's organizational authority. Plans had no idea where this type of structure comes from but it does understand that the structures create potential inconsistencies in the public model, and that the inconsistencies need to be reconciled if the rhetor is to continue to tell predictable truths and falsehoods about the social world.

The reconciliation of an inconsistent public model is a substantial undertaking that Plans has the leisure to take on at a slower rate than the events of the debate. The Tactics, Events, and Presentation modules,[4] on the other hand, must keep pace with debate events. This means that a speaker with an inconsistent public model must continue to perform, even perhaps try to work on the inconsistency in the course of local tactics and presentation, while waiting for the Plans module to work on the inconsistency more globally every time it gets a chance to look at the design structure.

Giving the different timing schedules of Plans and Tactics in repairing the effect of Lincoln's response to Douglas' dilemma, we would expect a latency between the time Lincoln fell into the dilemma and the time he actually shows evidence of efforts to restore consistency in his organizational authority. We do see signs of such a latency. After he responds to Douglas and creates an inconsistency in his organizational authority, he never in the remainder of his Freeport opening takes action to restore it. Douglas makes him pay for that delay. In his Freeport response, he continues to take tactical jabs at Lincoln's loss of organizational authority. He uses the word *foundation* as a code for a leader's representative power and he claims that his answers to Lincoln have a foundation whereas Lincoln's to him do not. Douglas tries to make Lincoln's lack of foundation a source of humiliation for him with the Republican audience at Freeport: "I just wanted to know whether he agreed with his party." "What do you think of Lincoln, who is your candidate and attempting to dodge the responsibility of this platform?"

In his rejoinder at Freeport, Lincoln manifests some behavior that is consistent with his doing a global repair of his organizational authority. Lincoln had tactically gotten into trouble when he had responded on the premise that to be a Republican was to be an abolitionist. On that premise, he could not object to abolition without forfeiting his representative power over Republicans. Now the Plans module has had time to work out how to predictively tell the truth about leading the Republicans. One can lead the Republicans without being an abolitionist. The power to represent the Republicans comes from being opposed to slavery. Throughout Freeport and the later debates, Lincoln tactically brings this realigned plan of organizational authority to the debates. He claims that Douglas has gotten the history of the Republican party wrong. The national and state party formed in 1856,

---

[4]For the rest of this chapter, we avoid repeating all the modules that bring plans to expression and just refer to them as Tactics and Events.

not 1854. Some Republicans in the North were abolitionist but abolition was not the uniform principle of the party. The Republicans were essentially antislavery and they opposed the Kansas Act because that act seemed to have resuscitated the institution of slavery. In his reply at Jonesboro, Lincoln can put his realigned organizational authority to work when he assures the Jonesboro audience that there was nothing deceptive about his Freeport answers, rejecting abolition. "I have never deceived anyone."

By the opening of the fifth debate at Galesburg it is Douglas who makes some tactical moves that put his organizational authority in jeopardy.[5] Douglas had turned his focus to justifying his opposition to the Lecompton convention and the follow-up English Bill. Both were divisive for the Democrats. Douglas himself had taken controversial stands that had alienated the southern-leaning Buchanan democrats. Douglas now portrays himself as being a member of a party that has failed him. He describes with disdain the "postmasters and federal office holders" in the Democratic ranks who, according to Douglas, are conspiring with Buchanan to elect Lincoln. Douglas, however, never criticizes the Democrats for long without finding a way to turn it into a criticism of Lincoln and the Republicans. What is bad about the wayward Democrats, according to Douglas, is not that they call into question his own entitlement to lead but that they inadvertently hand to the hapless Lincoln and the ragtag Republicans a slim hope to win the election. What is bad about the split in Douglas' own party is not that the Democrats have caused it but that the Republicans would be desperate enough to take advantage of it.

In his reply at Galesburg, Lincoln offers more of his realigned organizational authority for the audience's consideration. Although Douglas has had much to say about the Republicans throughout the debates, Lincoln notes, he has yet to say anything true about Republican principles. "If he had great confidence that our principles were wrong, he would take hold of them and demonstrate them to be wrong. But he does not do so." Douglas never responds to Lincoln's revamped organizational authority, this being a blind spot in Douglas' Tactical module we take occasion to review in the next chapter. In his rejoinder at Galesburg, Douglas repeats the organizational authority structure—Republicans as abolitionists—on which he had caught Lincoln the first time. "You Republicans cheer for the slogan 'no more slave states' and yet Lincoln at Freeport says his conscience won't let him live up to that doctrine."

---

[5]Douglas does split briefly with the Democrats earlier than Galesburg, in his Freeport reply, when he attacks the Buchanan printer, Cornelius Wedell; but he quickly represents Wendell as in cahoots with the Republicans.

In addition to this dated understanding of Lincoln's organizational authority, Douglas added another. By the Galesburg rejoinder, Douglas had heard Lincoln say that the Republicans were more variegated in belief than the imputation of abolitionism had allowed. By the time of his reply in the fourth debate, at Charleston, Douglas begins to (mis)represent the variability of the Republican rank and file as opportunism. The Republicans fall from wrong principle to any principle that gets them elected.

His revamped organizational authority untouched by Douglas' tactics, Lincoln pushes ahead with it. In his opening at Quincy and then again in his rejoinder, he offers a minitreatise on Republican party principles. He devotes more space to a history and statement of principles of the Republican party in this round than in any of the other nine debate rounds in which he spoke. He dichotomizes the category membership of Republicans and Democrats in starkly simply terms: "[It is] the difference between the men who think slavery is wrong and those who do not think it is wrong." "The Republican party thinks it is wrong."

Studying a speaker's systematic use of a particular plan over time yields a first glimpse at a speaker's strategic behavior. A strategy is a repertoire of plans, tactics, and events that a speaker uses over the course of interaction. Because any specific plan is an intersection of goals, structure, and lexicalizations of structure, a strategic repertoire also includes regularities about the speaker's selection and scheduling of plans, tactics, and events. The fact that the Democratic party was well established and the Republican party was not seemed the main factor in setting Lincoln's and Douglas' strategy with respect to organizational authority. Douglas believed, correctly, that he could use the fledgling youth and unproven status of the Republican party to keep Lincoln on his heels. Lincoln probably believed it would be much harder to discredit Douglas as a Democrat despite the rifts in that party. Lincoln knew he would need to address misinformation about his new party before he could set the record straight about its reason for organizing. Lincoln thus had a strategic reason to externalize stereotypes about the Republicans (as abolitionists) in order to dissolve them. Lincoln's fall into Douglas' dilemma was hardly the most opportune way to realize this strategy. It was a tactical miscue serious enough, arguably, to put the first three debates in doubt for Lincoln.

### Public Confessional.

The public confessional is a focus on a public model that both creates tensions with and corrects biases in an organizational authority focus. Organizational authority presumptively cements the representative voice of the speaker with the constituent group. There are occasions, however, when the speaker and, more importantly the audience the speaker seeks to persuade renounce beliefs and commitments identified with the speaker's organization. An organizational authority plan is a tactically inappropriate plan in such a context, as the speaker's immediate interest is to unalign from the organization rather than align with it. The public confessional plan, depicted in Fig. 7.3, allows a speaker just this distance from his or her own organization.

Notice that this plan shares much of the structure of the organizational authority plan. The main difference is that the speaker disavows rather than avows (circles rather than squares) the information associated with the group in the mundane, entitlement, and public spaces. To make this disavowal public, the speaker builds a direct link from the sensory to the public space, in effect making an open confessional of a split with his or her group on a salient event class.

A public confessional focus allows the Plans module to tell its impersonal story about the social world with the courage of conviction, with the speaker able to rise above the conforming expectations of those who conferred leadership in the first place. In this regard, the public confessional focus creates tensions with organizational authority.

Yet the public confessional also serves as an important corrective to the bias of organizational authority when it comes to widening the source of representative power, for organizational authority does not hold a notion of representative power that takes account of the necessity that the leader in the public space be a person beneath the entitlement; it does not take account of the fact that representative power can only be held and applied by one who is human, making humanness a not incidental source of representative power for anyone who is independently entitled. The public confessional brings into closer alignment the sensory spaces and the public space by allowing entitled individuals to bring public abstractions into the public space with a representative power inherited not from their constituents but directly from what is in their hearts and minds as persons.

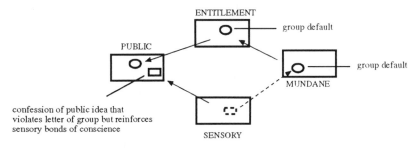

FIG. 7.3.   The public confessional plan.

Providing an alternative source of representative power to an entitled individual, the public confessional accords a speaker a story about how representatives are empowered to lead, even when their on the record actions are taken over the objections of constituents. The public side of the confessional takes a distancing step from the represented group. The confessional side invokes the personal source of representative power that maintains the presumption of leadership and a group bond to its leader.

When Lincoln falls into the trap of organizational authority at Freeport, he relies on the public confessional to explain how he can consistently disagree with many Republicans and, nonetheless, lead them. Consider how he juxtaposes his open pledges against Republican doctrine (the public side) and what he "really thinks" (the confessional side) as a Republican at heart: "Now, my friends, it will be perceived upon an examination of these questions I answer that so far I have only answered as to whether I was pledged for this, or that, or any other thing...but I am disposed at least to take up some of these questions, and state what I really think upon them."

What Lincoln "really thinks" is telegraphed through the lexicon of private sensory and emotive attitudes, a lexicon rich with words like *freely, frankly, reluctantly, exceedingly sorry,* and *glad*. Lincoln contrasts what he is reluctantly pledged to do (in the public space) with the resistance that would accompany the pledge in his interior, sensory life:

> In regard to these other questions of whether I am pledged. I state to you freely, frankly, that I should be exceedingly sorry to ever be put in the position of having to pass upon that question I should be exceedingly glad to know that there never would be another slave state admitted into the Union...[I am not pledged to the abolition of slavery in the District of Columbia but] I should be exceedingly glad to see slavery abolished [there]...I confess that I should be exceedingly glad to see congress abolish slavery in the District of Columbia.

In his reply at Freeport, Douglas sees himself as beating Lincoln in a contest of organizational authority. He can continue to press his advantage only if he can keep Lincoln from appealing to the alternative source of representative power that the public confessional affords him. Consequently, Douglas' tries to turn the tables on Lincoln by mispresenting Lincoln's shift to the public confessional into a personal (and indirect) admission that the conditions for entitlement no longer hold and that the Republicans ought to find a leader with a more eager attitude for their cause. Douglas says in mock innocence that he had raised his original questions at Ottawa only to know whether Lincoln agreed with his own party. Because (in light of his

Freeport answers) Lincoln apparently does not, Douglas goes on to offer, "out of kindness, " to relieve him of the responsibilities of representation. After all, the Republicans who voted for the abolitionist resolutions in conventions across the state of Illinois were firm in their conviction and pledged themselves to vote for no man who was not equally committed to them. By a strange irony, Douglas observes, the Republicans have unanimously agreed to elect as their leader perhaps the only Republican in Illinois who now confesses not to be pledged to them!

Douglas concocts the further mispresentation that Lincoln's public confessional is a sign of deeply conflicted mind, too frail and fragile for the decisiveness required for public office. For Douglas, Lincoln's house divided is an expression for abolition. So when Lincoln now publicly confesses that he would tolerate more slave states and rejects abolition, there is a problem of voice and credibility. Which Lincoln to believe? "There [when articulating house divided], he says he won't vote for another slave state." "Yet he now [in his public confessional at Freeport] says he will vote for another slave state." If he believes in no more slave states, why not just say so? If he believes in more slave states, why not just say that? Little wonder, Douglas observes, quoting Lincoln's public confessional as if a damaging personal admission "he says he would not like to be put to the test." Lincoln refuses to be pledged but he is "exceedingly sorry" not to be. "Why be a candidate with that attitude?" Douglas asks the audiences at Freeport and Jonesboro.

As Lincoln gains momentum with his revamped organizational authority focus in the later debates, the need for the public confessional as an explanation disappears. We never see it after Freeport.

Douglas avoids the public confessional across the debates. He fronts organizational authority as his chief plan focus and, from this focus, the public confessional marks a unambiguous failure of public definition. As we mentioned earlier, even when Douglas addresses Lecompton in the later debates, divisive for the Democrats, he never betrays his category membership as a Democrat. On the contrary, he portrays himself and his popular sovereignty doctrine at the center of category identity for a Democrat. When he depicts other Democrats as attacking him, it is they, not he, who left behind the Democratic party and its true principles. They, not he, threaten the Democratic party by forging "ruinous alliances" with Republicans. They, not he, subvert the intentions of Jefferson and Jackson.

Lincoln's and Douglas' disparate stances toward the public confessional reflect a difference in their public models. The strategic considerations, as before, seem to play off the perceived differences in party strength. The Democrats enjoy the heritage of Jefferson and Jackson and, despite current divisions, Douglas is simply unwilling to "confess" against his party. In the face of intraparty division, Douglas' strategy is to keep his own person at the definitional center of the Democratic party and to banish dissenting Democrats from that center. Wrapping his person and his principle of popular sovereignty in the tradition of the Democrats, the public confessional is not a focus available to Douglas. Lincoln, by contrast, enjoys no such party strength from the Republicans, and some Republicans, in addition, come to the party with platforms (abolition) that (for Lincoln) are neither defining for membership nor credible to the swing vote. For this reason, Lincoln has little to lose by confessing against his party when an occasion opens for him to do so.

### Precedent and Counterprecedent.

The plans we have considered thus far deal with links between the public space and supporting spaces. We have yet to consider plans that focus on the interior of the public space itself and on the public abstractions that comprise that space. The most important plans that fit this description are precedent and counterprecedent. These plans construct a blueprint for a truth founded on right-thinking principles and falsehoods fabricated on wrong-thinking ones. A precedent/counterprecedent focus allows the Plans module to tell its impersonal story about a world of public abstractions that fill both a temporal horizon, from past to future, and a moral horizon, from an ideological history based on good principle and the agents seeking to uphold it, to alternative histories based on bad principles and the counter-agents seeking to follow them. Through precedents, a speaker links a series of public event classes, separated in time and place, through a common principle that makes each event class "teach" the same positive lesson. Through counterprecedents, the event classes in question share a common counterprinciple that makes them "teach" the same negative lesson.

An individual must have special entitlements to instigate or continue precedents and counterprecedents. Such individuals have the standing to "make history." We need to distinguish this history-making entitlement from the entitlement to engage in public discourse, the latter entitlement being defined in an organizational authority plan. These two entitlements overlap in practice, but they need not. Public agents are typically public spokespersons, but not all spokespersons are agents. To make history, individuals must be kings, religious authorities, appointees, elected officials, judges, and so on. They must have some recognized authority.

Although only individuals can make history, the description "history makers" can be more diffuse than a reference to individuals. Precedent and counterprecedent plans can be instigated and reinforced by aggregates or diffuse practices with no special standing. Social custom and cultural practice can have as much to do with precedents and counterprecedents as discrete individuals in discrete moments of decision and action. Locutions, associated with canonical event-telling (chapter 2), allow us to make standard references to history makers, either as persons or practices from a remote and unwitnessed past. Phrases like "the Founders" or "the intent of the settlers" are such locutions. On some occasions, the reference is to actual persons: Washington, Jefferson, Madison, Adams. On others, it is to the diffuse practices of colonial days, as if such practices had emanated from a single intelligence.

Precedents and counterprecedents define a plan that shares some of the objectivity, or distance from a sensory self, of organizational authority and some of the subjectivity, or closeness to a sensory self, of public confessionals (Fig. 7.4). Like an organizational authority focus, precedents and counterprecedents require that the speaker view the public space from the constituent group as the source of representative power. Like the public confessional focus, precedents and counterprecedents at least weakly indicate that the principles put in motion by precedents and counterprecedents are also the speaker's personal principles, abiding in the sensory space of lived experience.

Precedent

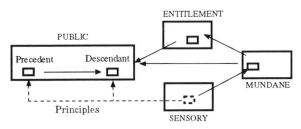

Counterprecedent

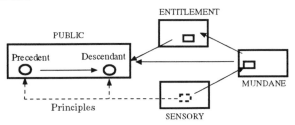

FIG. 7.4.   The precedent and counterprecedent plans.

In a precedent and counterprecedent focus, the past and the future are mapped with well-marked landmarks annotating ideological history. The precedent and counterprecedent plans make the unfathomable past a known and familiar entity. The primary uncertainty is the present, unclassified exigence under discussion, and the singular challenge is to fit this current unknown to the familiar blueprints of history. The effort to make this fit provides a rhetorical design with a historical teleology, moves the speaker toward the goal of on the record predictability about what has been and should be. Through this fit, argument interfaces with ideology.

In constitutional democracies, institutionalized state narratives derive not from detailed accounts of the past but from precedents and counterprecedents. They are the well-told, sometimes apocryphal, often mythologized stories of kings, princes, generals, and founders sacrificing for large ideas through decisive and courageous action. Such accounts are often more tale and legend than accurate descriptions of the past. For school students acculturated into civic religion, the historiography of publics is constructed out of precedent and counterprecedent plans. Precedent and counterprecedent plans, as public abstractions, necessarily simplify event classes into marble snapshots so that they may have public lessons to teach.

We now turn to precedent and counterprecedent plans as they are expressed in the debates. In his opening at Ottawa, Douglas lays out the historical precedent for his principle of popular sovereignty on the slavery question. The canonicity of Douglas' event-telling resembles that of the Encyclopedia piece on Bull Run we examined in chapter 2. Precedents require a history that can be very carefully controlled, and the need for such control encourages events to be lexicalized canonically.

> Prior to 1854, this country was divided into two great political parties, known as the Whig and Democrat parties—both national and patriotic in their principles—both advocating principles which were universal in their application. An old line Whig could proclaim his principles in Louisiana and in Massachusetts alike....While the Whig and the Democratic parties differed in regard to a Bank, and in regard to a Tariff, and in regard to Distribution, and in regard to the Specie Circular, and in regard to the Sub-Treasury, they agreed on the great question that now agitates the Union, known as the slavery question... "to leave the people...perfectly free to form and regulate their domestic institutions in their own way, subject only to the Federal Constitution."

The reference to 1854 is meant to signal the rise of the Republican party and its divisive interest in abolitionizing the country. According to Douglas' story, the founding political parties in America, Whigs and Democrats, both national in their outlook, jointly adopted popular sovereignty as the correct resolution of the slavery question. Each state was to decide whether it was to be free or slave. Slavery was never to be a national issue but one local to each state. The nation had traditionally enjoyed peace on the slavery question. It is only the new Republican party that in the past four years has come to disrupt that peace by insisting on a new counterprecedent, a uniform antislave policy (i.e., abolition) as a national platform.

Douglas reprises this plan in slightly different variations many times throughout the debates. In his opening at Jonesboro, he gives almost a verbatim rehash of the precedents and counterprecedents of his Ottawa openings, with only slight alternations at Jonesboro to accommodate the more southern audience (chapter 9). Hardly a debate goes by when Douglas, in at least one round, does not invoke the names of Washington, Jefferson, Madison, Webster, and Clay as history makers who put the principle of popular sovereignty first for the country. In authoring the Kansas Bill with that same principle foremost, Douglas effectively makes himself a scion of this legacy.

In his opening at Galesburg, he mentions that he has been working tirelessly on behalf of popular sovereignty for the past four years, both as a matter of conviction and commitment, "in public and private." He categorizes his opposition to Lecompton as opposition to a counterprecedent, for, as he saw it, Lecompton flagrantly violated the popular sovereignty of the voters of Kansas. In his opening at Alton, he affirms that no power on earth has the right to force a constitution on an unwilling people. In his rejoinder, he claims to care more about popular sovereignty "than all the negroes in Christendom." He starts the debates avowing the principle of self-government and he ends them declaring self-government "our only hope."

Lincoln also brings a blueprint of history to the debates, but the blueprint differs radically from Douglas'. In his rejoinder at Freeport, he briefly raises the anti-slavery platform that unites the Republicans on a history-making course. In his Jonesboro reply, he claims that the Founding Fathers did not make slavery, but found it, found it to be evil, and set it on a course of gradual extinction. In his Charleston rejoinder, Lincoln allows that the country has never had peace with slavery and the only way to maintain peace is to keep it on the same course of containment and gradual elimination that the Founders intended for it. In his Galesburg reply, Lincoln is more direct about the principles that animate positive history for the Republicans. Slavery is a moral wrong, and if one does not believe that history needs to evolve in consonance with that premise, one need not seek membership in the Republican party. In his rounds at Quincy and Alton, Lincoln describes the founding of the Republican party as a history-making event, one intended to correct the wrongs of the Kansas Act and to restore slavery on the course the Founders set for it.

By the end of the debates, the precedents and counterprecedents of Douglas and Lincoln have been clearly laid out. Douglas' precedents are popular sovereignty and state's rights, and his counterprecedents are the efforts to impose uniform policy across the territories and states. Lincoln's precedents are the evils of slavery, and his counterprecedents are policies that seek to advance the union cause while remaining morally insensitive to slavery.

Precedent and counterprecedent plans represent the speaker's decision about how the historical world can be coherently filtered, regardless of whether the speaker has convincing historical data to support the filter. Speakers may and often do push certain historical blueprints well beyond their historical understanding. Neither Lincoln nor Douglas was an expert in American history. Both formulated their blueprint of history as much from their political imagination as from their knowledge of the actual past. The debates gave both an appreciation of how much more history they needed to understand before they could feel they could defend their precedent and counterprecedent plans credibly before the most exacting of audiences. After the debates, both realized they needed more information about American history in order to support their special take on it. And both sought out such information prior to the 1860 presidential campaign (Johannsen, 1989).

From a strategic point of view, speakers must lay out precedent plans if they want to indicate the basic furniture of their historical "position" in public discourse. A strategy to avoid a precedent plan is conceivable when a speaker has more to gain by attacking a standing position than to formulate a position of one's own. This strategy, however, leaves the speaker with the capacity to be responsive without being predictive. Political candidates must be predictive for their audiences. Consequently, neither Lincoln or Douglas could avoid tactics to express precedent plans.

Speakers must lay out counterprecedents if they want to acknowledge the furniture of positions that counter their own. A strategy to avoid counter-precedents is conceivable when a speaker has a good reason to focus only on constructive solutions. This could happen when the audience has little patience to hear alternatives rejected or does not know to expect them. In the heat of a contentious campaign, at a time when political argument, constructive and refutative, was entertainment, and when each was an agent of the other's counterprecedents, Lincoln and Douglas could scarcely have avoided making counterprecedents part of their public models.

## Conspiracy

The conspiracy plan describes public space abstractions in the historical world, in the manner of precedents and counterprecedents. The conspiracy plan, unlike precedents and like counterprecedents, always depicts a negative focus on a public model. The conspiracy plan is a charge that others have participated in a deceptive plot to deform a public model in predictable ways. A conspiracy focus is what allows the Plans module to tell its impersonal story about a social world where the counteragents of counterprecedent history use the public mask and motive of precedent to get their private purposes accomplished. The conspiracy focus is a consolidation of the precedent and counterprecedent foci into a single public focus (Fig. 7.5). The covering relationship between the precedent and counterprecedent focus is made possible under four conditions. First, the conspirators and their counterprecedent motives are secret, at least not widely shared as public space abstractions. Second, the conspirators are themselves agents who have the role qualifications and even representative power to make credible the motions of shepherding through legitimate precedents as public space abstractions. Third, the conspirators have the cunning and deceptive intent to use legitimate public argument as a cover for the unleashing of the counterprecedent scenario. Fourth, perhaps most importantly and most overlooked in definitions of conspiracy, the precedent and counterprecedent structures are themselves coextensive, can be realized through the same set of external event classes. For example, suppose we allow that Congress raising the funding to the National Endowment for the Arts will lead to more artistic initiatives in the country. In the conspiratorial mindset, the same material act must be stuffable into a contradictory and darker narrative: Congress raising the funding to the National Endowment for the Arts will incense the taxpayers, who will demand that the Endowment be eliminated—which was the Congress plan all along: Funding it better will kill it. In a conspiracy plan, contrary principles in contrary stories are threaded through common

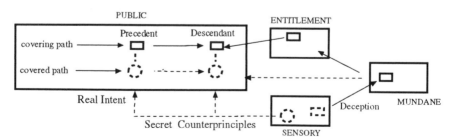

FIG. 7.5.   The conspiracy plan.

event sequences. The representation of conspiracy always requires this take of doubles working their way through a single convergent series that diverges only at the very end.

Conspiracy representations do not require human agents as instigators of the conspiracy.[6] Laws against monopoly and unfair trade assume that these practices are illegal conspiracies against the invisible hand of blind market forces. The precedent structures used for cover are not discrete human actions in discrete situations. They are rather abstract market forces used to represent aggregations of human behavior pooled across thousands and tens of thousands transactions. The inside trader is a conspirator who manipulates the market in the legitimate guise of risk-taking capitalist, seeming to remain vulnerable, like everyone else, to the market's invisible hand.

Conspiracy plans abound in the Lincoln/Douglas debates and they tactically express themselves throughout. In the opening at Ottawa and many rounds thereafter, Douglas portrays the rise of the national Republican party as a cover for a sectionalist effort to abolitionize the country. He indicts Lincoln and Senator Lyman Trumbull as the agents of the conspiracy in Illinois.

In his reply at Ottawa and again at Freeport, Lincoln constructs an alternative conspiracy plan, one where Douglas and the Democrats use the Kansas Act, the defeat of the Chase Amendment, and Dred Scott as a cover for a clandestine effort to nationalize slavery. According to Lincoln, Douglas all but admitted such a conspiracy was in the works when Douglas has a falling out with the southern Democrats on the Lecompton affair.

In his opening at Charleston, Lincoln opens a third conspiracy plan against Douglas. He repeats Trumbull's charge that Douglas and the Democrats, ostensibly public champions of popular sovereignty for the citizens of Kansas, in fact conspired behind the scenes to deprive these citizens of a free referendum on the slavery question. According to Lincoln's Charleston argument, Douglas is a conspirator and a hypocrite besides, because the principle he preaches everywhere, popular sovereignty, is the very one he denies to the people of Kansas when no one is looking.

In the Galesburg debate and thereafter, Douglas opens a fourth conspiracy plan against Lincoln and the Republicans, accusing them of conspiring with the Buchanan Democrats to elect Lincoln and to defeat Douglas. In his opening in the final debate at Alton, Douglas complains that every Democrat office holder "loses his head" when he dares back Douglas instead of Lincoln.

We can summarize these four conspiracy plans as follows:[7]

---

[6]We are indebted to Phil Tompkins for this point.

[7]Zarefsky (1990) chronicled these four sites of conspiracy in the debates.

Douglas' conspiracy representations against Lincoln:

1. Lincoln and his cronies are using "Republican party" principles to further abolition.
2. Lincoln and Buchanan are using "Democratic party" principles to defeat popular sovereignty.

Lincoln's conspiracy representations against Douglas:

1. Douglas and his cronies are using "popular sovereignty" to nationalize slavery.
2. Douglas and his cronies are using "popular sovereignty" to diminish "popular sovereignty."

When there are alternative conspiracy plans, how does one make a decision about their respective plausibility? The question is a challenging one because both the legitimate cover and the illegitimate goals sought trade on a common sequence of events. Curiously, Lincoln rises to the challenge. He raises an interesting argument about why his conspiracy plan (1) is more plausible than Douglas' conspiracy plan (1). The argument involves Occam's razor: the fewer assumptions needed for a series of event classes to unfold in a conspiracy plan, the more plausible the plan. Douglas' conspiracy plan, constructed against Lincoln, requires that the Republicans risk a war between the states in order to see their secret plans evolve. But, as Lincoln points out, the conspiracy plan he constructs against Douglas requires no such drastic assumptions:

> There is no danger of the people of Kentucky shouldering their muskets to bring slavery upon us. There is no danger of our going there to make war upon them. What is necessary to make slavery national? It is simply the next Dred Scott decision. It is simply for the Supreme Court to decide that no state under the constitution can exclude slavery, just as they and the territorial legislatures cannot exclude it from the limits of the territory.

Strategically, conspiracy is not at all effective as a plan of rhetoric because it suggests a public model that is systemically paranoid. It creates a world where nothing is as it seems. The forces of truth and goodness are really forces of falsehood and evil. Its most direct strategic function in the debates is to bog down the tactical opponent in charges that need to be addressed but that can never be refuted. The result of such plans is to steal the time the opponent has to develop a constructive public focus of his or her own.

## Historical

Historical plans provide yet another focus on a public model, this time on the alignment between mundane and public spaces. The historical plan directly links information from the detailed mundane space to the public space (Fig. 7.6). It provides mundane detail with which to fill in public space abstractions. A historical focus allows the Plans module to tell its impersonal story about truth and falsehood with the benefit of specific "factual" detail.

Historical plans are easily confused with precedent and counterprecedent, so it is useful to distinguish them right away. When we think of historical arguments as undergirding public space abstractions, our conventional way of thinking about historical argument is less from the vantage of historical plans (as we define them here) than from the vantage of legal precedent and counterprecedent. Statutory, constitutional, and case law are rules of language that construct a public sphere through their restrictiveness, their closing off of other possibilities of language, interpretation, and interaction (White, 1973, 1984). History, as a plan of rhetoric, consists in efforts to stabilize existing public space abstractions by furnishing them with the credibility of fleshed out detail and descriptions involving actual persons engaged in concrete events. In this sense, historical plans live symbiotically in rhetorical design with precedent and counterprecedent plans.

If historical plans need to be distinguished from precedent and counter-precedent, they also need to be distinguished from the practice of writing history from a disciplinary point of view. Disciplinary history need not service rhetoric at all; it may involve only finding and organizing archival information from the past, previously unnoticed. White's image of the ideal legal mind, in essence, is the imaginative historian who can draw on a dense and noncanonical narration to expose the inadequacy of reigning public abstractions. White's (1984) insistence on the importance of the lawyer's doing history as part of legal research, rather than falling back on scripted historical plans of rhetoric, is that it allows the lawyer to come up with descriptions of events that do not easily fit into the existing categories of interpretation. It thus provides the lawyer with the basis for new interpretations, new laws,

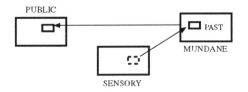

FIG. 7.6.   The historical plan.

and new publics. White's ideal of the lawyer/historian is not to be mistaken for the speaker relying on history as a plan of rhetoric in the sense we are now discussing. The speaker using historical plans (of rhetorical design) may, at one extreme, approximate White's ideal historian if he or she seeks to put forth a public model that is entirely new to the audience and to the larger culture it inhabits.

But more often, the speaker using history as a rhetorical plan only wishes to undergird the designed stereotypes of an existing public model with supporting detail. Maintaining the past through stable ideological filters, the speaker employing historical plans relies on canonical more than noncanonical event-telling, a form of event-telling where the past can remain objective, stable, predictable, controllable, and so serviceable for an existing set of public abstractions.

Consider briefly the role of the historical plan in the debates. In his opening at Ottawa, Douglas uses an interesting manifestation of the historical plan that we call the public autobiography. In the public autobiography, the speaker goes into his or her own personal past and raises details that bear on the public space.

The public autobiography bears some resemblance to the public confessional but with an important difference. In the public confessional, the speaker bares for the record information that runs counter to the speaker's inherited pledges to a constituent organization. In public autobiography, the speaker unearths heretofore private information that is not directly aligned with any of the speaker's public commitments. Despite the lack of a direct alignment to the public space, the public autobiography remains public discourse (controlled by Plans) and not event-telling from one's personal past or, more artistically, literary autobiography, neither of which requires explicit public models. The public autobiography conditions opportunities for placing information in the public space that would otherwise not be conditioned. We call this conditioning alignment the "no-malice" alignment. A no-malice alignment requires that information be known about the immediate opponent to support his or her face. This face support is then used as a basis for launching an attack on the opponent in the public space that seems credible and disinterested.[8] The no-malice alignment in effect dampens the suspicion that the speaker's public representations against the opponent are

---

[8]The "no-malice" alignment is, strictly speaking, an intricate coordination between Plans and Tactics. It requires that information be known about the immediate opponent to support his or her face. The immediate opponent and the potential of face support are known only to the Tactics module. Tactics conditions opportunities for the Plans module. We say more about Plans/Tactics coordination in the next chapter and again in chapter 10.

personally motivated. In the no-malice alignment, it is unsurprising to find the harshest public words against the opponent followed by the kindest personal utterance. In his Ottawa opening, Douglas trashes Lincoln in a conspiracy plan for plotting to destroy the American party system:

> ...for I quote them from the platform of the Republican party—the platform made by himself and others at the time the Republican party was first formed...and the bargain was made to dissolve and kill off and destroy the old Whig and Democratic parties, and transfer each of their members, bound hand and foot, into the Abolition party, under the directions of Giddings and Chase...

but immediately after, unleashes a historical focus to pay his personal respects to Lincoln:

> In the remarks I have made upon this platform, and the positions of Mr. Lincoln upon it, I mean nothing personal, disrespectful or unkind to that gentleman. I have known him for nearly twenty-five years. We had many points of sympathy when I first got acquainted with him. We were both comparatively boys—both struggling with poverty in a strange land for our support. I am a humble school teacher in the town of Winchester, and he a flourishing grocery keeper in the town of Salem. He was more successful in his occupation than I, and thus became more fortunate in this world's goods. Mr. Lincoln is one of those peculiar men that has performed with admirable skill in every occupation that he ever attempted.

The no-malice alignment is not only a useful way of using personal history to soften a preceding attack; it is well suited as a credible platform with which to launch into one. After crediting Lincoln with being an admirable fellow in his youth, Douglas turns to the darker side of Lincoln's personal past, where he describes Lincoln as riding a wave of abolition sentiment and selling out his country while a congressman in the war against Mexico.

It is instructive to distinguish the public autobiography and its attendant "no-malice" alignment from the satisfaction of humanness goals. Many politicians, in the heat of battle, launch into public autobiographies in order, eventually, to slam the opponent harder than they normally would be able to get away with. But before the slam, their depictions of life with the opponent can seem warm, down-home, and friendly. This leads to the satisfaction of humanness goals with the audience. Once the slam comes, and often before, the audience is likely to recognize that they are not listening to a spontaneous outpouring of affection. They are rather being led through the space of the sensory with the opponent in order to intensify the magnitude of the opponent's personal betrayal in committing public harm. The public autobiography exposes the opponent's humanness only to diminish his or her public predictiveness. If the public autobiography works as intended, then it should do little or nothing to satisfy the speaker's own goals to appear human and humane.

Lincoln himself uses historical plans often in order to undermine many of Douglas's public representations against him. In his reply at Ottawa, for example, he goes into minute detail about the Springfield convention in order to refute Douglas' representation that he had sponsored the resolutions passed there. His reading of his speech of 1854 that rejected abolitionism was another tactical use of a historical plan structure to counter Douglas' representation of himself and the Republicans as embracing abolition. And Lincoln uses historical plans at Ottawa to correct some of Douglas' autobiographical description of him—about his congressional actions during the Mexican War and even whether he ever worked in a saloon.

Historical plans are used to explore American history from a fixed ideological perspective. Did the Founders believe in a uniform slave policy (one implication of the house divided doctrine)? Did the signers of the Declaration intend to include blacks in the "all men equal" clause? Because neither Lincoln nor Douglas was a historian, their historical plans contain more hypothetical supposition and hearsay than factual detail.[9] In his Ottawa and Jonesboro opening, for example, and in his Alton finish, Douglas conjectures that if the Founders had wanted a uniform slave policy, they would have forced slavery in all the colonies, as 12 of the original 13 colonies allowed slavery. In his opening at Jonesboro, Douglas surmises that if the signers of the Declaration believed that negroes were equal, they would have freed them. And at Galesburg, he wonders whether they could have been "hypocritical" enough to declare blacks equal and then keep them in slavery.

Lincoln in his reply at Galesburg, his rejoinder at Quincy, and his reply at Alton sets up a contrary history of the signers. He claims that even southern sympathizers, like Brooks, admitted that slavery as an economic institution was moribund until the cotton gin made slavery more profitable.

---

[9]Zarefsky (1990, p. 154) reported that both Lincoln and Douglas were probably "unsatisfied" with their histories, as both relied at key points on "assumption or unsupported inference rather than evidence."

He notes that until the Kansas Act, no one would ever hear talk of blacks not being included in the Declaration. He reports that many southerners opposed the Declaration because they had assumed all along that document had insisted on the equality of blacks. Interestingly, both Douglas and Lincoln mention Henry Clay as a champion in their divergent histories of slavery in America.

Strategically, historical plans are necessary for speakers who want audiences to take their precedents and counterprecedents seriously. No speaker who argues from a constructive position can afford not to have "history" on his or her side. As we have seen from the preceding examples, Lincoln and Douglas resurrect history less from authoritative documents than from signs, isolated testimony, hearsay, and hypotheticals. For both speakers, history is not a way to establish their precedents in axiomatic fashion. It is rather a mode of recollection to be summoned when the precedents they offer are put under stress.

### Principle

The Principle plan represents yet another focus on a public model, in this case on the direct alignment between the sensory and public spaces (Fig. 7.7). A principle focus allows the Plans module to tell its impersonal story about truth and falsehood with the benefit of correct principles from the heart and the gut.

The principle plan is a construction not necessarily indicative of the speaker's real convictions, any more than the public confessional plan is truly indicative of what the speaker "really thinks." Speakers deploy a principle plan to indicate an immediacy between their principles and their public commitments.

As one can see from the visual depiction of all the plans so far discussed, the principle plan carves out a focus of alignments that is contained in many other plans. The result is that the principle plan is highly interactive with

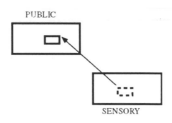

FIG. 7.7.   The principle plan.

many other plans, meaning that the principle plan is active when many other plans become active. For this reason, it is worthwhile to examine some of these interactions.

Consider the principle focus as an adjunct to organizational authority. Organizational authority, we recall, melds the voice of the speaker with the voice of the group, which leaves a trail of suspicion that the individual speaker may have made compromises in assuming leadership in the group. The use of a principle focus, as an adjunct to organizational authority, defeats this suspicion. It indicates that the speaker's commitment to the public space is personal as well as civic or professional, a matter of conviction and not just camaraderie.

The public confessional, which also aligns the speaker's sensory states to the public space, is mainly a preemptive structure. Speakers use the public confessional to offset the fear that their inheritance from the group that empowers them is blind and uncritical. Activated with the public confessional, the principle focus can make the speaker seem more than a human being in charge of a group; it can also make the speaker seem like a public leader hewing to a standard higher than the group over whom one has official representative power. This case does not occur in the Lincoln/Douglas debates, but imagine a case when the individual is saddled with a group that seeks a more expedient, less principled organization of the public space than the speaker desires. Or, more realistically, the individual wants to show him- or herself to be a public citizen over and above a leader of an interested group. In these cases, the speaker can deploy a principle focus as an adjunct to the public confessional. This allows the speaker a way of indicating that the public space sought after is principled even beyond the standards of the groups now trying to seek and maintain recognition within it. An example is a chief executive officer (CEO) of Acme tuna fish company who boasts that Acme obeys all federal guidelines for catching tuna in a way that is not dangerous to dolphins, but then goes on to "confess" that the guidelines in place remain far too lax and that the entire industry, including Acme, will need to do better.

We now further examine the interaction between principle and precedents and counterprecedents. Precedents and counterprecedents can be described in terms of the event classes that constitute them. Moreover, these event classes can leave concealed, moreover, the principles that they are meant to instantiate. We need the precedent and counterprecedent focus to be accompanied by the principle focus to know exactly what lessons the precedents and counterprecedents are supposed to carry. Douglas saw the Kansas Bill of 1854 as an important precedent, but we do not in actuality understand the event as a precedent until we know the principle (popular sovereignty) Douglas meant it to embody.

When the precedent/counterprecedent focus is decoupled from the principle focus, the understanding of the focus can remain murky. As a result of such decoupling, precedents can be contested, especially when there is no agreement on the principle they are supposed to carry. Douglas maintained that the 1850 Compromise was a precedent Clay established to affirm the principle of popular sovereignty. Lincoln retorted that Clay, the Great Compromiser, took the 1850 Compromise to mean exactly what its name implied: a compromise forcing all parties to get some things in return for giving up others. Further, sometimes speakers can leave their opponent and audience at sea because they delay revealing the principles underlying certain precedents. The "founding of the Republican party" is an event structure put on stage in the first minute of the debates. Douglas gives it a principled meaning (the nationalization of abolition) within the same time frame. But as we have seen in his delay in revamping his organizational authority, Lincoln is restrained, if not slow, to bring forth his own meaning of the principles that were founded when the Republicans were. Not until the later debates, as we have seen, is Lincoln expansive about what makes a Republican a Republican. Precedents are very unstable events structures without a principle focus to pin them down.

Finally, we examine the interaction between the principle and the conspiracy plans. As with normal precedents and counterprecedents, the events in a conspiracy structure can be described entirely in terms of the event classes that make them up. The principles and secret counterprinciples that indicate both the "meaning" of the conspirator's cover and the secrets covered up can remain hidden. Speakers can use a principle focus to indicate what values they are seeming (contrary to fact) to further and what values they are furthering in fact, under cover. At Charleston, for example, the bulk of Lincoln's discussion can be understood as Douglas' conspiracy to change one version of a Senate bill for another without fair consultation. Yet it requires the addition of an explicit principle focus to understand why anyone would think this—or any—conspiracy, apart from its secrecy, is wrong. Without a principle focus, Lincoln cannot communicate how this conspiracy offends his basic convictions; he cannot communicate how, in his view, Douglas is restricting voter choice under the pretext of promising it to the citizens of Kansas without restriction.

Let us briefly review the principle plan through the debates. Douglas traps Lincoln, we recall, by imputing abolitionist principles to Lincoln and the Republicans. We also indicated above that Douglas does not touch Lincoln's principle about the immorality of slavery once he revamps the organization of the Republicans around that principle.

The case is not symmetrical because Lincoln does great tactical damage to Douglas' seeming invincible (at the start of the debates) principle of popular sovereignty. Douglas opens a principle plan for himself that links him to the positive principle of popular sovereignty. "I publicly own up to my principles and can avow them everywhere" is a frequent refrain of Douglas throughout the debates. When Douglas finally gets around to answering some of Lincoln's questions about popular sovereignty, the seeming clarity and integrity of Douglas' principle plan starts to come undone. Although affirming popular sovereignty in the principle plan, Douglas also supports the Dred Scott decision, as a good Buchanan Democrat, in an organizational authority plan. The problem is the two plans do not easily cohere. The Dred Scott decision affirmed that territories do not have the right to exclude slavery from their limits. Douglas' popular sovereignty doctrine affirmed that the citizens of a territory do have that right, as well as the right to include slavery if they wish. Being a good Democrat seemed to threaten Douglas' personal principle of popular sovereignty and vice versa.

To reconcile these plans, Douglas offers a structure to the design called unfriendly local legislation. The idea is that, despite Dred Scott, citizens of a territory, appealing to unfriendly local legislation, can agree to exclude slavery if they find it anathema to local custom and practice. Lincoln logically deduces that if one upholds the letter of Dred Scott, and Dred Scott affirms the right of property in a slave, then no other decision, certainly not laws of unfriendly local legislation, can overrule this right. Lincoln performs the deduction as follows:

> I think it follows, and I submit to the consideration of men capable of arguing, whether as I state it, in syllogistic form, the argument has any fault in it?
>
> Nothing in the Constitution or laws of any State can destroy a right distinctly and expressly affirmed in the Constitution of the United States.
>
> The right of property in a slave is distinctly and expressly affirmed in the Constitution of the United States.
>
> Therefore, nothing in the Constitution or laws of any State can destroy the right of property in a slave.
>
> I believe that no fault can be pointed out in that argument; assuming the truth of the premises, the conclusion, so far as I have capacity at all to understand it, follows inevitably.

What had started the debates as Douglas' trump card, popular sovereignty, as part of a principles plan, the principle from his gut he could declare anywhere north and south, seemed, after Lincoln's deduction, nowhere to be found. It was a principle fitting onto no noncontradictory public abstraction. Dred Scott, according to Lincoln's deduction, had obliterated it out of existence. In his rejoinder at Quincy, Lincoln calls Douglas' defeated popular sovereignty principle "as thin as the shadow of a starving pigeon used to make homeopathic soup."

What is the strategic difference between Lincoln's use of principle and Douglas'? Strategically, principle is an effective plan for a speaker to use when the speaker's own principles are societally accepted, clear, uncompromised, and well substantiated through events, and when the opponent's principles are societally repudiated, muddy, conflicted, and poorly substantiated. In the early debates, Douglas operates from the assumption that his principles (popular sovereignty) are highly accepted and Lincoln's (abolition) are highly repudiated. On this assumption alone, Douglas would expect principle to work as a useful plan on his behalf. Lincoln wiggles out of the assumption that he is an abolitionist, but then turns the tables on Douglas in the later debates by showing that his motivating principle (to limit slavery) is far clearer and more implementable than Douglas' popular sovereignty. Dred Scott has made popular sovereignty not only unclear but seemingly unconstitutional on every clear interpretation. Lincoln knew what he was defending and Douglas did not. Why did Lincoln wait until the end of the debates to make this apparent? The least interesting hypothesis, that Lincoln did not realize the clarity of his own position over Douglas' until the end, cannot be ruled out. There are more interesting hypotheses, however, having to do with Lincoln's self-conscious reliance on the print audience. Knowing that the debates were to be as an unfolding drama for the print audience, Lincoln may have wanted his most damaging plan against Douglas—principle— to be unleased as part of a climactic effect near the end.

### Venue

Venue is the only plan focus to involve the local space, more specifically, the alignment of the public and local spaces. A venue focus allows the Plans module to tell its impersonal story about truth and falsehood with an understanding that only necessary public abstractions are being dealt with; unnecessary ones can be dispensed with. We mentioned earlier that, tactically understood, the venue plan means that certain public abstractions can be deferred to later rhetorical situations.

Public spaces, as abstractions and to a large extent speaker defined, have flexible boundary conditions. Further, speakers can gerrymander boundaries to fit their situational circumstances, which include their power in the situation to define the venue unilaterally, without requiring the input from others, including opponents.

An important function of the venue plan is to control the structure put at issue, to control the makeup of the game board and the pieces put at issue in rhetorical design. Speakers will want the object classes that favor their own interests to fall within the venue of the public space as they define it, and as they think the opponent should define it. Conversely, they will want, if possible, the object classes that favor the opponent to fall outside the venue of the public space of the interaction. They will want the opponent's agenda to be found "out of bounds" if they can seize the opportunity to make such line calls. When speakers make efforts to do this, the plan of venue becomes a visible part of rhetorical design.

All along, our discussion has presupposed that speakers and opponents are fairly accepting of the other's determinations of venue. They have thus far seemed to agree that the basic furniture in the public space for one is furniture for the other. What does it mean, then, for this presupposition to be suspended? It means that the speaker seeks to defer the opponent's concerns to a later time or place when other decision-makers can then pick it up. It means that the speaker seeks to defer the opponent's concerns, insofar as they seem valid, from the public to the local space. We call this space of deferred concerns "local" because to designate an issue "a local matter" means deferring it to another time or another decision-making body that is closer to the issue. A space for deferrables can go beyond the strict meaning of local to indicate a higher body, like the Supreme Court, as well as a more proximate one. Either rendering of a local space is depicted in Fig. 7.8.

We now examine the course of venue plans in the Lincoln/Douglas debates. We have seen in examples about abortion how it makes a significant

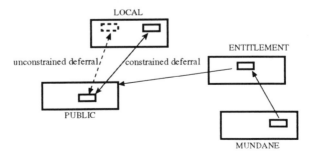

FIG. 7.8. The venue plan.

difference whether a speaker is perceived as making a constrained or unconstrained deferral of public space objects to the local space. Lincoln is keenly aware of the difference, and Douglas would have held his side more impressively had he been.

In his reply at Ottawa and at later places in the debate, Lincoln raises an issue that turns on whether a deferral to a local space was meant as constrained or unconstrained. To understand the issue, some background is useful. Douglas' principle of popular sovereignty had involved defining the slave issue as belonging to a local space. For Douglas and many Democrats, slavery and the agitation surrounding it were caused in the first place by mapping it into a public space, giving it attention and priority on the national agenda. Popular sovereignty was a way of deferring the slavery question in the territories to local spaces, where the issue could be disposed of across a distributed range of local venues. The sloganistic content of popular sovereignty was "let the people [in each locality] decide."

A point of contention was the following: In deferring slavery to a local issue, was the deferral to be constrained or unconstrained? A constrained deferral meant that local bodies had very limited control over the terms of their decision making. An unconstrained deferral meant that the issue would be given over completely to local control, and that localities had total freedom over the terms in which to dispose of the issue.

Lincoln's position on deferring slavery to a local issue was unambiguous. He did not reject local control, but only the idea of deferring slavery to local control in an unconstrained way. He uses historical plans throughout the debates to show that a territory, left to its own course, becomes a slave state when settlers are allowed to enter the territory with slaves. As long as slavery is allowed in a territory during the time of its settlement toward statehood, Lincoln contends, it is a foregone conclusion that the citizens will ratify a state constitution that allows slaves. For this reason, Lincoln associated the unconstrained rendering of popular sovereignty with a systemic bias toward creating more slave states. Lincoln wanted to eliminate this bias toward more slave states. This did not make Lincoln against more slave states, period. He allows at Freeport that if the citizens of a territory forbid slavery during its settlement, he will (reluctantly, as part of a public confessional) support their ratification of a slave constitution when they are admitted as a state. Lincoln thus offers clear grounds for supporting a constrained version of popular sovereignty as a local principle deferred to a local space.

Douglas' position on popular sovereignty, with respect to venue plans, was ambiguous, and the ambiguity of venue is what gives Lincoln the cause to doubt that Douglas has any clear principle in mind in the principle plan when he goes about defending popular sovereignty.

At times, Douglas associates popular sovereignty with an unconstrained deferral to the local. The issue of slavery is local and there are no strings attached in its forever remaining so. This rendering is evident in Douglas' rejoinder at Ottawa when he defends his interpretation and rejection of the Chase Amendment. Recall (chapter 5) that after the Kansas Act extended the right of the people in the territories to "include" slavery, Chase, a Senator from free Ohio, had asked for amended wording giving the people to right to "include or exclude" slavery. Chase had effectively asked that the possibility of "excluding" slavery be made into a marked category alongside the marked category of "including" slavery. Douglas rejected the amendment, claiming that the right to exclusion was implicitly covered in the generic designation of inclusion. We saw in chapter 5 that Chase had interpreted the Kansas Bill as "verbatim on the record" language, meaning that to commit to the right to "exclude" slavery was to make no firm commitment to the implied right to "include" it. We have also seen earlier in this chapter how the verbatim on the record is related, within the tactical view, to constrained deferrals to the local space.

Lincoln, following Chase, supported only constrained deferrals to the local space and only the verbatim on the record account of the Kansas Bill. He understood that Chase's proposed addition of the "exclude" clause was not redundant. Douglas interpreted the language of Kansas as an unconstrained deferral, a deferral to local control without recourse to a public should the local forum decide matters a certain way. Such an unconstrained deferral is apparent in Douglas's doctrine of unfriendly local legislation. This doctrine allows all jurisdictional control over slavery to revert permanently to the local territory, with no further recourse to the federal government. At other times, however, Douglas seems to define the slavery question as part of a constrained deferral, one permitting further recourse to the federal government. He endorses Dred Scott, after all, which imposes a constraint on slavery in local territories. Dred Scott denies territorial legislatures the right to exclude slavery from their limits. Violation of this local constraint would lead to severe federal recourse against the perpetrator. A citizen in the territories who found his or her slaves being confiscated would have recourse to the highest court in the land.

In his Jonesboro reply, Lincoln shows how Douglas, in refusing to pin down the slavery issue as a constrained or unconstrained deferral to the local, has boxed himself into a contradiction of venue. He says that the people can decide for themselves whether they will permit slaves; and he says they cannot decide for themselves, the decision having been made by the Court. How, Lincoln asks, can one agree to uphold the constitution under Dred Scott ("slaves can't be excluded from the territories") and then, in the same breath, agree to let the constitution be rescinded ("slaves may or may not be excluded from territories") in local venues? This is the contradiction of venue that Lincoln charges Douglas with committing. Douglas had indiscriminately juxtaposed constrained and unconstrained deferrals to the local space in ways that committed contradiction (Fig. 7.9).

Douglas' internal contradiction affords Lincoln the opportunity to explain how his mutual deployment of organizational authority and the public confessional is anything but contradictory. Lincoln announces that as a member of the federal legislature, he is duty bound to uphold the constitution and the courts (organizational authority), even on matters with which he personally disagrees, like the fugitive slave law (public confessional). According to Lincoln, one violates one's oath if one does not uphold what the law is, regardless of what one would like it to be. And if the law through Dred Scott protects slave property and forbids the exclusion of slaves from a territory, one is obligated to uphold it as law. Personal regret for Lincoln. But not the public contradiction it had become for Douglas.

Tactically, the venue plan is useful for dealing with points of contention that the speaker cannot win or control in the immediate situation. Much of the tactical cat and mouse of the debates happens because Lincoln and Douglas cannot agree on the public abstractions to be debated. Douglas sees much to lose and nothing to gain by keeping slavery a central issue. He

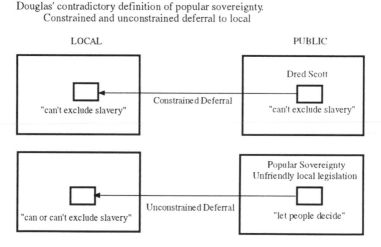

FIG. 7.9.   Douglas' contradictory venue arguments over slavery.

cannot wrest the northern vote from Lincoln, and trying to appease the northern vote will just alienate the South. Slavery is a structure he cannot win with or control so he tries to defer it. Lincoln, on the other hand, is silenced from public discourse if he goes along with deferring it. It is the one issue that, to him, accounts for his party organization, the southern conspiracy he now finds himself opposing, the violation of historical precedents, and many other factors giving weight to the moment of the debates. In such a contest over venue, the speaker who wishes to defer wins by getting the audience to go along; the speaker who wishes not to defer wins by getting the audience to reject deferral. When the audience is split, so are the winners. Put another way, any voter who thought the debates should be about slavery had to support Lincoln; any voter who wished to defer the slavery question to another day had to wear a Douglas button.

To sum up, the Plans module works to create a consistent story about truth and falsehood in the social world. It does this by focusing on patterned alignments within or across component spaces. These foci function as plans to organize the design structure according to an emergent model of the public. The emergent public model implicit in converging plan foci allows the Plans module to find truth and falsehood for its story. The Plans module relies on plans with positive value, namely, organizational authority, precedent, history, and principle, as structure to fill in truth in its story; it relies on the public confessional to harmonize two positive plans, principle and organizational authority, that would not otherwise fit within a consistent tale of social truth. It relies on venue to define the scope and range of its statements about truth; it relies on plans with negative value, namely, counterprecedent, counterprinciple, and conspiracy, as structure to fill in falsehoods.

## THE PUBLIC SPACE AS THE ANCHORING FOCUS OF A PUBLIC MODEL

Plans are views of an entire public model, but every view is designed to give greatest luminance to the public space. Like a cook more interested in having the food savored than giving away the ingredients, the Plans module generates plans that are designed to make the public space seem to stand alone, autonomous. Precedent, principle, organizational authority, and other positive plans are designed to mask their dependencies in supporting spaces. The mask is functional for enhancing the speaker's goal of on the record predictiveness, as a speaker's predictability erodes when it is understand how much fleeting contingency it is based on. Only counterprecedent, counterprinciple, conspiracy—the plans that can include the live opponent as a member of the abstracted class of counteragents—are designed to lead the audience back to the contingency of the opponent's existence in supporting spaces, explaining their actions through greed, error, bias, prejudice, the hunger for power, lunacy, false consciousness, and other variations on the motif of the bad motive. The opponent's plans can be traced back to his or her feet of clay. But the speaker's plans rest in revealed truth. They are offered to leave audiences thinking that the speaker's positive plans are one and the same with the stand-alone furniture of the speaker's public space.

The asymmetry assumed by Plans is not confined to political rhetoric. Gilbert and Mulkay (1984) documented the same asymmetry when academic scientists reason about their own work and the work of competitors from a Plans perspective. They found, specifically, that scientists tend to explain their own results through natural law, the inexorable process through which the truth reveals itself to the patient and trained mind; yet they explained the findings of competitors with which they questioned or disagreed as rooted in short-lived contingencies that were more tactical than principled, results that they assumed would be proven wrong over time when the truth of the matter finally revealed itself.

In the realm of academe, conventions for the academic paper evolved just so writers could preserve this asymmetry between the basis of their own reasoning (in Plans) and the basis of their opponent's reasoning (in Tactics) (Geisler, 1994). These conventions marked academic writing's transformation into a rhetoric of antirhetoric (chapter 1), a kind of rhetoric that sheltered the writer (but not necessarily opponents) from having to assume the appearance of an interested tactician. In the antirhetoric rhetoric of academic writing, writers new to the genre learned to signal their own plans as falling along a "main path" (a precedent plan) of revealed truth, whereas the plans of competitors had to be explained away as contingent and shorter lived "faulty paths" (counterprinciple; counterprecedent plans), the site of disapproving elaboration and citation (Geisler, 1994; Kaufer & Carley, 1993a; Kaufer & Geisler, 1989). As we see in the next chapter and revisit in chapter 10, conventions of academic rhetoric have tended to eclipse the tactical as a legitimate dimension of knowledge production. Tactics are attributed only to the opponent moved by self-interest more than truth. But conventions of academic writing also pressured writers to intellectualize the tactical dimension, to abstract opponents into faulty paths, to forces of reasoning, groups, desires, or "isms" that were historically wrong-headed.

## RHETORIC AND THE RESCUE OF PUBLICS?

In this chapter, we have identified publics with realist abstractions that guide a speaker's decision making and design. We have not claimed that publics are cognitive reals but reals in the weaker sense that they account for the complexity of rhetorical design, and any attempt to reduce or operationalize them into a nominal reality is to miss important generalizations about the complexity of rhetoric. At the same time, our endorsement of publics as reals is not to be confused with the liberal notion of publics as normative reals, as embodiments of positive civic values poised to monitor the unchecked accumulation of private interest or advantage. Ours is a different realist position about publics, and a different project, from those who seek to reify publics as guides for curbing the accumulation of private advantage. Some prominent writers in this last group (Bitzer, 1978; Dewey, 1946; Farrell, 1993; Habermas, 1962) begin with a liberal narrative of "the general public" having its decision-making function eclipsed with the rise of bourgeois, technocratic, and special-interest groups. Rhetoric, within this narrative, plays a potentially heroic role in the recovery and restoration of a general-interest public. We have two comments to make about this liberal narrative.

First, there is nothing wrong with the narrative as long as one does not assume a simplistic opposition between public and nonpublic interests. Our analysis suggests that a plan for rhetoric is always a focus on a public model, which itself is composed by aligning spheres of public with nonpublic concerns and considerations. It is an illusion to think of a "pure" public interest naturally opposed to the "evil" of individual or nonpublic interests. The private sphere cannot "corrupt" the public sphere (a motif of the liberal narratives) because the public space is already built on the foundation of many nonpublic concerns.

Second, the narrative of rhetoric rescuing the public sphere is implausible if we confuse the public with the clients of rhetorical design. The public is not the client of the speaker; the public, as it exists in the abstraction of a public model, is rather a precondition of planning the design. One hopes that rhetoric does well in the world, but doing well cannot be built into the preconditions of any design art. If there exists such a measurable thing as "serving the public interest" through communication, then no doubt a person expert in rhetorical design will do it. Yet rhetoric can also be designed to do much worse. The narrative of a rhetoric rescuing the public interest is inspirational and compelling drama, but unmistakably wishful if we assume the best case scenarios always work out in the end.

If rhetoric is to change the world in positive ways, it is not only because we have a hopeful rhetorical tradition to look back on, but also because we have a constructive notion of rhetorical design to work toward and an empirical interest in understanding when and why we like the products it produces.

# Eight

# Tactics

Harry Truman was known to quip that he never intended to hurt his political opponents—only to tell the truth and let the truth hurt them. This quip, denying the need for tactics, the need for live give and take with an opponent and audience, indicates the sometimes elevated and aloof vantage of the Plans module in rhetorical design. Although the Plans module may adapt itself during a rhetorical situation in order to maintain consistency, the Plans module adapts as a consequence of changes in structure that result from the Tactics and Events modules foraging into the rhetorical situation. The Plans module never directly forages into it. It remains behind the lines and above the fray, innocent of a battle or a contest, working in solitude on constructing and maintaining a consistent picture of what is true and false about the social world. Plans must remain relatively inert and unresponsive if it is to keep the speaker predictive. Issues are rife with small, complex detail. Were Plans to vary with every variation in detail, the speaker's plans would be as complex as the detail and the speaker would become enigmatic. Consequently, Plans must resist assimilating too much detail if it is to remain effective on the speaker's behalf.

It is left for tactics to manage the small detail in the course of a speaker's being asked to respond to the opponent's call for clarification and elaboration. To achieve responsiveness, a speaker shows how an ever increasing amount of detail can be adjusted to a plan; or how a plan can remain intact without having to handle certain details because of their irrelevance. The speaker in any case cannot possibly anticipate all the relevant detail to which a plan may be held to account to or judge the relevance of detail a priori. The speaker must be agile enough to make these adjustments in interaction with an opponent.

From the Plans view, there is a representational inequality between the abstractions for truth and those for falsehood. The speaker, looking at structure through plans, stands for truth, whereas counteragents are allowed to stand only for falsehood. From the view of Tactics, the structures associated with the speaker and the live opponent are viewed in more symmetrical fashion. Unlike Plans, Tactics does not discriminate the design structure into public and nonpublic spaces. Consequently, unlike Plans, Tactics has no capacity to bestow special luminance on the public space abstractions, which emphasize the speaker's predictability and gray out the social, personal, and private contingencies that compromise that emphasis. The contingency of the social, personal, and private are as much fair game—and, typically, more interesting game—for tactics as the austere abstractions of the public space.

Further, unlike Plans, which knows nothing about the live opponent, Tactics does have the capacity to view the opponent's structure as part of the design space. The tactical speaker leaves the pose of aloofness to enter the fray, to engage an opponent on a more level playing field. This is not to say that the Tactics module views the speaker's design structure and the opponent's from some assumption of fairness. On the contrary, the tactical speaker is focused on beating the opponent in a self-interested, often self-serving, way. It is to say, however, that the Tactics module proceeds from the assumption that beating the opponent requires convincing the audience (perhaps even the opponent him- or herself if included in the audience to be persuaded) that one has been responsive. Unlike Plans, which is content to work on stories to present truth and falsehood, the Tactics module understands that winning requires more than telling truths and dismissing falsehood. The audience must appreciate that the speaker can hold one's own in the give and take of exchange. And holding one's own with an opponent requires positing certain symmetrical assumptions between the self and the opponent, assumptions contrastive with Plans.

Tactical speakers, for example, recognize that their motivation to win can be, must be, no less than the opponent's. They recognize themselves as tactically motivated no less than their opponent. They see, unlike the Plans perspective, no long-term interest in truth—only a shorter lived and competitive interest in winning rhetorical situations or contests of rhetoric that span multiple arenas. They acknowledge that their own point of view, no less than the opponent's, can be represented as pieces on a game board seeking positional strength and, eventually, domination. The Plans module, knowing social truth only as a Homeric epic, is blind to how an opponent's involvement can degrade the conditions of audience receptivity within a specific rhetorical situation. The Tactics module, in contrast, views the design structure only as it references the self and the opponent's competitive involvement with one another. The Tactics module knows that to win the contest with the opponent, it needs to be responsive by making sure that the self does more damage to the opponent's structure than the opponent does to the structure belonging to the self.

## ENTERING THE RHETORICAL SITUATION

Tactics marks one of the interfaces between rhetorical design and rhetorical situations. A host of assumptions follow from this that we need to elaborate before going further.

As a forager through the rhetorical situation monitoring the competitive involvement with the opponent, the Tactics module takes a very different view on the design structure than Plans. In some ways, the Tactics module "sees" more in the design structure than Plans. In other ways, it "sees" less. We consider each case in turn.

Consider first what Tactics can see in the design structure that Plans cannot. Tactics can see the structure of the design contributed by the opponent. For Plans, rhetorical design is a solitary activity, one person constructing a social world of truth and falsehood. The only structures of the design viewed are structures associated with the self, what the self thinks about truth and falsehood. For Tactics, rhetorical design is a competitive activity, a speaker and an opponent doing battle over who can produce the design with the fewest vulnerabilities. To take action on this assumption, the Tactics module can discriminate between the design structure contributed by the speaker and the structure contributed by the opponent.

Now consider what Tactics cannot see in the design structure that Plans can. The Plans module can take intricate and integrated views of the design structure. Plans can see the design structure in terms of an intact public model. It can see the various patterned subsets of these models known as generic plans and can integrate these plans with the specific design structure to make specific plans. It can register whether a public model is consistent or inconsistent. It can take action to recompose the alignment of object structures across component spaces to restore an inconsistent public model into a consistent one.

The views Tactics takes on the design structure are less intricate and integrated. The Tactics module knows nothing about intact public models, or the tools needed to create them as emergent designs: spaces and plans. The vision of Tactics is more short-term and myopic. The Tactics module recognizes in structure only abstracted patterns of a scalar attribute called *vulnerability*. It has the capacity to recognize and reference vulnerability in the design structure and to increase or decrease the vulnerability of the referenced structure along a scale of more or less. It can, for example, recognize a vulnerable structure and take action to make it more vulnerable; or recognize a vulnerable structure and take action to reduce its vulnerability. Tactics identifies actions in the class "repairs" when the action makes patterns in the self's structure less vulnerable. Conversely, it identifies actions as "attacks" when the action makes patterns in an opponent's structure more vulnerable. Tactics also knows how to couple the recognition of vulnerability with repair and attack actions. Given a structure in the design space, in sum, the Tactics module knows how to recognize abstracted patterns of vulnerability in structure associated with self and to attempt repairs; it knows how to recognize abstracted patterns of vulnerability in structure associated with the opponent and to attempt attacks.

Were we to attempt a computer implementation of the tactical Lincoln/Douglas, we would need to make some firm assumptions about the communicative conditions of the rhetorical situations within the debates. Because the Plans module has an intact reality apart from rhetorical situations, we did not have to concern ourselves with the conditions of communication. Nor did we have to worry about the Plans module's ability within a rhetorical situation to recognize a set of prior moves and formulate a next move. However, stating these assumptions becomes a key consideration for specifying tactics.

## Communication Assumptions

We start with assumptions about the conditions of communication underlying Tactics. For simplicity, we make a transparency assumption, namely, that both speakers are capable of learning one another's emerging design. This assumption is already reflected in the way we represented structure in chapter 6. The representations in that chapter considered the structure of the debates by the end of the debates, not at their beginning. Typically, at the beginning of rhetorical interaction, speakers have not discriminated what the structures are, who owns what, and what is shared. Answers to these questions emerge in the course of interaction. We further assume that both speakers are able to recognize patterns of vulnerability in the designs. This means that as interaction continues, they become increasingly prepared to initiate repairs and attacks.

From the Tactics perspective, neither speaker will unwittingly advance the tactical interests of the other. Neither will initiate repairs for the opponent; neither will initiate attacks against oneself. This is not the same as saying that a speaker will never repair structure associated with the opponent, or never attack structure associated with self. As we saw with Plans, some structure associated with each speaker is negative, structure the speaker disavows and does not embed into a constructive position. So to classify the range of generic tactics available to a speaker we need to take positive and negative structure into our account of repair and attack.

## Types of Tactics

There are four kinds of generic tactical actions, dividing according to whether the structure in question is positive or negative and whether the action taken on it is repair or attack. These tactical types are easiest to discriminate when we understand how they can coordinate with plans:

1. Positive offense: lay out self's positive structure interactively.
2. Negative offense: recognize vulnerability in self's negative structure (i.e., self's image of the opponent as a counteragent in self's plans) and attack.
3. Repair defense: recognize vulnerability in self's positive structure (as opponent has recognized it) and repair.
4. Attack defense: recognize vulnerability in opponent's positive structure (i.e., self's image of opponent as agent in opponent's own plans) and attack.

Such coordination with plans is not necessary for these tactics to fire, but the intent to make this coordination will make attacking moves—negative offense and attack defense—seem more purposive and matters of public discourse. Without such coordination, attacks degenerate into face threats and other personal modes of attack based on insult scripts from the face-to-face culture. We have more to say about face threats later.

Offensive tactics are proactive and reference structures diffusely; they introduce or reinstate structure into a rhetorical situation before they are known or well established (positive offense); and they reinstate (positive offense) or attack (negative offense) structure at a rough level of granularity as they become better known. Defensive tactics are reactive and reference structure only after they been narrowly referenced as anaphors. They refer backward to fine-grained structures that have emerged in the interaction. The conditions for defense, as a result, are relevant only when such structures have established themselves as narrow reference points in the rhetorical situation. Defensive tactics are used to reference this anaphoric structure, either to repair the damage the opponent has sought, through earlier moves, to inflict on the self's positive structure (repair defense), or to use these anaphoric patterns to inflict damage on the opponent's positive structure (attack defense). We next consider each type more specifically.

A tactic is used on the positive offense when the pattern recognized and acted on is the self's own positive structure referenced diffusely, without the narrowing provided by intense interaction and cross-examination. No previous interaction is needed to launch this tactic. Consequently, the tactic is typically associated with the first affirmative of debate, the openings of particular rounds of speaking. Although tactics are most responsible for the speaker's satisfying the goal of responsiveness, tactics used on the positive offense bring the speaker's goal of predictiveness down to the interactive level of the rhetorical situation. Positive offense is the tactical type supplying a situational mouthpiece to the Plans module. Recall that nothing in the Plans module is situational. Plans knows how to go on about truth and falsehood but knows nothing about the rhetorical situation at hand. Insofar as a speaker needs to bring an emergent public model to the rhetorical situation, it must be done tactically, through a positive offense. At the beginning of a debate, a powerful positive offense can "seed" the rhetorical situation with all the focal elements needed to "grow" plans in later interactions and, along with those interactions, an elaborate and impressive public model. In this sense, all tactical types can be seen as potential agents directing the development of a speaker's plans and public model and doing so from the foundation laid by a powerful positive offense. Of all the tactical types, Douglas is Lincoln's superior in positive offense. He is much better than Lincoln in laying the foundation of his public model tactically. Unfortunately for Douglas, he is Lincoln's inferior at most of the other tactics, especially the defensive ones. The result is he doesn't grow his plans and public model much more effectively or impressively than the model he lays out in his first affirmative in the first debate at Ottawa.

A tactic is used on the negative offense when the pattern it recognizes and acts on is the speaker's negative structure, also diffusely referenced. Negative offense consists of tactics used to characterize and attack structure the speaker disowns or disavows. The emphasis remains offense-minded because the locus is proactively the speaker's structure, not the opponent's. But it is negative because the focus is on the rejected aspects of the speaker's structures.

Defensive tactics are reactive and narrowly referenced through prior interaction rather than proactive and diffuse. Setting the grounds for defensive play, each speaker seeks in the interaction to establish finer patterns of vulnerability associated with the positive structures of the other. The conditions for defense are relevant, then, when a structure has been introduced and narrowly referenced in the rhetorical situation. More than offensive tactics, defensive tactics are better vehicles for satisfying responsiveness goals in a rhetorical situation. The element of pinpoint responsiveness to structures contributed by the opponent in interaction is what distinguishes defense from negative offense.[1] Lacking this element, the self's efforts to repair or attack vulnerabilities established in previous moves with the opponent and in fine, comparative brushstrokes (defense) would be indistinguishable from the self's efforts, with a diffuse and indiscriminate brush, to call attention to and attack existing vulnerabilities in negative structures that had been associated with the self even before the rhetorical situation (negative offense).

A tactic is used for repair defense when the self repairs vulnerabilities that have, as a result of the opponent's actions, emerged in the self's positive structure. A tactic is used on attack defense when the self is interactively responsible for creating patterns of vulnerability in the opponent's positive structure and then attacking them.

Tactical speakers are not limited to offense or defense. They can also call "foul" on the opponent and so try to suspend play, seeking a victory by forfeit. In such cases, the tactical speaker charges that the opponent has failed some precondition that disqualifies him or her to share the platform with the speaker. We call such tactical charges face threats. Face threats were a frequent tactic of Douglas, as we see later.

We now summarize the relationships between the type of tactic chosen and the communication condition: Offensive tactics can operate on patterns that are diffuse and of large grain size and can take actions of similar proportion. Tactics used in positive offense require no previous interactive context. They are a good place to begin, although not to culminate, an argument. Tactics used in negative offense operate to discredit the speaker's own negative structure with a broad brush. The use of defensive tactics requires finer patterns of discriminations and they initiate actions that are themselves finer grained. A speaker cannot play defense until, as a result of interactive moves with an opponent, narrowly referenced structures emerge in the rhetorical situation that can be recognized and reacted to. Repair defense acts on emergent aspects of the speaker's positive structure that the

---

[1]Defensive play is sometimes associated with the height of rhetorical skill because it requires the social reasoning necessary to closely monitor, for purposes of independent confirmation, or refutation, the reasoning of an opponent. Johnstone (1959) thought that such close refutative skill was the essence of the skill underlying philosophical argument. Booth (1974) called this skill the ability of the rhetor to have a "meeting of the minds" with an interlocutor. More recently, Deanne Kuhn (1991), studying argument from a cognitive perspective, found that close refutation associated with what we call defensive play is one of the hardest skills of argument for novices to acquire. We explore this claim further in chapter 10 when we discuss refutation as an art par excellence requiring the coordination of modules.

opponent has tried to attack. Attack defense acts on emergent aspects of the opponent's positive structure which the speaker tries to damage. Face threats challenge the opponent's capacity or credentials to participate as a principal in the rhetorical situation. They challenge the opponent's right to share the platform with the speaker.

## Intelligence Assumptions

Although tactics "know" nothing about the public model as a discrete and intact entity, tactics can increase in intelligence when some of the patterns it recognizes when it sees "vulnerability" in structure contain elements of the patterns that Plans recognizes when it sees "truth" and "falsehood" about the social world within a public model. Tactics notices a vulnerability in the opponent's structure—thinks "aha" and starts to frame an attack. Tactics has a limited repertoire of "attacking a structure." Left to its own repertoire, it might engage in name-calling, ridicule, ad hominem, and other scripts of face attack that people develop in the world of face-to-face interaction. A more intelligent tactic knows (or, better, the designer who uses tactics intelligently knows) that this repertoire of attack can be greatly expanded and generalized if the Plans module can be woken up and called on to "notice" that same structure. Plans has a more general, abstract, and conceptually sophisticated repertoire for talking about what is false in the social world and why. Plans won't know anything about the difference between the speaker's structure and the opponent's. For Plans, there are no opponents, only general counteragents who are responsible for falsehood. Nonetheless, if the speaker, using tactics to forage the rhetorical situation, finds a vulnerable structure of the opponent's to attack, and can somehow coordinate Plans to look at the same structure in the same few moments as a piece of social falsehood within a public model, then the speaker will be able to go on at much greater length, abstraction, and historical depth about why the opponent's position is wrong-headed.

As we discuss in more detail when we look at the coordination of modules in chapter 10, the challenge of coordinating Plans and Tactics is to teach Plans how to be sensitive to changes in a public model that suddenly and starkly arise (unbeknowst to it) from an opponent's actions. Another challenge is to teach Tactics how to recognize vulnerability and react to it with information that Plans can also utilize to further develop a focus on a public model. In their native state, Plans are integrated but slow to respond to change. Tactics are sensitive to changes but isolated and without direction. Intelligent Tactics are those trained to fill out more integrated path-like connections; intelligent Plans are those trained to notice and respond to change more quickly.

It is apparent from what we have said that for a module to be intelligent is to increase the fluency with which it coordinates with other modules. The intelligent coordination involved here between Plans and Tactics is analogous to the tactics of the chess master, which know nothing per se about the larger goals of chess, the long-term agendas to control position (strategies), or the repertoire of abstract board patterns that fill in these agendas (plans). Nonetheless, the chess master's tactics are increasingly intelligent when, in any local move, the patterns through which the master recognizes and responds to "vulnerability" are part of larger patterns on the playing board (structure) that match at least some of the interior pattern of an abstracted plan, some of the interior conditions of a strategy, and so on. The smarter the tactics in chess, in sum, the more the chess master's goals, strategies, and plans will be represented in the actual movement of physical pieces on the structure of a 64-square board.

Analogously, the smarter the tactics in rhetorical design, the more the patterns (defined on the design structure) that the speaker uses to win the contest with the opponent will fit into larger patterns (over that same structure) that also allow him or her to actualize goals and plans through well-crafted linguistic events. Mastering rhetorical design poses the challenge of coordinating many heterogeneous modules that, left on their own, would remain radically unaligned, go their separate ways. This is the very same challenge of mastery we saw obtaining in any art within the family of design arts (chapter 2). It is the challenge of making a designed artifact with radically different segments appear, nonetheless, seamless.

Novice behavior in any design art is a problem of coordination as much as mastery of the individual modules. Novices can know one module or another but can fail to coordinate them with mastery. To understand the difficulties of coordinating tactics with plans in rhetorical design, we have done some pilot work with a few first-year college students, untutored in argument. We asked them to read a short article about abortion, capital punishment, or some other public policy. We then asked each student to "criticize" the article, in effect to generate a first move in a tactical game with the author. The results are interesting. In many cases, the students offer criticism about punctuation, tone, the sequence of paragraphs, the author "twisting things around," and many other aspects of the article that have no direct involvement with the public model the author brings to it. One hypothesis is that the students have no incipient public models of their own on the issues they are reading about. But oral conferences suggest that this is not the case. The students often turn out to be sophisticated in their understanding of the issue. They are not without plans of their own. A second hypothesis is that students lack the goals of rhetorical design and so do not translate the instruction to "criticize" the author with the goal of responding to the author's plans. They may interpret the goals of criticism as incidental to responding to the author's blueprint for social truth. But when students are questioned about their criticism, they claim to offer it as a direct response to what the author is trying to get a reader to believe. A tentative conclusion we have drawn from this informal work, and a hypothesis for future testing, is that students lack smart tactics (in written argument, in any case) for seizing on the plans of authors and using these patterns to make tactical moves. Students fail to see and evaluate the opponent's structure from a tactical perspective so they don't know how to attack, or defend themselves, in ways that are sensitive to that structure.

Unlike the freshman writers we have studied, Lincoln and Douglas are masters of coordinating their tactics with their public models. To be sure, our culture came to appreciate this fact long before our investigation, but our investigation yields a more systematic understanding, we suggest, of the skills that we have long appreciated. Lincoln's and Douglas' tactics home in on patterns of vulnerability that overlap with much of the interior of their respective public models. Consequently, when they want to seize on a vulnerability for offense or defense, for repair or attack, they also are never far from telling their abstracted stories about truth and falsehood in a historical world.

We now turn to the tactical description of Lincoln/Douglas. We classify the action of the debates within each of the four tactical types, from Ottawa to Alton. Normally, we have been careful not to confuse the vocabulary of Plans (truth, falsehood, public model, plans) and that of Tactics (speaker, opponent, attack, repair, positive structure, negative structure). However, when we make assumptions about Lincoln's or Douglas' rhetorical expertise and, more specifically, their ability to coordinate Plans and Tactics, we mean precisely to speak to their capacity to coordinate these vocabularies for positive effect, and so seamlessly that the naked eye (or ear) cannot notice that the speaker is in fact orchestrating disparate and essentially noninteractive realms of experience and thought. In chapter 10, we make some speculations about how such coordination takes place in rhetorical design.

## Tactics and the Design Structure

As we saw in chapter 6, for experts like Lincoln and Douglas, offensive and defensive potential can be built directly into structures of the design. The

Plans view, knowing nothing about offense or defense, does not make use of notations in structure indicating offensive and defensive potential. However, these notations are central discriminations for facilitating tactical perception. Without offensive or defensive potential built directly into the design structure shared by both speakers, we would imagine Lincoln and Douglas having to spend many rounds learning about the issues and their positions in them before they could launch tactics against one other.

## OFFENSE

Both debators offer much positive and negative offense. We trace their use of each offensive type separately.

### Positive Offense

Positive offense is a special case, the only tactic that does not strictly rely on recognizing and responding to patterns of vulnerability in a structure. Positive offense rather recognizes structures as "sayables" merely because they are part of the speaker's positive structure, because they constitute object and event classes that the speaker affirms. When coordinated with Plans, speakers rely, in part, on positive offense to lay out the interior of their public space for audiences. The chess analogy to an expert on positive offense is players who can use their own "pieces" to fill in board positions needed to take strategic control of the game. Douglas and Lincoln are both admirably expert in positive offense. This should be not too terribly surprising. The power of a good positive offense played by an expert derives largely from power of the public model organized and maintained by Plans. Both Lincoln and Douglas have rich and distinctively different public models to bring to and maintain within the debates, yet they use positive offense with markedly different styles. Douglas' positive offense is powerful, concentrated, and repetitive.

Unlike the freshman who doesn't do tactical justice to an otherwise good plan, Douglas is masterful at using a positive offense to lay out the major parts of his public model succinctly and systematically in the early minutes of the debates. Within the span of the first two debates, we know all of Douglas' "chess pieces," we know how he intends to use them, and we watch, during the course of the debates, as he uses them to lay out the same public model with little variation. Lincoln's positive offense, in contrast, is slow to unfold, uneven, and cumulative. We know few of his pieces early in the debates, we know little about how he will use them, and we watch, during the debates, as he fills in his pieces incrementally and at different rates, sporadically in the early debates and in more concentrated form in the later ones.

In the Ottawa opening, Douglas leads with all offensive guns firing. He invokes precedent, principle, venue, and organizational authority on behalf of popular sovereignty. Popular sovereignty represents Douglas' deep conviction about slavery in the territories (principle plan); it is the fundamental principle of local control on which the country was founded (precedent and venue plan); it is the principle reinforced in the 1850 Compromise and ratified by the major political parties of the time, Whigs and Democrats, shortly thereafter (organizational authority plan). Douglas declares popular sovereignty as the basis of his own Kansas Act, thereby anointing himself a history maker, one with the power and entitlements to further precedents in his own person. He concludes the Ottawa opening noting that popular sovereignty is the basis of the nation's past and future. It promises peace to the country and growth (precedent projecting into the future).

To this offensive salvo, Lincoln's reply at Ottawa is folksy and human, but tactically diffuse and ineffective on both offense and defense. Fehrenbacher (1962, p. 126) wrote in his history of the debates that even Lincoln's friends "thought he had done too much backpedaling," and Zarefsky (1990, p. 55) observed that "the debates began with momentum favoring Douglas."

Lincoln's Freeport opening offers barely a whimper of offense. Using a repair defense, he disputes some of Douglas' history of the Republicans, noting they were founded in 1856, not 1854. Yet Lincoln never connects this dispute to an offense-minded organizational authority plan of his own about the Republican party. He uses the dispute only in passing, to add backing to his contention that he was never at the Springfield convention of Republicans in 1854.

In his Freeport reply, Douglas regroups his offense in the face of Lincoln's questions. He contends that popular sovereignty holds in the territories, regardless of Dred Scott. According to Douglas, Dred Scott, like any federal ruling, posits only an abstract dictum that the people in their local settings must ratify. According to Douglas, no ruling of any federal body can be forced down the throat of an unwilling people "for even a day." This is Douglas' doctrine of unfriendly local legislation. In his rejoinder at Freeport, Lincoln repeats that the Republicans organized in 1856 (not 1854) and that the judge is "afraid" of Republican unity. But again the mention is in passing and not developed into an organizational authority plan on Lincoln's offense. To a detached observer of the first two debates, the dominant definition of the Republicans belongs to Douglas, not Lincoln. Douglas' offense is getting through faster and more effectively than Lincoln's.

In his opening at Jonesboro, the third debate, Douglas repeats the offensive barrage he had delivered in his Ottawa opening, with some important adaptations in his offense for the benefit of the southern audience at Jonesboro (see chapter 9 for an analysis of adapting designs to local audiences). At Ottawa, Douglas had portrayed Lincoln's opposition to Dred Scott chiefly as a sign of his disloyalty to the federal court system. Yet Douglas in the North of Ottawa and Freeport had not portrayed the Dred Scott ruling as part of his positive offense. In the North, Douglas is clear about ignoring race directly, saying "[I] don't care" about it in comparison to the more pressing issues of national development and expansion. Yet at Jonesboro, Douglas does incorporate Dred Scott and race into his positive offense, cryptically observing that Dred Scott "covers the whole question" when it comes to the question of negro citizenship and slavery in the territories. And at Jonesboro, unlike Ottawa, he makes gestures of conciliation toward Buchanan and the southern Democrats, noting that Buchanan recently backed a bill requiring constitutions to be submitted to the people. Douglas remarks that if Buchanan stands by that, "there will be no division in the Democratic party."

In his Jonesboro reply, Lincoln begins to hint that Douglas' characterizations of the Republicans are false. He refrains, however, from telling the true account of the Republicans. He keeps his positive offense muffled, under wraps. In his rejoinder at Charleston, Lincoln finally takes some positive offensive moves by countering a strength in Douglas' offensive position. Douglas had made his offense depend on deferring slavery to a local issue. But Douglas' offense also uses as precedent the notion that slavery has never been a national problem, that the Founders always meant to defer it to local control. In an effective counter, Lincoln responds that if this precedent history is true, and the Founders always classified slavery as local, how has it come to so persistently surface throughout American history as a recurrent source of national agitation? Lincoln uses the opportunity of the counter to unfold an alternative precedent history in which his house-divided doctrine figures. According to Lincoln's precedent, slavery has always been a source of national division, one the Founders sought to heal by putting slavery on a course of ultimate extinction. As Lincoln says, there is no way to end the division other than to put slavery "back on the basis our fathers left it" and to let the public mind once again "rest in the belief" that it is on a course of extinction.

Although exposing some of his precedent plan at Charleston, Lincoln continues to hold back other aspects of his public model. He does not lay out his own organizational authority and personal conviction tying him to the Republicans until the fifth debate at Galesburg. Not until that debate does he make clear who the Republicans are, what they stand for, who he is, what he stands for, and, not incidentally, why he is a Republican. He identifies slavery as the "evil" of American history and the Republican platform as a platform chartered by persons with little in common except the conviction that the institution is evil. In a single stroke laying out the intersection of organizational authority and principle plans, he utters, "I confess I belong to those who think slavery is a moral and political wrong." In this case, his confession is not part of a public confessional, where he would be claiming to put his heart ahead of his inherited responsibilities. His personal confession in this case aligns with his organizational authority as the Republican leader. The Republicans are a group whose members confess, one heart at a time, to the evils of slavery.

Not until his opening in the sixth debate, at Quincy, does Lincoln chart the history of the Republican party, chronicling the meeting times and places the Republicans themselves consider authentic calendar events. He documents how the Illinois Republican party was born at Bloomington in May 1856, how the national Republicans first convened in Philadelphia a month later, and how the Illinois Republicans had reconvened in June 1858 and updated their platform to meet the pending issues of the day. As if to express indignation that Douglas from the early debates forced him to choose between party and principle, Lincoln says that "in entering this canvass, I assume [all along] I have been standing on their [the Republican] platforms." He emphasizes that no one has given him cause to doubt his foundations, that he is "unaware in this canvass, from the beginning till today, of anyone who has found anything wrong with our platform." Lincoln concludes his Quincy opening with his most sustained discussion of the history and immorality of domestic slavery and the organization of the Republican party as a response to this wrong. He closes with a statement indicating that he thinks he has in this round mounted his most sustained and direct offense thus far: "This, gentleman, is the plain statement of our principles in all their enormity."

Lincoln is not finished on the offense. In his rejoinder at Quincy and again in his reply at Alton, he provides further briefing about how the Founders wanted to extinguish slavery and how their intent was to include blacks in the Declaration. He offers as signs of this intent that the Founders cut off the African slave trade in the first 20 years of the nation's life, forbade slavery in the new territories, and mentioned slavery only obliquely in the constitution, in passages that would not need revision were slavery to disappear in an instant. As a further sign of the founders' intent, he cites the testimony of Brooks of South Carolina, a proslaver, who publicly conceded that only the cotton gin, technology, had saved the institution from the Founders' plans for it. In his reply at Alton, Lincoln offers signs the Founders meant to include Blacks in the Declaration. He repeats a statement made at Galesburg that, no more than three years before, it would have been heresy to think the founders had not included Blacks in the Declaration. At Alton he adds an important disclaimer to give this statement more credibility. He notes that before 1854 many who supported slavery never questioned the Founders' intent. They simply "denied the truth" of the Declaration.

Releasing the speaker from any pressure to respond to previous discourse, openings, especially in an oral setting, are the natural place to press a positive offense. Douglas had shown his superb offensive skill in his openings at Ottawa, Jonesboro, and Galesburg. Throughout the early debates, Douglas' devastating openings allowed him to dominate the terms of the public models being contested. Lincoln's openings are not nearly as offensively minded. His opening at Freeport is bogged down in Douglas' challenges at Ottawa. His wastes his opening at Charleston reviving an arcane charge that Trumbull, his political ally, made against Douglas two years before. And it didn't help Lincoln that he picked the unluckiest of places, nonopenings—the rejoinder at Charleston and the reply at Galesburg—to begin his positive offense in earnest.

Lincoln's late offensive surge, however, seems to have bested Douglas at his very strength. Douglas' opening offense at Alton is less focused and confident than his earlier openings. He offers many of the principled arguments on behalf of popular sovereignty he has offered before. But instead of confidently proclaiming his own solidarity with the Democrats, he seems to be calling for their support, lest their divisiveness elect Lincoln: "There never was a time for Democrats to stand together as there is now."

Why would Lincoln wait so long to show his offensive hand? There are many possible answers but the most interesting, perhaps, is his understanding of the print audience. Because he believed the influence of the debates would be greatest among the class of opinion leaders who could hold the debates in their hand as a single text, Lincoln seemed to believe that, like drama, it is more important how the play ends than how it begins. Lincoln dramatic sense suggests he wanted both power and surprise at the end. He couldn't achieve power without opening up his offense at the end. But he couldn't have achieved surprise if he had given away his offense from the start. Contrastively, Douglas' powerful, but unsurprising, offense may have reflected his choice of media more than a weakness of tactics. He may have believed that the local listening audience was the main audience to be persuaded and so he couldn't afford to let a single debate go by without making visible the entirety of his offense. Another complementary possibility, also related to print, is that Douglas, thinking himself performing in a nonpermanent medium, understood that he was constructing a single message for each debate, so he had to remain consistent within the confines of each debate site. Lincoln, on the other hand, thinking himself addressing a single message across seven sites, understood that he didn't need to reveal a full public model, much less a consistent one, within the span of single site. He had seven debates across which to accomplish a consistent message.

## Negative Offense

Negative offense, as we have seen, involves actions speakers take to turn their own negative structures into "sayables." They say what they fail to affirm or avow. For masters like Lincoln and Douglas, negative offense is tightly coordinated with their public stories about falsehood in the historical world. The analogy between negative offense and chess is how well players recognize and act on an opponent's pieces from within the plans that they themselves are trying to achieve. In an expert rhetor's negative offense, speakers are seeing the opponent's pieces and moves, but egocentrically, for they are seeing the opponent's pieces and moves but only within their own public stories about falsehood. Negative offense thus represents a pattern of attack that tends to stereotype the opponent from the distance of the speaker's own categories of falsehood. The expert on negative offense recognizes and launches attacks against the opponent from a perspective that is alien to the opponent. Consequently, the use of negative offense in an expert's repertoire predisposes the designs toward plans that include the opponent as an abstracted counteragent whose beliefs have been molded from a stereotypical distance: counterprinciple, conspiracy, and organizational authority. Each of these plans can be used to retrofit counteragents within complex plots and positions that require no personal acquaintance with their actual words or ways of thinking.

Not surprisingly, when Lincoln or Douglas go on the negative offense, they almost always coordinate their action of "attacking their own negative structure" with (within Plans) identifying one another as counteragents within conspiracy scripts or as leaders of treasonous organizations within negative organizational authority scripts.

In his opening at Ottawa, Douglas implicates Lincoln in a conspiracy: Ostensibly Lincoln is a leader in the new national party of Republicans. But in reality, the Republicans are a sectionalist party of northern abolitionists and Lincoln, with his friend Trumbull, is trying to abolitionize the old Whigs and Democrats of Illinois. The secret counterprinciple driving the Republican conspirators is abolition. Had Douglas applied only the conspiracy charge to Lincoln, Lincoln could perhaps have wiggled out. Conspiracies are easy to charge because they assume a grand design behind seemingly independent events. They are also hard to defend against (now a commonplace about conspiracy) because there are no grounds for proving that one wasn't conspiring. But (less a commonplace) they are exceedingly difficult to prosecute because the prosecutor must show how so few of the conspirator's words are what they appear and how so few of the conspirator's actions align with the public description of them.

Douglas set ups a trap for Lincoln much more elaborate than the standard conspiracy charge. He adds an organizational authority charge to the attack to set up a dichotomous category of Republican. Within Douglas' conspiracy attack, the Republicans are necessarily quiet about their abolition. Within his organizational authority attack against Lincoln, they proclaim it to the world. Sandwiching Lincoln between these two attacks, Douglas creates the dilemma that boxes Lincoln in for the first three debates. Lincoln can't answer the conspiracy charge without coming off a traitor to his party. He can't answer the organizational authority charge without seeming to endorse a principle (abolition) that will lose him the election.

In his reply at Ottawa, Lincoln attacks with a conspiracy charge of his own, one that has Douglas working with Buchanan, Pierce, and Taney to nationalize slavery. Lincoln offers history to support the conspiracy. He notes that the Democrats' notion of popular sovereignty is biased in favor of extending slavery to the territories, for it allows the people of a territory to hold slaves prior to their taking a formal vote on slave-holding at the time when they have enough settlers to seek admission as a state. The bias occurs, according to Lincoln, because of a historical trend that once an economy makes provisions for slaves, it remains a slave economy. And so the question of what the settlers of a territory will decide when it comes to slave-holding will already be decided, in Lincoln's view, if the settlers are permitted to hold slaves prior to their formal decision. Lincoln maintains the pressure of the conspiracy charge against Douglas but he girds it with an organizational authority charge when the hold of conspiracy weakens. Lincoln recalls that Douglas had previously squirmed out of the conspiracy charge by denying he had ever talked with the persons with whom he is supposed to have conspired at the time the conspiracy was supposed to have taken place. Lincoln retorts that Douglas was in the same political organization as the coconspirators and for this reason could have been just an unknowing dupe of their plotting.

The combination of conspiracy/organizational authority as parallel stronger or weaker charges against an opponent also serves Douglas. In his reply to Douglas' conspiracy charge, Lincoln had denied he was physically present at Springfield. Yet Douglas shifts the hold from a conspiracy to an organizational authority charge, one that can implicate Lincoln for his category membership with the Republicans more than his bodily presence and cognition. Douglas now claims that he never charged Lincoln with being a member of the steering committee at Springfield. He charges that it was the Republican party platform, the party of Lincoln, that the committee meant to uphold. Denying being on the committee avoids the main issue. The main issue is the Republican platform, which is by implication Lincoln's platform.

Pressing the attack on organizational authority, Douglas, in a constructed monologue of his questions and Lincoln's responses at Freeport, mimics Lincoln responding evasively:

> I asked Lincoln if he favored the repeal of the fugitive slave law and Lincoln just responds, I wasn't on the committee at Springfield. I repeat the question and Lincoln still just answers, I wasn't on the committee. I ask Lincoln whether he will vote down slavery in Washington D.C., but when I ask him, he won't answer. I want his answers. I want to know whether he will arrest the acquisition of more territory unless slavery shall have been prohibited.

In his rejoinder at Freeport, Lincoln returns to the negative offense to secure Douglas within the conspiracy charge he had set up at Ottawa, aligning Douglas with those Democrats conniving to nationalize slavery. And again repeating from Ottawa, he shows that Douglas himself spilled the beans about the conspiracy when he split with the southern Democrats over Lecompton. "I am trying to show, judge, that you are a witness on my side." Lincoln points out that Douglas's charges made against the editor of the *Washington Union* for his pro-Lecompton stand were really charges Douglas was making against the Buchanan administration.

Throughout the remainder of the debates, Lincoln and Douglas create small variations on these same themes, in each case trying to yoke one another within charges of conspiracy/organizational authority. Little "progress" is made in the debates when either or both speaker is on the negative offense against the other. This is because negative offense is not used to explore issues with the opponent for confirmation or refutation. It is rather used to keep opponents on their heels, occupied cutting their way through a thicket of stereotypes, so they cannot make progress on their constructive argument.

Although Tactics is a foraging module that can see into elements of the rhetorical situation, offensive tactics remain egocentric, and so myopic, about the opponent in the situation. Offensive tactics home in on the self's structure, positive or negative. In positive offense, the opponent tends to fill the role of intellectualized counteragent; in negative offense, the role of a living stereotype. In both cases, the speaker sees the opponent on the speaker's terms and on the speaker's turf. The speaker retains the home-court advantage, as it were. Not until we understand defensive tactics can we understand how a speaker can break the confines of this egocentricism and begin to take on the opponent on the opponent's terms and turf.

## DEFENSE

Experts play defense,[2] coordinating tactics and plans, when they act on precise pieces of one's own structures, to be repaired, or precise pieces of the opponent's structures to be attacked. In either scenario, defensive play requires the close intermingling of opposed points of view, and the tight juxtaposition of the speaker's structure with comparable elements of the opponent's. The speaker playing defense must do a mental simulation[3] comparing the self's and opponent's structure in narrow and circumscribed ways. Even for the expert, this simulation takes place at the level of tactics where the speaker and opponent are discrete and knowable presences. It does not take place within Plans, for Plans knows nothing about opponents or of the conceivability of there existing public models other than the one whose consistency it is trying so hard to maintain.

The coordination between Plans and defensive play within Tactics is indirect, at best. In a repair defense, the opponent has established vulnerabilities in the speaker's positive structure. The speaker, operating tactically, now notices this vulnerability and tries to repair it. These repairs change the

---

[2]We distinguish defensive play, as we define it here, and being defensive, as used to describe the behavior of an arguer. An arguer who plays on the defense is responsive to the opponent's representations. An arguer who is defensive fails to be forthcoming about the strengths of the opponent's representations or the weakness of his or her own representations. The two are very different notions and should not be confused.

[3]The assumption of transparency assures that this mental simulation of the other's mental state is accurate; see the beginning of this chapter.

very same design structure Plans views when it attempts to maintain its public model of truth. When Plans next views this structure, it will notice the changes wrought by its own Tactics module (not knowing where they came from) and will make its own adjustments, if necessary, to maintain consistency about truth. In an attack defense, the speaker has established vulnerabilities in the opponent's positive structure. The Plans module registers nothing happening because there is no such entity within Plans as an "opponent" or an "opponent's public model." Suppose, however, that the opponent issues a repair defense, elaborating changes in his or her own positive structure to reduce the vulnerability. There may be an overlap in the structures changed by the opponent and the structures that the speaker's Plans module maintains to tell stories about falsehood in its public model. When Plans next views its public model, it will notice the changes wrought by the opponent's Tactics module (not knowing where they came from) and may make its own adjustments to maintain consistency about falsehood.

Given the potential of Plans/Tactics coordination, to engage in tactics against opponents either with a negative offense or an attack defense is to seek to introduce inconsistencies in their public model. It is useful at this juncture to consider what the Plans module can do to restore consistency in a public model against the attack of an opponent. It has two options. First it can block, or nullify, alignments that are the source of inconsistency. Should a certain alignment not fit within other existing designs, Plans can restore consistency by finding information that directly cancels out the offending alignment. Second, it can seek to offset offending alignments by elaborating new structures that override the original inconsistency. If the offending alignment introduces an inconsistency in a speaker's story about truth, Plans can elaborate additional information that gives contra-indication to the offender. The advantage of nullifying resolutions is that they eliminate the offending alignment. The disadvantage is that they do not set in motion processes for elaborating a public model further. By way of contrast, offsetting resolutions elaborate a public model but at the same time risk introducing more inconsistencies into it (leaving the speaker even more vulnerable for attack). We see examples of both nullifying and offsetting resolutions in Lincoln/Douglas later in this chapter.

Shifts to defensive play are often signaled by establishing agreements with an opponent and then developing disagreements while referring back to the contested point at the site of the rupture. Leading with agreement identifies an intersection between the speaker's rhetorical design and the opponent's. Moving away from the similarity at a single contested point has the effect of creating a precise and focused juxtaposition between the opponent's positive structure and the dissenting structure of the speaker. Having established the context for precise juxtaposition, speakers can go on and indicate why it is that (in the case of a repair defense) they can block, or reduce, the damage done to the self's positive structure, or why it is that (in the case of an attack defense) they can block or damage the opponent's positive structure.

We now consider Lincoln and Douglas on the defense. Defense is less frequent than offense in the debates, unevenly distributed across the debators (Lincoln does it more), and uneven in the types used (more repair than attack defense, except in the later debates when Lincoln crests with a strong attack defense). Lincoln and Douglas differ little in their style of negative offense, and differ more in their use of positive offense. Yet they divide dramatically in their use of defense. For all his prowess on offense, Douglas is a feeble tactical debator on the defense. Lincoln, a very good offensive debater, is an master of defensive play, especially the attack defense that manifests in the later debates.

### Repair Defense

Repair defense indicates actions speakers take to block the opponent's attacks against their own positive structure. In expert repair defense, coordinating plans and tactics, speakers will try to defend attacks perceived (by Plans) to have thrown inconsistency into their public model. The analogy of expert repair defense with chess is how well players can use their own pieces from their own plans and their knowledge of the opponent's pieces from within the opponent's plans to anticipate and block the opponent from achieving positional strength on the player's own side of the board. Douglas issues more diffuse offensive attacks than Lincoln, and Lincoln spends more time, especially in the early debates, on the defense repairing them. For both speakers, more repairs are made against conspiracy charges than against any other pattern of "vulnerable structure" in the debates.

In his reply at Ottawa, Lincoln answers Douglas' conspiracy charge by revealing the mundane truth about the Springfield conference—"I wasn't a participant in the Springfield convention"—which he uses to repair Douglas' conspiracy charge against the Republicans. As another gesture of repair from the conspiracy charge, he reveals a "Lincoln" in 1854 who gave a decidedly anti-abolition speech, who indicated he had no interest in interfering with slavery where it exists, and who indicated he believed that Blacks did not deserve social equality, although they do deserve the right to formal equality as guaranteed by the Declaration of Independence. Lincoln also plays repair defense against Douglas' attempts to cast him in a favorable autobiographical light, insisting that he acted honorably in congressional debate on the Mexican War. He further repairs Douglas' characterization of the house-divided doctrine that equates the doctrine with abolition. He fashions house-divided doctrine into a historical doctrine, that the Founders found the country divided between free and slave and knew that this condition was unstable for the country over the long term.

One of Douglas' few signs of defense in the beginning of the debates occurs when he seeks to repair Lincoln's conspiracy charge against him. In his rejoinder at Ottawa, he indicates that the vote against the Chase amendment was an independent event and does not fit into Lincoln's conspiracy plan. "Lincoln wants to know why I voted against Chase." The bill "already conferred all power Congress had." Against Lincoln's charge of a conspiracy to spread slavery to all the states, Douglas explains why the Kansas Act he authored included the provision that states, not just territories, had the right to vote on slavery. Douglas notes that the Missouri Compromise was itself a case of a state seeking admission as a slave state with the majority of Missouri's Free-Soiler citizens seeking to vote her out because she had slavery. So, Douglas concludes, the mention of "state" in the Kansas Bill was a perfectly appropriate mention, free of conspiracy implications.

In his opening at Freeport, Lincoln again repairs Douglas' Ottawa characterization of the Springfield convention. "There was never in the fall of 54 any convention calling itself Republicans." "The judge was so precise I could not bring myself to say that what he was saying was not true." "I contented myself denying my connection to them, not denying the existence of the whole event."

In his Freeport reply, Douglas continues to repair Lincoln's conspiracy charge against him vis-à-vis the Chase Amendment. According to Douglas, Chase wanted his own amendment rejected rather than insisting on a fair wording. The wording of the Kansas Bill was already fair, neutral between freedom and slavery. At the end of his reply, Douglas also repairs Lincoln's charge that has the leading Democrats using the Kansas Act and the Dred Scott ruling to spread slavery throughout the land. Douglas remarks that orchestrating Kansas and Dred Scott from a conspiracy was an impossibility because Dred Scott was not even a pending case during the time of Kansas. In addition, Buchanan, one of the reputed conspirators, was in England and out of touch during the time in question.

In his rejoinder at Freeport, Lincoln responds to Douglas' attack against his giving different messages north and south. He appeals to the fact that his statements said at different times and places can be easily checked for consistency in the spatial copresence of print. Lincoln claims that when people compare his speeches "laid side by side," they will see that the message is the same north and south.

Through the first two debates, both speakers use defense for mainly repair purposes. They seek to block the other's conspiracy plans that indicted the insidious doings of the other's party. In Douglas' conspiracy plans, Lincoln and his friends are conspiring to abolitionize the country. In Lincoln's conspiracy plans, Douglas and his friends are conspiring to extend slavery to all the states. Defense for both speakers through the middle of Jonesboro, the third debate, means repairing the damage of the conspiracy charge. For Douglas it means rejecting any conspiratorial designs with the Democrats, and for Lincoln, rejecting any conspiratorial designs with the Republicans.

In his rejoinder at Charleston, Lincoln initiates some further defensive repairs regarding Dred Scott and negro citizenship. Prior to this point in the debates, Douglas had used Dred Scott multiple times on the negative offense, identifying Lincoln's rejection of it with his support for negro citizenship. Now at Charleston, Lincoln, finally responding to Douglas' repeated inquiries, says "he shall have no occasion to ask again for I say frankly I am not in favor of negro citizenship." Lincoln offers that Douglas "keeps saying I objected to Dred Scott because it denied black citizenship." Establishing agreement on Douglas' own principle of self-government, Lincoln cites his personal opposition to Dred Scott (which rescinds territorial choice on the slave question) as following from Douglas' own principle: "I believe that states have the right to decide on negro citizenship." Yet Dred Scott denies that the local citizens have the right to decide.

In his reply at Galesburg, Lincoln repairs what Douglas had called the "slander" of thinking that negroes were included in the Declaration of Independence. He follows his repair with offsetting information that allows him to elaborate his own public model further. He retorts that, until three years before, the entire record supported the negroes' inclusion in the Declaration, and Lincoln challenges Douglas to come up with any quote more than three years old of a person saying otherwise. He casts an image of the venerable Jefferson as himself having "trembled" when he thought condoning slavery in the face of a "just God."

In his rejoinder at Alton, Douglas closes with some uncharacteristically good points on a repair defense. He takes reasonable exception to Lincoln's statement that slavery has been the only or even principal source of the nation's divisions. He asks, "Didn't nullification disturb the peace in 1832?" "Was that the slavery question, Mr. Lincoln?" "Didn't the last war with

Britain divide the country?" Lincoln's argument that slavery is the only source of disunion in this county, Douglas offers, "falls to the ground." Douglas also has an interesting defense against Lincoln's report that the cotton gin altered the course of slavery in the country. The Founders, according to Douglas, could not envision many new technologies, including the telegraph or the railroads. Is it realistic to think that the vagaries of technological change could be used to undermine the founding principles of government?

## Attack Defense

Attack defense consists of actions a speaker takes to damage the opponent's positive structure. The analogy between expert attack defense and chess is how well players can use their own pieces from their own plans and their knowledge of the opponent's pieces from within the opponent's plans to anticipate and block the opponent from achieving positional strength on the opponent's side of the board.

In his reply at Jonesboro, Lincoln makes an important tactical shift to a more attack defense, one that seeks to block Douglas' more offense-minded positions. He signals this shift by establishing a beachhead of agreement within Douglas' positive structure. From Douglas' earliest salvo at Ottawa, Douglas had tried to present his prize principle of popular sovereignty as if he championed it and Lincoln perversely opposed it. In Lincoln's Jonesboro reply, for the first time in the debates, a zone of agreement is established. Lincoln states that, on the issue of popular sovereignty, he can "cordially agree" with Douglas. By offering his cordial agreement with popular sovereignty, Lincoln signals that the debate for too long had been conducted in terms that have left Lincoln's positive structure misrepresented and that have left Douglas' positive structure free from scrutiny. Lincoln will henceforth conduct the debate more on his own terms, seeking to expose what Douglas' own positive structure comes to, for if the issue is just popular sovereignty as self-government, the debate might as well be called for lack of an issue. Lincoln avows his agreement with state sovereignty and "he won't find anyplace in print [where] I argued against [it]." What must be at issue, if there is an issue at all, Lincoln signals at Jonesboro, is Douglas' particular take on popular sovereignty.

Landing on Douglas' positive structure associated with his precedent plans, Lincoln charges that Douglas has "changed [American] history." According to Lincoln, the Founders did not choose slavery but inherited it and with great misgivings. They intended to leave slavery in the course of extinction by prohibiting its spread in the new territories. Far from offering an authentic precedent history of slavery, Douglas and his friends have "put slavery on a new course." What they offer as a precedent is a counterprecedent in disguise. Invoking the seeds of his own precedent, Lincoln offers, "I just ask it be restored to where the Fathers put it."

Lincoln tightly coordinates his attack defense (within Tactics) with expansive development of his own public model to offset Douglas' previous attack. He claims that the southerner Brooks admitted that slavery was on its way out until the cotton gin made it profitable. He illustrates how Douglas has made a career of charging his enemies with abolition. The Whigs, Lincoln insists, got their good name with Douglas only after they disbanded. He shows how, contrary to Douglas' history, Clay's 1850 Compromise did not repeal the Missouri Compromise. As Senate chairman of the Committee on Territories, Douglas had repealed it, under cover, when getting the Kansas Bill passed.

Lincoln further employs his attack defense as interference for elaborating the Republican stand on slavery. Using agreement to train on Douglas' principle of popular sovereignty, Lincoln acknowledges that diversity "is a cement of the union." But slavery, Lincoln insists, is different. We had peace on slavery until we debated whether and how to extend it into the territories, first with the Missouri Compromise, then with the annexation of Texas, and most recently the Mexican War. And then in a quick turnaround from a defensive action to the invocation of a precedent with his offense, Lincoln observes that we cannot expect this agitation to stop until we return to where the Founders placed slavery.

Lincoln's more focused use of an attack defense comes when he stalks the compatibility between Douglas' views on Dred Scott and his principle of unfriendly local legislation. He mentions that the Supreme Court, through Dred Scott, has ruled against the right of a territory to exclude slavery and that the Judge "adheres to their decision most firmly." Lincoln then questions the accuracy of unfriendly local legislation. But, says Lincoln, slavery implanted itself without local police protection. The issue over Dred Scott arose because a slave was taken into free territory, proving there is "vigor enough in slavery to implant it even against unfriendly legislation." Moreover, even when unfriendly legislation is effective at keeping slavery out, its effectiveness cannot come without question or cost; for if the courts allow slavery as property and that property is denied, the owner surely has a right of appeal.

Lincoln now conjures a thought experiment to see if Douglas' position can create a consistent model for thinking about how to reconcile Dred Scott and the principle of unfriendly local legislation. An elected member of a territorial legislature is sworn to uphold the constitution. Now suppose the constitution guarantees to your neighbor the right to hold slaves, as property, in the territory. Through organizational authority, one is bound to support the neighbor's right to slaves, regardless of what one thinks about the merits of slavery. After all, Lincoln explains, many of us who are opposed to slavery nonetheless feel duty bound to support the fugitive slave law because it is the law of this country. One must go along with the law, even when one does so reluctantly. (In this reasoning, Lincoln in effect reproduces the reasons for the public confessional as a plan.) Yet, according to the principle of unfriendly local legislation, a legislator can lawfully violate this duty if the people in the territory decide to violate it. Dred Scott and the principle of unfriendly local legislation define no consistent model for what a legislator should do when faced with the situation of ruling on slaves in the territory.

## LINCOLN AND DOUGLAS AS TACTICIANS

How do Lincoln and Douglas fare as tacticians? One test of the adequacy of our understanding of a Tactics module in rhetorical design is that it provide a representation of rhetorical "moves" that makes it easy to shift from is to ought, from description to normative evaluation. In this spirit, we evaluate Lincoln and Douglas as tactical designers of rhetoric.

### Lincoln on the Offense and Douglas on the Defense

On the offense, Lincoln is slow and plodding but nonetheless steadily evolving. His positive structure remains eclipsed by Douglas' in the early debates and reveals itself only in the later ones. Even when he is decisively on the offense, furthermore, his offense is never as potent and concentrated as the offensive burst of Douglas in the opening at Ottawa.

On the defense, Douglas is weak and inconsistent. He forfeits many opportunities to play defense when a good defense would be helpful. One of the best examples of a missed opportunity is Douglas' reply at Quincy. Defense is most important when an opponent comes out with a compelling view of the world that remains unchallenged. The Quincy opening is among Lincoln's finest offensive minutes in the debate. He uses the opportunity to go into depth about the Republican party, its history, and its principles. As leader of the party, Lincoln uses this opening to elaborate his organizational authority, historical, and principle plans. If there was ever a time for Douglas to play good defense, it is in his Quincy reply.

That is not what Douglas does. He stays with his negative offense and rehearses the now much hashed themes about the 1854 Republicans and abolitionist resolutions, many if not most of which Lincoln has answered. He again explains how he ended up with erroneous information about the Springfield convention; again challenges Lincoln to show how he used this information knowing it was untrue; again recounts Lincoln's public confessionals at Freeport, that Lincoln said he would not be pledged to the Republican resolutions seeking "no more slave states" but that he'd be "sorry" to have to vote on the question; again accuses Lincoln of holding no position on the self-government options of territories that have not eliminated slaves from their territories—even though Lincoln's responses at Freeport do cover this case. Lincoln had been clear about the conditions (the elimination of slaves) under which he would accept a territory coming into statehood with a slave constitution. So Douglas' remark is off the point. So too is his response to Lincoln's reply to the charge of giving different messages north and south. In the Quincy opening, Lincoln had showed that some of his strongest anti-abolition statements were made in Ottawa, abolition country. This response indicates that Lincoln makes no ideological partitions in his speeches based on geography. Douglas' replies overlook the fact that Lincoln had been responsive to him. Rather than conceding Lincoln's point, Douglas continues to misrepresent and attack it. Douglas would have been better served by a more pinpoint defense than a repetitive negative offense.

Figure 8.1 is a schematic to help us visualize Douglas' meager repertoire as a defensive tactician. The top half illustrates two plans Lincoln coordinates with his tactical offense: precedent and a conspiracy plan. In the precedent plan, used for positive offense, Lincoln threads the events of the Founders at the time of the Declaration (1776), the Missouri Compromise (1820), and the new Republicans (1856) through the principle that slavery is evil and should be contained and eventually eliminated. In the conspiracy plan, which Lincoln uses on the negative offense, Douglas and the Democrats have been involved in a 3-year conspiracy, from the Kansas Act (1854) to Dred Scott (1857) and beyond, to nationalize slavery.

The bottom half of the schematic illustrates the defensive moves Douglas makes, across the seven debates, to attack the information in these two offense-minded plans. Douglas' attack defense is denoted within rectangles. Any text below a rectangle indicates Lincoln's responses to repair the consequences of Douglas' attack.

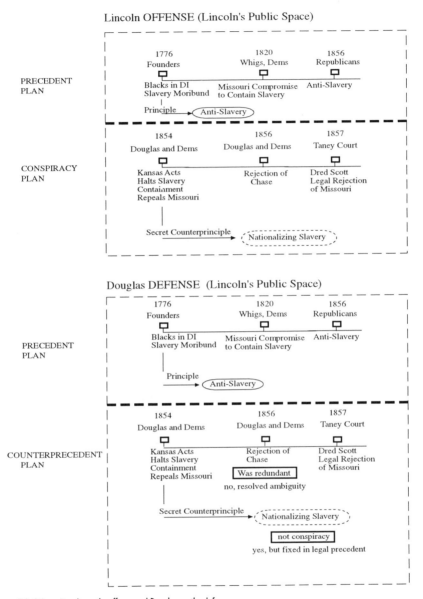

FIG. 8.1.   Lincoln on the offense and Douglas on the defense.

Note that there are few rectangles in the lower half of the schematic, and every rectangle is answered by Lincoln in a counter. Douglas' most sustained defense throughout the debates is that the Democrats could not have conspired to nationalize slavery. Dred Scott was an unknown at the time of

Kansas, Buchanan was in England, and so on. The events Lincoln threads into a conspiracy could not have been intended. Lincoln, however, anticipates this defense in the first debate, at Ottawa. In the later debates he withdraws his conspiracy charge in favor of a legal counterprecedent set by Dred Scott that makes the nationalization of slavery inevitable. An agile tactician, Lincoln changes his offense under the pressure of an effective defense.

Douglas seldom defends against Lincoln's positive structure dealing with the founder's moral aversion to slavery and their effort to contain, and gradually eliminate, slavery. The absence of Douglas' defense is apparent, and curious, to Lincoln himself. At several times through the debates, Lincoln claims a forfeit of sorts, because, as he says, he has never heard one word of criticism or refutation from Douglas about the principles of the Republican party or the reasons for its founding. Douglas is so silent on the moral issue of slavery that it is Lincoln who must infer that Douglas just "don't care" about the morality of slavery and that it is his lack of care that divides Republicans from Democrats.

### Douglas on the Offense and Lincoln on the Defense

Now we use a similar schematic (Fig. 8.2) to consider Lincoln on the defense with respect to two of Douglas' most often used offense moves. One is his ubiquitous association of popular sovereignty with a series of events: the founding of the country, the solution to the slavery question, the inspiration of the 1850 compromise, and Douglas' own Kansas Act. The second is his ubiquitous association of the Republicans with a conspiracy to abolitionize the country.

Rectangles again indicate places where Lincoln responds on defense. The X mark *in a box* indicates a place where Lincoln's response seems ample and pointed enough to effectively attack the event. The X mark *on a line* indicates a place where Lincoln's response seems ample and pointed enough to effectively attack the inference that Douglas' precedent events are in fact common instantiations of a single principle.

Note how thoroughly Lincoln attacks Douglas' major offense-minded structures. Douglas offers very few counters to Lincoln's defensive blocks. When we focus on defense maneuvers, one is justifiably led to ask, where is Douglas?

A defensive scorecard is useful at this point. Overall, both speakers play offense more than defense. That is to be expected, because the requirements for defense are more stringent. Defensive play, after all, is reactive, requiring a communicative background with well-delineated and narrowly referenced

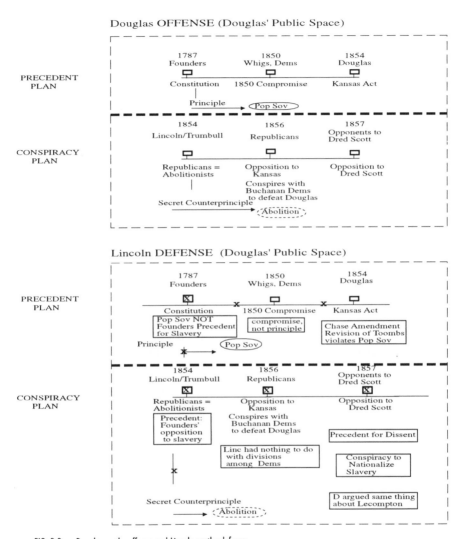

FIG. 8.2.  Douglas on the offense and Lincoln on the defense.

patterns for tactics to work from. Overall, Lincoln plays defense far more than Douglas. Defense is Lincoln's strength. It is Douglas' weakness. Overall, repair defense is far more common in the debates than attack defense.

Lincoln and Douglas spend more time repairing the damage done by the other's offense than they do causing their own damage by dismantling piece by piece the offense of the other. Douglas almost never plays attack defense. As the debates wear on, Lincoln shifts his dominant defense from a repair to an attack defense. From Galesburg, he homes in on the chief contradiction in Douglas' offense, takes it apart syllogistically and in other ways, and never seems to let go. Although we had no strong rooting interest going into the debates, we find it hard not to imagine picking Lincoln the more consummate designer of rhetoric, in light of his capacity to mount a ferocious attack defense coupled with furnishing a great deal of offsetting information against Douglas that allows Lincoln to elaborate his public model without jeopardizing its consistency.

To return to the question of where is Douglas, Douglas doubtless spends most of his time on offense, positive and negative. But much of his time is spent on a kind of negative attack that veers from public discourse per se. It is a kind of negative attack that challenges the opponent's qualifications to engage in public discourse. It is a kind of attempt to knock the opponent out of the game, to threaten Lincoln's face.

## THREATENING FACE

Public discourse is "faceless" (Brown & Levinson, 1987) in the sense that speakers and opponents interact from role relationships rather than from their unique individual identities. The speaker and the opponent are usually persons entitled and entrusted to speak out of a role: a senator, a dean, a toastmaster, a candidate for office, and so on. Because their roles are institutionalized, it is often thought inappropriate for a public speaker to "get personal" with the opponent as it were—to express the spectrum of feelings, emotions, rushes, twinges, and twangs that intense personal friends, lovers, family members, or enemies feel when confronting one another face to face. Getting personal in our personal lives leaves us open—and vulnerable—to channels of information we consider sacred and hidden from the public world. We thus choose partners for these nonpublic relationships with care and trust.

The sensory space (chapter 7) pipelines directly into the realms of experiences we consider personal and private. A sensory space offers a speaker a great deal of creative potential in formulating public models. This potential, however, can be exploited for ill purposes at the tactical level. A speaker can dredge up material from the sensory space in order to compromise the opponent as a public person, to show that the opponent either lacks the qualifications to be a public spokesperson or has engaged in some behaviors so illicit, outrageous, or inappropriate that they disqualify him or her (an otherwise qualified person) from a public forum (Fig. 8.3). In politics at large such potential is often referred to as "dirty tricks."

Threatening Face

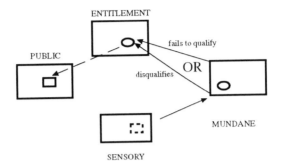

FIG. 8.3.   Weakening entitlement alignments in a face threat.

In rhetoric, we might call this behavior "threatening the opponent's face" or more simply the *face threat*. The reason for the name is this: In public discourse, the norm is that both speaker and opponent will remain institutionally faceless or with a face that is given personal support insofar as it is visible. Although many plans of rhetoric are faceless, some are not. Douglas' "no-malice" alignment in an autobiographical narrative requires the speaker to support the face of the opponent in order to justify "fair" public and faceless attacks on him or her. Douglas needs to support Lincoln, the person, in order to gain credibility and distance on his attack of Lincoln, the opponent.

We must be clear at this juncture to distinguish face threats from Plans that weaken an alignment in an agent's entitlement space. Suppose Professor Smith, a noted scholar in Asian policy, makes a public statement about our funding of European nations. A speaker may question Professor Smith's qualifications to speak about Europe without threatening his face. Face threats, being tactical, with the opponent in the immediate vicinity, have an element of sabotage about them. To threaten the opponent's face, the speaker must first have made some implicit agreement to share a platform, an arena, with the opponent. The fact threat is the sudden, unexpected suspension of this agreement during the course of rhetoric. Douglas could threaten Lincoln's face only by accepting to debate him, and, in so doing, offering implicit support for his standing to be an opponent.

Douglas squanders many opportunities to play serious defense in favor of ridiculing Lincoln's qualifications to appear on the same platform with him. In his opening at Ottawa, we learn little about Douglas' regard for Lincoln because Douglas casts Lincoln less as a tactical opponent than as an agent of counterprecedent and conspiracy. Douglas' low regard for Lincoln as an opponent is first made known to us in Lincoln's reply at Ottawa, where Lincoln himself complains, and at the same time makes fun of, Douglas' feeling of aloofness and superiority toward his challenger. Hearing Lincoln's charge that Douglas and the Democrats are conspiring to nationalize slavery, Douglas (reports Lincoln) admonished him that making such an unsubstantiated charge is the same as lying. At other times, Lincoln notes at Ottawa, Douglas has made it known that he "honorably" restrained himself from calling Lincoln a "liar" because, as he puts it, Lincoln could not conceivably attack Douglas without trying to make a joke. Lincoln indicates he is caught between a rock and a hard place when it comes to public discourse with Douglas. By making a charge against Douglas, he is, within Douglas' logic of disrespect, violating a principle of evidence or just having fun.

In his rejoinder at Ottawa, Douglas demonstrates the dismissive attitude that Lincoln portrayed. Like a child looking for a compliment for form over substance, Lincoln is cast by Douglas as a person whose pride is hurt because Douglas will not respond to the elegance of a "house" analogy Lincoln used to make his conspiracy charges. "His vanity is offended because I won't go into that beautiful passage about building the house." Douglas associates Lincoln's engagement in public discourse with "getting personal" in a face to face world of fragile moralities. Lincoln's bids for occupying a shared public space with Douglas get deflected by the incumbent to a shared sensory space and, finally, to Lincoln's private sensory space. Lincoln's openness to discuss the "problems of the day" with Douglas becomes, in Douglas' formulations, "Lincoln's (personal) problem with Douglas" and, finally, "Lincoln's problem."

Douglas seems to think himself deserving of engaging public matters without Lincoln's intrusion. He justifies the asymmetry on the basis of his longer, continuous experience holding public office. "I'm not green enough to let [Lincoln] make a charge he doesn't know to be true and I know to be false." Experience, presumably, entitles Douglas to public discourse without risking the fragile human trusts required to maintain it. Douglas claims a public zone that is distinct from a personal one, and yet conveniently dismisses much of Lincoln's best attack defensive as personal attack. For example, instead of defending Lincoln's conspiracy charge involving Douglas and the Democrats, Douglas tries to shame Lincoln for offering it: "Lincoln has not character enough for integrity, merely on his own ipse dixit, to arraign me and the rest for conspiracy."

In his reply at Freeport, Douglas has the opportunity to respond to Lincoln's responses to his key questions about slavery in the territories. Douglas uses two face-threatening gestures to indicate he does not see himself in a debate among equals. For one, he presumes that Lincoln had a purpose not to be specific and became so only under Douglas' coercion: "I am glad I've gotten Lincoln to be specific." For another, he assumes that some of Lincoln's questions are more symptomatic of the character of the questioner than useful in airing public views. When Lincoln asks about the possibility of Dred Scott providing a legal basis for permitting slavery in all the states, Douglas replies, "I am amused he would ask such a question." "No person of intelligence or decency would endorse that doctrine." "For the Supreme Court to do that would be an act of moral treason."

In his reply at Charleston, Douglas turns Lincoln's use of Trumbull's speech as an indication of Lincoln's incapacity to make a speech of his own. "Why, I ask, doesn't Lincoln make a speech of his own instead of taking up his time reading Trumbull's speech at Alton?" Lincoln's opening gambit at Charleston becomes, in Douglas' stern eyes, a disappointment of the expectation that he was dealing with an opponent capable of public discourse: "I supposed Mr. Lincoln was capable of making a public speech on his own account or I should not have accepted the banter from him for a joint discussion." Douglas later indicates he was lured into the debate under false pretences: "I had supposed we had assembled here today for the purpose of a joint discussion between Lincoln and myself upon the political questions that now agitate the country." But "what question of public policy" has Lincoln put forth before you? Lincoln's real motives are personal and time-wasting, to hide his revolutionary principles, which he cannot defend. "I am not going to allow them to waste much of my time with these personal matters." He has not yet "uttered a word about the politics of the day." Lincoln's object in the debates "is to conduct this on personal matters." Lincoln "is a man of bad character."

According to Douglas, when he is proved wrong—at Springfield for example—he retracts the charge like a gentleman. But Lincoln, Douglas complains, refuses to retract his words, as if Lincoln's refusal were merely a matter of personal ill will. Lincoln answers in a latter debate that when the public evidence is there for him to retract, he will do so. But as it stands, he must work with the logical accumulation of premises and evidence drawn from them. This is why they cannot be withdrawn simply because of personal good will and the lack of malice. In his rejoinder at Galesburg, Douglas again complains that when he is found wrong, he retracts charges. But Lincoln dares to put forth charges and then dares not to retract them when he is answered.

After delving into a history of his mistaken account about Springfield and how any "honest man" would be fully satisfied with his voluntary retraction,

Douglas shifts into how "any honest man would be disgusted by Lincoln's charge of forgery at Charleston." Where is Lincoln's retraction? Douglas wonders aloud, "[D]oes Lincoln want to push things to the point of personal difficulty here?" "I began this contest treating him kindly and with courtesy."

In his opening at Quincy, Lincoln reminds Douglas that the charges of "forger," "conspirator," and other personally damaging charges in the debates began with Douglas himself. The Ottawa debate, he recalls, began with Douglas placing Lincoln square in a conspiracy to topple the American way of life. Because he well understands the conventions of tactical debate, Lincoln hints that he does not take personal offense when he is put in the midst of conspiracy and his basis as a leader is called into question. But Douglas is also mistaken, Lincoln goes on to suggest, if he thinks Douglas has been handling him across the debates in a gentle, dignified way, as Douglas now claims.

Lincoln often responds to Douglas' face threats with self-deprecation, as if to turn into a positive Douglas' appraisal of him as a mere human. One of Lincoln's standard reactions to Douglas' threat of face is to disarm the threat by effacing himself. "Douglas asks me if I wish to push this to the point of personal difficulty. I tell him, no." "He did not make a mistake when, in one of his earlier speeches, he called me an `amiable' man, though perhaps he was mistaken to have called me `intelligent.'"

Douglas saves some of his darkest personal venom when he discusses how Lincoln will not go along with the Supreme Court decision on Dred Scott. He attacks Lincoln across the debates for this show of disrespect to the court, but in his Quincy reply he is careful to link Lincoln's public display with a "sour-grapes" disposition that has bedeviled Lincoln throughout his professional career. When I used to practice law with Lincoln, Douglas says, I never knew him to get beat when he didn't get mad at the judge and go out on the stump seeking the support of the mobs for his anger. Douglas, on the other hand, holds himself up as a consummate professional who is willing to live with any judgment of the court. "When I got beat I never dreamed of making a stump speech to the people." "I take the decisions of the Supreme Court as the law of the land and do not question them."

In his rejoinder at Quincy, Lincoln retaliates at the personal level. He sarcastically remarks that Douglas wants to know how we will reverse Dred Scott. Taking a page from his Ottawa reply, Lincoln repeats that the Judge "ought to know" because he himself enlisted his friends to overrule the Supreme Court on a national bank and on the power of a governor to remove a secretary of state. And he got his title "Judge" by persuading the legislature to have the state court add five new judges, including himself, over the protests of the original four. If there is villainy in opposing court decisions, Lincoln concludes, Douglas' record indicates he must be a chief villain.

Douglas relies on face threats more than Lincoln, and his behavior seems related to his incapacity or unwillingness to play defense. To play defense, a speaker must take the opponent's plans seriously enough to repair them. A speaker who threatens the opponent's face, who shows a low regard for the opponent, who questions the public import of the speaker's positions, will see a diminished need to play defense. Conversely, a speaker with a diminished capacity to play defense will substitute defense by engaging in personal attack, tactics lacking coordination with plans and drawing from personal insult scripts in the world of everyday interaction. Playing poor defense and threatening face are associated, although the causality can go in both directions. Whichever direction the causality flows, the association between poor defense and face threats in Douglas' rhetorical design is apparent.

A tempting view on face threats is that they lie outside rhetoric as an art of design. The tactic, as we just suggested, seems to derive directly from insult scripts in the culture and has little to do with education. No challenging or interesting rhetorical design, it seems, requires speakers to threaten the opponent's face. When a face threat is initiated, the speaker seems to stop designing events for the here and now of an audience in favor of bullying another human being who has been stripped of the insulating role of opponent.

Nonetheless, there are various explanations of how face threats can play a legitimate role in rhetorical design. They can be classified as venomous misfires on a conspiracy, organizational authority, or some other plan driven by a negative offense, where the armor of being an abstract "counteragent" or "opponent" is accidentally (or deliberately) penetrated and the self beneath the armor is hit. In such cases, face threats are just an occupational hazard of rhetorical design, a reason why we sometimes caution that the entrance to public arenas is best taken by folks with thick skins. In such cases, face threats are the personalization of formal (impersonal) attack. In other cases, face threats, meant with no malice, can be seen as a legitimate extension of the entitlement and venue plans. In civic rhetoric, where any fit adult can supposedly climb the stump, the qualifications for public discourse must remain open and threats to face discouraged. But in most venues, and certainly the Lincoln/Douglas debates, there need to be filters on who can speak. Viewed as a filter to define entitlement and venue, face threats merely arise as a personalization of the consequences of an impersonal and nonprejudicial exclusion.

In suggesting that face threats are a debased, if not altogether dispensable, form of rhetorical design, we don't mean to argue against the discretionary decision of a speaker to personalize what is otherwise an impersonal process; nor do we mean to dispute that there are often impersonal and nonprejudicial reasons for exclusion from speaking before the fact. We only mean to argue against the high-mindedness of the face threat when a speaker uses it only for tactical advantage, as a way of beating an opponent by complaining, after the fact, that the opponent lacks the credentials to compete. Any theory of rhetoric needs boundary conditions on legitimate and debased uses, and the boundaries we draw are that artful rhetoric requires either the lack of face or the support of face, but not face threats issued *only* in the pursuit of a tactical advantage. Face threats in this bold form indicate fissures, failures, in the Tactics module; not ability.

## MUST TACTICS RESULT IN A MALE COCKFIGHT?

Our description of tactics has been undertaken mainly through competitive, even pugilistic, game metaphors. Tactics have an offense and defense like chess and bridge. They expose and threaten face, like boxing. Many who read this chapter on tactics are likely to understand why they do not like rhetoric. Tactics may serve up the worst reminders of the silly zealousness of high school debate, where speakers and their audiences may think the object of rhetoric is to beat the opponent in a brutal game of one-upmanship. Kathleen Jamieson, in her PBS commentaries on campaign rhetoric during the 1992 Presidential election, in her book *Dirty Politics: Deception, Distraction, & Democracy* (1992), and in more recent empirical work she is conducting with Joseph Capella at the University of Pennsylvania, noted that the press's fascination with reporting elections as competitive games, horse races, associating candidates with rising or dipping polls and Q-factors, may dampen the electorate's interest in the (plans-based) issues and policies that divide candidates on substantive grounds.

These are worthy reminders but they throw the baby out with the bathwater if they are used to condemn, wholesale, the place of tactics in rhetoric. First, as we have mentioned all along, Tactics are but one part of rhetorical design. They are not the whole enterprise and certainly not part of the goal structure of rhetoric. The goals of rhetoric are to be predictive, responsive, and human with an audience. A speaker cannot create a successful rhetorical design if the focus is to "get" the opponent at all costs. The opponent fits into the process of rhetorical design in only an indirect way: The speaker needs to engage the opponent to show that his or her position can be responsive to many cases that are of interest to an undecided audience. The principal reason for being responsive to opponents, then, is not to beat or humiliate them but to acknowledge the limits of monological predictiveness and to honor the interest of an audience member seeking to come to a decision by benefit of a full exchange. Jamieson is surely right to worry that the tactical dimension of American political rhetoric can overwhelm, and to a large extent has overwhelmed, plans-based issues as a basis for press reporting and so, indirectly, audience decision making. But the correction to this imbalance—one Jamieson would likely endorse—is to call for a change in tactical styles rather than an elimination of tactics. There is nothing wrong with reporting on elections as a horse race as long as the speed of the horses is gauged by the clarity and comprehensiveness with which they can reveal their plans for the country, both through direct presentation and cross-examination.

Second, were the speaker not to credit the opponent with the capacity to persuade, the speaker would do best to ignore the opponent altogether and focus only on putting the best positive case forward. Indeed, in rhetorical settings, ignoring an opponent is considered less respectful than engaging him or her. Attending to the opponent is a necessary side effect of having respect for the opponent's capacities. Such attention, however, is a side effect of rhetorical design, not the point of it. A speaker who forgets that fact falls out of rhetoric and into interpersonal warfare. Unfortunately, it is all too true that many public figures have forgotten this lesson and have collapsed the tactical dimension of rhetoric with face threats, verbal assaults on character. Commenting on the breakdown of civility in our public discourse, Meg Greenfield (1995) noted that our political rhetoric has too often degenerated into "endless sneering and snickering and reducing others to a caricature of unworthy motives." But she wisely understood that the alternative is not a "namby-pamby toothless public discourse" but rather a tactical style that, although "rough" and "skeptical," nonetheless insists on a "frontal" engagement into the opponent's argument, not his or her face.

Third, even when attending to the competition with the opponent, the target of the rhetor's attack is not[4] the opponent as a person, but the representation of the opponent's public model, which the speaker perceives as contrary in at least some operative respects to his or her own. As we saw with the "no-malice" alignment, a design of rhetoric is arguably more effective as public argument when it grants the opponent personal respect and deference than when these personal elements are withheld or denied.

---

[4]This assumes we have ruled out face threats as part of rhetorical design. It is too strong if we rule them back in. Our position is to keep them in, conditionally, so long as the speaker's attack of the opponent has an interpretation within the speaker's public model.

In sum, the rhetor is after predictability, responsiveness, and humanness to persuade. The reason to persuade is to create the common alignments that are needed to carry out productive collective action in the world. The actions of the opponent threaten these alignments and so these projects. Responding to the opponent's public model, the speaker tries to mitigate, if not neutralize, their influence on the audience's decision making. The speaker does so in order to fight for his or her worldly projects. But this hardly needs to be a dirty fight or a fight among or on behalf of stereotypical male styles and values. It is certainly not a fight to bully or beat another human being into submission. Unlike a boxing match or a cockfight, it is always a fight for something larger than the interaction. The element of winning is there, but only because something more than winning is at stake. And, in the case of Lincoln, the more that can be at stake are public abstractions of great intrinsic value, such as increased social and racial justice.

That said, one scarcely wants to deny that the Lincoln/Douglas debates are examples of rhetorical design conceived and crafted by stereotypical White male voices and styles. The tactics of the debates are notoriously bloody, face-threatening, competitive, and sledgehammer explicit. Other tactical styles can be far more bloodless, face-saving, cooperative, and gesturally subtle. The style and signature of a designer that defines a particular tactical style are not incorporated into the Tactics module per se. They are rather part of the large and complex story about how the various modules of rhetorical design are coordinated (chapter 10). In conjunction with rhetoric and the diversity of coordinative styles, there now exists a substantive, impressive, and growing literature that seeks to revisit the rhetorical tradition from nonwhite (Walker, 1992) nonmale (Campbell, 1989; Poulakos, 1993; Solomon, 1991;) and nonwestern (Liu, in press) perspectives. The value of this literature is to define multiple cultures, personalities, styles, and signature voices through which rhetoric can be designed. Against the background of this literature, a useful distinction to bear in mind is that between accommodating diversity and difference in a single theory of rhetorical design, and seeking new theories for each different site of rhetoric studied. For reasons of generality and minimalist parsimony, we prefer to think that a single theory of rhetorical design should accommodate many culturally diverse sites of rhetoric. Given our own limited data source, this remains a preference more than a claim we can now defend.

However, we do think that various efforts to frame a gender-or culture-specific rhetoric have suffered because their proponents have not sought to generalize a unified theory of rhetorical design prior to specializing it to the gender or cultural group. Efforts, for example, to define a "feminist" rhetoric, in opposition to the Aristotelian tradition, have tended to take less than satisfying directions. One example is to define a "feminist" rhetoric by removing the tactical component altogether from rhetorical design. This removes conflict from a theory of rhetoric. But it also threatens to make rhetoric solipsistic and monological, incapacitating opponents and audiences from interrogating a speaker's public model that they would like to understand better but cannot. Western rhetorics tend to confuse tactics with a conflictual style of interaction, but tactical interaction can also be very cooperative, even when the speaker and opponent have opposing interests. More cooperative tactics, male or female, would approximate dialectic, where the search for truth is the dominant interest, and where speakers and opponents agree to engage in constructive fact-finding before deciding how to adjudicate the competing interests in the situation.[5]

A second direction, sometimes used to define a militant "in your face" rhetoric for politically marginalized groups, is to restrict the range of acceptable tactics to negative offense, an offense that attacks the opponent through caricatures of the opponent's actual words and reasoning in context. The Plans most often associated with this negative offense are conspiracy and an abstraction of organizational authority, where the opponent inherits the values of the politically correct (viewed from the political right) or the dominant culture (viewed from the political left). As we saw in the previous chapter, from the example of Lincoln and Douglas, these plan types are easy to apply to the opponent from a distance. Lincoln and Douglas do not use this tactical/plan combination to make serious progress on the issues within the debates. They use it to throw one another on the psychological defensive so that the target will not have time to display his actual reasoning and positions. This kind of rhetoric, once known as the rhetoric of paranoia, has become disturbingly mainstream in American society. It now fills much of the programming on "Talk TV" and radio. It has become increasingly evident in the writing of academics and accepted by the editorial boards of respected academic journals. Whatever one thinks of the merits of this rhetoric, our principal point is that it is hardly a "new" turn on the rhetoric we already have. Indeed, it is a stilted narrowing of it.

---

[5]A penetrating example of such fact finding, problem analysis, and reframing is Jamieson's (1995) account of women and leadership.

# Nine

# Events

The Events module makes word, phrasal, and clausal lexicalizations part of the rhetorical design. From the view of Events, the design structure is not organized into public models, nor into the positive and negative structures of the speaker and the opponent. From the vantage of Events, the design structure is organized into conceptual structures with the potential of uniquely tying the design structure to the immediate audience. The Events module, like the Tactics module, forages the rhetorical situation, searching for opportunities to elaborate the structure in ways to connect with the immediate audience; searching for ways to make the structure seem the personal possession of the immediate audience; Events searches for ways to make the audience feel as if the design structure were custom tailored to fit the uniqueness of the rhetorical situation that it now occupies; and Events looks for ways to make the immediate audience feel that the rhetorical design is relevant to it, so thoroughly does the lexicalized structure reflect *its* take on things.

Identifying tight connections between structure and the immediate audience is hard, even if the speaker wants to adapt to the audience only to amuse it. It is arguably just as hard, if not harder, to find connections that make the speaker more substantively persuasive. Substantive convergences of this kind require a three-way coordination between Plans, Tactics, and Events, with Events uniquely lexicalizing aspects of plan and tactical structures to fit the immediate audience. Events must work behind the scenes to mitigate the otherwise jarring cognitive demands that Plans and Tactics place on audiences. For example, to comprehend a plan, the immediate audience must be mentally transported to the center of situations far displaced in time and space, situations embedding abstractions about social truth and falsehood, without the audience sensing artificiality, without things seeming forced, without causing the audience to notice how far in abstractive space it is being asked to surrender itself. Yet, if the structure is well adapted to the audience, the audience will remain under the illusion that the relational dynamics are just the reverse, that the speaker has surrendered to it. Insofar as there is an opponent to challenge the speaker's plans, the comprehension of tactics requires the same jarring effort, as the audience must referee a contest between the speaker and opponent over and above understanding their utterances. Yet the adaptation of a tactic through unique lexicalization can have the same mitigating effects on audience comprehension as adapting a plan, making the immediate audience think that it is has chosen of its own free will to referee a contest when in fact the speaker had all along cast the audience into the role of referee.

Events look for ways to turn abstract structure into live and engaging lexical performances. Although the output of both Events and Presentation are object classes, the output of Events are uniquely lexicalized objects and events, swaths of discourse that strike the audience as performed, what we call rhetorical performatives. Coordinated with Plans or Tactics, a speaker can involve Events to satisfy humanness goals in the midst of concurrently satisfying predictability and responsiveness goals. Yet a speaker can generate rhetorical performatives independent of Plans and Tactics, indicating a speaker who, for a moment at least, is willing to step outside the burdens of public discourse and address the audience as one human being to another. The speaker uses uniquely lexicalized events in such a case to divert the audience away from the task at hand in order to wink at it.

To summarize, Events sweep over the design structure in search of unique lexicalizations to engage the immediate audience. Unlike our discussion of Plans and Tactics, where we recreated continuous segments of the debates in the chronology in which they unfolded, our discussion of Events reconstructs the Lincoln/Douglas debates in a more scattered fashion. This is not accidental. To track how plans get introduced over time in rhetorical situations is to track how a reporter, listening for on-the-record discourse to quote, would report on them. The Events module, on the other hand, knows nothing about Plans and Tactics per se. It knows only about the rhetorical situation and how to lexicalize anything in the design structure that would give the immediate audience a feeling of connection, a sense of ownership, over that structure.

Any object or event class in the design structure is a candidate for unique lexicalization. Two consequences follow. First, the potential of relating the structure to audience is vast and diffuse. Second, the Events module can, and often must, act opportunistically. It creates rhetorical "performances" whenever it can, with no necessary relationship between where a performance might occur and the current state of a rhetorical design as monitored from the view of Plans and Tactics. As we observed earlier, Events can be coordinated with Plans or Tactics to allow a speaker a spark of playful humanness amid the work of being predictive and responsive. But rhetorical performances can function as stand-alone performances, and often stand out most, although not necessarily most effectively, when they function in a stand-alone fashion.

## RHETORICAL PERFORMATIVES

We now survey classes of rhetorical performatives. Our survey is not exhaustive. Our goal is to review enough classes of performatives and in enough detail to suggest both the broad and profound ways the Events module can alter, and so impact a rhetorical design.

### Lexical Elasticity: Making Events Scalable

Lexical elasticity involves scaling the public space addressed in Plans to the proportions of the immediate situation. To follow the effect of this performative, we must appreciate the differences between public spaces and rhetorical situations. Public spaces are abstract and endure across situations. Situations are concrete, temporally and spatially bounded, and, at best, furnish a specific illustrative site for a public space. The unanchored abstractions of any public space seem less immediate, concrete, timely, and heart-wrenching than when they are anchored in a rhetorical situation. Conversely, the dense and often confoundingly complex detail of any situation muddies the pure abstractions needed to crystallize the relevance of public space entities. Were speakers not able to take performative steps to scale public spaces and rhetorical situations to comparable proportions, the impact of bringing to expression any abstracted public space for the attention of a situated audience would not have the virtuoso potential it does have. The performance of a speaker in bringing about this comparable scaling can take one of two directions. The first abstracts the situation to the scale of the public space. This process makes the rhetorical situation a symbol for the public space brought to it. The second concretizes the public space down to the particulars of the situation. This process makes the public space a camera lens trained to focus on the sensory experience of the audience that instantiates, and so brings home to it, key public space abstractions.

Both processes rely on the elasticity of lexicalized events, their capacity to be scaled upward or downward on a ladder of abstraction.

### Scaling the Rhetorical Situation to the Public Space: Abstracting Events

In this form of adaptation, concrete elements of the situation are called on to stand in for public space abstractions. Douglas has spent much of the

Ottawa debates establishing a Republican conspiracy to abolitionize the country, grant negro citizenship, and allow intermingling among the races. Freeport, a city in the north of Illinois and the locale of the second debate, provides a site to demonstrate the truth of the conspiracy in action. He offers to the Freeport gathering that he has sighted Frederick Douglas escorted about town by a White woman, in a carriage driven by a White man.

> I have reason to recollect that some people in this country think that Fred. Douglas is a very good man. The last time I came here to make a speech, while I was talking on the stand to you people of Freeport, as I am today, I saw a carriage, and a magnificent one too, drive up and take its position on the outside of the crowd, with a beautiful young lady on the front seat, with a man and Fred Douglas, the negro, on the back seat, and the owner of the carriage in front driving the negro.

Douglas recalls the same story at Jonesboro (in the South), where he places Frederick Douglas not with one White woman, but two: "Why, they brought Fred Douglas to Freeport, when I was addressing a meeting there, in a carriage driven by the white owner, the negro sitting inside with the white lady and her daughter."

The local reference is designed not only to anger the White audience but to stand in as a reference to the national abolition sentiment that Douglas opposes.

Sometimes the generalization of events is triggered more through the juxtaposition of local conditions and public space abstractions than through direct resemblance. Using this kind of event generalization, a speaker can tie the minute and typically invisible detail of an audience's everyday life to larger abstractions. Lincoln uses such contingent generalization at the very start of his Charleston opening.

> While I was at the hotel to-day, an elderly gentleman called upon me to know whether I was really in favor of producing a perfect equality between the negroes and white people. While I had not proposed to myself on this occasion to say much on that subject, yet as the question was asked me I thought I would occupy perhaps five minutes in saying something in regard to it. I will say then that I am not, nor ever have been, in favor of bringing about in any way the social and political equality of the white and black races.

What is interesting about this story is not that Lincoln thought to talk about the race question but that a random meeting with a nondescript "elderly" gentleman in the hotel gave him the thought. Event abstraction in this form mingles the contingent and taken-for-granted of the audience's lives with the importance of public space universals. It gives the audience the sense that Lincoln has taken notice of their local context, and, more importantly, that he recognizes in their local conditions an immediacy and gravity of concern that can only be answered by moving into his public abstractions.

On occasion, the abstraction of events can occur through an analogy drawn from history. The most memorable and effective is Douglas' analogy before the Alton audience. Throughout the debates, Douglas had associated popular sovereignty with the founders' commitment to self-government. But Douglas had never made a concrete association between the situation faced by any of his audiences and the situation faced by the beloved generation of the Revolution. At Alton he does. He likens those who oppose self-government to George III and English control over the American colonies. What had been an abstraction restricted to slavery in the territories becomes a cross-reference between the concrete situation of the American colonists and the situated audience at Alton.

### Scaling the Public Space to the Rhetorical Situation: Concretizing Events

Concretizing scales down public abstractions to the particulars of the imme-diate audience and its experiences. There are two major processes of concre-tizing in the debates: regionalizing and home-spunning.

### Regionalizing Events

Regionalizing is a performative in which public space abstractions are adapted to the regional biases of the audience. Generally speaking, a regionalizing device will be markedly different if we are talking about southern Illinois in 1858 or southern Italy in the late 16th century. The point in regionalization is to offer language that is "around here" where "around here" cuts off more possibilities than the national discourse. Although Douglas never stops complaining that Lincoln changes his message North and South, Douglas is more guilty of giving specially regionalized perform-ances. He adapts for region when he moves from Ottawa, in the North, to Jonesboro, in the South. In the North, the Illinois "Republicans" are the chief troublemakers because they adopt abolition as their platform. In the South, the enemy is no longer identified as Republicans but as "ambitious North-erners." In both North and South, Douglas does not fail to mention Trumbull's "double-cross" of Lincoln that won Trumbull the election in 1856 and now makes Trumbull beholden to Lincoln in the current senatorial election. But only in the South does Douglas regionalize the double-cross by condemning it as a "Yankee trick." In the North, Douglas uses the Republican opposition to Dred Scott to condemn the Republicans for endorsing full negro equality. Yet, significantly, he attaches no positive significance to the Dred Scott verdict itself. In the South, Douglas strengthens the positive meaning of Dred Scott, as an affirmation of the Democratic party's founding principle of states' rights. In the South, more than the North, Douglas makes gestures of conciliation toward Buchanan and the southern Democrats. At Jonesboro, he notes that Buchanan recently backed a bill requiring constitutions to be submitted to the people. Douglas remarks that if Buchanan stands by that, "there will be no division in the Democratic party." At Alton, the other southern site, Douglas declares that "I have no personal difficulty with Mr. Buchanan or his cabinet." The real enemy, according to Douglas speaking to southern audiences, is the North, for "the moment the north obtained the majority, ambitious northern men started a scheme to abolitionize the country."

Like Douglas, Lincoln regionalizes events, but his manner of connecting to the southern audience is more through gestures of friendliness than arousing their fears of Northerners. At Jonesboro, with wry humor, Lincoln notes that by geography of birth and rearing, in Kentucky and Indiana respectively, he is more a Southerner than Douglas, who was raised in the Green Mountains of Vermont. In anticipation of the Jonesboro debate, Douglas often chortled that Lincoln would be demolished by the Southern audience. Now Lincoln, citing his Southern background at Jonesboro, accuses Douglas of failing to comprehend Southern graciousness and hospitality: "Did the Judge talk of trotting me down to Egypt to scare me to death? Why, I know this people better than he does. I was raised just a little east of here. I am a part of this people. But the Judge was raised further north, and perhaps he has some horrid idea of what this people might be induced to do."

Noting that no less a Southerner than Brooks conceded that the Founders believed slavery a moribund institution, Lincoln is quick to praise Southerners for their candor: "That was but the opinion of one man but it was such an opinion as we can never get from Judge Douglas or anybody in favor of slavery in the North at all. You can sometimes get it from a Southern man."

In his Jonesboro rejoinder, Douglas does not let Lincoln's Southern regionalizations pass without comment. He admits to being born in Vermont, but that New England is only a fine place to be from. He identifies the place of one's rearing more with youthful indiscretion than hardened roots: "I discard all flings where a man was born." Where principles are concerned, Douglas insists, place is finally not important.

> The worst Abolitionists I have ever known in Illinois have been men who have sold their slaves in Alabama and Kentucky, and have come here and turned Abolitionists whilst spending the money got for the negroes they sold, and I do not know that an Abolitionist from Indiana or Kentucky ought to have any more credit because he was born and raised among slave holders. I do not know that a native of Kentucky is more excusable because raised among slaves, his father and mother having owned slaves, he comes to Illinois, turns Abolitionist, and slanders the graves of his father and mother, and breathes curses upon the institutions under which he was born, and his father and mother.... I wish to be judged by my principles, by those great public measures and Constitutional principles upon which the peace, the happiness and the perpetuity of this Republic now rest.

To be sure, what Douglas offers here is a tactical response to Lincoln, trying to repair certain connections with the Jonesboro audience that Lincoln had tried to loosen. Yet the structures involved in Douglas' tactical response are the ties that bind Douglas to the Southern audience, suggesting that Douglas' tactical response is influenced by Events and the humanness goals as well.

### Home-Spunning Events

Events are home-spun when they are couched in the homey and homely language of the sensory world of audiences. Home-spunning is a specialization of regionalizing, that is, a special kind of concretizing elasticity that turns the abstract principle of the public space not only into the mundane of the regional audience, but in the earthiness of their mundane life—the "manure" of their mundane, so to speak, their grounded horse sense. As with regionalizing, events that are home-spun for the Illinois audience of 1858 will take different twists from other audiences in other times and places. Like regionalizing, the language of the home-spun will be from "around here" but in ways that are even more restricted and earthy than regionalized discourse. The sense of restrictiveness here is important because home-spunned language is not necessarily a dialect spoken and understood only by the locals. Home-spunned discourse, on the contrary, is often invoked to make endearing points considered universally applicable. What makes home-spunned discourse so restrictive is that its meaning is thought not to be independent of the local character spitting it out. We are supposed to hear more than what's said. We are supposed to hear what members of the town or village would hear—not the words of Abraham Lincoln alone, but "that's old Abe running his mouth again," or "Mrs. Lincoln's boy, who can never get pants long enough and can't keep his shirt buttoned, just told a number of folks about...." From the lens of sensory experiences caught in the local time and place, home-spunned performatives draw out latent universals as nuggets of wisdom. There are various categories of home-spunned performatives in the debates, a few of which we overview.

### Simple Profundities

Performatives of this type are used to endear audiences through the recitation of obvious but cleverly said wisdoms, often with a tactical edge, to cut through the heart of an opponent's pomposity. In the case of Lincoln and Douglas, the abstractions are not typically hard to capture, but Douglas sometimes tries to make them so, through obfuscation. In the Charleston debate in particular, Lincoln home-spuns Douglas' obfuscations through simple profundity to keep them crystal clear for the audience. For example, in his Charleston opening, Lincoln recounts Douglas' defense against Trumbull's charges. One of Douglas' points is that Trumbull is now trying to cover himself because he was in on the plot. Lincoln retorts with a bit of horse sense about accusation and defense, namely, the accuser's sins don't absolve the defendant's:

> I repeat, that if Trumbull had himself been in the plot, it would not at all relieve the others who were in it from blame. If I should be indicted for murder, and upon the trial it should be discovered that I had been implicated in that murder, but that the prosecuting witness was guilty too, that would not at all touch the question of my crime. It would be no relief to my neck that they discovered this other man who charged the crime upon me to be guilty too.

Douglas further charges that the Toombs' bill was forged, although he never denies the authenticity of the bill's every version. Again applying horse sense, Lincoln lectures Douglas on how, appropriately, to make the charge of forgery: You can't charge forgery if you can't show what was forged.

> Then the question is, how can Douglas call that a forgery? How can he make out that it is a forgery? What is a forgery? It is the bringing forward something in writing or in print purporting to be of a certain effect when it is altogether untrue. If you come forward with my note for one hundred dollars when I have never given such a note, there is a forgery. If you come forward with a

letter purporting to be written by me which I never wrote, there is another forgery. If you produce any thing in writing or in print saying it is so and so, the document not being genuine, a forgery has been committed. How do you make this a forgery when every piece of the evidence is genuine?

In his Charleston reply, Douglas repeats that Trumbull has been inconsistent in his charges against him. At one point, Douglas offers, Trumbull had accused him of deleting a passage in the Toombs bill that was better left in. At another point, he accused him of inserting a passage that was better left out. Douglas argues, incredibly, that the accusations against him are incoherent because they are inconsistent. Lincoln sprinkles more horse sense on the matter, noting that, in altering a document, there is nothing preventing a person from making both wrongful insertions and deletions. Professor Lincoln illustrates the point, as if teaching the law of torts to third graders:

> To illustrate: A man brings an accusation against another, and on trial the man making the charge introduces A and B to prove the accusation. At a second trial he introduces the same witnesses, who tell the same story as before, and a third witness, who tells the same thing and in addition, gives further testimony corroborative of the charge. So with Trumbull. There was no shifting of ground nor inconsistency of testimony between the new piece of evidence and what he originally introduced.

Also at Charleston, Douglas had defended himself against the charge that he inserted a clause into the Tombs' bill because (at another time) he had ordered the clause deleted. Lincoln home-spuns Douglas' explanation to expose the fact that one person can do two things (delete and insert) at different times. As if the point is not clear enough, Lincoln probes the everyday world for examples:

> I assert that you [pointing to an individual] are here to-day, and you undertake to prove me a liar by showing that you were in Mattoon yesterday.

> I say that you took your hat off your head, and you prove me a liar by putting it on your head.

> That is the whole force of Douglas's argument.

### Sayings

When simple profundities have a frozen surface form, they are known as sayings, adages, or maxims. The most recognizable saying in the debates is "thus saith the Lord," a religious expression indicating the deepest of sensory conviction. Lincoln uses this performative tactically, to characterize Douglas' zealous commitment to Dred Scott, a commitment beyond all legal or even political reason. In the past, Lincoln richly illustrates, Douglas had fought to overturn high court decisions. Now, with Dred Scott, Lincoln says, Douglas has turned the verdict of the high court into a "thus saith the Lord," a matter of infallible gospel. Lincoln home-spuns Douglas' political commitment with the religious saying to heighten the suspicion that the Judge is too badly compromised in a conspiracy plot depending on Dred Scott to leave an opening for its repeal. The juxtaposition of political and religious themes in unexpected ways is also the basis for humorous performatives, as we discuss more fully later.

### Sensory Analogies

Sensory analogies are another kind of concretizing elasticity, used to scale an issue down to the sensory understandings of the immediate audience. If the sensory analogy seems apt, its sheer familiarity can make it compelling for the immediate audience. More importantly, if the speaker—a stranger from out of town—knows enough about the immediate environs to connect with a sensory analogy, then the audience can reason that the speaker is a person of "my" world and can be trusted to lead me down paths of inference that I wouldn't know to go down on my own. The power of the sensory analogy increases as it indicates a speaker who has lived among the natives, not just one who has been briefed to talk to them and will be briefed tomorrow in another town.

Sensory analogies are legion in the debates. Some of the most colorful involve animals, a familiar aspect of 19th century agrarian life. When Lincoln finds Douglas' adherence to Dred Scott suspicious, he likens the Judge to a tenacious canine who will cling to a victim at all costs.

> But when I speak of all these things, I cannot make the judge fall loose from his adherence to this Dred Scott decision. If I may say so, and I mean by it no disrespect, he is like some creature that will hang on which he has got his hold to a thing ... you may cut his arms and limbs off and he is still hanging on. He is bespattered from the beginning of his life with war upon the courts and at last he hangs with desperation to the Dred Scott decision. (Ottawa, reply)

In frontier Illinois, there was little worse than a horse thief. In his Freeport opening, Lincoln had asked Douglas point blank if he would sanction a court ruling to permit slavery in every state. In his reply at Freeport, Douglas tries to indicate the absurdity of Lincoln's question:

> Mr. Lincoln knows that reply was made on the subject a year ago and now he wants to put the question, Suppose the Supreme Court of the United States shall decide that the States can't exclude slavery from their limits, would I sanction it? He might as well ask you, Suppose Mr. Lincoln should steal a horse, would I sanction it? It would be as gentlemanly in me to ask him what, in the event of his stealing a horse, ought to be done, as for him to ask me such a question.

At Charleston, when Lincoln wants to indicate that Douglas had full editorial control over the passages being inserted and deleted in the Toombs' bill, he likens Douglas' smothering and protective relationship to the controversial clauses as a mother bear to her cubs. The mother who carries her cubs in her mouth is always primed to put them down or sweep them up. "It was in regard to that thing precisely that I told him he had dropped the cub. Trumbull shows you that by his [Douglas] introducing the bill it was his cub."

In the same debate, Lincoln, incredulous at Douglas' wailing that documents have been forged while never denying their authenticity, likens Douglas' obfuscation to a fish that survives by blackening the water and scampering from prey: "Judge Douglas is playing cuttle-fish, a small species of fish what has no mode of defending itself when pursued except by throwing out a black fluid, which makes the water so dark the enemy cannot see it, and thus it escapes. Ain't the Judge playing the cuttle-fish?"

Not to be outfished, Douglas, wanting to take a picture of Lincoln's own backsliding, returns with a fish known for swimming with a backward motion. He says in his Alton opening, "After having pressed these arguments home on Mr. Lincoln for seven weeks, publishing a number of my speeches, we met at Ottawa in joint discussion, and he then began to crawfish a little, and let himself down."

### Anecdotes

Anecdotes expand events into humorous narratives. In his reply at Freeport, Douglas indicates that he had worried about a Southern conspiracy to nationalize slavery after Lecompton. Senator Toombs, he recalls, allayed his concern by indicating that no one could have such audacity to try it. In his rejoinder, Lincoln home-spuns Douglas' response to Toombs in an anecdote used to illustrate Douglas' gullibility.

[Douglas' charge of southern conspiracy] all went to pot as soon as Toombs got up and told him it was not true. It reminds me of the story that John Pheonix, the California railroad surveyor, tells. He says they started out from the Plaza to the Mission of Dolores. They had two ways of determining distances. One was by a chain and pins taken over thr ground. The other was by a "go-it-ometer"—an invention of his own—a three-legged instrument, with which he computed a series of triangles between the points. At night he turned to the chain-man to ascertain what distance they had come, and found that by some mistake he had merely dragged the chain over the ground without keeping any record. By the "go-it-ometer" he found he had made ten miles. Being skeptical about this, he asked a drayman who was passing how far it was to the plaza. The drayman replied it was just half a mile, and the surveyor put it down in his book—just as Judge Douglas says, after he had made his calculations and computations, he took Toombs' statement. I have no doubt that after Judge Douglas had made his charge, he was as easily satisfied about its truth as the surveyor was of the drayman's statement of the distance to the plaza.

In his Galesburg reply, Lincoln comes up with a choice anecdote to explain how Douglas and his cohorts stood to gain by repeating the same false story about an 1854 Springfield convention of Republicans that never took place:

As the fisherman's wife, whose drowned husband was brought home with his body full of eels, said when she was asked, "What was to be done with him?" "Take the eels out and set him again"; so Harris and Douglas have shown a disposition to take the eels out of that stale fraud by which they gained Harris's election, and set the fraud again more than once.

In the chapter on Plans, we referred to the sensory space as that region of experience that calls to the mind a world of the senses, a world not of language but a world that language abstracts and makes generic. Because of language's inherent abstractness, speakers routinely hint at the sensory world rather than refer to or invoke it directly. Hinting is often good enough from the Plans view, because in Plans the function of the sensory, and other secondary, spaces is to highlight the abstractions of the public space. From the Plans perspective, as long as the public space abstractions are on view, the resolution of the sensory space undergirding those abstractions is of less moment.

Things are different from the perspective of Events. In Events, there are no partitions between the public and secondary spaces. There is no partitioning in terms of spaces at all. The whole idea is to connect with the audience in the here and now. And this motivation puts a high value on entering the sensory world of the audience, for this is precisely the world where the audience lives, and where the densest, most conductive, and most consensual (Kaufer & Carley, 1993a) connections can be drawn with it. Being the system of abstraction that language is, the speaker's capacity to use language to refer to this sensory world is limited. But this limitation rests mainly with a literal language that tries, in abstract terms, to depict it through categories and predicates. It rests less with language that seeks to "paint" the audience's sensory world with a multisensory brush of indigenous words that breathe through them the sensory experience of the natives, what they see, hear, and smell in their everyday, unspoken, reality. The elasticity of language, especially the ability to scale its meaning down to the rush of an audience's experiences, is crucial for the kind of lexicalizations that go on in Events. We have seen that lexical elasticity often interacts with Tactics, as a way of responding to an opponent. But more centrally, lexical elasticity brings the speaker's public space abstractions, the essence of his or her plans, sterile and austere, into worlds that the audience can confirm with its senses.

### Lexicalizing Emotion: Making Events Affective

Efforts to create emotion, Aristotelian pathos, must be understood as performatives inasmuch as the creation of an emotion goes hand in glove with artfully lexicalizing an event offered to put the hearer in a certain emotional state. We need to distinguish seeking to create an audience emotion through a unique lexicalization—a matter of rhetorical design—and the situation of occupying a particular emotional state—a matter of emotive cognition. The two are different but related, for to craft an emotional lexicalization as a matter of rhetorical design, the speaker must know, tacitly, the principles of emotive cognition to which any emotive lexicalization much adhere. These principles have been explored by Ortony, Clore, and Collins (1988), and we draw on their principles here. And yet, despite the cognitive status of emotions, without the capacity to lexicalize an emotion as part of rhetorical design, there would be no way to use the human emotional system as an enhancer for collective action.

Suppose I am in a room of parents and want to experiment with the emotional system. I decide I want to distress them. I begin to throw rocks. They are distressed but are probably too bewildered for anger. They may flee or all come at me to disarm me. In both cases, their emotions have moved them to act. But their actions are not deliberated about, are not the source of what we normally think of as collective action. It is very common for human action to be based in emotion. It is much rarer to use the human emotional system as a controlled enhancer for principled collective action. Only within rhetorical design is the human emotional system ever used in this principled way.

To make the human emotions an instrument for controlled collective action almost always requires lexicalization. Most of the stimuli in the world that affect emotion—thrown rocks, bad drivers, barking dogs, provocative pictorial advertising without words and captions—are simply too open-ended in the emotions they arouse to control cognition and coordinated behavior at the level of groups. The beauty of words is that they can sculpt out situations worded only to arouse some emotions and not others. Show a person a captionless photograph of a traffic jam and a driver in the foreground with a distinctly irritated expression. Ask the person, "What's going on?" Some might say "the driver is having a bad day" indicating the driver's distress. Others might say "the driver can't believe those in front of her are moving so slowly," indicating the driver's anger. The picture can't help us disambiguate. Now suppose we add a caption "Driving on Memorial Day Weekend." The words become a framing device for the irritation; they show us how to "read" the irritation of the driver in the foreground. As a frame, further, the words offer a distance on the actual situation that allows us to step back and reflect on the emotion as a basis of coordinated action. To be sure, the words put us in the situation enough to respond to the emotion it conveys. We can, in some sense, feel the frustration of driving on Memorial Day weekend, when everyone is skipping town. At the same time, the words are sufficiently displaced from the situation in time and space so that we do not lose sight of the need to deliberate on the matter about what, if anything, to do about holiday driving of this kind.

Lexicalization is thus central to the use of the emotions as a basis for collective action. It is for this reason that, despite being cognitive and unattached from surface language, the emotions are, within a theory of rhetorical design, controlled within the Events module, where unique lexicalization takes place. In this section, we adapt various elements of the Ortony et al. cognitive theory of emotions to survey the range of affect-producing rhetorical performatives. Ortony et al. defined three categories of emotion that are most pertinent to a theory of rhetoric. They are prospect, attribution, and compound emotions, with each of these categories overseeing subcategories of emotions. We next review each category and its subcategories. We discuss each category and subcategory as it functions as an enchancer or, in rarer cases, an inhibitor of rhetorical design. When appropriate, we relate the conditions of each emotional state to emotive performatives in the Lincoln and Douglas debates.

### Prospect Emotions

Prospect emotions involve prospects for the future and how these prospects bear on the emotional system. Different categories of this class follow.

### Happy-for Events

Happy-for events please the audience because of the desirable prospects that befall third parties. Happy-for events are intensified when we share a value for happiness with the persons for whom we are happy. We are not likely to be happy for the masochist who inflicts self-injury; we are more likely to be happy for the person who wins the lottery. Happy-for events are also intensified when we think the persons for whom we are happy are deserving. We are more likely to be happy for persons who overcome misfortune than for the lottery winner. Neither Douglas nor Lincoln seems to compose happy-for events for their audiences. They are both happy to have the audience's vote, but not in any relevant sense do they lexicalize expressions to make their audiences happy for anyone.

### Sorry-for Events

Sorry-for events displease the audience because of the undesirable prospects that befall third parties. Being sorry for another is intensified when we share the same sense of sorrow with the victim. A rich matron may see grave misfortune in a broken fingernail, but that is not likely to provoke a sorry-for event in most of us. Sorry-for events are intensified when the victim's suffering seems undeserved. The more liked and undeserving the victim is, the more intensely sorry audiences will feel. Douglas sometimes lexicalizes sorry-for events on behalf of the South, at times portraying the region as an undeserving victim of the abolitionists' efforts to destroy the slave economy. He also tries to block the negro from being the object of too intense sorry-for events, insisting that each state treats the negro with charity and humanity. Douglas' uses of sorry-for emotions have tactical value, as Douglas wants to make it harder for Lincoln not to show sympathy with the South, and harder to show it for the negro. But his sorry-for lexicalizations are also aimed at the immediate audience, as they seek to condition the emotional state through which it comes to respond to the slave economy and the negro.

### Resentment Events

Resentment events displease the audience because of the desirable prospects that befall third parties. Resentment intensifies when the resenter and the target of resentment share a sense of the desirable. We resent a person who steals a job we wanted more than we resent a person who was never our competitor. Resentment events intensify with the extent to which the target of resentment seems undeserving of the good fortune. We resent a pay raise to an incompetent more than to an employee who has worked hard and well. Douglas lexicalizes events to make his White audiences resent the abolitionist's efforts toward racial equality. Douglas' depiction of Frederick Douglas at Freeport occupying a carriage with a white woman driven by a white man is carefully crafted to produce resentment in the crowd.

## Gloating Events

Gloating events please the audience because of the undesirable prospects that befall third parties. Gloaters find joy in the misfortunes of others. A gloating event intensifies when the gloater identifies the other as a rival, someone whose good fortune threatens his or her own prospects. As rivals in debate, Douglas and Lincoln seem to gloat at one another's missteps. Neither seems particularly to rely on putting their audiences in a state of gloating.

## Satisfaction Events

Satisfaction events please the audience because of the desirable consequences that befall them. Satisfaction intensifies with the investment of hope and effort that people put into realizing the events that give them satisfaction. It also intensifies with the extent to which the satisfying event is actually realized. We are more satisfied (but not necessarily more happy or joyous) when we win a contest we have worked hard to win than when we win the lottery. Satisfaction events are related to the rhetorician's understanding of presumption and burden of proof. Generally speaking, a speaker favoring the status quo will want to leave audiences satisfied with the world the way it is. To be sure, the speaker favoring things as they are can acknowledge audience discontent and even instigate some. But such a speaker cannot afford to leave the audience less satisfied with the present than with an altered, but unknown, future. Of the two speakers in the debates, Douglas favors the status quo more than Lincoln. As we have seen, a key issue of the debates is the placement of slavery in a public model. Douglas claims that it belongs in the local space, as it always has been placed. Lincoln claims that it belongs in the public space, as the Founders intended it to be placed over the eventual course of time. Lincoln is forced to appeal to the Founders' evolutionary intentions to explain how he can have the founders on his side but still need to fight an uphill battle against the status quo. Douglas, in brief, tries to make his audiences satisfied with the long course of American history and the present state of affairs, which in his view still follows that course. He needs to make audiences dissatisfied with the recent efforts to undermine the Founders by nationalizing abolition. Lincoln, conversely, needs to make his audiences satisfied with the overall course of American history, and then make his audiences dissatisfied that politicians in Douglas' generation had turned their back on the Founders' long-term plan that slavery be gradually done away with.

### Fears-Confirmed Events

Fears-confirmed events displease the audience because of the undesirable consequences that befall them. Fears-confirmed events intensify with the extent of the fear, the effort the person expends in trying to avoid it, and the degree to which the anticipated condition causing the fear is realized. Our fears are confirmed when our house is destroyed by an earthquake, and more intensely so if we took every precaution in the book against that outcome. Lincoln and Douglas are concerned in the debates to give their audiences a sense of impending fear for the future. The fear is real, but both offer hope that the audience's "effort" (a vote) would do much to avoid the worst scenarios. For Douglas, the worst case future to avoid is a confederation of states that has lost the power to manage its own affairs, including its right to slaves. For Lincoln, the worst case to avoid is a nation so torn apart on the slavery issue that it can never reconcile itself into a functional whole. Although both speakers create fear for the future, neither wants the audience to become resigned to a hopeless situation. It is worth pointing out that what an audience fears is an inducement for rhetorical design, not an inhibitor. For a speaker seeking an emotional connection with an audience, the greatest emotional inhibitors are doubt, fatalism, and cynicism. Doubt robs an audience of its ability to believe in any plans to connect with; fatalism robs it of its ability to think that connecting with a single plan will make a difference in outcomes; and cynicism robs it of its ability to think that any of the outcomes makes a future worth striving for.

### Relief Events

Relief events please the audience because of the undesirable prospects that are avoided (against expectation). A relief event intensifies as the future apprehended is expected and dreaded and as the effort to avert it increases. We are more relieved when we successfully fight off a bear than when we skip over a puddle (degree of apprehension). We are relieved to hear that we can get a tax deduction on an expense that we thought the Internal Revenue

Service might have questioned. But we are even more relieved if we hear the news after battling the IRS for a year (degree of effort). Lincoln and Douglas offer their plans as relief against an expected and unwanted future. Each tries to impress upon his audiences the effort that must be collectively expended in order to avoid calamity. Each offers his audiences, as a result, the promise of joyous relief as a payoff for accepting his point of view.

### Disappointment Events

Disappointment events displease the audience because of the desirable prospects that did not befall them (against expectation). Disappointment intensifies with the desirability of the future prospects lost. We are disappointed when we lose a small bet; and more so when we lose a large one. Disappointment, like relief, also intensifies with effort. We are disappointed losing a couple of hours of work, but more so when we lose a year of work. Disappointment also intensifies with the amount of control we had over alternative outcomes that would have offset the disappointment. The more control we had, the more disappointed we are. We are more disappointed to lose a job from a poor performance review than from a recession. There is little in the debates to suggest that Lincoln and Douglas are out to make their audiences feel disappointment. Neither have lost a future they barely missed having. The futures they portray themselves to be seeking come across as near and attainable. Nor do Lincoln and Douglas come to the debates on the assumption that the audience is already disappointed. This is in noticeable contrast to the modern political temper, where speakers address audiences who are used to being lied to and who have come to be disappointed in politicians to the point of cynicism. In chapter 5, we mentioned that audiences often confuse a speaker's on-the-record claims (taking a predictive stance toward the future) with moral promises (opening oneself to the charge of "liar" if the future does not turn out as planned). This confusion, it seems, is the result of modern audiences having lost faith in political authority and making leaders personalize their political commitments as moral obligations.

### Attribution Emotions

Attribution emotions involve events that affect the audiences' feelings with respect to the agents responsible for these events happening. Different categories of this class follow.

### Admiration Events

Admiration events are events about which an audience approves and for which a third party is responsible. More simply put, we admire those who are responsible for events for which we approve. Our admiration intensifies with the concentration of responsibility and the degree of approval. We admire the single genius responsible for curing polio (concentrated responsibility, high approval) more than the committee that wrote the municipal litter law (diffuse responsibility, mild approval). Our admiration also intensifies with deviations from expected role type. We admire an old lady saving a drowning child even more than a healthy lifeguard doing so. Throughout the debates, Lincoln and Douglas lexicalize events that put their audiences in a state of admiration for the founding fathers and Henry Clay. They want to make their audiences admiring of the agents who are responsible for the precedents on which they base their precedent plans. Conceivably, one might include as precedent agents persons whom an audience does not personally admire (e.g., Machiavelli, Napoleon) but who are nonetheless magnified by history. But having precedent agents with whom the audience can also emotionally connect, like the beloved Henry Clay, makes persuasion that much more effective.

## Reproach Events

Reproach events are events about which an audience disapproves and for which a third party is responsible. Like admiration, reproach intensifies with the concentration of responsibility and disapproval. We reproach a lone madman more than a committee that puts red tape in our path. Like admiration, reproach also intensifies with deviations from expected role behavior. We reproach religious authorities who do bad things more than hardened criminals. Throughout the debates, Lincoln and Douglas try to put their audiences in a state of reproachful feeling toward the agents of their counternormed plans, especially the agents behind the counterprecedents and conspiracies they reference. Lincoln wants his audiences to feel reproach for those trying to nationalize slavery; Douglas, for those trying to nationalize abolition. The reasons for having audiences admire the agents of one's positive plans mirror the reasons for having them reproach the counteragents of their negative plans. The world of Plans is an emotionally sterile one. The more the speaker can coordinate Plans and Events, especially emotive lexicalizations, the more the audience can become a fan of the speaker's Plans, with specific interests to cheer and others to boo.

## Pride Events

Pride events are events of which the audience approves and for which it is directly responsible. Pride intensifies with the degree of approval and concentration of responsibility, and also varies with deviations from role expectation. We take more pride when what was accomplished was done against great odds and given a small chance of success. We take more pride in tutoring a very slow student to a passing grade than in helping an already excellent student get an A. Although pride is directed toward the self, it can be projected onto outside persons and things for which the self feels a strong bond. Pride in self thus becomes extendable to pride in children and pride in country as long as one can invest in the objects of pride. Both Lincoln and Douglas are interested in making their audiences feel pride in country, although the pride has different sources. For Douglas, audiences are meant to feel pride in a country that is expansive and prosperous. For Lincoln, audiences are meant to feel pride in a country that can live up to the full promise of the "all men equal" clause of the Declaration.

### Self-Reproach Events

Self-reproach events are events of which the audience disapproves and for which it is directly responsible. Self-reproach is the mirror image of pride and so mirrors its characteristics. Like pride, it can be projected onto outside persons and things for which the self feels a bond. Because the country belongs to the audience, is a reflection of them, the audience can take pride in it when the country lives up to expectations and reproach itself when the country does not. Both Lincoln and Douglas want their audiences to feel a personal responsibility for the elements in the country that are "subverting" its true traditions.

### Compound Emotions

Compound emotions combine an audience's feelings of joy and distress with persons responsible for events. Different categories of this class follow.

### Gratitude Events

Gratitude events are instigated by third parties and fill audiences with a combination of joy and admiration. When others do admirable things that also give us joy, we feel gratitude to them. Lincoln and Douglas use the Founding Fathers and Henry Clay as sites of audience gratitude as well as admiration. Both want their audiences to feel indebted to the agents of their precedent plans.

### Gratification Events

Gratification events are instigated by the self and fill the self with a combination of joy and pride. When we do something that gives us pride and that makes us feel joy, we feel gratified within ourselves. Although gratitude is other-directed, gratification is a self-directed emotion. But when the self and the other are strongly identified by bonds of blood and country, the boundaries between gratification and gratitude become indistinguishable. Insofar as we feel the Founders are distinct from us, we give them our gratitude. But inasmuch as we make their accomplishment our own accomplishment, our gratitude toward them becomes a kind of gratification within ourselves for embracing them. Lincoln and Douglas use the Founding Fathers and Henry Clay as sites of audience gratification as well as gratitude. Both want their audiences to feel pride as well as admiration for the agents whose plans for the country they are stewarding through history.

### Remorse Events

Remorse events combine distress and self-reproach. They cause the audience distress as well as a feeling of self-reproach. When we do something that makes us feel self-reproach and distress, we feel remorse. Although Lincoln and Douglas want their audiences to take a certain personal responsibility for the bad that is happening in the country, it is clear that neither wants their audience to feel the distress associated with remorse. Although remorse is a very powerful emotion, it is more a rhetorical inhibitor than enhancer. Remorse often implies a self-absorption that diminishes the capacity for collective action. It is hard to change a world when one blames oneself for the need to change. The self-reproach of remorse must have a chance to dissipate before one is able to act constructively on the distress. Neither Lincoln nor Douglas is interested in making their audience as self-absorbed as remorse requires.

### Anger Events

Anger combines distress and reproach. When others do reproachful things that cause us distress, we feel anger. As Aristotle well knew, anger is one of the more potent rhetorical enhancers, especially when it leaves the audience clear-headed and focused to act. Lincoln and Douglas want their audiences to feel anger at the elements that each envisions are destroying the country. Typically, they want their audiences to target anger at the agents that cause fear. For Douglas, this anger is directed at Lincoln and the Republicans, who threaten the nation with abolition. For Lincoln, the anger is directed at Douglas and the Democrats, who threaten the nation with slavery in all the states.

## Emotion in the Context of Rhetorical Architecture

Consider the lexicalization of emotion in the broader context of our architecture. Earlier we saw how the elasticity of language, the ability to scale meaning to the audience's experiences, is important for the type of lexicalization that happens in Events. In the case of concretely scaled experience, the abstractions of a plan are brought home to the sights and sounds familiar to the audience authorized to judge it. Now we can see how Event lexicalization can also be used to coordinate the abstract conditions of truth and falsehood (within Plans) into lexicalizations (with Events) that pique the emotions of the immediate audience. The level of abstraction typical of a plan is autistic, outside a world of emotion. In such an autistic world, it may be hard to discriminate truth and falsehood. Truths, after all, become easier to identify and sanction when they make us joyful, satisfied, or relieved; falsehoods, when they make us distressed, disappointed, and angry. Coordinated with Event lexicalization to give emotion to an autistic truth and falsehood, truths can be lexicalized to arouse positive emotion; falsehoods to arouse, negative. If lexical elasticity can make the abstracted states of Plans more experientially real and concrete for audiences, the lexicalization of emotion can bring Plans down to the level of an audience's emotive reactions and feelings.

## Lexicalizing Audience Collaboration: Making Events Interactive

The types of performatives we have seen thus far, elasticity and emotion, put the plans of a speaker into words that reflect the worlds of the audience. The crucial coordination for these devices lies between Plans and Events. The class of performatives we now consider, interactives, tends to coordinate more with Tactics. The goals associated with Tactics is responsiveness, and interactives are central performatives to use when one opponent solicits information from the other. Interactives, like all performatives, also matter to making connections with the immediate audience. How do we reconcile the Tactics focus of interactive events, responding to the opponent with the Event focus, connecting with the immediate audience?

Thus far, we have made a hard distinction between the opponent and the audience. The opponent is the person to beat; the audience, the one to persuade. We must now admit that the distinction is not that hard. Sometimes, though not in the Lincoln/Douglas debates, the opponent is a member of the audience. The opponent must be persuaded as well as beaten. But whether this is the case or not, it is almost always true that to regulate its own decision making, the immediate audience must role play each speaker's opponent in order to understand what it would be like to respond to him or her. The way to decide with a speaker is to decide that one has no cause to respond to him or her further; the speaker's position, although not complete, as none can ever be, has nonetheless been filled in enough to act on favorably. The way to decide against a speaker is to decide that there are still many ways to respond to him or her, and the speaker has been too stubborn or obtuse to understand that.

Using interactives, a speaker puts pressure on the opponent (and vicariously the audience role-playing the opponent) to respond. Interactives need to be distinguished from declaratives, which do not directly put the pressure of response on an opponent. Declaratives bring events to the rhetorical situation intact. Interactives are nondeclaratives that decompose an event into parts whose completion is based on the immediate audience, or the opponent, responding in an appropriate way. Interactives differ in what they ask of the audience or opponent in "completing" the event. Let us now consider a range of interactives.

## Queries

Queries are bids for the audience or opponent to fill in information about an event raised by the speaker. The query may be real—the speaker does not know the information being sought. Or it may be leading—the speaker may offer the question as a device to arouse or hold the audience's attention or to make the opponent participate in his or her own hanging. In either case, queries exert pressure, in form if not substance, for the audience or opponent to respond.

The Ottawa and Freeport debates are marked by Lincoln and Douglas making queries of one another. Each speaker tries to get the other to participate in completing events that fill in his specific structures. Douglas tries from Lincoln's mouth to extract the events needed to confirm the Republicans' involvement in an abolitionist conspiracy. Lincoln tries to extract from Douglas' mouth the events needed to confirm a Democratic conspiracy to nationalize slavery. For the remainder of the debate, Lincoln and Douglas both use the other's responses at Freeport as "first-hand" sensory evidence from the enemy camp for the truth of their own plans.

Lincoln's and Douglas' queries to the audience (not to one another) tend also to be leading. They are used to hold the audience's attention and to help the audience anticipate where they are going next in their argument. In some cases, both speakers make audience queries in order to build powerful emotions, as we will see below. Tactically, queries keep the speaker on the offense and the opponent on the (repair) defense or the (psychological) defensive. They allow speakers to hold the floor on their own terms while keeping opponents distracted from their own offense.

## Denials

Speakers can become aware of potential interference or conflict that would keep the immediate audience from embracing their plans. They may further perceive that the only way to clear a path for their own version of events is to clear away the interference. Bids to clear away these interfering events are denials.

Events denied can key into very subtle maneuvers. For example, in his Ottawa opening, Douglas reads the abolitionist resolutions associated with the Republican convention at Springfield. Douglas then queries Lincoln about his own beliefs. Douglas' intent, we have seen in previous chapters, is to trap Lincoln in a dilemma. If his answer converges with the Springfield resolutions, he will be an abolitionist; if his answer fails to converge, he will fail to represent his party. Lincoln is caught in a no-win dilemma as long as a certain mental event—the presumption of his "party membership"—remains part of the immediate context of response. This event, the presumption of Lincoln's party membership, interferes with Lincoln's effort to answer Douglas without hanging himself.

When Lincoln does come around to answering these queries, at Freeport, the first thing he does is deny the obstructing event. He mentions that at Ottawa Douglas had read from some Republican resolutions passed at Springfield. He also mentions that Douglas had asked him about his own views. He denies the linkage between his answers and any implications about his party affiliation. He indicates that he does not answer Douglas' questions because they sprang from the Springfield resolutions. He answers Douglas only because Douglas asked. The effect of Lincoln's denial is to avoid Douglas' trap. Lincoln does not want to be understood as responding from an organizational authority focus. He responds, he implies, because it is responsive to answer an opponent's questions, not because of any pressure he feels to align or not to align with Republicans. As this example indicates, denials assist speakers playing repair defense, by blocking negative plans opponents try to pin on them.

## Challenges

A challenge is a performative that directly or inferentially casts doubt on the opponent's or the audience's sense of responsibility. Let us say, by way of

illustration, the opponent holds down a role—senator or senatorial candidate—that requires knowledge and honesty. A speaker challenges the
opponent by calling forth an event—"you should have known, but did not";
"you lied"—that indicts the opponent's capacity to live up to these requirements. In light of Lincoln's alleged abolition and spotty political record,
Douglas often questions whether Lincoln has the qualifications to be Senator.
In light of Douglas getting so many facts wrong about the Springfield
convention, Lincoln makes the same issue of Douglas.

Speakers can challenge audiences by making them feel responsible for the
negative consequences if they agree to follow their opponent's vision of the
future. Douglas challenges the Ottawa audience in just this way:

> Now, I ask you, are you in favor of conferring upon the negro the rights and
> privileges of citizenship? Do you desire to strike out of our State constitution
> the clause which keeps slave and free negroes out of the State, and allow the
> free negro to flow in and cover out prairies with his settlements.
>
> Do you desire to turn this beautiful State into a free negro colony, in order
> that when Missouri shall abolish slavery, she can send us these emancipated
> slaves to become citizens and voters on an equality with you?

A speaker can reverse an opponent's challenge to an audience by indicating that the opponent him or herself is more culpable than the audience.
During his Freeport reply, Douglas challenges the raucous "black Republicans" to remain silent in light of the fact that no Democrat had been "vulgar"
enough to interrupt Lincoln during his opening. When Lincoln returns to
the podium for the final rejoinder, he seizes the opportunity to make clear
that the "vulgarity" was evidently the fault of the speaker, not the audience,
because when he (Lincoln) was first speaking, he had used no vulgarity
against any Democrat and had suffered no disruption.

A speaker can challenge an opponent to answer questions that the speaker
considers unanswered or only partially answered. After Freeport, Lincoln
continues to challenge Douglas to answer more fully how he can reconcile
his principle of popular sovereignty with his support of Dred Scott. At
Galesburg, Lincoln complains that when he had asked Douglas that question
at Freeport, Douglas just sneered. At Quincy, still stalking Douglas for an
answer, Lincoln challenges Douglas to point out in the language of the Dred
Scott decision where it protects the right of popular sovereignty: "I have the
Dred Scot decision here, and I will thank Judge Douglas to lay his finger
upon the place in the entire opinions of the court where any one of them
[protects popular sovereignty]."

Challenges can also put pressure on the internal consistency of an opponent's plans. The opponent is made to feel responsible for not being as open, forthcoming, or mindful about his or her position and its ramifications as he or she needs to be. At Galesburg, Douglas rejects the idea that the founders included blacks in the Declaration. In the same debate, Lincoln challenges Douglas to come up with any quote more than three years old that supports that position. Throughout the debates, Douglas allows that the people have the right to ignore federal law in the name of popular sovereignty. At Alton, Lincoln argues that Douglas's position comes to anarchy, allowing people to overturn laws protecting slavery. This makes Douglas an abolitionist of sorts. Lincoln concludes his Alton speech with a serious challenge garnished with levity, "Why, there is not such an Abolitionist in the nation as Douglas, after all."

Tactically, challenges, like queries, keep the speaker on the offense by pointing out the responsibilities that the opponent has failed to live up to. They are stronger than queries (but weaker than traps) in causing the opponent to backpedal. A speaker queried can respond without missing a beat. A speaker challenged who stays on the offense without missing a beat seems less responsive.

## Traps

Traps are performatives specifically designed to place the opponent in a dilemma. A dilemma is created when an opponent is involved in a plan containing entanglements in both truth and falsehood, such that the opponent's positive involvement (in truth) cannot escape a negative outcome (in falsehood). We have seen in the chapter on tactics how Douglas, in the first three debates, tries to keep Lincoln trapped between two losing identities: either (a) a Republican (positive) abolitionist (negative) or (b) a nonabolitionist (positive) who has turned his back on members of his own party (negative). Whichever horn Lincoln chooses has a positive involvement followed by a negative implication. In his Freeport reply, sure that Lincoln is now safely caught, Douglas for the first time brags about the trap he has set:

> Either Mr. Lincoln was then committed to these propositions, or Mr. Turner violated his pledge to you by voting for him. Either Mr. Lincoln was pledged to Mr. Turner, or else all the Black Republicans from this District violated their pledge of honor to their constituents by voting for him. Now, I ask you, which horn of the dilemma will you take? Will you hold Lincoln to the platform of the party or will you believe that every member you had in the House of Representatives with two exceptions violated their pledges of honor

to their constituents? So you see their is no escape for Mr. Lincoln on this pledge. He was committed to this proposition or your members violated their pledge. Take either horn of the dilemma. There is no dodging of the question.

Tactically, traps are designed to keep the speaker on the offense by pointing out inconsistencies in the opponent's plans. A speaker trapped can go on the defense to repair the plan, can elaborate one's positive story about truth to show the trap is to narrow to catch anything, and/or can challenge the legitimacy of the trap on the strength of the opponent's misinformation or bad will. Lincoln does all three.

## Promises

Promises are performatives that commit the speaker to a future action on behalf of the audiences to whom it is made. In the chapter on goals, we took care to distinguish going on the record from promising. We mentioned there that promises are audience specific, whereas a speaker who goes on the record makes a claim about the predictability of his or her behavior into the indefinite future and does not commit a moral fault merely by failing to live up to the record. We also indicated that in an age of suspicion against politicians, speakers have found it necessary to make promises above and beyond going on the record. The concept of on-the-record predictability provides a useful way of understanding not only what promises are but why they happen. Promises are events that commit the speaker to a specific future. They are issued when it is perceived, by the speaker, audience, or both, that the speaker's on-the-record predictability is not sufficiently binding or of sufficient reward to make the kind of contract for the future that the speaker and audience are prepared to make. Promises in sum become necessary because of the limitations in on the record predictability in bringing collective futures about.

The Lincoln/Douglas debates seem to have taken place in a time of less political distrust than our own. Although both debaters indicate that their (on-the-record) positions will bring futures of "calm," "peace," and "prosperity," we find no evidence in the debates of their promising these futures as some politicians would do today.

## Threats

Threats arise when a speaker issues events that project negative consequences affecting the audience, that portray the speaker's taking responsibility for these consequences, and that hold out the option that the speaker will refrain from these consequences if the audience alters its present behavior. Threats are the mirror image of promises. In a promise, the speaker obligates him- or herself to a future on the audience's behalf. In a threat, the speaker tries to get the audience to obligate its present behavior on the speaker's behalf so as to avoid the speaker's causing it a specific painful future.

We saw earlier that public promises result when the speaker's on-the-record predictability proves an insufficient reward for the audience. Public threats result when a speaker judges that the opponent's on the record predictability proves an insufficient cost. The speaker is not content to project the world implied from the opponent's on the record behavior. The speaker feels the additional urgency to threaten the audience with the opponent's world's coming into existence—thus putting the audience under the gun to make sure the opponent never gets rein on the future.

Threatening an audience with an opponent's world is a form of face threat against the opponent, because it centers the threat in the opponent's very ascension to power, the opponent's opportunity to shape a future. As we saw in the chapter on tactics, Douglas is a master of the face threat. It is thus not surprising to find him threatening the audience with a future led by Lincoln more than Lincoln threatens audiences with a future led by Douglas.

From the time of Lincoln's nomination speech two months before the debates, Douglas had threatened that Lincoln would end slavery, grant full citizenship to Blacks, condone intermarriage, ruin the Southern economy, and foment civil war. Lincoln does not return the threats but makes light of them at the very beginning of the debates. In his first speech at Ottawa, for example, he references Douglas' threats with humorous understatement, "he goes on and draws out from that speech this tendency of mine to set the states at war, and to set the negroes and white people to marrying with one another," and a sense of the absurd:

> I had no thought in the world that I was doing anything to bring about the absolute equality of the white and black races. It never occurred to me that I was doing anything to reduce to a dead uniformity all the local institutions of the states. But I must say in justice to the judge, that if I am really doing something that leads to these bad results, it is just as bad to the country, whether I wished it or not. But I ask you, can it be true that placing this institution of slavery upon the original basis upon which our fathers placed it, that it can have any tendency to compel the people of Vermont to raise sugar corn because they can raise it in Louisiana, or to compel the people of Grand Prairie to cut pine logs off the prairie where none grow, because they cut them in Maine?

The fact that Lincoln does not present his opponent as a threat seems to make him more likeable than Douglas, who is never bashful about offering up Lincoln to audiences as one.

## Concessions and Disclaimers

Concessions and disclaimers are performatives that fill in the small brush-strokes needed to keep an audience on the same course as the speaker. We have already suggested how issues are replete with small detail and the audience is often challenged to retain the detail while not losing sight of the evolving plans and tactics. Concessions and disclaimers are designed to keep audiences on course through the trees while not losing their way in the forest.

Concessions anticipate and contain events that reveal strengths in the opponent's ideas and weaknesses in one's own. When presenting his political history of the country in his opening at Ottawa and again at Jonesboro, Douglas tries to paint a utopian picture of America's traditional parties, the Whigs and Democrats. He depicts them as living in relative harmony. His objective is to show that America's political landscape did not begin to shake at its foundations until the Republicans came on the scene in the 1850s promoting abolition. Douglas' historical picture is obviously too simple and, more importantly, he knows it. There are many counterexamples, including the clashes between the Whigs and Democrats over the bank, tariffs, and taxes. By composing these counterexamples as part of a concessive "while" event, Douglas is able to retain the simplicity of his history, acknowledge the contra-indicators, and at the same time contain them. He accomplishes all this when he offers: "[W]hile the Whig and the Democratic parties differed in regard to a Bank, and in regard to a Tariff, and in regard to Distribution, and in regard to the Specie Circular, and in regard to the Sub-Treasury, they agreed on the great question that now agitates the Union, known as the slavery question."

Disclaimers anticipate and contain audience inferences that venture beyond what the speaker sanctions and that, left unchecked, could do the speaker potential harm. One repeated Douglas disclaimer pertains to his regard for blacks. He does not want to grant them rights of any kind. Yet he wants to uphold a standard of human charity for them, lest the audience think him without feeling. Avowing the first, he fears, implies disavowing the second. Douglas thus sees the need for a disclaimer, a way of avowing the first and disclaiming the idea that he also disavows the second:

> The fact is he [the black] belongs to an inferior race and must occupy an
> inferior position. I do not hold that merely because the negro belongs to an

inferior race, therefore he ought to be a slave. By no means can such a conclusion be drawn. On the contrary, I do hold that humanity and Christianity both require that the negro should have and enjoy every right, every privilege, and every immunity, consistent with the safety of the society in which he live.

Another common use of the disclaimer is to implement a "no-malice" alignment (chapter 7), in which the speaker indicates a personal bond with the opponent to justify savage public attacks. The opposite of the no-malice disclaimer is the no-bias disclaimer, used to show that one has no special closeness to a person supporting one's own argument. In his Freeport speech, Douglas uses this disclaimer toward Tom Turner, a Republican abolitionist who supports Douglas's view that the Republicans are an abolitionist party. Just to show that Turner is a true abolitionist, and no ideological friend of Douglas in disguise, Douglas asks the "black Republicans" in the audience to "give Turner three cheers for drawing the resolutions, if you approve of them."

Lincoln finds he needs an important disclaimer in the Alton debate. At Galesburg he had made the bald statement that no more than three years ago, it was unheard of to think the Founders had not included blacks in the Declaration. This statement, Lincoln must have thought, is easily confused with the statement that, three years before, no one could be heard to criticize the Declaration. Lincoln comes to Alton with the following disclaimer: He begs not to be misunderstood, for he knows there have been persons who, wanting to spread slavery, declared the Declaration a false document. He clarifies that only in the environment of the Dred Scott ruling (making negroes property under the Constitution) did interpretations of the Declaration begin to emerge that excluded Blacks.

## Lexicalizing the Design Space: Making Events Diversions

Speakers can use performatives to call attention to their own rhetorical performance. Through such reflexivity, the speaker creates a diversion from the normal business of public discourse. The diversionary performative offers a respite or interlude for the speaker and the audience and, if successful, one they can make a social moment, sharing a ground as humans interacting. Although speakers can satisfy humanness goals through concretizing events, nondeclaratives, and the emotions, it is only through diversionary events that speakers can stand apart from their own activities and take a wink at the audience as one human to another. The purest satisfaction of humanness goals comes from a speaker's willingness to take such diversions with an audience.

Figure 9.1 explains how a diversionary event alters the relational dynamics between speaker, opponent, and audience. In discourse guided by Plans and Tactics, the speaker inhabits the "now" with the opponent and the audience awaits in the near future as a judge. Through diversionary events, the speaker shares the " now" with the audience and holds the opponent in the wings until public discourse is resumed.

There are two kinds of diversionary events, controlled and reflexive diversions. We look at each kind in turn.

## Controlled Diversions: Self-Conscious Retreats from Public Discourse

Controlled diversions suspend public discourse momentarily. The speaker breaks the expectation to address public space abstractions and reverts instead to information that has no, or minimal, bearing on the issues at hand. Simple diversions express themselves as puns and other forms of linguistic play, as when Lincoln at Ottawa says that to think he believes in a perfect equality between Whites and Blacks is to think a horse chestnut is the same

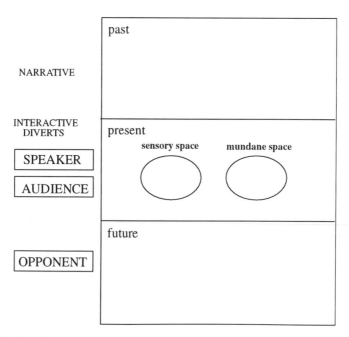

FIG. 9.1.   The reorientation of the speaker—audience dynamic when the speaker issues a diversionary event. The audience is engaged in the moment and the opponent is held off.

as a chestnut horse. Feedback from a voice at Ottawa allows Lincoln to define a serious debate into an everyday situation of an old man needing to put on his spectacles:

> Lincoln: Permit me to read a part of a printed speech that I made then at Peoria.
> Voice: Put on your Specs.
> Lincoln: Yes Sir, I am obliged to do so. I am no longer a young man.

### Reflexive Diversions: Exposing the Insides of Rhetorical Design

Reflexive diversions work on two levels. They have the appearance of public discourse whereas at the same time they allow the speaker to stand back and expose the inside assumptions out of which public discourse is designed.

### *Lexical Reflexiveness: Privatizing the Opponent's Public Words*

Speakers entrust their depictions of public realities to words. For the most part, when we hear public discourse, we focus on the realities to which the words point rather than on the words themselves. But at times, speakers can remind us that their opponent's realities are, finally, words. And by doing so, they can help us see that the opponent's public realities may be no more than the private semantic choices of an individual speaker.

Consider the way Lincoln picks up on Douglas' use of the word "conscientious" in the Ottawa debate. In his Ottawa opening, Douglas had first used the word in the following context: "I do not question Mr. Lincoln's conscientious belief that the negro was made his equal, and hence is his brother. But, for my own part, I do not regard the negro as my equal."

The word *conscientious* seems at first like a compliment but it is meant as a putdown. Conscientious is ambiguous. One meaning is a public meaning, in which a person with entitlement is praised for fulfilling a public role with hard work. A second meaning is a sensory-mundane meaning, in which a person works hard but fails the entitlement to make the hard work amount to anything that matters. Douglas appears to offer the public meaning as a mask for offering the private one.

Lincoln, aware of the putdown, returns it in his Ottawa reply. "Well, all I have to say is, that Judge Douglas cannot prove that because it is not true, nor nothing like it. I have no doubt he is conscientious in saying so."

What is true for the word *conscientious* is also true for the word *dare*. One meaning of dare is public, indicating what a public official can do when he or she has the courage to do it (the Senator dared to ask for a vote). A second meaning of dare is private, belonging to the sensory-mundane, in which a person attempts something foolishly, with no substantive reason or entitlement to succeed (the moron dared to cross the highway blindfolded).

In his rejoinder at Galesburg, Douglas criticizes Lincoln for "daring," at the Charleston debate, to talk of Douglas' committing fraud and forgery. Douglas uses the public meaning of dare as a cover for the sensory-mundane meaning. In his opening at Quincy, Lincoln defiantly confirms that he "dared" to say forgery, this time insisting on the public meaning, that he had the evidence to dare. Douglas had boasted that he would not "dare" to maintain a charge once it had been proven false. But Lincoln, offering a lesson in the semantics of *dare*, suggests that there are some things you can dare to charge (when you have public proof) and some things you cannot (when you have none), and "I do dare to say forgery when it is true and don't dare when it is not true."

A third item that is bandied in the debates between public and sensory-mundane senses is actually a pair: public/mob. The public is who a speaker addresses when the speaker is authorized; when the speaker lacks public entitlement, he or she can only "incite mobs." In his reply at Quincy, Douglas accuses Lincoln of being consumed with two questions that are beyond the public's prerogative to change, the morality of slavery and Dred Scott. In his rejoinder at Quincy, Lincoln, citing Douglas' attacks on the courts throughout his career, echoes Douglas' criticism back at him: "Didn't Douglas appeal to the 'mobs' then?"

Through the play and counterplay of public and sensory-mundane senses of words, Lincoln and Douglas expose rhetorical design as a parlor game of words—even in the midst of making dead serious arguments about the world beyond.

## Tactical Reflexiveness: Wit

Before defining wit, we look at what we think is Lincoln's most crafted use of wit in the debates:

> When my friend Judge Douglas came to Chicago, on the 9th of July, this speech having been delivered on the 16th of June, he made a speech there in which he took hold of this speech of mine and showing that he had carefully read it... he complimented me as being a most kind, amiable and intelligent gentleman. Notwithstanding I had said this, he goes on and draws out from that speech this tendency [understatement arising from juxtaposition of Public and Event/Sensory Spaces] of mine to set the states at war, and to set the negroes and white people to marrying with one another.... The judge

thereupon, at Bloomington, where I heard him speak, said... "unless he [Lincoln]... shall have extinguished slavery in all the states, the Union cannot stand." Now, I did not think that was exactly the way to treat a kind, amiable, and intelligent gentleman. (Ottawa reply)

Wit is a lexicalized performative and, at the same time, a tactical way of playing attack defense against an opponent. It is also a type of diversionary event and its involvement in lexicalization and diversion makes it more noticeable, as compressed expression, than a conventional attack defense. Although coordinated with the Tactical module, wit also reaches out to the immediate audience in a way that normal tactics do not. Behind the expression of wit lies a mild populism, inviting the audience not to be afraid to approach a revered opponent with a certain irreverence. As a literary form, wit is often associated with an irreverence to the subject matter, even if the irreverence is understood to be more affectionate than nasty. Stephen Pinker's *The Language Instinct* (1994) was an immediate bestseller because it explained in wondrously engaging prose the intricacies of scientific neurolinguistics. The book was widely praised for its "wit," and the target of that wit included the very linguistic scientists, like Chomsky, that Pinker set out to explain. Before going into a discussion of Chomsky's X-Bar theory of syntax, for example, he shows that he is not above poking fun at the atrocious naming conventions "that has made generative linguistics so uninviting" (p. 107).

Beyond a stylistic irreverence for a forbidding subject that welcomes an audience into it, there is a more intellectual use of wit, like Lincoln's, that involves combining audience populism with a more serious attack defense, one that uproots the fragile soil within which the opponent has constructed a public model. Lincoln's wit involves catching, through verbatim mimicry, Douglas committing contradiction/equivocation through the inadvertent crossing of component spaces within his public model. Lincoln reproduces Douglas' verbatim across the incompatible assumptions of the public and sensory/mundane spaces. His wit is made possible precisely because component spaces within a public model are rooted in contradictory assumptions. In the foregoing excerpt, Lincoln's wit takes advantage of the fact that a speaker's opponents in the public space do not have the same properties as flesh-and-blood persons in the sensory/mundane spaces. A debaters' public opponents are social abstractions that can cause war, ruin the economy, and still not face a jail term. Even in the view of Tactics, opponents are not morally held to account as everyday persons in a face-to-face world. Similar exaggeration against the flesh and blood person would be less socially acceptable. Lincoln's wit arises when he juxtaposes Douglas' verbatim reference to "Lincoln" in the face-to-face sensory/mundane world ("a kind, amiable, intelligent gentleman") and his references to Lincoln, the opponent, in the public space. Every alignment of component spaces within a public model is fragile, likes plates along a geological fault line. When speakers use plans, the fault lines are typically invisible. With wit, a speaker seizes the opportunity to bring major fault lines of an opponent's plan into direct collision at the surface of a short and highly compressed lexicalization.

To follow Lincoln's wit through the details of his rhetorical situation, we need to appreciate what Douglas was trying to do and the fault lines in his public model he left available for Lincoln to exploit. To show he was an unprejudiced critic of Lincoln, Douglas had sought a "no-malice alignment" to explain his friendship to the "kind, amiable gentleman" in the sensory-mundane spaces. This left Douglas open, according to his plan, to attack Lincoln publicly as the "destroyer of the country." But the fault lines produced by Douglas' plan opened the space for more inferences than Douglas had intended. For example, if a person is really intent on destroying the country, why think well of him or her at all in a face-to-face world? Why think of Lincoln as a "kind gentleman" in the sensory/mundane spaces if he is so dastardly in the public space? Douglas was trying to humanize Lincoln to make himself credible as Lincoln's public critic. But in the process Douglas overlooked—and Lincoln exploited through wit—that the same connection catches Douglas in the act of making a public menace look sympathetically human.

Wit, in its finest manifestation of coordinative skill, like that Lincoln could muster, exposes the shaky foundations of all internal maneuvers that result in plans.

### Event Reflexiveness: Humor

Humor can have a serious rhetorical purpose, as when used to soften or diffuse the full impact of a plan or tactic whose use would otherwise seem mean-spirited.[1] But humor can also allow speakers to distance themselves from the pressing business of plans and tactics and to simply share a human moment with the audience. In this capacity, humor is another reflective diversion contrived by the juxtaposition of incongruous events. This definition is broad enough to explain how all diversionary performatives can be humorous, relying as they do on juxtaposition of unexpected, and so incongruent, lexicalized events. But the definition is also specific enough to

---

[1]For an example, see our reference to Senator Biden in chapter 7.

explain what can be humorous about a performative even if it does not meet the specialized requirements of one type of diversion or another. Our account here converges with that of Raskin (1985), who defined humor as the juxtaposition of events within opposing "frames" of knowledge. In Raskin's theory of humor, these frames are cognitive scripts in the tradition of Schank and Abelson (1977). Raskin's account works well for humor based in short jokes based on semantic ambiguity. But the theory does not explain rhetorical humor that involves the plans and tactics of speakers and opponents. In our account, when the humor is plan centered, the frames in question are the component spaces of the Plans module; when it is tactics centered, the frames in question are the positive and negative structures of Tactics.

Often we must await the punchline of the humor to realize that an expected component space of the event has been crossed into another, unexpected space. Consider Douglas' use at Ottawa of "brother," an object structure seeming in the public space, and then shifting, only at the last moment, to the sensory-mundane: "I do not regard the negro as my equal [public space] and positively deny that he is my brother ["brother" in public space as "fellow citizen"...latent sensory-mundane space interpretation... "brother" as sibling] or any kin to me whatever [latent mundane-sensory crossing recognized as punchline]."

Douglas employs a similar shift when, at Ottawa, he describes the role of God toward the negro. He begins with a supremely entitled role in the public space, divine intent. He then shifts unexpectedly, for humorous effect, to the nonentitled mundane space in which divine intent is contrasted with an average plodding intent: "Now, I do not believe that the Almighty ever intended [public space active] the negro to be the equal of the white man. If he did, he has been a long time demonstrating that fact [latent sensory-mundane spaces activated]."

Lincoln also produces humor through such shifts, sometimes by turning abruptly from a public space abstraction to the earthy terms of the sensory-mundane: "I have no way of making an argument up into the consistency of a corn cob and stopping his [Douglas'] mouth with it. [Jonesboro reply]."

In his reply at Alton, Lincoln pulls off a more extended shift, from Douglas' debate opponent in the public space to his debate coach, in the sensory-mundane:

This is the seventh time Judge Douglas and myself have met in these joint discussions, and he has been gradually improving in regard to his war with the Administration. At Quincy, day before yesterday, he was a little more severe upon the Administration than I had heard him upon any occasion, and

I took pains to compliment him for it. I then told him to "Give it to them with all the power he had;" and as some of them were present, I told them I would be very much obliged if they would give it to him in about the same way.

I take it he has now vastly improved upon the attack he made then upon the Administration. I flatter myself he has really taken my advice on this subject. All I can say now is to re-commend to him and to them what I then commended—to prosecute the war against one another in the most vigorous manner.

## Strategic Reflexiveness: Irony

Irony is another manifestation of reflective diversion, but this time a manifestation capable of involving the speaker's self-aware control of the strategic element of rhetorical design. In its simplest form, irony is localized to Events, a mild form of diversion by lexicalizing the conventional opposite of the lexicalization that truly matches one's communicative intentions. This localized form of irony can become so conventionalized, moreover, that it may reveal no greater level of reflexiveness than that revealed in direct lexicalization. Irony diverts from the Strategic module of rhetorical design when it is used recurrently to express an attitude of detachment and experimental play toward the business of alternating between Plans, Tactics, and Events in order to satisfy the goals of predictiveness, responsiveness, and humanness. Rather than evincing strategic behavior in rhetoric, the chronic use of irony brings to the surface the speaker's aloof attitude on being strategic in rhetorical design. It is a speaker's effort, perhaps, to insist that being human is a condition of life, a fact, rather than a goal for getting one's way with an audience.

This sense of routinized, rather than occasional, diversion, a sense nourished by the habitual use of irony and the commitment to train audiences in its reception, provides a regular signal to audiences that a human being outside the "game" of competitive design is also standing in the role. The ironic attitude fosters a conscious split between action and reflection, between the deadly sincere process of persuading an audience about a public model and a spirited sense to poke holes in the tenuous and too rigid abstractions needed to compose one. To admit to audiences the limitations in the very abstractions one needs to persuade them is a human confession. To feel comfortable enough with the audience to think that making this confession can actually help, not hurt, persuasion is the essence of creating a community of reflective intellectuals. Listen to Lincoln at Quincy:

When the Judge says he wouldn't have believed of Abraham Lincoln that he would have made such an attempt as that, he reminds me of the fact that he entered upon this canvass with the purpose to treat me courteously; that touched me somewhat. It sets me to thinking. I was aware, when it was first agreed that Judge Douglas and I were to have these seven joint discussions, that they were the successive acts of a drama—perhaps I should say, to be enacted not merely in the face of audiences like this, but in the face of the nation, and to some extent, by my relation to him, and not from any thing in myself, in the face of the world; and I am anxious that they should be conducted with dignity and in the good temper which would be befitting the vast audience before which it was conducted. But when Judge Douglas got home from Washington and made his first speech in Chicago, the evening afterward I made some sort of a reply to it. His second speech was made at Bloomington, in which he commented upon my speech at Chicago, and said that I had used language ingeniously contrived to conceal my intentions, or words to that effect.... Now, I understand that this is an imputation upon my veracity and my candor....As soon as I learned that Judge Douglas was disposed to treat me in this way, I signified in one of my speeches that I should be driven to draw upon whatever of humble resources I might have—to adopt a new course with him. I was not entirely sure that I should be able to hold my own with him, but I at least had the purpose made to do as well as I could upon him; and now I say that I will not be the first to cry "hold." I think it originated with the Judge, and when he quits, I probably will.

Lincoln shows just how he could step out of the debate role, refer to himself as the "Abraham Lincoln" in the debates, to his own understanding of himself in a public drama, to his insecurities about how he would come off, to his personal surprise and anger at Douglas' behavior and his resolve to fight back. Such reflexive distance is very effective toward the satisfaction of humanness goals in rhetorical design. Neither Lincoln nor Douglas could have won the debates on the satisfaction of humanness goals alone. However, in the company of a consistent and compelling public model and a strong tactical defense to support it, knowing the human side of Lincoln could hardly have hurt his chances with the Illinois audiences. We know much less of Douglas' human side. Which becomes a greater liability, it seems, as Douglas' plans come undone and his tactics express themselves as face threats.

## EVENTS FOCUS, HUMANNESS GOALS, AND THE HUMANITIES

The Events focus, we have seen, searches, exploits, and extends connections between the speaker and the immediate audience. The primary goal focus of Events is the satisfaction of humanness goals, enabling the speaker to share a culture with the audience by sharing a language. The language- and culture-sharing aspects of Events are themselves tied to the traditional mission of the humanities. In the second chapter, we argued for the lack of fit between rhetoric and the humanities because of rhetoric's disinterest in universals. Our discussion of Events in this chapter indicates how one can turn the argument around and claim that, because rhetoric is concerned with the stark contingency of language use, because it can be used to interiorize the here and now of persons, to distance speakers from their abstract designs and to enter the moment with an interlocutor, it is the essence of a human view of language.

Richard Lanham has been perhaps the most eloquent writer to advocate a reinvorgated place for rhetoric in the humanities. In work over a decade old, he noticed a key relationship between rhetoric's vital relationship to the humanities and the goal of humanness that we satisfy as reflexive users of the language. He argued that our reflective capacities with language depend on our being able to divorce what language means on the surface from the underlying mechanics of how it works to mean anything at all. Lanham (1983) called this distinction the difference between looking *through* language and learning to look *at* it. All inquiry requires that we look *through* language to meaning. But only inquiry in the humanities bids us look *at* the language itself to understand the very possibility of meaning at all. Humanistic inquiry in this sense, moreover, is identical to the satisfaction of humanness goals that comes with sharing the pleasures of language in the moment with an audience (including only oneself). Thus, the regimen and discipline that is central to inquiry in the humanities is, to Lanham's way of thinking, a rhetorical regimen and discipline.

A decade later, Lanham (1993) elaborated his view of rhetoric and the humanities further. The central tie between the two remained. But rather than tie rhetoric and the humanities mainly with the humanness goals of an Events focus, Lanham's understanding of rhetoric and the humanities seemed more explicitly to comprehend the oscillation of our Events focus with Plans and Tactics as well. He tied this comprehension to the "extraordinary convergence of social, technological, and theoretical pressures" (p. 117) that have once again caused us to think through the future of the humanities. This convergence, he suggested, especially the electrification of the word, brought out the various oscillating "faces" or modules of rhetoric that bear a striking resemblance to the views of Plans, Tactics, and Events we have been developed here. As Lanham (p. 111) saw it, rhetoric has always seemed theoretically fragmented because it held together oscillations of different world views that were seldom caught in the same theoretical snapshot: "Rhetoric as a theory has proved so exasperating and unsatisfactory precisely because it oscillated from one world view to the other." The western tradition, Lanham affirmed, has preferred arts that sought timeless truth. This has been the basis of philosophy's triumph over a temporal rhetoric. But as Lanham contended, art, by its very nature, is caught in time. And to overlook the art behind the statement of timeless truth, "generations of thinkers" had to "tak[e] the oscillation out of time, stopping it to point out how immiscible" truth and rhetoric are. For Lanham and for us, "Rhetorical man [sic] was a dramatic game-player but he was always claiming that the ground he presently stood upon was more than a stage." This points out, precisely, the tensions between the Plans and Tactical views of the world required in rhetorical design. But the rhetor's gaming and play are not confined to the competition with the opponent. They also spill over, as Burke well knew, into a game of solidarity and cooperation with the audience. To understand rhetoric is to comprehend these ostensible contradictions as not at all contradictory when these views are seen in what Lanham calls "perpetual oscillation." From Lanham's point of view, to understand rhetoric as housing these multiple faces is necessary to revitalize a humanities that has come to split the seriousness of truth-telling from the challenge of competitive play and the pleasures of sharing a culture with others. From our point of view, the fact that rhetoric's nature is to house these multiple faces (or modules) is basic to its fit within the arts of design. These points of view, happily, are complementary. Moving rhetoric closer to the arts of design need not move it away from the humanities. We have talked about how the traditional humanities has tended to push rhetoric aside. But if the traditional humanities now finds that it has relied on rhetoric all along, that its claim to express timeless truth was but an oscillating moment (within Plans) of rhetoric, then one can imagine a rhetoric, as Lanham, McCloskey (1985, 1990), Simons (1990), and now many others imagine a rhetoric, that can be "gracious" enough to help nurse the project of the humanities back to a renewed vitality.

Ten

# Putting It Together and Leaving It Undone: Threads and Loose Ends

In this final chapter we explore the remaining threads of the rhetorical design process and loose ends that remain. The threads represent the components of our architecture that we have yet to discuss, namely, the Strategic and Presentation modules. A third thread is the question of coordination across modules, how the various modules of our architecture are woven together (or coordinated) within the design process. The loose ends are a collection of issues, ideas, and directions that arise from our theory of rhetorical design. They do not fill in information about our architecture per se, but furnish jumping off points for further inquiry over a range of issues in which our architecture might be applied and extended.

## THE COORDINATION OF DESIGN MODULES

Coordination across modules, either within the design space or across different aspects of the design, is a crucial issue for all the arts in the family of design arts. In this section, we discuss the role of coordination in rhetorical design.

### Coordination and Anthromophorism

It is easy to misunderstand what we mean by coordinating across modules, so we quickly dispel a naive understanding. The naive understanding is to think that modules can "talk" to one another and have "intentions" to do so when they "recognize" that they "need" information from the other. Another aspect of a naive understanding is to assume that the process of design is strictly sequential, that the problem of coordination is simply the problem of "deciding" what needs to be said first, next, and so on. We have quoted the mentalistic terms in the last two sentences to indicate how easy it is to anthropomorphize modules as embedding little human communicators within them, as if every module were a stand-in for the whole speaker being assisted through a rhetorical design.

We acknowledge a partial anthropomorphizing, that is, anthropomorphizing within a module. Within a module, we have relied on an anthropomorphic intelligence to provide the mechanism by which a specific module, within the limits of its own knowledge and action potential, "decides" or "does" something. We have described Plans, Tactics, and Events as making decisions on structure within the design space of rhetoric. The decisions each makes are limited by their internal logic. The Plans module can only "decide" how to partition the design structure into a finite set of spaces, how to link the spaces to form the skeleton of a public model, and, using generic and specific plans, how to elaborate the model in order to speak about truth and falsehood in the social world. The Tactics module can only recognize vulnerabilities in design structures, and on the basis of that "decide" whether to change the design through offense or defense, repair or attack, all for the purpose of beating the opponent. The Events module can only "decide" on what structures should be uniquely lexicalized as rhetorical performatives and "choose" the type of performative, in the interest of connecting with the audience through the sharing of language.

We have ascribed a "cognition" to the modules within the design space. Were our aim a computer model of Plans, Tactics, and Events, our partial anthropomorphism would be a starting point but not an end. We would need to go many levels lower in refinement to translate the decisions of these modules into the detailed mechanisms, stripped of metaphor, that is required for creating a machine understanding. Within our focus in this book, which has been a general theory of rhetoric within the family of design arts, our partial anthropomorphism is not a limitation. We have argued that the challenge of rhetorical expertise is centered in the management of the set of modules as it is the application of any one module. A key burden of our theory is to focus on the sources of rhetorical expertise in a way that relates it to design expertise in general. This relationship is not dependent on any module specific to rhetorical design but on the coordination of modules required for effective performance. We have thus have had no reason to rid individual modules entirely of an anthropomorphic element. Our hope is that the anthropomorphic elements we have relied on to describe the internal logic of the modules can serve as a foundation for the further development of these modules and can provide for an integrative framework for prior theory.

Yet for us to allow for an anthropomorphic understanding of the coordination across modules would have more serious consequences for our project.

Moving rhetoric from a practical art to a design art, we have argued that (a) the challenges of performing rhetoric are similar to that of other design arts. We have suggested that rhetoric relies on a "complexity" of production no less than is found in the other arts of design. Developing an architecture of rhetorical design, we further argued that (b) even though rhetoric expresses itself as complex performance, we can explain, or at least describe, the challenges associated with that performance through a modular breakdown. Now, if we anthropomorphize the whole process of rhetorical design by adding an intelligent homunculus to the design process we are throwing out argument (b), for to allow for a nonanalyzable "intelligence" that rises above individual modules would be to claim one of two things. First, we might be claiming that rhetorical coordination is common to all people, or linked to general intelligence if it is not. The challenge of rhetoric would be learning the individual modules and then leaving it to nature and other factors of the environment (unrelated to rhetoric but related to intelligence) to determine the extent to which one can acquire rhetorical expertise. Second, we might be claiming that rhetorical coordination is a mystical art that some just inherit and others do not. In either case, we would be claiming—conceding—that a central challenge of rhetorical design is unanalyzable on its own terms, at best filters into other general considerations. This is precisely the claim we want to avoid if we are to open, rather than close, inquiry into the challenge of rhetoric as an art of design. Once we allow that, intelligence and inheritance in place, a hidden homunculus underlying the design "knows" the right thing to do at the right time, we implicitly concede much of the ground we have tried to take in reclassifying rhetoric from a practical to a design art. We would be assuming that some modules of rhetoric are easy even for novices to accomplish and that rhetoric's standing as a practical art would be assured by that fact alone. Any further efforts to explain why so many novices fail at rhetoric and never touch the expertise we can glimpse in a Lincoln or Douglas, could not appeal to a "higher challenge" of rhetoric that begged for a precise description. For once we leave the "challenge of rhetoric" unanalyzable or diffused into other general factors, we cut off the idea of rhetoric per se presenting that higher challenge, of rhetoric as an art that we perceive on par with the arts of design.

## Skilled Refutation: An Example of Successful Coordination

Were rhetoric truly a practical art lacking an analyzable coordinative challenge, we would not expect to find certain aspects of rhetorical behavior very hard for novices to acquire. But we do. Kuhn's (1991) research suggests that novices have a very difficult time learning fair refutation of an opponent. To understand the challenge posed in learning such a skill, we consider the coordination that is involved even in a simple manifestation of refutation. Assume that Douglas says (as he did) words to the effect of "the Founders made slavery a state's decision" and Lincoln seeks to refute him, as he did, with words to the effect of "even a Southerner such as Brooks admitted that, but for the cotton gin, slavery would not have politically survived." These two statements are intricately tied to one another, but how? What was Lincoln's decision making that allowed him to respond with his statement in the environment of Douglas'?

Let's trace how the refutation might work. Lincoln's Plans, Tactics, and Events must view the same structure impacted by Douglas' statement, but these modules view it in different ways and prime Lincoln's behavior according to these differences. In Plans, Lincoln is primed to tell stories from his public model; in Tactics, he is primed to respond to Douglas' offense; and in Events, he is concerned with the audience's reaction to Douglas' lexicalizations.

No module, working alone, can change the rhetorical design reliably. After Douglas' statement enters the design structure, Lincoln's Plans may go on telling its stories from his public model, some of which make Douglas a counteragent of certain social falsehoods. But Lincoln's Plans knows nothing about opponents or responding to an opponent in a rhetorical situation. And his Plans certainly knows nothing about Douglas' immediate words, his exact lexicalizations as a target of response. Lincoln's Tactics, on the assumption of transparency, can recognize and respond to Douglas' offense but not in a way that assures preserving consistency in Lincoln's public model. Lincoln's Events can lexicalize structure that is relevant to the audience's reaction to Douglas's previous statements. But these Event actions, left on their own, might create more vulnerabilities, tactically, for Lincoln and may create inconsistencies in his public model.

To figure out how to make the refutation, Lincoln's Tactics had to understand that a good way to attack an opponent's structure is to respond with one's own structure that both corresponds to and offsets it. Tactically, for the speaker's structure to correspond with the opponent's is to say they are comparable along certain criteria. For the speaker's structure to offset the opponent's is to say that the tactical action either addresses/repairs the vulnerability that was created by the opponent or it creates/increases a vulnerability for the opponent that mitigates some, if not all, the strength the opponent accrued from it in the first place.

Tactics can find the initial pattern for a refutation but is very limited in its ability to act on it. However, before giving up, Tactics starts a chain of actions leading to a refutation, the results of which are ultimately visible to the other modules. Lincoln's Tactics sees that structure dealing with Brooks is negative structure for Douglas and can offset some of the advantage he has tried to press with his earlier statement. Lincoln's Tactics elaborates the design structure to reflect this knowledge. Lincoln's Plans sees the newly elaborated structures and attempts to integrate them into the public model it maintains. The Plans module focuses on the public model in a new way, perhaps applying a new plan, pursuing a new focus based on actions taken by Tactics. The benefit of Plans coordinating with Tactics is that only Plans has a ready way of elaborating the design in a way that maintains consistency across the public model. The result of Lincoln's Plans is to assimilate Douglas' rhetorical action as a social falsehood. But thanks indirectly to the knowledge initiated by Tactics, it has come to focus on elaborating the design structure as part of a precedent plan to tell the truth about the history of slavery in America. The snag for Plans is that it knows many truths to tell about slavery in America, and there are far more truths to tell than good refutations of Douglas. Plans, after all, knows nothing about good refutation; only about telling stories from a consistent public model.

Lincoln's Plans changes the design structure, elaborating it with many stories about the origins of slavery. Influenced by Tactics and Plans, the design structure now contains information pertaining to "respond to Douglas" and public narratives about the history of slavery. Events views the rhetorical design in its present state and finds it can begin to sculpt part of it into a statement with recognizable audience effect by lexicalizing the structure to make it similar to Douglas' earlier statement. Events retrieves Douglas' prior lexicalization "the Founders made slavery a state's decision" and adds to the rhetorical design a lexicalization that balances Douglas' words. Events knows that the lexicalized pattern of "state's decision," which implies, for the audience, no uniform outcome to slavery across the states, can lexically balance against a statement affirming a national policy for slavery, as indicated in the Brooks example. The result of this complex interaction between Plans, Tactics, and Events is a refutation. But no single module, significantly, has the whole view of what a refutation is, for a refutation spans knowledge across all three views. More specifically, a well-done refutation tells the truth (Plans) in a way that corresponds (viewed from Tactics, corresponds = responds to opponents; viewed from Events, corresponds = connects with the audience) with the terms (Events) in which the opponent (Tactics) has told a falsehood (Plans). Or it offers a falsehood as a counterbalance to the speaker's alleged "truth." Lincoln decided in this case to return Douglas' statement with a truth in his public model. The decision for this preference is beyond our scope here.

It is through this independence, and yet indirect interdependence, of Plans, Tactics, and Events that Lincoln creates a refutation that responds to, and attacks, Douglas, is understandable (both to the opponent and audience) as a refutative "correction" to Douglas' previous statement, and remains informed by and consistent with Lincoln's public model. Given our simplified description, the flow between Plans, Tactics, and Events may seem assembly-line and linear. But it is not. Plans, Tactics, and Events operate concurrently, as independent "experts" that look for opporunities to change a design as the state of the design changes.

The idea of concurrently operating "experts" that indirectly influence one another may seem strange. However it describes a well-known cognitive science paradigm called blackboard architectures (Erman, Hayes-Roth, Lessor & Reddy, 1980; see Engelmore & Morgan, 1988, for a comparative survey of 30 such blackboard systems). Blackboard architectures are especially robust for modeling systems, like design, where a task requires the opportunistic application of many heterogenous "experts" all looking at the same problem (represented in a common workspace called a "blackboard") but with each expert looking at the problem from a specialized set of competencies and goal priorities. Craw and Tock (1992), to cite one example, implemented a blackboard system to recognize a human face, with one "expert" knowing how to extract lines and shapes from a photographic image; another expert knowing the prototypical shapes and relative position of facial features, eyes, ears, nose, mouth; and yet a third expert knowing how to fit the information of the first two experts together so that lines and shapes from a specific input photoimage can be identified in terms of discrete features.

In our architecture, the design structure is the common blackboard that each module knows how to "read" and "write on." Each module brings to the design structure specialized expertise needed to succeed at rhetorical design. Plans knows how to speak the on-the-record truth about the social world, satisfying predictiveness goals. Tactics knows how to win the local debate with the opponent, being responsive to the opponent. Events knows how to satisfy humanness goals by bringing the concerns of the immediate audience into the design. Initially, the blackboard, or design structure in our case, contains only a statement of the problem or initial goal priority. As the experts read the data on the blackboard, they contribute to the global understanding of the problem by writing additional information on the blackboard for all the experts and to see and process. A key aspect of blackboard systems is that much of the coordination of the modules is implicit in the evolving design itself. What is written on the blackboard can precondition the expert who is best able to look and act on it in a directive way. Because each expert is autonomous and each has access to the design structure, there is nothing to preclude implementations of rhetorical design as parallel processes, with each module taking its view of the design structure simultaneously. In an expert refutation, the shifting perspectives of Plans, Tactics, and Events on the design structure are so automatic and lightning quick that it is hard to imagine them not working in parallel.

From an intuitive point of view, it seems as if the modules of rhetorical design should be able to attend to the same object as a single intelligence. Up close, however, the modules rely on more primitive, distributed, and yet more precise and describable mechanisms to coordinate themselves as they do. The advantage of blackboard architectures is in the description of complex skilled behavior, where, in terms of coordination, failure is as much the norm as success. We believe this nonromanticized mechanistic description is more realistic and informative for rhetoric because failure at rhetoric, like failure in all the arts of design, is as common as success. We also believe the nonidealized story because it opens up rhetorical expertise as an object of inquiry rather than shutting it down abortively. Viewed as a practical art, the one typically taught in high school and to college freshman, rhetoric is a matter of presumed competence that needs only to be accredited. The design of rhetoric is complex but our approach suggests that it is complex in ways that are nonetheless describable. Viewed as an art of design, rhetoric is a matter of gradient expertise and it opens up the potential for theory to explain the gradients from a novice to a Lincoln.

## The Role of the Strategic Module in Coordination

The coordination of Plans, Tactics, and Events in rhetorical design can determine that a highly integrated design is produced, like that required by a refutation. However, although the coordination of the modules within the design space assures an integrated design, it does not necessarily assure a design that evolves in conjunction with rhetorical goals. In many blackboard systems, as well as in our theory of rhetorical design, a Strategic module coordinates the actions of the modules in the design space with the goals of the design. Like the head of a nonheirarchical organization, the Strategic module keeps a record of goal priorities at any point in the design process.

To appreciate what the Strategic module can and cannot see, we start by considering the relationship of the Strategic module to goals. The outside environment, including the larger culture and rhetorical situation, as well as the speaker's intentions, determines the speaker's goals. Goals are dynamic, and goal priorities change as the situation changes. The goals component represents what goal should be the highest priority, given the state of the speaker's intentions and the outside environment. The Strategic module does not strictly "decide" on goal priorities per se. Like a manager who must communicate the priority of the Board of Directors down to every level of the organization, the Strategic module must try to "direct" the behavior of the internal design modules in line with the current priority. To do this, the Strategic module is cognizant of the general "job descriptions" of each of the internal design modules in terms of the goals it is best at turning a design toward: Plans, Predictiveness; Tactics, Responsiveness; Events, Humanness.

In addition, the Strategic module knows how to "give support" to the module whose job description seems most to accord with the current priority. The less complex and dynamic the context of rhetoric is, the more stable the goal priorities and the more straightforward it is for the Strategic module to give support to the relevant modules. To support a monologic lecture, for example, where the speaker must be predictable, Strategy can set Plans at the highest speed and at the highest level of alertness, provided that the same context dominates the design throughout the presentation. To support a stand-up comedy act, where the speaker must cater to the audience, Strategy can hand the design process over to Events to create designed lexicalizations. Yet to support more variegated and difficult environments, like the debates, Strategy must keep shifting priorities dynamically to accomplish the shifting goals of design. The refutation we considered above is a micro-accomplishment of Plans, Tactics, and Events all working convergently across the same design structure. The details of refutation, however, appear to rely on a level of coordination that is too low level for Strategy to direct. In our architecture, Strategy knows little about each module beyond their job descriptions, the goals of a design they are most likely to help a particular design move toward.

We have spoken of Strategy giving support to modules whose job description best meets the current goal priority. Let us specify what it means to "give support." The Strategic module can give support to some modules over others by influencing three properties in the way that Plans, Tactics, and Events behave. The first property is the speed or frequency of operation. The Strategic module can allocate the speed or frequency with which a particular module gets to view and change the design structure. For example, the Strategic module can translate a priority to be responsive into a decision to "run" Tactics on the design structure at a higher speed, or a more regular frequency, than the other modules are run. This is like an executive in charge of a project requiring an engineer and a lawyer and who finds that the project is technically strong but legally underspecified. To indicate that the project team needs to strengthen its focus on the legal dimension, the manager puts the lawyer in charge of the project for the next couple of weeks. This assures that the lawyer will have more time on task than previously and should correct some of the expected shortcomings of having the engineer in charge for too long. Having the lawyer in charge does not mean there will no input from the engineer, just as having the engineer in charge never silenced the lawyer. It just means that the lawyer will get disproportionate control over the project for the near term. Similarly, increasing the speed or frequency with which Tactics views the design structure does not leave the design structure beyond the access of the other modules. It just increases the chances that the design will evolve in a way that weights it toward the Tactical dimension of rhetoric.

The second property the Strategic module can influence to "give support" is the alertness of a particular module. A module is alert to the extent that it notices and is quick to respond to changes in the design structure produced by any module. A module that is very unalert only notices and responds to changes in structure that it produces. On the project team mentioned earlier, an alert lawyer notices and acts on changes in structure regardless of who produced it. An unalert lawyer only notices and acts upon changes in structure that he or she produced as legal changes. Alert and unalert are poles on a continuum and there are many settings in between. One can imagine very unalert modules that do not know how to represent what is new in a structure since they last spied it; one can imagine an even more alert module that would know how to represent "the latest changes" in structure since the previous viewing. A more alert module still would know not only to represent the latest changes but to attend to them and make them focal for further action. The alertness to newly introduced structures is one mechanism behind how modules seem able to "share" information. One module A alters structure S out of a large set of possible structures. When module B comes to view the design structure, B is alert enough to know that S is the structure most recently changed. It thus attends to S and makes it focal for further alteration. Such an alertness factor can explain how a structure S in Plans gets classified as a social falsehood, how that same S in Tactics can get classified as the opponent's positive structure, and how

Events, focusing on that same S, can choose a negative lexicalization like "false" or "will ruin the country."

Alert modules can keep a shared focus on the same structures. But just as important is how the Strategic module can direct a design by changing the relative alertness of modules. By making a module more alert relative to others, the Strategic module increases the chances that a module will play a leadership role in the evolution of the design. Should the Strategic module want to increase the priority of responsiveness within the rhetorical design, it can make the Tactics module more alert than the other modules in addition to, or as an alternative to, increasing the relative speed and frequency with which it views the structure. As an important aside, rhetorical strategy operating in writing is more difficult because the writer's external environment is largely artificial. The writer must simulate the external environment against which goals and strategy are formed. The flow of a written text often depends on the internal cues the writer gives to "wake up" different modules as they become more important. The actual realization of a writing environment—and the final text of whether the writer's simulation has an empirical effectiveness—takes place in the reader's displaced context.

The third and final property that the Strategic module can affect to "give support" to a module is the resistance of a module to the design structure. A module's level of resistance affects its interrelatedness to the actions of other modules. A module that is low in resistance, other things being equal, will tend to notice and create change in the design structure caused by other modules. But a module that is high in resistance will tend to avoid noticing and taking action on the structure shaped by other modules even when others factors would precondition it. A fast and alert but highly resistant module will notice the existing structure and be eager to act, but to act by creating new structures rather than elaborating existing structures built by the previous actions of other modules. A module with a high resistance to the existing structure, like a writer with a high resistance to a working draft, is likely to start from scratch rather than do detailed revisions. By contrast, a module with a low resistance, like a writer with a high commitment to a draft in progress, is less likely to start fresh than to keep working on what is there. A module with a high resistance to existing structure will tend to act in what designers call a "top-down" fashion. A module with a low resistance to existing structure will work "bottom-up."

There are interactions between a module's resistance to existing structure and particular goal priorities. For example, the Strategic module knows that the goal of responsiveness requires a module to work bottom-up, hewing closely to the existing structures produced by the opponent. The tactical speaker who wants to play defense has no choice but to work from the bottom up relative to the opponent's current structure. The goal of responsiveness cannot be satisfied apart from the commitment to working from the input of the opponent. A speaker, like Douglas at times, who does not have this commitment cannot be responsive. At the same time, the Strategic module knows that truly inventive and nonclichéd lexicalization will be highly resistant to existing lexicalizations. For strategic rhetoric, low resistance seems a preferable default for the Tactics module and high resistance, a preferable default for Events. Unlike speed and alertness, then, where a module is given support by having these properties increased, there is no simple relationship between resistance and the favoring of one module over others. Whether a module is more or less likely to be used in a design by changing its resistance to the current structure depends on the particular module.

To summarize, rhetorical strategy, we should see, provides only a weak constraint on the actual design of rhetoric. It gives support or "resources" to modules it wants to be in charge but otherwise exerts very little direct influence. Consequently, it is difficult to predict behavior only knowing the strategic choices of a rhetor. However, understanding these strategic choices can clarify behavior after the fact. For example, after tracking the behavior of Lincoln and Douglas, the differences in their strategies as the debates unfold become useful markers for explaining differences in their behavior. As strategists, Lincoln and Douglas pose an interesting contrast. Douglas uniformly assigns the highest priority to Plans across the debates. He has a story to tell about true and falsehood in America and he wants to show himself utterly predictable in light of this story. However, as the debates wear on, he has to give higher—not necessarily the highest—priority to tactics, when he finds Lincoln attacking the consistency of his plans. By changing the environment, Lincoln forces Douglas to assign a higher priority than before to responsiveness (an alteration in goal priority within the goals component), which forces in turn a strategic change, having Douglas give greater support to Tactics. Were Strategy able to micromanage the individual modules, Douglas would never have chosen offense and face threats as his main tactical actions. But we assume that Douglas' strategy can only give support to the tactical dimension of his argument, not tell him which tactics to choose. As a tactician, either Douglas is limited in his tactical repertoire—many of his tactics, we have seen, express themselves through an unresponsive offense or face threats—or he makes a strategic error, leaving Tactics a fairly low priority, which implicitly encourages him to think of tactics only as a way to grumble at Lincoln for rudely interrupting his plans for America. In either case, one presumes that Douglas had no good counter to Lincoln's charges. He didn't know how to resolve the inconsistency between popular sovereignty and Dred Scott that Lincoln demonstrated syllogistically. Yet he wanted, in any case, to keep telling his same story about truth and falsehood in America—and he did. Lincoln shows more evidence of a complex dynamic strategy, of shifting priorities as the debates unfold. In the early debates, he assigns to Events and Tactics a higher priority than Plans. He wants his audiences to feel like he is one of them even before they know what a "Republican" is and how they are supposed to fit into Lincoln's story about truth and falsehood in America. By satisfying human-ness goals early in the debates, Lincoln seems to understand that he would have a foundation when he became tactical with Douglas. It is not until the end of the debates, however, that Lincoln makes Plans a high priority, seeming to think that if audiences have a rooting interest in him, they are more likely to accept his story about social truth and falsehood.

## THE PRESENTATION MODULE

A second thread to explore is the Presentation module. We have mentioned this module in passing, but have yet to discuss it at any length. We begin by distinguishing the Events and the Presentation modules. Linguistic aspects of a rhetorical design that are not part of the design per se are assigned to the sentence and discourse grammar implementing it. The Presentation module is our name for this implementation mechanism. Conceivably, many if not most of the lexicalizations that get expressed in a rhetorical design are never acted on by Events. They come straight from Plans or Tactics and are lexicalized directly by the Presentation module. Although the Presentation module cannot influence or change a rhetorical design, it, like Plans, Tactics, and Events, is a module that can "look" into the design space and can forage the rhetorical situation. Like the Events module, the Presentation module can lexicalize structure in the design space. Unlike the Events module, it can only lexicalize structures whose rhetorical significance is considered "satu-rated" prior to lexicalization. Lexicalization can only implement the design, not add to or modify it further.

The Presentation module makes decisions about the structure as a "rhe-torically complete" design that is ready for expression. Some of this decision making is content and context driven, determined by the nature of the information and the rhetorical situation. Other aspects are driven by the tempo and rhythm of communication. At regular intervals for a speaker and (to a lesser extent) for a writer drafting, expression must come forth or there will be no tempo of expression. The Presentation module is regulated by the need to establish a rhythm and tempo of expression regardless of other content and context constraints on a "finished design."

What part of language results from unique lexicalization (Events)? What part results from the routine lexical implementation of structure outside the rhetorical design (Presentation)? In some sense, these are empirical questions to be adjudicated in a disinterested way. In a more important sense, it seems, they are questions that investigators need to use to focus issues more than to settle them. Whatever chunks of language a theorist is interested in explaining from within a rhetorical design must be explained as unique lexicalizations. Whatever chunks a theorist is not interested in explaining from within the design can be explained through a standard grammar, accommodating much lexical variation but without a loss of power in one's base theory of rhetorical design. In chapter 2, we considered variant expressions on a World Series outcome and called them separate events. We did so because we assumed that their wording was intrinsic to the rhetorical design. We thus treated them as unique lexicalizations and hence unique events. A theoretical focus based on different assumptions, classifying both as acceptable variants, would have treated them as alternative expressions of the "same" (nonunique) event.[1]

It is left to the Presentational module to turn the rhetorically saturated structure into a full presentation of rhetoric. The Presentation module is responsible for lexicalizations and larger organizations of expression considered nonunique. In contrast to the Events module, which handles unique lexicalization artfully performed, and timed, to the moment of utterance, the Presentation module handles the lexicalization and organization of linguistic structures that implement a rhetorical design into linguistic expression but whose implementation is thought to lie outside the design proper. This module is obviously necessary for bringing many aspects of a rhetorical design to expression. Still, it is a module studied by the discipline of linguistics more than rhetoric.

The Presentation module, implementing a rhetorical design into the materiality of routine and unremarkable language, exhibits the same conceit of concealment on which all good art is based. Insofar as the rhetorical art

---

[1] To be distinguished from the unique events created by the Events module. Notice that our definition of rhetoric (chapter 2) as the strategic organization and communication of events does not specify the uniqueness or nonuniqueness of the events organized and communicated. Rhetoric results both from language that is judged to be part of the design, as well as language that is not so judged.

conceals itself, as good design art does, then when audiences are with the speaker, they will not notice that the speaker is making manifest to them a human artifice. They will not notice artificial or constructed worlds, surely not "mere" rhetoric. They will think the speaker has put them in touch with the world head on, as it exists without mediation, without the intervention of minds, without design. They will think the world framed through rhetoric is the world as it is, a world far-ranging in time and space, replete with voices, positions, and counters. And, until an opponent happens along, it may well be the only world they will know to explore and act on.

A question often asked in discourse generation models within computational linguistics and artificial intelligence is, how do discourse plans translate into actual sentences? This looks like a question we should ask of the Presentation module. However, we will not pursue this "how" question for several reasons. First, and not least, it is beyond the scope of this project. Second, the how question is a much harder, and different, question to pursue when the grain size of a plan spans public discourse and not simply something the size of a single object structure. In computational linguistics and artificial intelligence (AI), "plans" are roughly the grain size of what we have discussed as single "object classes" (chapter 6) in the design structure. Object classes are molecules of meaning that require the addition of connective syntax—auxiliaries, categories, ordering rules, case, conjunctions, prepositions, articles, suffixes, prefixes, particles— to become well-formed clauses and sentences of English. This level of knowledge is quite important for expanding paragraph-level plans into English sentences (Dorr, 1991; Hornstein, 1990; O'Keefe & Lambert, 1995), but it is seriously incomplete if one's grain size for plans spans the structures of a public model through which speakers assemble public discourse.

Third, the how question is best left to the details of a psychological and accompanying computational model. Despite our analytic framework, we offer no psychological or fully operational computational model of how speakers translate the structure of a design into events. If our analytic study has merit, we will have made progress describing, in analytic terms, that the structure of a design, under the controlling lens of Plans, Tactics, and Events, and under the supervision of rhetorical goals can be embodied as streams of events. This characterization is in line with our effort to understand the minimal level of complexity required for rhetorical design (chapter 1). None of it is to address the how question in psychological or computational terms.

At the discourse level, the Presentation module must perform an organizing, as well as a lexicalizing, function. It must organize multiple-clause structures into patterns of nonunique events that are understandable to an audience. It seems that much of this organization can be taken directly from the organization of structure in the design structure. But other forms of organization may be more specific to presentation, such as the dramatic narrative, transforming one's internal rhetorical plans and tactics into a setting, conflict, and resolution. The Plans module is responsible for much of the macro organization that takes place in a rhetorical discourse associated with the speaker's monologic position. But much of the presentational implementation of plans will be based on a highly abstracted, edited, and compressed view of events, events more likely told in canonical than non-canonical fashion.

Such presentation often requires a dramatic narrative that is organized more in terms of holding an audience[2] than in the terms of audienceless Plans (telling truths and falsehoods about the social world). Speakers typically provide setting or background events to prepare audiences to understand conflicts that have arisen or that are imminent. They typically compose conflict events, events manifesting instabilities demanding short- or long-term attention, in the hopes of stirring an audience's attention and concern. And they sometimes provide resolution events in the hopes of recommending to audiences what they believe are useful ways of resolving the conflicts.

These regularities indicate that compelling rhetoric requires a compelling presentation in terms of the classic categories of dramaturgy. Different presentational sequences of events ensue from variations in the dramatic slots to which speakers wants audiences to attend. For example, some novice audiences, lacking in much of the basic background to understand the conflict events, may require whole discourses that do no more than provide settings. Some expert audiences, well versed in the conflict events and in many detailed, but failed, resolutions, may be impatient to hear anything but resolutions that take very narrow pathways. Audiences lying between these poles require ever differing proportions of setting, conflict, and resolution events.

Certain controls that govern plot sequencing in event-telling, such as the linguistic difference between settings, conflicts, and resolutions, must belong to the Presentation module. It falls to this module, for example, to understand that settings result from descriptions of general, generic, routine, and ongoing states and activities; that conflicts result because of clashes in principles in settings that are particular, concrete, unique, and discrete; and that resolutions result when conflicts are resolved, transforming conflict

---

[2]Holding a generic audience. If the Presentation were tailored to holding THE immediate audience, there would be a basis for explaining the expression as designed through Events.

situations back into the ordinary and mundane. All of this knowledge must belong to the Presentation module. How it belongs remains unknown to us and requires the examination of complex discourse across a larger sample of genres and situations than we have undertaken here.

The Presentation module views the design structure only from the property "completed design" or a partial design that the tempo and rhythm of speech makes "ready for expression." The completed design expressed by Presentation is an amalgamation of actions taken by Plans, Tactics, and Events. That is to say, the Presentation module never presents isolated Plan, Tactics, or Events actions or structures that are annotated from the purified views of any one of these modules. The Presentation module just brings to expression "completed designs." At the same time, there are stronger or weaker traces of Plans or Tactics in particular presentations.[3] These traces lend some independent support to Plan and Tactical information living as distinct modules prior to their presentation in discourse. To highlight the connection between Plans and Tactics and Presentation, it is instructive to discuss the extreme cases where a presentation expresses strong traces from Plans, and then strong traces from Tactics.

### Presenting Disourse with Traces from Plans

We consider here how structure interpreted by Plans might be lexicalized through the Presentation module. Plan-interpreted structures indicate displaced[4] situations from a public model, states of the world that lie outside the rhetorical situation. Their lexicalization through Presentation requires assigning to such structure information considered more linguistically elemental than the assignments we first think of when Events lexicalizes rhetorical performatives. It includes, importantly, tense/aspect information.[5]

Consider some of the regularities that underlie these assignments, as plans from a public model default to different requirements for tense/aspect marking. These defaults are illustrated in Fig. 10.1. Of the plans discussed in chapter 7, none is bound to an orientation fixed by the English pluperfect

---

[3]The same is least true for Events because Presentation is often an alternative, not an accessory, to Events.

[4]See Chafe (1994) for a discussion of displacement in narrative.

[5]Events also assigns tense/aspect to structures it lexicalizes. But this assignment is usually eclipsed by the assignments that are more immediately associated with the structure's performative status.

or past perfect ("had been"), an orientation that is locked in the past, cut off from the present. Rather, for every plan in a public model, past-oriented tense/aspect markings have the potential to bear some direct relevance to the present. The perfect ("has been") signals a present still affected by a past rushing up toward it. To say that Jane has been to Paris is to imply much about Jane now (e.g., she speaks French, she is sophisticated in culinary experiences, etc.). Speakers often use the perfect to signal autobiographical information that has current relevance for the immediate situation. Douglas praises Lincoln as a youth good in sports, storytelling, and drinking. This offering would seem most irrelevant in the context of the debates were it not interpretable as relevant history, intended by Douglas as part of a "no-malice" alignment (i.e., I have known Lincoln 25 years and take no personal issue with him). By showing a firsthand acquaintance with Lincoln that was amicable and of long standing, Douglas gave himself a shield from which to attack, with greater credibility and impunity, Lincoln's public record as an adult.

As we mentioned earlier, only the past perfect ("had been") unambiguously signals a dead past, a past with no current heartbeat. The simple past

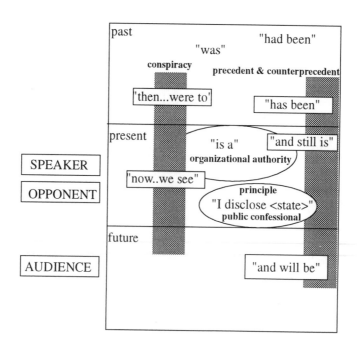

FIG. 10.1.   Overlaying plans on a tense/aspect grid for generation as linguistic events.

("was") is ambiguous in its present relevance. In the Ottawa debates, for example, Douglas reminds the audience that the Democratic party "was and is" the historical party of the country. The coupling of the past and present is not a redundancy. The auxiliary "was" does not preclude the present but only weakly implies that continuation into the present is in some doubt. The addition of "is" dissipates all doubt.

Still other plans are designed to overlap into a present and future time horizon. From our vantage in the here and now, the future is radically indeterminate and unknowable. Rhetoric could not move audiences to action if the only future audiences had to decide on was the future economists contend for, with their mathematical models and computer simulations. Rhetoric, rather, offers audiences a glimpse of the future as defined from the past. Through precedent, counterprecedent, and conspiracy plans, audiences are asked to retrofit interpretations of the past as forks into the present and future. Precedents urge acceptance of a future that reinstates the past. Counterprecedents urge rejection. To charge a conspiracy is to point out a counterprecedent that has been worked out in a secret past when a cabal then (past) decided what was to (future) happen. Secrecy nourishes the plan and exposure starves it. The audience is bid, having detected such a plan, to use the present or future as an opportunity to expose the secret and thwart the plan. The speaker charging conspiracy, in other words, urges the audience to reject a future that continues to shelter the cabal's private dealings from public scrutiny.

Some plans seem to reside in the present. Organizational authority, the public confessional, and principle are the plans with a heightened sense of presentness. Befitting their rootedness in the present, they are also the plans whose effectiveness is most likely to change with changes in the living speaker. For example, individuals inherit the entitlements of an organization as long as they enjoy official standing with it. But once an individual leaves the organization, the standing changes. Persons rely on public confessionals to indicate they are more than, and so can rise above, the sum of their inherited roles. But to be effective, the public confessional relies on the speaker's seeming to be a worthy person apart from such roles. Should that assumption change, should the speaker suffer a personal fall from grace, be exposed as a crook or a lunatic, even the public confessional will ring hollow. The confessional, in such a case, is better left private, for the ears of the priest perhaps, but not the voter. Individuals avow principles that may last a lifetime. But principles must also be reinforced and reinvigorated through private conviction as well as public conduct. As the circumstances of life change, a person's principles may change with them. These various observations illustrate how plans centered in presentness are most sensitive to the personal contingencies of the speaker. This means they are also the plans most in need of reinforcement through ritual. People must offer recurring allegiance to their organizational alignments ("I am a Republican, after all"), their capacity to speak nobly out of turn ("To be perfectly honest, let me tell you..."), and make recurring public avowals of their private principles ("Let me tell you what I believe...").

Let us turn to a specific example of the interplay between plans, clausal events, and tense/aspect markings. Consider a passage of Douglas' opening at Ottawa. Because the event-telling is mostly canonical, the verbal events seem discrete and bounded, as in a simple narrative. For ease of reference, we have numbered the events and put them in boldface type.

Prior to 1854, this country [1] **was divided** into two great political parties, known as the Whig and Democrat parties. Both [2] **were** national and patriotic, [3] **advocating** principles that were universal in their application. An old line Whig [4] **could proclaim** his principles in Louisiana and in Massachusetts alike. Whig principles [5] **had** no boundary sectional line— they [6] **were** not limited by the Ohio river, nor by the Potomac, nor by the line of the free and the slave States, but [7] **applied** and [8] **were proclaimed** wherever the Constitution ruled, or the American flag waved over American soil. So it [9] **was** and so it [10] **is** with the principles of the great Democratic party which from the days of Jefferson until this period, [11] **had** [12] **(has?)** proven itself to be the historic party of this nation....The Whig party and the Democratic party jointly [13] **adopted** the Compromise measures of 1850 as the basis of a proper and just solution of this slavery question in all its forms.... In 1854, Mr. Abraham Lincoln and Mr. Trumbull [14] **entered** into an arrangement, one with the other, and each with his respective friends, [15] **to dissolve the old Whig party on the one hand, and** [16] **to dissolve the old Democratic party on the other,** and [17] **to connect the members of both into an Abolition party, under the name and disguise of a Republican party.**

We examine each verbal form in three ways. First is the form it takes, whether a finite verb, indicating an event with temporal endpoints, or an infinite verb, indicating a space of continuous duration or activity that fills the temporal span of whatever finite event happens to control it. Second is the tense/aspect structure— for tense, whether the event form is past (was), present (is), future (will), perfect (has been) past perfect (had been), future perfect (will have been), or future in past (then...was to), and for aspect, whether the structure is progressive (being) or an unmarked punctual form.

Finally, we are interested in the specific plan made most active and seemingly most responsible for the lexicalization of the verbal form. In some cases, this is more than one plan.

We have tabulated the results of applying these observations to the 17 verbal forms in Douglas's passage (Table 10.1). The reader should consult this table while reading the discussion that follows.

Event 1, "was divided," is a finite passive and nonprogressive form. Nevertheless, it implies continuous duration because "divided" functions as a state adjective with no temporal start or stop points. Douglas' meaning is that "being divided" is a continuous state description of America for the first 67 years of her existence—from 1789 to 1854. From the standpoint of an

TABLE 10.1
Plans Brought to Presentation Through Events

| Event | Lexicalization | Form | Tense/Aspect | Plan |
|---|---|---|---|---|
| 1 | was divided | Finite | Past | Precedent |
| 2 | were | Finite | Past | Precedent |
| 3 | advocating | Infinite | Past | Precedent |
| 4 | could proclaim | Infinite | Past | Precedent |
| 5 | had | Finite | Past | Precedent |
| 6 | were | Finite | Past | Precedent |
| 7 | applied | Finite | Past | Precedent |
| 8 | were proclaimed | Finite | Past | Precedent |
| 9 | was | Finite | Past | Precedent |
| | | | | Precedent |
| 10 | is | Finite | Present | Principle |
| | | | | Org. authority |
| 11 | had | Finite | Past perfect | Precedent |
| | | | | Precedent |
| 12 | has | Finite | Present perfect | Principle |
| | | | | Org. authority |
| 13 | adopted | Finite | Past | Precedent |
| 14 | entered into an arrangement | Finite | Past | Conspiracy |
| 15 | to dissolve | Infinite | Future in past | Conspiracy |
| 16 | to dissolve | Infinite | Future in past | Conspiracy |
| 17 | to connect | Infinite | Future in past | Conspiracy |

audience member who does not know where Douglas is going, the "was divided" event seems to be part of a historical plan with no evaluative meaning.

We learn later that this parsing is incorrect. The 1854 reference is to Douglas' dating (contested by Lincoln) of the birth of the Republican party. The "Prior to 1854" phrase is a temporal anchor activating a counterprecedent and conspiracy plan against Lincoln and the Republicans. Douglas offers the "was divided" event as part of a precedent plan, carrying the principle of popular sovereignty but in a form that stresses how the freedom to choose produces difference and, more specifically, the historical state of the country's being divided over slavery.

Douglas offers the event of "was divided" to describe the country in its halcyon youth, when the principle of self-government was an unrivaled precedent. Later, Douglas reveals Lincoln's house-divided doctrine as a radical counterprinciple that strikes at the heart of the "was divided" precedent. He also distinguishes the event of "was divided" and the current state of national "division," a state caused by the Republicans/abolitionists insisting on a uniform slave policy throughout the nation.

"Was divided" is a precedent event propelled by the principle of self-government. Both national parties, Whigs and Democrats, were faithful adherents to this precedent. This fact made these parties "historic," makers of history entitled to move the principle of self-government forward in time. The next two verbal events continue to activate precedent plans by showing the precedent-setting entitlement of Whigs and Democrats as political parties. Event 2, "were," is a finite past linking both parties with descriptors—national and patriotic—intended to reveal the common precedent they fielded from first principles. Events 3 and 4, "advocating" and "could proclaim," are infinite forms that focus on the capacity of Whigs and Democrats to advocate and proclaim precedents that are "universal," ranging from "Louisiana to Massachusetts." Event 5, the past finite "had," continues the focus on precedent principles, but the source is more the Whigs (the group) than specific Whigs. This continues with events 6 ("were") and 7 ("applied"). Event 8 ("were proclaimed") shifts the focus back to individual Whigs and their function as agents of precedent.

Event 9 ("was") uses the simple past to declare that what was true for the Whigs was true for the Democrats. Douglas immediately follows in the next clause with Event 10 ("is"), indicating with the present tense that the Democrats, unlike the Whigs, are still alive and kicking at the time of the debates. The shift to the present, the first appearance of that tense in this fragment, brings into play other plans that rely on presentness. Besides crediting the Democrats with furthering the principles of the founders, Douglas's shift to present makes available the interpretation that Douglas, himself a democrat, is avowing his own principles (principle) and, himself a leader of Democrats, is representing the authority of the group (organizational authority).

Events 11 and 12 speak to an interesting hermeneutic controversy. We digress into the controversy a bit because it makes an instructive point about how a theoretical focus demarcates the difference between the Events and Presentation modules. We start with a bit of background. The Lincoln/Douglas debates were the first debates covered verbatim by print. But the means for transcribing speech were error prone and the reporters who transcribed them introduced much bias in their transcriptions, depending on the political leanings of the papers for which they worked. Lincoln and Douglas also introduced their own written versions, edited words that were more polished and tighter than the raw oral transcripts. In light of there being no authoritative edition of the debates, no fully authentic account of what Lincoln and Douglas said on the days of the debates, it has become a minor issue to determine what the content of the debates were when transcripts differ.

Both Paul Angle's centennial (1958) edition of the debates and Harold Holzer's 1993 edition record Douglas as uttering Event 11 ("had"). Robert W. Johannsen's 1965 Oxford edition has Douglas saying Event 12 ("has"). We have little to say about which, if any, edition is right; but we can say something about what the difference means in regard to the higher-level plan structures of Douglas.

The past perfect "had" indicates a boundary of time that does not survive into the here and now of audience decision making. According to this interpretation, Douglas' relationship to the Democrats is not much more immediate than his relationship to the Whigs. The Democrats once carried precedents, but they are a party of precedent no longer. Bringing "had" to lexicalization means that Douglas associates the Democrats with precedent but the association, like that of the Whigs, is now only historical rather than a living principle.

The perfect "has," in contrast, indicates a boundary of time that permeates the present moment of audience decision making. According to this event meaning, Douglas associates only the Democrats with his present principles. Bringing "has" to lexicalization opens the possibility that Douglas is not just reporting on the precedent history of the Democrats but avowing their beliefs, via a principle plan, and also claiming his present representative solidarity with them, via organizational authority.

Although the "has" seems better motivated than the "had" for Douglas' own purposes, there is a case to be made for the "had." Douglas' relationship to the Democrats is as much dissociation (in the later debates) as association (in the earlier ones). He did believe that the Democrats had abandoned popular sovereignty on the Lecompton issue and the debates began in the context of his falling out with Buchanan democrats over that issue, so it is not out of the question to think he could have lexicalized events that wrote off the present Democrats as the party of precedent.

At the same time, the "had," were it actually uttered, could have been a slip. Douglas may have intended to say "has" but slipped into "had." Holzer's edition is based on accounts of what Lincoln sympathizers thought Douglas had said. If Douglas did say "had," intending "has," then Lincoln sympathizers would have had no reason to edit the slip. Indeed, Lincoln sympathizers, wanting to wedge Douglas from his own party, would have had a prior interest in hearing Douglas say "had" even if he actually uttered "has." Johannsen's edition ("has") is based on accounts of what Douglas sympathizers reported. Had Douglas make a slip into "had," these listeners would have had an interest to edit it out. Had Douglas said and meant "had," these listeners, not wanting Douglas to alienate his own party, would have had an interest to change the transcript to "has."

Exegesis of what Douglas said and meant is a fascinating topic but not our main point. Our point is that this site of controversy illustrates the interesting way the theoretical focus one brings to a rhetorical discourse can demarcate the Events module versus the Presentation module. If we assume that this elemental tense/aspect information is part of Douglas' designed structure, a possibility opened by the exegetical controversy, then we need to explain tense/aspect as undertaken by Events. On the other hand, if we judge that Douglas' meanings are (for theoretical purposes) invariant across tense/aspect renderings, then we assume that the lexicalization belongs to Douglas' presentation, a matter of linguistics more than rhetoric proper.

Let's now move further through Douglas' clauses. Event 13 ("adopted") returns to the historical precedent Douglas used in the first eight events. This event turns out to be transitional because the subsequent events chart a new course. We get a sense of this new course in the form of Event 14 ("entered into an arrangement"). All the earlier event forms in this passage have been generics, events that recur over and over at unspecified times and places. Event 14 represents the first unique event form. Lincoln and Trumbull did not keep entering into a arrangement. They did it—and it was done. But who are they to do anything? They do not act from any preestablished precedent; nor do they belong to a group with high organizational authority.

So they cannot stand in for a public. They are a clique. This is an indicator of the start of a conspiracy plan. Like precedents and counterprecedents, the temporal realization of conspiracy is the "then...were to" structure, a collusion was made in the past to bring about a certain future. Event 14 supplies the "then" part of this temporal structure. Events 15, 16, and 17 supply the "were to" part.

In chapter 7, we saw that conspiracy plans involve a series of covers to disguise the secret plot. To fill out the conspiracy plan, Douglas had to express this cover in some way. Significantly, he does not use a verbal form at all but the prepositional phrase "under the name and disguise of a Republican party." This is a significant observation because it means that the lexicalization of key event classes within a plan will not always center on verbal forms.

## Presenting Discourse with Traces from Tactics

From the presentation of Plans to that of Tactics, we must shift the linguistic consciousness through which the rhetorical design is implemented. In the Plans module, the speaker's consciousness is at most a steward of a world that existed prior to and independent of that consciousness. In the Tactics module, the speaker's consciousness, and especially its agility and responsiveness in the face of the opponent's, becomes more marked.

Significantly, Lincoln's habit is to present most of his thinking about American history through his own consciousness, as part of tactic-driven presentation that confronts Douglas' thinking on the subject straight on. That is to say, we seldom get from Lincoln an "objective" description of reality over which his consciousness now stewards. We get fewer of the canonical backgrounds of which Douglas is so fond—backgrounds out of which the speaker's consciousness eventually discovers itself. We rather learn from Lincoln about slavery in the American past directly from the seat of Lincoln's own consciousness. Consider at Alton how Lincoln describes the negro being included in the Declaration of Independence:

> Allow me while upon this subject briefly to present one other extract from a speech of mine, more than a year ago, at Springfield, in discussing this very same question, soon after Judge Douglas took his ground that negroes were not included in the Declaration of Independence: "I think the authors of that notable instrument intended to include all men, but they did not mean to declare all men equal in all respects. They did not mean to say all men were equal in color, size, intellect, moral development or social capacity. They

defined with tolerable distinctness in what they did consider all men created equal—equal in certain inalienable rights, among which are life, liberty, and the pursuit of happiness. This they said, and this they meant. They did not mean to assert the obvious untruth, that all were then actually enjoying that equality, or yet, that they were about to confer it immediately upon them. In fact they had no power to confer such a boon. They meant simply to declare the right, so that the enforcement of it might follow as fast as circumstances should permit. They meant to set up a standard maxim for free society which should be familiar to all: constantly looked to, constantly labored for, and even, though never perfectly attained, constantly approximated, and thereby constantly spreading and deepening its influence and augmenting the happiness and value of life to all people, of all colors, every where." There again are the sentiments I have expressed in regard to the Declaration of Independence upon a former occasion—sentiments which have been put in print and read wherever any body cared to know what so humble an individual as myself chose to say in regard to it. At Galesburgh the other day, I said in answer to Judge Douglas, that three years ago there never had been a man, so far as I knew or believed, in the whole world, who had said that the Declaration of Independence did not include negroes in the term "all men." I reassert it to-day. I assert that Judge Douglas and all his friends may search the whole records of the country, and it will be a matter of great astonishment to me if they shall be able to find that one human being three years ago had ever uttered the astounding sentiment that the term "all men" in the Declaration did not include the negro. Do not let me be misunderstood. I know that more than three years ago there were men who, finding this assertion constantly in the way of their schemes to bring about the ascendancy and perpetuation of slavery, denied the truth of it.

Lincoln never disguises the fact that the Founders' thoughts and actions vis-à-vis the negro and the Declaration are constructions of his own consciousness. But by his narrating events from his particular thoughts, the audience comes directly into contact with the way Lincoln thinks and the agility with which he thinks on the subject compared to Douglas. The risk of avoiding plan-driven narrative and bringing tactical structures directly to lexicalization is to make the speaker seem self-interested, subjective, contentious, and petty, more focused on beating the opponent than resolving the larger issues of the country. The benefit, however, is to front one's own consciousness as a more reliable, trustworthy, and agile guide than the opponent's.

When both speakers have tactical agility, as Douglas and Lincoln surely do, their lexicalization takes on the appearance of dueling consciousnesses. The speakers lexicalize noncanonical events more fine-grained than plans. Consider the first words of Lincoln's reply at Jonesboro:

Ladies and Gentleman:

There is very much in the principles that Judge Douglas has here enunciated
that I most cordially approve, and over which I shall have no controversy
with him. In so far as he has insisted that all the States have the right to do
exactly as they please about all their domestic relations, including that of
slavery I agree entirely with him…. He places me wrong in spite of all I can
tell him, though I repeat it again and again, insisting that I have no
difference with him upon this subject. I have made a great many speeches,
some of which have been printed and it will be utterly impossible for him to
find any thing that I have ever put in print contrary to what I now say upon
this subject. I hold myself under constitutional obligations to allow the
people in all the States, without interference, direct or indirect, to do exactly
as they please and I deny that I have any inclination to interfere with them,
even if there were no such constitutional obligation…. While I am upon this
subject, I will make some answers briefly to certain propositions that Judge
Douglas has put. He says, "Why can't this Union endure permanently, half
slave and half free?" I have said that I supposed it could not and I will try,
before this new audience, to give briefly some of the reasons for entertaining
that opinion.

At the end of this passage and beyond, Lincoln tries to show that his
house-divided doctrine is a prediction more than a preference or a threat.
That slavery will eventually doom the country is not a consciousness he seeks
to incite but is natural law recognized by the Founding Fathers. Thus it
should not be used, as Douglas uses it, to implicate him (Lincoln) in
conspiracy plans to abolitionize the country. The main part of the passage,
however, is devoted to a much more fine point—to recount his personal
struggle to get Douglas to acknowledge their common ground on states'
rights and Douglas' stubborn refusal to do so. The point is to indict Douglas'
nonresponsiveness.

Sometimes the presentation can be so convoluted that its value as a
structure of argumentative design, plan or tactic, becomes diluted. It thus
becomes an easy target for a countertactic that cries irrelevance. This is what
Douglas does to Lincoln at Charleston. In the Charleston opening, Lincoln
tries to show that Douglas is hypocritical about popular sovereignty because
he edited that principle out of the Toombs bill. But Lincoln's account of the
events surrounding the Toombs revisions are so painstakingly detailed that
their argumentative significance is easy to lose. Douglas is able to open his
Charleston reply with the following complaint:

Ladies and Gentlemen:

I had supposed that we assembled here to-day for the purpose of a joint discussion between Mr. Lincoln and myself, upon the political questions that now agitate the whole country. The rule of such discussions is, that the opening speaker shall touch upon all the points he intends to discuss, in order that his opponent, in reply, shall have the opportunity of answering them. Let me ask you what question of public policy, relating to the welfare of this State or the Union, has Mr. Lincoln discussed before you?

## Presentation and the Organization of Narrative

The purpose of the Plans module, as we have said, is to tell stories about publics. The knowledge to use plans for narrative is part of the Plans module. But the knowledge of how to express events so that they take on the surface appearance of narrative belongs to the Presentation module. As a surface form, narratives require settings, conflicts, and resolutions. The setting is needed to provide a ground against which the story's plot stands out as figure. The plot of the story rests on conflict, and the speaker's "stand" can be viewed as an effort to move the story along to a resolution.

There is an initial temptation to think that the discrimination between settings and conflicts in narrative lexicalization is driven primarily through differences in plans. After all, some plans seem to represent norms (viz., precedent, organizational authority, principle, venue) and others counter-norms (viz., counterprecedent, the violation of organizational authority, counterprinciple, the violation of venue, conspiracy). Normed plans would seem the stuff of settings and projected resolutions, and counternormed plans, the stuff of conflicts. There is a grain of truth to this preliminary observation. It does seem to be the case that all events of conflict have, as their source, the imputation of one or another counternormed plan. But the reverse is not the case. Being a counternormed plan is not sufficient to create a conflicting event. One can read an encyclopedia account of the conspiracy to assassinate Lincoln and no conflict event is produced, no call to resolution is invited, at least for the average reader. The information is a historical tidbit, not a problem for rhetoric. Counternormed plans, as well as normed ones, can provide the background for stories about publics.

What rather seems the case is that we bring different epistemic orientations to narrative settings and conflicts, differences that only become fully evident within the Presentation module. Narrative settings depend on a perception of the world as it is, with minimal dependence on minds or plans.

Even when we speak of the Founders' "intent" in establishing precedent, the luminosity of this event in setting a baseline for rhetoric is not that Jefferson had a cognition of a particular sort but that, endowed with the status of "Founder," we assign to Jefferson's cognition the status of revealed truth. Settings always present a picture of the world that is meant to be initerial and stabilizing, a picture that, in order to retain the aura of stability, must remain distant, impersonal, detached, sparsely detailed, decontextualized, and mainly unwitnessed. This is the very epistemic stance adopted in canonical event-telling, where events are traversed from afar as bound entities uncontaminated by the struggle of a human consciousness to work through them (on this point, see Hopper, 1995). Normed plans, insofar as they describe settings and hoped-for resolutions, though mental constructions, nonetheless can be portrayed as instances of a public truth working its way through history. Speakers in other words do not need to describe and defend their norms as if they were rooted in fragile cognition. They can describe and defend them as if part of revealed truth, a descriptive portrait of natural law. This does not foreclose speakers from openly wrestling with positions they hold—as they certainly must when showing themselves responsive to the opponent and human for the audience; it does mean, however, that describing their position as canonical events of revealed truth always remains open to them.

Events stirring conflict, typically the counternormed plans of opponents, are rooted in a different epistemic stance. These events do not have the sanction of natural law. They have only an existence in the minds and plans of wrong-thinking individuals. They can only be explored and criticized in terms of the consciousness of the persons who seek to foist them on innocent audiences. Having no existence apart from consciousness, conflict events are deeply entangled in the social scenes in which they have been concocted. Exploration and criticism of these events require exploring the scenes and their ties to the consciousness implicated in them. The scenic exploration requires a move to noncanonical event-telling. Although the self's positions can move back and forth between canonical and noncanonical event-telling, the self can only describe the opponent's thinking in noncanonical terms, as the opponent's position has no validity outside the concrete scenes of the opponent's consciousness.

To this point, we have implied that narrative backgrounds and ideal resolutions are conveyed through canonical event-telling, and narrative conflict, through noncanonical event-telling. As a generalization, this moves in the right direction but it elides much interesting detail. We now consider some of the detail this generalization misses.

### The Flow of Events from Narrative Background to Conflict

True, simple narratives (chapter 2) created from canonical event-telling do contain events that have been completed prior to speaking. But for reasons we discuss later, the simple narrative never constitutes a stand-alone story about publics. Simple narratives, we see later, provide useful settings and backgrounds for rhetoric, but they are never enough by themselves to complete a rhetorical design. The simple narrative only becomes implicated in a full story about publics when it is coupled with noncanonical event-telling. We argue next that noncanonical event-telling is necessary for bringing conflict into a story, and any well-formed story about publics requires conflict.

The details of moving from a narrative background to narrative conflict are best appreciated through a specific example. We return to Douglas' opening at Ottawa, where he paints a canonical background of the mechanisms that make American history work.

### *Background*

Prior to 1854, this country was divided into two great political parties, known as the Whig and Democrat parties—both national and patriotic in their principles—both advocating principles which were universal in their application. An old line Whig could proclaim his principles in Louisiana and in Massachusetts alike. Whig principles were not limited by the Ohio river, nor by the Potomac, nor by the line of the free and the slave States, but applied and were proclaimed wherever the Constitution ruled, or the American flag waved over American soil. So it was and so it is with the principles of the great Democratic party which from the days of Jefferson until this period, had proven itself to be the historical party of this nation. While the Whig and the Democratic parties differed in regard to a Bank, and in regard to a Tariff, and in regard to Distribution, and in regard to the Specie Circular, and in regard to the Sub-Treasury, they agreed on the great question that now agitates the Union, known as the slavery question, while they differed on those matters of expediency to which I have referred.

Notice that the events are vague, diffuse, generic, and unwitnessed. The canonical description promotes a view of reality that is too far away to be contested, which is exactly the point of canonical event-telling. One may think that a speaker moves directly from background to conflict, from canonical to noncanonical event-telling. But that is too abrupt for the significant change in epistemology that such a transition in fact represents. What we tend to find, instead, is a sequence of event-telling that gradually slides from the canonical to the noncanonical, preparing us for conflict information prior to giving us any. After the narrative background, the next step toward conflict, found in Douglas' lexicalization, is plot initiation.

## Plot Initiation

The Whig party and the Democratic party jointly adopted the compromise measures of 1850 as the basis of the solution of the slavery question in all of its forms. Clay was the great leader, with Webster on his right and Cass on his left, sustained by the patriots in the Whig and Democratic ranks, in devising, and adopting, and enacting the compromise measures of 1850. Again, in 1851, in Illinois, the Whig party and the democratic party united in resolutions endorsing and approving the compromise measures of 1850 as the proper adjustment of this question. In 1852, when the Whig party assembled at Baltimore, for the purpose of nominating its candidate for the presidency, the first thing it did was to adopt the compromise measures of 1850, in substance and in principle, as the satisfactory adjustment of the question.... I was saying, when the Democratic convention assembled at Baltimore, in 1852, for the purpose of nominating a candidate to the Presidency, they also adopted the Compromise measures of 1850 as the basis of Democratic action. Thus you see that up to 1853–4, the Whig party and the Democratic party both stood on the same platform in regard to the Slavery question which now agitates the country. That platform was the right of the people of each State and of each Territory to decide their local and domestic institutions for themselves, subject only to the Federal Constitution.

Notice how Douglas' language becomes more scenic. What were diffuse and dispersed events become proximate in time and space. What were generic and anonymous events now become named and dated with a specific cast of characters. What were unwitnessed events are now witnessed and documented. We are still learning about the background of Douglas' argument, but the greater scenic resolution hints to us that the information we are getting is the kind of information that can convey conflict. There remains a missing step, however, between the initiation of plot and the presentation of conflict. Conflict arises only with the clash of consciousness, a speaker and an opponent's. To understand how the opponent's consciousness goes wrong, we need to have exposure to the speaker's consciousness. Thus far Douglas has given us his version of American history in increasingly scenic terms, but not his own consciousness as an active force in that scene. His further lexicalization acknowledges his consciousness.

## Acknowledging One's Consciousness in the Scene

At the session of 1854, I introduced into the Senate of the United States a bill to organize the territories of Kansas and Nebraska on that principle, which had been adopted in the Compromise measures of 1850, approved by the Whig party and the Democratic party and the Democratic party in Illinois in 1831, and endorsed by the Whig party and the Democratic party in the national Conventions of 1852. In order that there might be no misunderstanding in regard to the principle involved in the Kansas and Nebraska bill, I put forth the true intent and meaning of the act in these words: "It being the true intent and meaning of this act not to legislate slavery into any State or Territory, not to exclude it therefrom, but to leave the people thereof perfectly free to form and regulate their domestic institutions in their own way, subject only to the Federal Constitution." Thus you see that up to 1854, when the Kansas and Nebraska bill was brought into Congress for the purpose of carrying out the principles which, up to that time, both parties had endorsed and approved, there had been no division in this country in regard to that principle, except the opposition of the Abolitionists. In the Illinois Legislatures, in the House of Representatives, upon the resolution asserting that principle, every Whig and every Democrat in the house voted for that principle.

We now understand how Douglas figures into the scene he has been setting for his audience. We understand how he has aligned his own cognition with the impersonal forces of history that set America into motion. We now see him as an agent of precedent. Had he started the narrative with his own conscious, we would have seen him in the conflict *in media res*. We would have seem him embattled rather than, as we see him now, standing above the battle in a world not of his own making, but a steward of the principles on which it was made. Speakers often portray their consciousness as a steward for the impersonal forces that animate societal norms. This becomes an appropriate setting for the introduction of a more reckless consciousness that would destroy or trample on what the speaker wishes to protect, giving us our first whiff of a complication.

## Plot Complication

Only four men voted against it, and those four men were Old Line Abolitionists In 1854, Mr. Abraham Lincoln and Mr. Trumbull entered into an arrangement one with the other, and each with their respective friends, to dissolve the old Whig party on the one hand, and to dissolve the Democratic party on the other hand, and convert the members of both parties into an Abolitionist party under the name of the Republican party.

The terms of the conspiracy are now introduced in great detail. Finally, we see evidence of the generalization of an opponent's consciousness being implicated in a counternormed plan. This is clearly a conflict situation described in noncanonical terms. But we have seen ample evidence of noncanonical event-telling that prepares the audience for conflict descriptions prior to the revelation of conflict.

## The Scene of Conflict

> The terms of that arrangement between Mr. Lincoln and Mr. Trumbull have been published to the world by Mr. Lincoln's special friend, Mr. James H. Mathenay, which was that Mr. Lincoln was to have Gen. Shields' place—then about to become vacant in the United States Senate—and Mr. Trumbull was to have my place. Mr. Lincoln went to work industriously to abolitionize the old Whig party all over the State, pretending that he was as good a Whig as he ever was. Trumbull went to work in his part of the State, down in Egypt, preaching Abolitionism in a milder and lighter form, and of not quite as dark a color, but yet trying to abolitionize the Democratic party and bring the old Democrats handcuffed, bound hand and foot into the Abolition camp. In pursuance of that arrangement, the parties met at Springfield in October, 1854, and proclaimed their new platform. Mr. Lincoln was to bring into the Abolition camp the old line Whigs, and transfer them over to Giddings and Fred Douglass, Lovejoy and Farnsworth, who were then ready to receive and christen them into Abolitionists. They laid down on that occasion a platform for this new Republican party, which was to be constructed out of the old whig party and the old Democratic party, by abolitionizing both and transferring them to abolitionism.

This completes our discussion of the remaining threads of our architecture, the Strategic and Presentational modules. To review, the Strategic module relates goals to the behavior of Plans, Tactics, and Events. The Presentation module makes decisions about how to bring the design structure to expression after it decides that the rhetorical interest of the design has been saturated. We now turn to the loose ends.

## LOOSE ENDS

In this final section, we take up loose ends, bits and pieces for further inquiry that the present study provokes.

### Styles of Reasoning

In the literature of rhetoric, rhetorical reasoning has been widely identified as originating in one of three dominant styles. The styles have no standard names, so we will assign them: (a) principled, (b) prudential, (c) relative similarity.

We start with principled reasoning. A speaker persuades through principle by adhering to principles which the audience also believes. Principled reasoning, the basis of rhetoric's tie to ethical and conceptual reasoning in general, can be very powerful in cases where the application of principle is clear cut. But in many cases, like situations for public rhetoric, the cases are gray, and competing principles can both seem compelling. Many rhetoricians have rejected the foundational assumptions of principled reasoning in favor of a more interactional, response-based mode of reasoning for rhetoric that is prudential. Perelman and Olbrecthts-Tyteca (1969) seem in this camp, as does Johnstone (1959). The work of Jonsen and Toulmin (1988) on casuistic argument shows the severe limitations of principled-based reasoning in ethics. Jensen and Toulmin called for a greater reliance in ethical theory on prudential reasoning. A speaker persuades through prudence by impressing the audience that he or she is wise and can remain reasonable in matters where the cases are not clear-cut. Prudential reasoning often allows an audience to choose between speakers when they both seem to have compelling principles on their side.

Some rhetorical theorists have recognized the limits of even this kind of reasoning in persuasion. Both speakers in a public deliberation can seem wise and reasonable, and in such a case, prudential reasoning fails to move an audience to one speaker or the other. Kenneth Burke is one theorist who recognized the limits of prudential as well as logically predictive thought in persuasion, espousing instead a criterion of "identification" or, as Kaufer and Carley (1993a) called it, relative similarity. According to Burke (1969, p. 55), "you persuade a man [sic] only insofar as you can talk his language by speech, gesture, tonality, order, image, attitude, ideas, identifying your ways with his." A speaker persuades through identification or relative similarity, in other words, by impressing the audience that he or she is more "like me" in the face-to-face world of interaction than the opponent is like me. Burke's notion captures the bridge between persuasion and satisfying humanness goals. His mistake was to have identified the whole of a theory of persuasion with identification. Identification is an ever-present criterion of persuasion, but as a criterion it lives alongside predictiveness and responsiveness goals. It becomes a decisive criterion of persuasion only when the speakers competing are equally principled and prudent. When this happens, audiences must fall back on the criterion of relative similarity, or degree of identification, to decide on one speaker over the other.

The rhetorical tradition has thus been split between principle, prudence, and relative similarity as the primary mechanisms of reasoning toward persuasion. Yet a worthy feature of our architecture is to integrate modules that account for the admixture of these types of reasoning within a single decision-making context. Our architecture suggests that principle, prudence, and similarity with the audience are different "faces" of the reasoning underlying rhetorical design. Our health as arguers requires that we not assign our principles an importance beyond our interest in furthering them; opportunism is, in the end, a good check on analyzing what we are doing when we think we are only doing the right thing. At the same time, healthy argument requires that we never shield ourselves from the general principles that may lurk in the noisiest of contexts; looking for the right thing to do may remain, in the end, a good way to get to the moral essence of a murky situation. Lanham (1993, p. 111) suggested that rhetoric's capacity to integrate principle, self-interest, and circumstantiality has helped it serve a peace-making, or irenic, function for just these reasons:

> In its natural oscillation, the rhetorical paidea is deeply irenic, would keep the peace by preventing us from filtering the self-interest and self-consciousness out of our most profoundly disinterested convictions and then committing atrocities in their name.... A rhetorical education, while reminding us of the inevitable circumstantiality of all human judgment, shows us how we can control and offset that circumstantiality.

The issue that should engage rhetorical theorists is not which mode of reasoning is the true mode underlying rhetoric. The question to address is rather, when should each mode be engaged? This question translates into, when should a speaker give priority in the design to Plans (principled reasoning), Tactics (prudential reasoning), or Events (similarity reasoning)? This question, in turn, further translates into a question about setting priorities for goals: When should a speaker make a priority of being predictive versus being responsive versus being human? In chapter 5, we offered detailed considerations to which any theory in pursuit of this question needs to account. We do not yet have that theory, so we cannot yet elaborate the Goals component as a true decision-making module. It is, however, both curious and significant to note that the information we need to fill in our architecture further dovetails with central issues in theories of rhetorical reasoning.

## Media Choice

The rhetor must make decisions about how to coordinate plans, tactics, and events based on the media assumed to be primarily in effect.[6] In the chapter on goals, we saw how media choice can make a difference in the speaker's understanding of on the record vs. off the record. But the media can further make a difference in the basic design of rhetoric. The effect of media on rhetorical design is a fascinating subject and deserves a book in its own right. In the present context, all we can do is suggest how it seemed to affect rhetorical design in the Lincoln/Douglas debates.

Douglas saw himself as addressing an oral audience. Perceiving the media this way would have led him, rationally, to repeat his on-the-record message as much as possible at each new debate site. Why? Because the oral medium keeps the exposure time of a message relatively brief compared to the print medium. As audience exposure time decreases, predictability will increase in importance as a goal of rhetorical design. If the audience misses the basic "plan" of the discourse, the speaker will not be able to set his or her discourse apart as a "public" discourse separate from the discourses of the everyday world of interaction. Douglas follows this rule and repeats his basic message many times over.

Lincoln's primary audience was the educated print audience. He says as much in his reply at Galesburg. And he criticizes Douglas for continuing to say at new debate sites what has already been published from old ones. Lincoln works under the assumption that print increases the exposure time of a message. As the exposure time of a message increases, the needs for predictability decrease. This may explain why Lincoln is so slow to go on the record with his own positive offense (chapter 8). He assumed that print afforded him the time (and space) to get his on-the-record positions across. He could afford to spend more time working on responsiveness and humanness goals, knowing full well he could open up his own positions later.

We probably will never know whether Lincoln and Douglas structured their rhetoric to meet the assumptions of the different media they thought they were addressing. But the difference in these assumptions is sufficient to account for Douglas and Lincoln's distinctive decisions as designers of rhetoric: why, for example, Douglas starts on offense and never changes until Lincoln shows that offense to be hollow, and why Lincoln starts on defense

---

[6]As we indicated in chapter 2, nothing in this book speaks to the choice of media when that choice determines the arena of rhetoric, the rhetorical situation itself. It merely speaks to the choice of media as implicit in the design of rhetoric once the rhetorical situation has been determined; see chapter 2 for a clarification of this distinction.

and only goes on the record after the audience knows and likes him as a person of practical horse sense. From our theory of rhetorical design, we can predict how Lincoln would understood that, with the greater exposure time of print, it was good to be predictable but it was even better if the audience had a rooting human interest in the person whose predictability was now an issue for them.

## The Economics of Rhetorical Design

Consonant with rhetoric and media choice, our own investment in the media of rhetoric has been severely restricted in this book. We have focused on a rhetoric of words. Words are the tools of the humanities and, insofar as rhetoric has been associated with humanism, words have been the tools of rhetoric. In the way words affect our thought and perception, words are expensive and dear. But in the economics of educational training, words are cheap. It costs much less to train a student with, in, and through words than it costs when other lab and studio equipment is involved. Taken as an art of design, rhetoric can hardly unalign itself with words. However, in the late 20th century, there is a host of electronic and visual media that make the presentation of the rhetor more palpable, moving, and engaging than words alone. Future models of rhetoric as design will need to combine "as naturally as breathing, effects that the university world does its best to keep apart" (Lanham, 1993, p. 123). The powerful rhetors of today and tomorrow know words, but they also know film, photography, typography, music, sound, animation, and video production. They know how to use words to write standard arguments. But they also know the written genres designed to interact with the static and kinetic visual arts, such as captioning, script writing, storyboards, and screenplays. Finally, the rhetor of today must know the digital computer, which is becoming the standard environment in which word, image, and sound are integrated. None of these media alters the need for the rhetor to think in terms of Plans, Tactics, and Events, but they equip the rhetor with a variegated, yet integrated, presentation environment, which makes available to the rhetor new alternatives for combining plans, tactics, and events with rhetorical designs. Bringing such new possibilities to the mix is exciting but expensive. Conservatively, training in the studio arts is anywhere from 5 to 20 times more expensive per student than training in the humanities.[7] To avoid the expense, it is easy to keep rhetoric the lowly

---

[7]We make this estimation assuming that students in the studio arts, unlike a humanities student, need a permanent work space, including a computer powerful enough to integrate word, image, and sound, and more contact hours per week with an instructor.

practical skill of the humanities, taught to freshman as a rite to passage to the college curriculum. But that is to reduce rhetoric to freshman composition and to miss rhetoric's potential as a member in good standing with the arts of design.[8]

## Reciprocity Between Design and Criticism

Evaluation is an inherent part of design, not an afterthought or a separate profession. There are, of course, professionals who call themselves critics who do not also design. There are book critics who do not write books, and movie critics who do not produce or direct movies. But to be a designer, professional or otherwise, is to already be in the business of criticism. Throughout this book, we have required our architecture to illumine both the productive choices of Lincoln and Douglas and the hermeneutical choices of those listening to, or reading, them. In this sense, we have tried to respond to the challenge of Gaonkar (1993) that existing accounts of rhetoric too often focus on production in the absence of rich interpretative theory or focus on rich hermeneutics in the absence of productive choice. Gaonkar's challenge, in our terms, is a response to the failure of theorists to think of rhetoric within the family of design arts, where the coupling of production and reception is a foundational requirement. Master graphic designers would not think of grounding production choices without studying archives of existing designs. Architects would not think of design choices for a building without studying the contrasting designs reflective in many standing structures. In the design arts, there is no meaningful separation between the theorist of productive choice and the critic of products. Every creative producer is expected to be a rich and powerful "reader" of previous designs. Production theory outside the context of criticism of prior products is judged to be hollow and uninformed; interpretation and criticism outside the context of production are judged to be armchair and wishful.

Rhetoric's separation from the design arts is underscored by the effort, especially in American schools of rhetoric, to distinguish rhetorical theory and rhetorical criticism as separate and noninteractive specialties. A move to bring rhetoric into the family of design arts, the move we have devoted this book to making, would question the value of this distinction. In the arts of

---

[8]It is probably no coincidence that the places where rhetoric has most flourished in the United States have been where it has had strong ties outside the humanities college on campus. Schools like Carnegie Mellon, Rennselaer, Minnesota, Michigan, Clarkston, Washington, and Purdue all have strong relationships between rhetoric and nonhumanities colleges, especially schools of design and engineering.

design, the tight feedback loop between criticism and production insures the increasing sophistication and maturity of the art. The reciprocity between production and reception allows for the expansion and refinement of theories about both.

## Continuities Between Public Rhetoric and Academic Writing

The framework of rhetorical design we have introduced can help teach us more about the relationship between civic and academic rhetoric. Now that we have mapped out the Lincoln/Douglas debates from a theory of rhetorical design, we first plot the academic persona within that map. Wanting to appear predictive, the academic persona elevates predictiveness in academic writing above the more interactive, off-the-record goals of responsiveness and humanness. Seeking to appear complete, the academic persona tends to eschew the need for tactics. Seeking to appear objective, offering a reality independent of expression, the academic persona avoids events. Seeking to appear specialized and restrictive, the academic persona tends to shorten and compress elemental stories about truth and falsehood in favor of the disciplinary-specific logic and evidentiary facts that yield "results." McCloskey (1990) wrote at length about the hidden stories of normative truth and falsehood that drive economic thinking but that remain outside the formal channels of formal economic reporting.

Rhetorical structures are clipped in academic writing, perhaps, because these structures represent a "political" underpinning that has low standing in a culture of expertise. In a culture of expertise, writers write only in the public spaces where they consider themselves, and in turn are regarded as, experts. This leaves the civic dimension of academic discourse mute insofar as no civic speaker can claim to be a legitimate expert in the unknown future. In cultures of expertise, the venue argument is suspended because it is assumed that if one cannot speak or write as an expert witness, one should not say anything. Conversely, only in writing to a civic public, where expertises cross and no single expertise dominates, does the venue argument come alive, and must speakers and writers appeal to venue to address how place and knowledge furnish their authority to speak responsibly and in an informed way, even if without the certainty of the expert. Academic writing, addressed to smaller, more cognitively and socially cohesive audiences, made it possible to assume rather than state important preconditions for the development and enactment of rhetorical plans, and further made it possible to compose an academic paper with much of the public model driving it left unspoken.

The transformation from civic to academic rhetoric, on this account, is one more of continuity than disjuncture. Deliberative rhetoric, the public rhetoric of Aristotle and Lincoln and Douglas, is, we suggest, a paradigm of civic discourse. Academic discourse, we further assert, is just a specialization of the paradigm. In deliberative rhetoric, the speaker, opponent, and audience face the uncertainty of the future. Academic rhetoric does not alter these fundamental dynamics. It simply restricts the terms for public abstractions and further restricts the mappings from the secondary spaces of a public model to the public space. As White (1972, p. 859) observed for legal rhetoric, the "central act of the legal mind" with respect to a more public rhetoric is "the conversion of the raw material of life—of the actual experiences of people and the thousands of ways they can be talked about—into a story that will claim to tell the truth in legal terms." It is not that academic specialists don't have a Plans module from which they talk about truth and falsehood in a social world. It is just that the terms of their talk about truth and falsehood become specialized in a way that restricts the audience. Like civic speakers, academics contrive to present arguments that seek to reinforce or change a public model for an audience. In academic rhetoric, however, reinforcing or changing a public model requires standards of evidence specific to the disciplinary audience addressed.

It is, of course, a simplification to treat academic writing as a unity. Although all academic rhetoric must contain a story element at the Plans level, there is much variation in who or what gets to fill the slots as agents of the story, and what sort of connective tissue is used to relate one event class of the story to another. In the chapter on Plans, we called these connective tissues "links" and "alignments." However, these designations are quite generic and we purposely left them that way. When we move from one discipline of academic writing to another, we often find that "links" and "alignments" have a more restricted and concrete semantics based on the discipline, even subdiscipline, in question.

For example, analyzing a sample of academic writing in literature, history, and psychology, Macdonald (1994) reported[9] that in disciplines that seek to be "scientific," like psychology, writers tend to restrict the agents of rhetorical plans to entitled groups (of researchers), and tend to restrict the agent's linking of events to the logical reasons they adduce for or against moving research in one direction or another. She found, however, that in a more diffuse discipline like literature, writers tend to restrict agents of their

---

[9]We describe only one trend McDonald found. We encourage readers to consult her original research for the appropriate qualifications on even the finding we cite here.

rhetorical plans more to particular individuals (topical authors), and are more likely to associate the logic linking the events of their paper with the experiences and reactions they share (or claim to share, through the use of the royal or oracular "we") with their readers. We can state these trends in terms of our architecture of rhetorical design as follows: In academic writing trying to look predictive, objective, and detached (like psychology), writers make sure there is a highly abstracted Plans module distinct from Events. But in academic writing where there is less effort to carry a persona of predictiveness or detachment (like literary criticism), Plans and Events are so highly coordinated as to make their boundaries hard to discriminate. MacDonald found from her sample of historical writing that historians evince a hybrid discourse structure between science and literature. They tend to waver between seeking scientific detachment (from readers) for their stories about truth and falsehood, and trying to connect with their readers based on their stories. As such, they tend to shift between the regularities of literary critics and psychologists in their surface discourse.

Regardless of the discipline in which the rhetorical plan is told, the academic writer cannot expect to change a reigning model of the public without rules of evidence approved by the restricted audience. Within an academic community, it may take years and decades just to change unnoticed events into precedents, or accepted precedents into counterprecedents, or to "de-center" and so let dissipate former precedents back into ordinary events. Nonetheless, despite these differences, the goals of the academic writer achieve success against the same considerations of a public model we found in the Lincoln/Douglas debates. The model of the disciplinary public prefigures the design of the academic paper no less than the model of a civic public prefigured the designs of Lincoln and Douglas.

## Monitoring the Dynamics of Cultural Change Through Changing Publics

Publics, a precondition of rhetorical design, are finite. They are born and die as a result of historical and linguistic change. Moreover, we tend to associate great rhetoric with rhetoric that has historical importance in changing the present configuration of public abstractions on the historical stage. This is the basis of White's (1984) definition of great rhetoric in the history of letters and law. According to White, great rhetoric exposes the limitations in a dominant set of public abstractions, and calls forth the need for a new conceptualization of the public space. Great rhetoric indicates that the impersonal forces that impel truth and falsehood in the social world (within Plans) are no longer descriptive of the concrete events of the here and now (within Events) that currently press and that must now be decided on. The result of this descriptive breakdown is that the existing public discourse is incapacitated to put on the record—to capture in direct or precise language—that which seems most important to bring to the surface. Arguably, one reason for describing Lincoln's rhetoric as great is that, in making slavery the issue of public concern, Lincoln was in effect trying to put on the national record a set of public abstractions that was still foreign to the national discourse of mid-century America in the 1800s. Given the distance between his public model and the reigning discourse of the day, he would have had strategic reason to delay a tactical offense until he had time to expose his own warm homespun character and the limitations of Douglas' public model.

Significantly, monitoring the dynamics of publics, understanding how rhetoric changes the topology of a public over time, is not a project of rhetorical design per se, but a project for the social historian interested in the changing representations of publics across time and space. Rhetors who wish to change the public space must use thick historical descriptions, not just canonically scripted historical plans, to bring about such change. But even here the rhetor's interest will be persuasion in the rhetorical situation. It remains for the person doing history, not out to win a rhetorical situation, to judge whether the rhetor has achieved historical importance through particular rhetorical designs.

## The Ethics of Rhetorical Design

From the classical world to the present, rhetoric is often stigmatized as relying on dirty tactics. The whole of rhetoric is often confused with such tactics. These negative associations, arguably, have had much to do with the decline of rhetoric in the post-Enlightenment world (chapter 1). Yet what post-Enlightenment critics of rhetoric missed is the functional interest of audiences in a fair exchange. The demand for such fairness is not a design consideration internal to the speaker or the opponent. It is a design constraint imposed externally by audiences who make the same empirical demands of rhetoric they make from any art of design. They want an empirical understanding of the results of rhetorical design that we like and why we like them. When we isolate positive and negative outcomes, we can isolate the design conditions associated with each outcome. We can then revise our constructive theories of rhetorical design to capture more of the positive and avoid more of the negative. This is how all the arts of design build in self-correcting mechanisms to improve the results of the design process. This is why the general public has an interest in furthering the study of engineering, architecture, software, and graphics. The public would like, collectively and as individuals, to live with sturdier bridges, safer buildings, more reliable computer programs, and easier to read manuals.

Rhetorical design should be no exception.

Yet all the design arts also suppose that the evaluation process needed to isolate positive from negative design outcomes will need to rely on an open market of information to avoid the incompleteness and bias of any single view. The best type of market to foster this exchange is one that strives for the norm of fair exchange. If the evaluation is based on incomplete or rigged information, then so will be the sort into positive and negative outcomes. If we cannot obtain relatively complete and untainted information about present outcomes, no useful information will be forthcoming about how to make the process better. The same is true for rhetorical design. The demand for a fair exchange is a precondition for guaranteeing that the information used to judge the outcomes of the design will be most complete. This understanding is necessary if we want to learn how to improve rhetorical design.

We may be accused of our own brand of wishful thinking insofar as we assume that an interested activity, like rhetoric, can somehow be judged fairly, without interest. But the same degree of wishfulness is tolerated in every design art. Bidding for a building design contract is highly interested. Yet architects, wanting to improve architectural design, understand that they cannot hope to do so just by studying the architects with the biggest contracts. Competing for a software design project is highly interested. Yet software engineers, wanting to improve software design, know that in many cases what makes a software firm successful has little to do with the principles that make software engineering a successful art or that promise to make it a more successful one.

The wisdom of this argument is as old as Aristotle, who worried that the art of rhetoric could never develop into a full fledged discipline as long as it remained associated with courtroom rhetoric. In forensic rhetoric, it is too easy to manipulate outcomes based on the whim and contingency of a single judge. The single judge can be biased and can be bribed. Worse, the single judge has no vested stake in the quality of the judgment rendering the outcome. What happens to the defendant has nothing to do with the judge's future. Consequently, the judge can decide outcomes without any intrinsic concern for the continuing improvement of rhetoric. For Aristotle, deliberative rhetoric was a different matter. Our individual interests move to a more level playing field when it comes to our collective future. We all have a stake in the collective future, but for most issues[10] none of us understands the future well enough to know what outcomes will further our individual interests or harm them. Given that uncertainty, the best we can do to move into the future is to care about the quality of the rhetoric that takes us there. Although the *Rhetoric* does not fully develop the idea of rhetoric as an art of design, Aristotle's opening remarks are extremely prescient about the importance of envisioning rhetoric as an art of design, in which outcomes are empirically assessed and the constructive art is iteratively improved as a result of that assessment.

Judging rhetorical outcomes fairly is thus necessary if we are to be able to gather the kind of complete information needed to improve rhetorical design. Many specimens of rhetoric will not meet this requirement for assessment and improvement, but the requirement is not threatened merely because of that contingent fact. All arts within the family of design work within this contingent constraint. Architecture that is rewarded through bias does not diminish the requirements to improve architectural design or society's interest in monitoring that improvement by judging fair outcomes. Analogously, rhetoric that succeeds as a result of bias or prejudice does not jeopardize society's interest in improving rhetoric generally, which comes only from sober and fair empirical assessments.

In the western tradition, the ethics of rhetoric has been assessed on the analogy of individual moral action. If an individual can use rhetoric badly, the practice is bad. The design arts, curiously, have never been judged by this standard. They have been judged by the morals of distributed collective action. We do not follow the behavior of a single architect. We study all the various architects distributed across society and wonder whether their collective action, aggregated across time and space, is consistent with the good society; we ask whether the good society is even thinkable without their collective action. Viewed as distributed collective action, the answer we must give for the ethics of rhetoric is no different from the answer we have always given to any of the arts of design.

## FINAL LOOSE END: HOW TO SHOW US WRONG

We have offered a analysis to show the minimal complexity needed to explain the rhetorical behavior of an emblematic rhetorical event, the Lin-

---

[10]In contemporary politics, Aristotle's ideal of deliberative rhetoric has been perverted somewhat by the turn to single issue politics. On most issues, we do not know how policy outcomes affect our interests. But on some we surely do. Increasingly, politicians confine their rhetoric to issues and constituencies where their interests are deeply entrenched.

coln/Douglas debates. We have argued that the complexity of rhetoric evinced by these debates shows rhetoric to be much more than a practical art, an art comprehended or captured by a handbook tradition. It is rather a modular art of design, fulfilling all the essential definitions of such an art. The topical traditions of classical rhetoric were, and remain, a convenient pedagogical stopgap to conceal rhetoric's fundamental modularity. In encouraging students to rhetoric for pedagogy, we have sometimes forgotten that rhetoric is not an art that only the poor students miss. It is rather an art in gradients that only the very best can develop with virtuoso control. In making rhetoric practical, we have sometimes forgotten that failed rhetoric is more than a near miss. It can go wrong in countless ways, and a modular theory can offer an extensive set of diagnostics for beginning to count and classify these breakdowns of the art.

We could be wrong, of course, in our minimalist analysis of the complexity involved in rhetorical design. Because we believe that theories of rhetoric are falsifiable, and improve when they are stripped of errors and omissions, we want to explain (at least) two important ways to prove us wrong. First, although we have tried to be simple while capturing rhetoric's underlying complexity, someone can object that we have not been simple enough. There may be ways of accounting for what we have described with a simpler theory. Perhaps we have missed opportunities to give a simpler account that is at least as comprehensive as the one we have offered. The burden of proof on an objector taking this route is an argument by demonstration: Show the simpler architecture.

Second, although we have tried to be simple in explaining complexity, someone can object that we are being too simple. Our analysis is radically incomplete and more needs to put in before we can claim a comprehensive architecture of rhetorical design. We started from the assumption that if we could account for large fragments of the Lincoln/Douglas debates, we could claim to have captured some fundamental prototype of rhetorical design. But perhaps what we have taken from Lincoln and Douglas has important gaps, or perhaps there are fundamental gaps we failed to anticipate by building our theory from the Lincoln/Douglas debates. In any case, the prescription for this second objector is much like our advice to the first: State what is missing and then offer the theory that includes it.

If we do our part and readers do theirs, we will all be working for the betterment of rhetoric. We will change rhetoric's practical mission, which has been to furnish the culture with literates, with a renewed mission within the arts of design, which is to furnish our thought, language, and practice with the cultures of literates.

# References

Angle, P. M. (Ed.).(1958). *Created equal? The complete Lincoln–Douglas debates of 1858.* Chicago: University of Chicago Press.

Aristotle. (1991). *On rhetoric* (G. Kennedy, Trans.). New York: Oxford.

Atwill, J. M. (1993). Instituting the art of rhetoric: Theory, practice, and productive knowledge in interpretations of Aristotle's rhetoric. In T. Poulakos (Eds.), *Rethinking the history of rhetoric: Multi-disciplinary essays on the rhetorical tradition* (pp. 91–117). Boulder, CO: Westview Press.

Austin, J. L. (1975). *How to do things with words.* Cambridge, MA: Harvard University Press.

Bazerman, C. (1988). *Shaping written knowledge: The genre and activity of the experimental article in science.* Madison: University of Wisconsin Press.

Bender, J., & Wellbury, D. E. (1990). *The ends of rhetoric: History, theory, practice.* Palo Alto, CA: Stanford University Press.

Bensman, J., & Lilienfield, R. (1979). *Between public and private: The lost boundaries of the self.* New York: Free Press.

Billig, M. (1987). *Argument and thinking.* New York: Cambridge University Press.

Billig, M. (1990). *Ideology and opinions.* Beverly Hills, CA: Sage.

Billig, M. (1992). *Ideology and dilemmas.* Beverly Hills, CA: Sage.

Bitzer, L. (1968). The rhetorical situation. *Philosophy and Rhetoric, 1,* 1–14.

Bitzer, L. (1978). Rhetoric and public knowledge. In D. Burks (Eds.), *Rhetoric, philosophy, and literature* (pp. 62–97). West Lafayette, IN: Purdue University Press.

Booth, W. (1970). The rhetorical stance. In *Now don't try to reason with me: Essays and ironies for a credulous age* (pp. 25–34). Chicago: University of Chicago Press.

Booth, W. (1974). *A rhetoric of irony.* Chicago: University of Chicago Press.

Brown, P., & Levinson, S. C. (1987). *Politeness: Some universals in language usage.* Cambridge: Cambridge University Press.

Buchanan, R. (1995). Rhetoric, humanism, and design. In R. Buchanan & V. Margolin (Eds.), *Discovering design: Explorations in design studies.* Chicago: University of Chicago Press.

Burke, K. (1969). *The rhetoric of motives.* Berkeley: University of California Press.

Cahn, M. (1993). The rhetoric of rhetoric: Six tropes of disciplinary self-constitution. In R. H. Roberts & J. M. Good (Eds.), *The recovery of rhetoric: Persuasive discourse and disciplinarity in the human sciences* (pp. 61–84). Charlottesville: University of Virgina Press.

Campbell, K. K. (1989). *Man cannot speak for her: Contributions in woman's studies.* New York: Greenwood Press.

Cherry, R. (1988). Ethos vs. persona: Self-representation in written discourse. *Written Communication, 5*, 251–276.

Craw, I., & Tock, D. (1992). The computer understanding of faces. In V. Bruce & M. Burton (Eds.), *Processing images of faces.* Norwood NJ: Ablex.

Dawkins, R. (1986). *The blind watchmaker.* New York: Norton.

Dewey, J. (1946). *The public and its problems: An essay in political inquiry.* Chicago: Gateway Books.

Dorr, B. (1991). *Lexical semantics and tense/aspect in machine translation* (Tech. Rep. No. CS-TR-2744). Bethesda: University of Maryland.

Dunaway, D. K., & Baum, W. K. (Ed.).(1984). *Oral history: An interdisciplinary anthology.* Nashville: American Association for State and Local History.

Einhorn, L. J. (1992). *Abraham Lincoln the orator.* Westport, CT: Greenwood Press.

Eisenstein, E. (1979). *The printing press as an agent of change.* Cambridge: Cambridge University Press.

Engelmore, R., & Morgan, T. (1988). *Blackboard systems.* Wokingham, England: Addison-Wesley.

Erman, L. D., Hayes-Roth, F., Lessor, V. R., & Reddy, D. R. (1980). The Hearsay-II speech understanding system: Integrating knowledge to resolve uncertainty. *ACM Computing Surveys, 12*, 213–253.

Farrell, T. (1993). *Norms of rhetorical culture.* New Haven, CT: Yale University Press.

Fauconnier, G. (1985). *Mental spaces.* Cambridge, MA: MIT Press.

Fehrenbacher, D. E. (1962). *Prelude to greatness: Lincoln in the 1850s.* Palo Alto, CA: Stanford University Press.

Fisher, G., Lemke, G., & McCall, R. (1991). Making argumentation serve design. *Human Computer Interaction, 6*, 393–419.

Fleischman, S. (1990). *Tense and narrativity: From medieval performance to modern fiction.* Austin: University of Texas Press.

Flower, L., & Hayes, J. (1981). A cognitive process theory of writing. College *Composition and Communication, 32*, 365–387.

Gaonkar, D. (1990). Rhetoric and its double: Reflections on the rhetorical turn in the human sciences. In H. W. Simons (Eds.), *The rhetorical turn* (pp. 341–366). Chicago: University of Chicago Press.

Gaonkar, D. (1993). The idea of rhetoric in the rhetoric of science. *Southern Speech Journal, 58*(4), 258–295.

Geisler, C. (1990). Toward a sociocognitive model of literacy: Constructing mental models in a philosophical conversation. In C. Bazerman & J. Paradis (Eds.), *Textual dynamics of the professions* (pp. 171–190). Madison: University of Wisconsin Press.

Geisler, C. (1994). *Academic literacy and the nature of expertise.* Hillsdale, NJ: Lawrence Erlbaum Associates.

Gilbert, G. N., & Mulkay, M. (1984). *Opening Pandora's box: A sociological analysis of scientific discourse.* Cambridge: Cambridge University Press.

Goel, V., & Pirolli, P. (1992). The structure of design problem spaces. *Cognitive Science, 16*, 395–429.

Goffman, E. (1959). *The presentation of self in everyday life.* Garden City, NY: Doubleday Anchor.

Greenfield, M. (1995, June 5). It's time for some civility: Good, frontal, rough, debate is what we should be about. *Newsweek,* p. 78.

Habermas, J. (1989). *The structural transformation of the public sphere: An inquiry into a category of bourgeois society.* Cambridge, MA: MIT Press.

Holzer, H. (Ed.).(1993). *The Lincoln–Douglas debates.* New York: Harper Collins.

Hopper, P. (1995). The category "event" in natural discourse and logic. In W. Abraham,T. Givon, & S. A. Thompson (Eds.), *Discourse grammar and typology: Papers in honor of John W. M. Verhaar* (pp. 139–150). Amsterdam: John Benjamins.

Hornstein, N. (1990). *As time goes by: Tense and universal grammar.* Cambridge, MA: MIT Press.

Jamieson, K. H. (1992). *Dirty politics: Deception, distraction, & democracy.* New York: Oxford.

Jamieson, K. H. (1995). *Beyond the double bind.* New York: Oxford.

Johannsen, R. (1989). *The frontier, the union, and Stephen A. Douglas.* Urbana: University of Illinois Press.

Johannsen, R. W. (Ed.).(1965). *The Lincoln–Douglas debates.* New York: Oxford University Press.

Johnstone, H. (1959). *Philosophy and argument.* State College, PA: Penn State University Press.

Jonsen, A. R., & Toulmin, S. (1988). *The abuse of casuistry: A history of moral reasoning.* Berkeley: University of California Press.

Kaufer, D. (in press). Techne and technology: Resolving Gaonkar's dilemma. In B. Keith & A. Gross (Eds.), *Gaonkar, hermeneutics & rhetoric.* Albany: SUNY Press.

Kaufer, D., & Carley, K. (1993a). *Communiction at a distance: The influence of print on sociocultural organization and change.* Hillsdale, NJ: Lawrence Erlbaum Associates.

Kaufer, D., & Carley, K. (1993b). Condensation symbols: Their variety and rhetorical function in political discourse. *Philosophy and Rhetoric, 26*(3), 201—226.

Kaufer, D., & Dunmire, P. (in press). Integrating cultural reflection and production in college writing curricula. In J. Petraglia-Bahri (Ed.), *Reconceiving writing, rethinking writing instruction.* Mahwah, NJ: Lawrence Erlbaum Associates.

Kaufer, D., & Geisler, C. (1989). Novelty in academic writing. *Written Communication, 8,* 286–311.

Kaufer, D., Geisler, C., & Neuwirth, C. (1989). *Arguing from sources: Exploring issues through reading and writing.* San Diego: Harcourt Brace Jovanovich.

Kaufer, D., Neuwirth, C., Chandhok, R., & Morris, J. (1992). Writing: A retrospective on computer support for open-ended design tasks. In D. P. Balestri, S. Ehrmann, & D. L. Ferguson (Eds.), *Learning to design; designing to learn: Using technology to transform the curriculum* (pp. 119–140). Washington DC: Taylor & Francis.

Kaufer, D. S., & Young, R. (1993). Writing in the content areas: Some theoretical complexities. In L. Odell (Eds.), *Theory and practice in the teaching of writing: Rethinking the discipline* (pp. 71–104). Carbondale: Southern Illinois University Press.

Kennedy, D. (1982). The stages of the decline of the public/private distinction. *University of Pennsylvania Law Review, 13,* 1349–1357.

Klare, K. E. (1982). The public/private distinction in labor law. *University of Pennsylvania Law Review, 130,* 1358–1422.

Kuhn, D. (1991). *The skills of argument.* Cambridge: Cambridge University Press.

Lanham, R. (1983). *Literacy and the survival of humanism.* New Haven, CT: Yale University Press.

Lanham, R. (1993). *The electronic word: Democracy, technology, and the arts.* Chicago: University of Chicago Press.

Leff, M. (1993, April). *Topics and paradigms.* Public lecture at Carnegie Mellon University.

Liu, Y. (in press). Three issues in the argumentative conception of early Chinese discourse. *Philosophy East and West.*

Lyne, J. (1985). Rhetoric of Inquiry. *Quarterly Journal of Speech,* 71(65–73), 65–73.

MacDonald, S. P. (1994). *Professional academic writing in the humanities and social sciences.* Carbondale: Southern Illinois University Press.

McCloskey, D. N. (1985). *The rhetoric of economics.* Madison: University of Wisconsin Press.

McCloskey, D. N. (1990). *If you're so smart: The narrative of economic expertise.* Chicago: University of Chicago Press.

McCloskey, D. N. (1995). Economics and the limits of scientific knowledge. In R. Goodman & W. Fisher (Eds.), *Rethinking knowledge: Reflections across the disciplines* (pp. 3–21). Albany, NY: SUNY Press.

Mnookin, R. H. (1982). The public/private dichotomy: Political disagreement and academic reputation. *University of Pennsylvania Law Reivew, 130,* 1429–1440.

Nelson, J. S., Megill, A., & McCloskey, D. N. (Ed.).(1987). *The rhetoric of the human sciences.* Madison: University of Wisconsin.

*Newsweek.* (1994, July). p. 62.

No HIts, A Lot of Runs. (1993). Rookie league: Magazine for Kids! *Major League Baseball,* p. 7.

Norman, D. (1988). *The psychology of everday things.* New York: Basic Books.

O'Keefe, B. J., & Lambert, B. L. (1995). Managing the flow of ideas: A local management approach to message design. In B. Berelson (Eds.), *Communication Yearbook* (Vol. 18). Newbury Park, CA: Sage.

Ong, W. (1971). *Rhetoric, romance, and technology: Studies in the interaction of expression and culture.* Ithaca, NY: Cornell University Press.

Ortony, A., Clore, G., & Collins, A. (1988). *The cognitive structure of emotion.* Cambridge: Cambridge University Press.

Perelman, C., & Olbrechts-Tyteca, L. (1969). *The new rhetoric: A treatise on argumenation.* Notre Dame: Notre Dame University Press.

Pinker, S. (1994). *The language instinct.* New York: Harper Collins.

Poppel, E. (1988). *Mindworks: Time and conscious experience* (T. Artin, Trans.). Boston: Harcourt Brace Jovanovich.

Poulakos, T. (Ed.).(1993). *Rethinking the history of rhetoric: Multi-disciplinary essays on the rhetorical tradition.* Boulder, CO: Westview Press.

Raskin, V. (1985). *Semantic mechanisms of humor.* Dordrecht: Reidel.

Ricoeur, P. (1988). *Time and narrative* (Vol. 3; K. Blarney & D. Pellauer, Trans.). Chicago: University of Chicago Press. (Original work published 1985)

Roberts, R. H., & Good, J. M. M. (Ed.).(1993). *The recovery of rhetoric: Persuasive discourse and disciplinarity in the human sciences.* Charlottesville: University of Virgina Press.

Ruegg, W. (1993). Rhetoric and anti-rhetoric in the nineteenth- and twentieth-century human sciences in Germany. In R. H. Roberts & J. M. Good (Eds.), *The recovery of rhetoric: Persuasive discourse and disciplinarity in the human sciences* (pp. 87–100). Charlottesville: University of Virgina Press.

Salazar, P.-J. (1993). The unspeakable origin: Rhetoric and the social sciences: A reassessment of the French tradition. In R. H. Roberts & J. M. Good (Eds.), *The *recovery of rhetoric: Persuasive discourse and disciplinarity in the human sciences* (pp. 101–116). Charlottesville: University of Virgina Press.

Schank, R., & Abelson, R. (1977). *Scripts, plans, goals, and understanding: An inquiry into human knowledge structures.* Hillsdale, NJ: Lawrence Erlbaum Associates.

Schon, D. (1983). *The reflective practitioner: How professionals think in action.* London: Maurice Temple Smith.

Simon, H. A. (1969). *The sciences of the artificial.* Cambridge: MIT Press. Simons, H. (Ed.).(1990). *The rhetorical turn: Invention and persuaasion in the conduct of inquiry.* Chicago: University of Chicago Press.

Smith, J., & Fink, M. (1988). *Off the record: An oral history of popular music.* New York: Warner Books.

Solomon, M. (1991). *A voice of their own: The woman suffrage press, 1840–1910.* Tuscaloosa: University of Alabama.

Sturrock, J. (1993). *The language of autobiography: Studies in the first person singular.* New York: Cambridge University Press.

Suchman, L. A. (1987). *Plans and situated actions: The problem of human–machine communication.* Cambridge: Cambridge University Press.

Toulmin, S. (1958). *The uses of argument.* Cambridge: Cambridge University Press.

Walker, R. J. (1992). *The rhetoric of struggle: Public address by African American women.* New York: Garland.

White, J. B. (1973). *The legal imagination.* Boston: Little, Brown and Company.

White, J. B. (1984). *When words lose their meaning: Constitutions and reconstitutions of language, character, and community.* Chicago: University of Chicago Press.

Will, G. F. (1982). *The pursuit of virtue and other Tory notions.* New York: Simon & Schuster.

Young, R., Becker, A., & Pike, K. (1970). *Rhetoric: Discovery and change.* San Diego: Harcourt Brace Jovanovich.

Zarefsky, D. (1990). *Lincoln, Douglas and slavery.* Chicago: University of Chicago Press.

# Author Index

# Subject Index